Postcolonial Copyright Law

This book appraises postcolonial perspectives to rethink the meaning of copyright and makes suggestions for its future within the global landscape of intellectual property law.

Drawing on the experience of Thailand as a case study, a country with a unique yet marginal position in discussions on colonialism, the book offers valuable insights for the international field of copyright law. Thai copyright law emerged in an era when the threat of European colonial powers inspired local ruling elites to embark on a quest for modernisation and establish a modern absolutist state. One can observe similar dynamics in the recent promotion of Thailand's Creative Economy. Contrary to these top-down developments, the book argues for greater attention to attitudes and practices on the ground. Taking an interdisciplinary approach informed by film studies, area studies, decolonial studies, and legal sociology, the book makes a case for redefining copyright as a community resource.

The book will be of interest to researchers in the field of copyright law, postcolonial and decolonial studies, and sociolegal studies.

Mespiti Poolsavasdi is a legal scholar specialising in copyright law and sociolegal studies. This book is based on his PhD dissertation from Queen Mary University of London (2023), which critically and constructively examined the development of copyright law in Thailand from a postcolonial perspective, offering fresh insights aimed at reshaping the law. He is currently a lecturer on the Thammasat University Faculty of Law, where he teaches and conducts research on intellectual property law with a focus on the intersections of law, culture, and society.

Intellectual Property, Theory, Culture
Series Editor
Johanna Gibson, Herchel Smith
Professor of Intellectual Property Law
Queen Mary
University of London, UK

This series presents theoretical and cultural examinations of intellectual property laws, developments, and policy. Volumes in the series may be identified by their innovative and critical analyses and their original contributions to international debate. Interdisciplinary in approach, the series will be of interest to intellectual property experts and stakeholders, policy advisors, and NGOs, as well as students and researchers in the very critical areas of intellectual property law, anthropology, and cultural studies.

Also in the series:

Patenting Lives
Life Patents, Culture and Development
Edited by Johanna Gibson
ISBN 978-0-7546-7104-6

Disrupting Copyright
How Disruptive Innovations and Social Norms are Challenging IP Law
Margery Hilko
ISBN 978-0-367-35497-8

Art and Copyright Law
An Interdisciplinary Study on Interpictoriality
Giulia Walter
ISBN 978-1-032-97448-4

Postcolonial Copyright Law
Lessons on Community and Coloniality from Thailand
Mespiti Poolsavasdi
ISBN 978-1-032-96111-8

https://www.routledge.com/Intellectual-Property-Theory-Culture/book-series/IPTC

Postcolonial Copyright Law

Lessons on Community and Coloniality from Thailand

Mespiti Poolsavasdi

Routledge
Taylor & Francis Group
LONDON AND NEW YORK

First published 2026
by Routledge
4 Park Square, Milton Park, Abingdon, Oxon OX14 4RN

and by Routledge
605 Third Avenue, New York, NY 10158

Routledge is an imprint of the Taylor & Francis Group, an informa business

British Library Cataloguing-in-Publication Data
A catalogue record for this book is available from the British Library

ISBN: 978-1-032-96111-8 (hbk)
ISBN: 978-1-032-97077-6 (pbk)
ISBN: 978-1-003-59203-7 (ebk)

DOI: 10.4324/9781003592037

Typeset in Times New Roman
by Apex CoVantage, LLC

Contents

Acknowledgements *vii*

Introduction: Copyright, Community, and Coloniality 1

PART I
Colonial Modernity 23

1 The Coloniality of Legal Modernity 25

2 The Quest for Civilisation 57

PART II
The Persistence of Coloniality 89

3 Thai Copyright in the Cultural Cold War 91

4 The War on Piracy 112

PART III
A Line of Escape 131

5 On Belatedness 133

6 The Cinema of Interactions 152

PART IV
Community After All 179

7 Copyright in (Inter)Action 181

8 Community Once More 201

Bibliography *214*
Index *236*

Acknowledgements

Writing is a solitary process. This gradually became clear over the years that I spent writing my PhD thesis at QMUL, which eventually became this book. During this time, I also learned that this solitude was both necessary and only made possible because of the people I had around me. Without them, the relentless force of chaos that is life would have pulled me into a black hole many times over. For the sense of order and safety I have had during these years, I must first thank both of my supervisors, Johanna Gibson and Jonathan Griffiths, for their kind, encouraging words and even more so for their patience. I still remember telling Jo that I wanted to find 'truth' through my research—it was embarrassing then, and it is still embarrassing now.

But that was the intensity with which I approached my PhD research, and I never quite managed to work smart rather than just work hard, despite once telling Jonathan that that was my goal. Somewhere along the way, the thesis grew into something both personal and political that demanded such investment. For someone born and raised in Thailand, it takes a village to have the opportunity I had, and I am indebted to everyone back home—especially to Mom, Dad, and Ji for allowing this indulgence and to Gib for always waiting and being there. This gratitude also extends to all the friends I have made in London. I will always be grateful to the versatile Yibo and incredibly thankful to the IPA crew—Abhijeet, Adela, Brian, Myriam, Oğulcan, Richard, Uche, and the honorary member Malcolm Langley—for making that place a welcoming little community.

Community is also central to this book, a theme shaped by my personal ties to that imagined community we call Thailand. It is hard not to be political when you are from there, with everything that has happened in the past two decades. But I find it necessary that being political means more than discussing politics, which raises the question of what it means to be a Thai scholar in this day and age. Although I do not yet have the answer, and this book can only begin to ask that question, I have found kindness and generosity in kindred spirits who have chosen the same path. Special thanks go to Munin Pongsapan, Natthanai Prasananam, Wikanda Promkhuntong, Oğulcan Ekiz, and Ying Thitirat for all their help along the way. I can only hope that more of your help will be needed—that this is only the beginning of a meaningful lifelong journey.

Introduction

Copyright, Community, and Coloniality

When a Thai filmmaker combines his dissatisfaction with copyright law and a broader resentment towards the country's politics, the result is a satirical documentary titled '*100 Times Reproduction of Democracy (100 TRD).*'[1] Released in 2019, when the military leaders who staged a coup in Thailand in 2014 were still in power, the director Chulayarnnon Siriphol presented this film as an attempt to address two parallel questions: Who owns this film, and who owns this country? Known for his satire and irony, Chulayarnnon does not intend these questions to be merely rhetorical. At its core, *100 TRD* interrogates the notions of artistic reproduction and copyright ownership while drawing a comparison with the state of Thai democracy. However, this is not simply a critique of excessive copyright protection as a threat to free speech. Instead, Chulayarnnon uses his film to connect two seemingly unrelated stories: his process of developing a video art project and the political fallout of the military coup.

Early in the film, it becomes clear that Chulayarnnon is less interested in ownership as defining our relationship with the things we own and more concerned with how it structures human relationships. He devotes the entire film to documenting the negotiations and struggles in human relationships over two notions of ownership. First, he examines the contested ownership of a film as a problem reflecting the broader issues of power dynamics in artistic production. Then, he shifts his attention to the contemporary struggle for democracy as a collective effort to reclaim ownership of the nation. In both cases, ownership is not viewed merely as a matter of individual possession but is reframed as a nexus of social and political relations.[2] Given that issues of exclusion and control always animate the notion of property, also implicit in Chulayarnnon's approach to ownership is the question of

1 *100 Times Reproduction of Democracy* (2019), dir Chulayarnnon Siriphol. This book follows the Thai norm of referring to Thai authors by first names except for citations in the bibliography.

2 This resonates with the anthropological concept of 'property relation,' which emphasises the relative character of property and often serves to shift the focus from the relationships between people and valuables to social relationships relative to goods and valuables. For an overview of the anthropological perspective on property, see Chris Hann, 'Property: Anthropological aspects' in James Wright (ed), *International Encyclopedia of the Social and Behavioural Sciences* (Elsevier 2015).

DOI: 10.4324/9781003592037-1

what ideological forces are at play in structuring and maintaining these property relations.

Viewed in this light, what emerges from the unlikely comparison is not merely a fanciful analogy between relationships in the artistic and political communities. Instead, Chulayarnnon appears to hold up a mirror to the state of social relations in contemporary Thai society. In doing so, more crucially, he inadvertently reveals the contradictions and ambiguities in how modernity is imagined in Thailand, a vision shaped by the allure and tensions in Thai–Western relations dating to the 19th century. A close reading of Chulayarnnon's film, therefore, offers new insights into the enduring influence of the 19th century and its implications for the future of copyright law.

I. A Jurisprudence of Thai Cinema

In *100TRD*, copyright and democracy remain two distinct domains, dividing the film into two parts that are linked by the metaphor of reproduction and the notion of authenticity. The first part of the film follows Chulayarnnon as he embarks on a new art project, which is ultimately a satire on the figure of the artist, or more precisely, the author of copyright law's artistic work. Central to Chulayarnnon's satire of the artist is a video experiment, in which he reproduces his award-winning short film 100 times using a video editing programme and exporting, a technical function of a video editing software that often results in a loss of video quality, rendering the image and sound unrecognisable after repeated reproductions.[3] Making the outcome unintelligible allows Chulayarnnon to dramatise the loss of context and the change in meaning when internet users reproduce films circulating online for various reasons.

As such, Chulayarnnon's video experiment illustrates how reproduction as such can create new meaning, not least because Chulayarnnon himself can produce a new work simply by 'reproducing' an existing one. Indeed, the project fundamentally challenges the concept of originality in copyright law, where a work must not be copied to be considered original. So what unfolds next serves to further sharpen the satire of the artist figure.

Chulayarnnon places the video for sale, allowing the public to purchase a DVD featureing a 'video art' with the title *100 Times Reproduction of a Cock Kills a Child by Pecking on the Mouth of the Earthen Jar.* Only 100 editions (100 DVDs) are available, and for each edition, the 'collector' will receive a certificate of authenticity bearing the signature of the 'artist' himself. As it turns out, the video art proves popular with friends and fans—many of them subsequently contact him with concerns about the 'quality' of the video, completely unaware of his experiment. More strikingly, they do not realise that the word 'reproduction' in the title is also unauthorised, as Chulayarnnon holds no rights to the original short film. It is

3 In technical terms, 'export a video' means to create a copy of the open video on your device or save the copy into a different file format required by a different application.

fair to say Chulayarnnon successfully turns a degraded counterfeit into an authentic edition. And it is here where *100TRD* begins to draw parallels between Chulayarnnon 'the artist' and the authoritarian Thai state.

Life Imitating Art

For Chulayarnnon, this unlikely comparison hinges on the metaphor of reproduction. Given that Thailand has seen a long series of military coups d'état—13 since the democratic revolution of 1932—he finds it pertinent to ask whether Thai democracy remains authentic even after so many reproductions.[4] The junta government apparently thinks so, but Chulayarnnon is not convinced, pointing specifically to the People's Party Plague incident. Here, the film refers to a controversy involving a commemorative plaque for the bloodless 1932 revolution that marked the end of Thai absolutism and the birth of Thai democracy.[5]

Unlike movements in former colonies, Siam's transition to democracy did not occur as a result of a peasant uprising. Instead, the democratic revolution in Siam was orchestrated by *khana-ratsadon* '('the People's Party'), a group of military officers, civil servants, and civilians frustrated by absolute monarchy.[6] Many of its members were Western educated and had formed the group while in Europe, aspiring to transform Siam into a civilised country.[7] In 1926, the group's leaders convened in France to plan a coup that they successfully executed in 1932, seizing power from the King without bloodshed.[8] A memorial plaque was laid to commemorate this event.

Fast forward to 2017: The memorial plaque mysteriously disappeared, and in its place appears a new plaque that is similar in design but different in meaning.[9] At the heart of the original inscription was the idea of the first constitution, which signified the end of Siam's absolute monarchy. In contrast, 'faithfulness towards one's king' is now engraved on the new plaque with no mention of democracy to be found.[10] Chulayarnnon thus compares the new plaque with his certificate of authenticity, and by doing so, he makes a mockery of the two authoritative figures.

Implicit in Chulayarnnon's satire on reproduction and authenticity are the intertextual relations of creative production. Indeed, one could even argue that *100TRD* is the embodiment of intertextuality, as Chulayarnnon quotes, parodies, and alludes

4 For a historical overview of Thai authoritarianism, see Suchart Bamrungsuk, 'The development of the hybrid regime: The military and authoritarian persistence in Thai politics' in Pavin Chachavalpongpun (ed), *Routledge Handbook of Contemporary Thailand* (Routledge 2020).

5 For more details on the 1932 revolution, see Chris Baker and Pasuk Phongpaichit, *A History of Thailand* (4th edn, CUP 2022) 128–134.

6 ibid.

7 ibid.

8 ibid.

9 Jonathan Head, 'The mystery of the missing brass plague' (*BBC*, 20 April 2017) <https://www.bbc.co.uk/news/world-asia-39650310> accessed 20 February 2025.

10 James Hookway, 'Why a stolen democracy plaque is gripping Thailand' (*Wall Street Journal*, 25 April 2017) <https://www.wsj.com/articles/why-a-stolen-democracy-plaque-is-gripping-thailand-1493112247> accessed 20 February 2025.

to his previous works and those of his predecessors. The film also touches on this topic, albeit briefly, when Chulayarnnon explains how exporting a video file one hundred times is comparable with how his work has been circulated and repurposed online. Just as his short film transforms into a video art through reproduction, a still picture from the same film also appears on a TV game show, stripped of the original context and given a new meaning. Here, Chulayarnnon seems to suggest that copying is a good thing as it allows the proliferation of meaning.

Yet the film does not end with satire. Instead, after drawing a parallel between the plaque and the certificate, it shifts to a sombre tone as it reflects on the state of Thai democracy. In the final scene—around one minute before the end—the film laments how the new plaque symbolises a fake 1932 revolution. At that moment, the entire analogy simply unravels. Moments earlier, the film was mocking the notion of authenticity, but in the end, it cannot resist using the People's Party as a reference point for 'authentic' democracy. How does it arrive at this paradox, and what are we to make of it?

Reproducing Authenticity

One could argue that there is no paradox if we view this film as a form of reproduction in itself. Chulayarnnon may see art and politics converge through his metaphor of reproduction, but it is actually his own reproduction of the Western frame of reference that does the trick. This is why the analogy, which appears effective until the final moment, suddenly collapses under the weight of the politico-historical reality of modern Thai society.

In this way, Chulayarnnon's video experiment must be situated within the Western discourse of originality. In this context, a work of art is perceived as originating from the artist and hence original.[11] However, multiplicity is inherent in digital media, complicating the assumed distinction between the original and the copy. There is no doubt that through the art project, Chulayarnnon aims to engage in a dialogue with those artists who question the notion of originality in art, but this is also where the problem arises as his art is also meant to be a satire of the Thai art market.

Notably, the cracks become most apparent at the moment when the film supposedly reveals the irony of authenticity in the art market. As previously mentioned, the scene in which friends and fans purchase his limited-edition art is meant to illustrate how the artist's signature can deceive the public into believing that they are paying for an original work of art, but this interpretation overlooks a crucial point: It is also possible that those who purchased his edition art simply view it as an investment in his authentic brand as an emerging filmmaker. It seems that the film might just be attacking a strawman here.

The same can be said of copyright ownership. Chulayarnnon is not alone in questioning the notion of originality and the authority of the artist. There has been

11 Rosalind Krauss, *The Originality of the Avant-Garde and Other Modernist Myths* (MIT Press 1986).

much discussion in Western scholarship regarding the relationship between Western Romanticism—a cultural and intellectual movement in Europe between the late 18th and early 19th centuries—and the development of the modern copyright framework.[12] The crux of these discussions is the argument that key principles of modern copyright law, particularly authorship and originality, are rooted in the Romantic conception of authorship.[13] This view portrays the creative process as a solitary endeavour, emphasising personal expression and elevating the author to the status of a unique and original genius.[14]

One might wonder to what extent Romantic authorship is actually responsible for the development of copyright law in Thailand. Notably, the Thai Supreme Court has no issue recognising a company—a legal fiction—as the author of a photograph, which is considered an artistic work under Thai copyright law.[15] Even the Romantics could not have predicted this, but this is not to suggest that there is no Western influence in Thai copyright law; that would be an absurd claim.[16] Instead, it highlights the fact that one cannot simply draw a straight line between Western Romanticism and Thai copyright law. And when someone attempts to do so, we must ask, why?

Of Ownership and Community

The 'why' question is particularly pertinent to copyright ownership. Comparing copyright ownership in film with that of the imagined community—commonly known as the nation—opens the possibility of reimagining what it means to protect copyright through the lens of community relations. This perspective promises to provide fresh insights, challenging our understanding of copyright as shaped by legal doctrine, but this approach remains unexplored in the film. After all, Chulayarnnon is more interested in deconstructing the myth of the artist than in examining the relationship between property and community.

If this film had been set in another country in Southeast Asia, the idea of colonialism would have immediately come to mind. However, Thailand's colonial history is shrouded in the myth of independence, with instances such as *100TRD*

12 See further discussion in 'Authorship and Ownership' in Chapter 2.

13 Peter Jaszi, 'Toward a theory of copyright: The metamorphoses of 'authorship'' (1991) *Duke Law Journal* 455; Jaszi, 'On the author effect: Contemporary copyright and collective creativity' (1992) 10 *Cardozo Arts & Entertainment Law Journal* 293; Peter Jaszi and Martha Woodmansee, 'Introduction' in Woodmansee and Jaszi (eds), *The Construction of Authorship* (Duke University Press 1994); James Boyle, *Shamans, Software, and Spleens: Law and the Construction of the Information Society* (Harvard University Press 1996).

14 Woodmansee, 'The genius and the copyright: Economic and legal conditions of the emergence of the 'author'' (1984) 17 *Eighteenth-Century Studies* 425.

15 In Thai Supreme Court Decision no 5259/2549, the Court ruled that a company, as a legal person acting through representatives, could be the author of a photograph, which is classified as an artistic work under Thai copyright law. That is, it recognised under Thai law, a company could own artistic copyright.

16 See further discussion of Western influence in the history of Thai copyright law in Chapter 1.

serving as a poignant reminder that the country must fully confront its colonial past. This could begin by raising some important questions: What does it mean to remain independent when Western influence permeated the country during the era of high colonialism? What happened to the country's power structures following the colonial encounter that could explain the ongoing struggle for democracy? Was it really possible for Thailand to opt out of the colonial world order?

These questions bring us back to Chulayarnnon's film, which aims to document the 2014 coup and reflect on this historic moment. Its main takeaway seems to be that the country does not belong to the people, just as the film does not belong to the audience. Indeed, those who study Thai politics have observed a concentration of political power in a pattern of relationships pivoting on the monarchy.[17] Notably, the alliance of the military and the palace had produced a crucial force in Thai politics since the Cold War years when military authoritarianism began to work in tandem with royalism.[18] It thus comes as no surprise that in 2014, the junta tried to justify the seizure of power with the claim that it had to protect the monarchy from corrupted politicians.[19]

To opponents of the junta, however, the 2014 coup represented above all a return to authoritarianism, one that sent democracy—and the country—backwards into retreat.[20] Supporters of democracy in Thailand often view the military and the monarchy as relics of a bygone era, criticised for failing to keep pace with modern times.[21] Many also argue that as long as power does not truly belong to the people, the country will be held back.[22] The struggle for democracy continues in Thailand, and necessarily so.[23] Yet this does not have to assume a linear trajectory marked by revolutions and historical breaks under which social change proceeds from tradition to modernity and from the West to the rest.

17 This presents a political order that Duncan McCargo refers to as network monarchy; see 'Network Monarchy and Crises of Legitimacy in Thailand' (2005) 18(4) *The Pacific Review* 499.

18 See further discussion on the revival of royal hegemony during the Cold War in Chapter 3.

19 Amy Sawitta Lefevre, 'Thai army chief calls on all to protect monarchy' (*Reuters*, 17 December 2014) <https://www.reuters.com/article/us-thailand-politics-idUSKBN0JV13K20141217> accessed 20 February 2025; Chris Baker, 'The 2014 Thai coup and some roots of authoritarianism' (2016) 46(3) *Journal of Contemporary Asia* 388.

20 **'เพื่อไทย' ชำแหละ 7 ปีรัฐประหาร ประเทศถอยหลัง 'ประยุทธ์' ไม่ทำตามสัญญา ปฏิรูปการเมือง-ปราบโกง ล้มเหลว** ('Pheu Thai' lambasts seven years since coup: Country going backwards, 'Paryuth' going back on promises, political reform-combating corruption floundering)' (*Thairath*, 22 May 2021) <https://www.khaosod.co.th/politics/news_6412448> accessed 20 February 2025.

21 Puangthong Pawakapan, '**ความล้าหลังของการเกณฑ์ทหาร** ("The backwardness of conscription)' (*Prachatai*, 19 February 2019) <https://prachatai.com/journal/2019/02/81102> accessed 20 February 2025.

22 Karoonp. Chetpayark, '**ไม่มีประเทศไหนที่ทำรัฐประหารแล้วเจริญได้: มองข้อสรุปทางรัฐศาสตร์ กับ อ.ประจักษ์ ก้องกีรติ** (No country has achieved progress after a coup)' (*The Standard*, 3 February 2021) <https://thematter.co/social/coup-in-pol-sci-with-aj-prajak/134759> accessed 20 February 2025.

23 'Thailand protests: Risking it all to challenge the monarchy' (*BBC*, 14 August 2020) <https://www.bbc.co.uk/news/world-asia-53770939> accessed 20 February 2025.

Arguably, the monarchy and the military are not mere relics of pre-modern times. This is particularly evident when one delineates the transition between pre-modern and modern times with the arrival of Western modernity in 19th-century Thailand—then known as Siam. The self-modernising Siamese monarchy, in particular, played a pivotal role in the well-known 'era of modernisation' in the nation's history.[24] Since then, this 'modern' institution has been a main pillar of the modern Thai state, which emerged in the late 19th century.[25] Interestingly, the late 19th century was also marked by the growing influence of Western colonialism in Southeast Asia, and it was no coincidence that Siam's modernisation unfolded amid the presence of the imperial West.

However, it is important to note that Siam's ruling elite did not seek to transform Siam into a 'civilised' nation simply to avoid colonisation. Becoming *siwilai* (a Thai transliteration of 'civilisation') was deeply tied to the process of internal colonisation, which allowed the ruling elite to centralise local power and build a modern nation-state.[26] Furthermore, one may be excused for wondering whether the bloodless revolution of 1932 was just a by-product of Siam's colonial encounter. After all, the monarchy never truly disappeared; it remained in the background until it was politically revived during the Cold War, thanks to Thai military rulers and the US anti-communist campaign. Once again, the Thai nation embarked on the quest for modernisation, but this time, modernisation was expressed in the then-political catchword of development.

Colonial Legacy in Thai Modernity

A 'seductive but dangerous Other' is how historian Thongchai Winichakul describes what the 'West' is to Thailand's ruling elite.[27] In one sense, it refers to the perception of Western knowledge as the sign of the times and the horizons of what is possible.[28] This relationship with Western knowledge points towards specific power dynamics that have persisted in Thailand ever since the encounter with European colonialism in the 19th century. The official narrative of independence manages to hide the legacy of colonialism in plain sight. Look carefully, and one will see how the bygone era of Western colonialism continues to cast a shadow over the ongoing history of Thai authoritarianism. This should be the backdrop for

24 See Chapter 1.

25 For a historical overview that explains a more recent authoritarian regime, see Baker, '2014 Thai coup' (n 19).

26 See further discussion on the relationship between *siwilai* and colonialism in Chapter 1.

27 Thongchai Winichakul, 'Coming to terms with the West: Intellectual strategies of bifurcation and Post-Westernism in Siam' in Rachel Harrison and Peter Jackson (eds), *The Ambiguous Allure of the West: Traces of the Colonial in Thailand* (Hong Kong University Press 2010) 135.

28 Janit Feangfu and Rachel Harrison, 'Contested modernities and spectres of progress in twentieth-century Siam/Thailand' in Susie Protschky and Tom van den Berge (eds), *Modern Times in Southeast Asia, 1920s–1970s* (Brill 2018).

examining the emergence and development of modern Thai law—including Thai copyright law—from the late 19th century.

Once again, it is worth recalling that Siam/Thailand emerged as a modern nation-state in the wake of Western colonialism.[29] Historians refer to the relevant period in Thai history as the era of colonial modernity.[30] This was the period when the Siamese ruling elite initiated numerous modernisation projects not only to address the threat of colonisation but also to centralise domestic monarchical power. Consequently, the pertinent question is not whether Siam was 'informally' colonised but how the ruling elite could refashion themselves as civilising agents, implementing aggressive internal colonisation policies predicated on Western models. Such was the agency of the local elite that eludes the colonised–coloniser model of explanation. And yet their pursuit of civilisation attests to the new global model of power that was concomitant with the expansion of Western colonialism.

As such, the historical era of colonial modernity resonates with the ideas of the Latin American scholar Aníbal Quijano, who posits the inseparability of modernity and coloniality as two sides of the same coin.[31] Likewise, the case of the Siamese ruling elite echoes the global relations of domination that Aníbal Quijano articulates through the concept of coloniality.[32] He argues that coloniality has outlived colonialism, and it constitutes 'the most general form of domination in the world today.'[33]

For Quijano, coloniality emerged in the 15th-century conquest of Latin America and has persisted to date in the confluence with a universal paradigm of knowledge that is, in fact, Eurocentric.[34] Expanding on Quijano, Walter Mignolo argues that coloniality is the dark side of modernity, and the coloniality of power persists as a form of domination even after political decolonisation.[35] Although he speaks from Latin American experiences, his arguments resonate curiously with Thailand, particularly because coloniality/modernity is not constrained by the colonised–coloniser binary.[36]

Thus, it is important to emphasise that 'learning from the West' does not necessarily work against Thai authoritarianism. For those in power, it simply counts

29 Thongchai Winichakul, *Siam Mapped: A History of the Geo-Body of a Nation* (Silkworm Books 1994).

30 Tamara Loos, *Subject Siam: Family, Law, and Colonial Modernity in Thailand* (Cornell University Press 2006) 2; Thongchai Winichakul, '*เมื่อสยามพลิกผัน: ว่าด้วยกรอบมโนทัศน์ของสยามยุคใหม่ (Siam at a Turning Point: On the Foundational Mentality of Siam in the Modern Era)* (Fah-diew-kan 2019) 6.

31 Walter Mignolo, 'Introduction: Coloniality of power and de-colonial thinking' (2007) 21(2–3) *Cultural Studies* 155.

32 Aníbal Quijano and Michael Ennis, 'Coloniality of power, eurocentrism, and Latin America' (2000) 1(3) Nepantal 553, 533; Aníbal Quijano, 'Coloniality and modernity/rationality' (2007) 21(2) *Cultural Studies* 168, 177.

33 ibid 170.

34 ibid 542.

35 ibid.

36 See further discussion in 'Modernity/Coloniality' in Chapter 1.

among their idioms of power, as the logic of universality—the same one that sent the Siamese ruling elite on the quest for civilisation—does not negate but rather constitutes the coloniality of power. Furthermore, it is important to note that the Siamese ruling elite did not always set out to imitate but oscillated between universality and identity. The notion of the nation—that 'imagined community'—is another source of power that emerged in the wake of colonialism.[37] Similar to the allure of the West, nationalism is another legacy of colonial modernity that constitutes a powerful logic through which relations of power are articulated.

Defining what it means to be Thai has been the cornerstone of Thai authoritarianism. Central to its narrative of Thai identity is the notion of 'Thainess,' which is encapsulated in the famous slogan *Chart, Sart, Kasat* ('Nation, Religion, and King'). This nationalist mantra has been in public circulation since the early 20th century, and it unmistakably resembles the British 'God, King, and the Country.'[38] This connection reveals much about the emergence of Thai nationalism and its connection with Western colonialism.[39] It is the paradox of aspiring to be civilised while remaining truly Thai that is key to understanding Thai nationalism as an ideology.

Nationalism did not emerge in Siam/Thailand through social movements. Unlike the history of popular nationalist movements in former colonies, Thai nationalism was born as a royal project inspired by European imperialism,[40] and before long, the Siamese ruling elite began to turn increasingly inward, in a purported repudiation of Westernisation, as the fruits of modernisation started to challenge their authority.[41]

However, the emerging notion of Thainess did not just become another source of authority. It also served as a pivot to regain control over the influx of Western knowledge and culture, as demonstrated by such imageries as 'a Thai way of life no less civilised than the life in the West.'[42] The same strategy also allowed a leader of a military dictatorship to devise the infamous claim of 'Thai-style democracy' to justify the absence of an elected government.[43]

Furthermore, Thai nationalism has largely been shaped by the enterprise of history writing, with the relationship between the nation and the monarchy serving as a long-standing theme in official historiography. According to official history, the self-modernising monarch was the main reason why Siam was able to secure its independence. This narrative illustrates how in the Thai context, 'official nationalism' constructs a relationship of indebtedness, portraying the imagined

37 Benedict Anderson, *Imagined Communities: Reflections on the Origin and Spread of Nationalism* (revised edn, Verso 2006) 99–101.

38 Baker and Pasuk (n 5) 118.

39 See further discussion in 'Keeping Up With the Emerging Public Sphere' in Chapter 1.

40 Anderson (n 37) 99–100.

41 See n 39.

42 Thak Chaloemtiarana, *Thailand: The Politics of Despotic Paternalism* (Silkworm Books 2007) 149.

43 ibid 209. See further discussion in 'Identity Politics' in Chapter 3.

Thai community as embodying the debt owed by its citizens.[44] This state–citizen relationship is closely tied to the pursuit of national development, which is itself imbued with deep political and cultural significance. Consequently, when creativity and innovation have been co-opted by the authoritarian Thai state, respect for copyright also becomes a duty arising from one's indebtedness to the nation.

II. A Decolonial Jurisprudence of Copyright

Thus, the legal field has long been entangled with the Thai predicament of colonial modernity.[45] In the 19th century, the adoption of a modern/Western legal system was central to a colonial-style state-building project, which was closely tied to the formation of an absolute monarchy.[46] This was the period when Siam found itself at the intersection between the height of Western colonialism in Southeast Asia and the pursuit of internal colonisation by the Siamese ruling elite. Occupying an intermediate position in this global–local dynamic was law. As a symbol of civilisation, law constituted a strategic domain for the Siamese elite to demonstrate Siam's civilisation to Western powers.[47] Meanwhile, the ruling elite also borrowed from the colonial West to modernise Siamese law for the purpose of governing its own subjects.[48]

In contemporary Thailand, this duality of law remains evident in public controversies surrounding copyright protection. By the end of the 20th century, the US-led global war on media piracy had created an image of Thailand as a lawless country plagued by rampant piracy.[49] Thai piracy was depicted as wild and dangerous, leading to the portrayal of the country as uncivilised and backward, but with the arrival of the new century came a shift in Thailand's policy landscape: the 'creative turn' in economic development policy.[50] Notably, notions such as creativity and innovation were being assimilated into the authoritarian language of legitimacy, as the creative economy emerged as a new national quest. From that point onwards, a gradual rise of a particular narrative surrounding IP can be observed—one that valorises ownership and exploitation, often at the expense of the otherwise significant notion of balance.

At the heart of the state's attempt to institutionalise copyright lies the issue of legitimacy. For while it remains wary of Western powers, the authoritarian Thai state has long thrived on selectively appropriating Western ideas for its own benefit: The 'Thai-style' democracy serves as a good example. Consequently, there is

44 See Anderson (n 37) 86, 99.

45 The concept of colonial modernity is further developed in Chapter 1.

46 This point is central to the historical discussion in Chapter 1.

47 Loos (n 30) 3.

48 ibid; Thongchai Winichakul, *นิติรัฐอภิสิทธิ์และราชานิติธรรม ประวัติศาสตร์ภูมิปัญญาของ Rule by Law แบบไทย (Legal-Privileged-State and Royalist Rule of Law: The Intellectual History of Thai-Style Rule by Law)* (Thammasat University 2020) 78–79.

49 See further discussion in 'Modernity/Piracy' in Chapter 4.

50 See further discussion in 'The Politics of Creativity' in Chapter 5.

a pervasive sentiment among progressive movements in Thailand that Thai modernity is belated and distorted, and understandably so.

Yet the problem with the desire for 'authentic' modernity is laid bare in *100RTD*. As seen earlier, Chulayarnnon's satirical take on authenticity assumes a particular conception of the creative process, one that valorises the individuality and autonomy of a true creator, the Romantic author. This raises a fundamental question: Does such a tradition exist in Thai culture to begin with? Indeed, before questioning the notion of originality, it may be more prudent to ask what it means to be an artist or an author in the Thai context. More importantly, this highlights the problem of fixing Euro-American experiences as 'the standard, the typical, the universal, and the centre.'[51] Implicit in this problem is a broader epistemological question: Can a Western perspective truly represent local experience?

Searching for a Vantage Point

Representation is a critical issue in postcolonial critique, a movement that developed around figures such as Edward Said,[52] Homi Bhabha,[53] and Gayatri Spivak.[54] These scholars explore the issue of identity through discussions of Orientalism, hybridity, and subalterns.[55] Meanwhile, in a different intellectual tradition, the problem of identity also animates the work of decolonial thinkers such as Aníbal Quijano. As seen earlier, his theory of modernity/coloniality traces the history of colonialism back to the European conquest of America, arguing that the concept of race emerged as a foundational aspect of the modern era.[56] According to Quijano, knowledge production and the totality of knowledge combine to create a form of oppression that cannot be displaced through a formal process of political decolonisation; rather, it requires epistemological decolonisation.[57]

Walter Mignolo expands on this argument and mobilises academic activities around the concept of modernity/coloniality. He also promotes the term decoloniality, contrasting it with (political) decolonisation, and describes it as an alternative to the totality of knowledge underpinning the coloniality of power.[58] In other words, Mignolo advocates for a decolonisation of the mind and imagination. He distinguishes this project from postcolonial critiques, which he views as attempts

51 Thongchai, 'Coming to Terms' (n 27) 151.

52 *Orientalism: Western Conceptions of the Orient* (Penguin 1995).

53 *The Location of Culture* (Routledge 1994).

54 Gayatri Chakravorty Spivak, 'Can the subaltern speak?' in Cary Nelson and Lawrence Grossberg (eds), *Marxism and the Interpretation of Culture* (Macmillan 1988).

55 Gurminder Bhambra, 'Postcolonial and decolonial dialogues' (2014) 17(2) *Postcolonial Studies* 115, 115–117.

56 Quijano and Ennis (n 32).

57 ibid.

58 'The geopolitics of knowledge and the colonial difference' (2002) 101(1) *South Atlantic Quarterly* 57.

to transform the Euro-American academy from within.[59] Unlike the work of scholars such as Edward Said, Gayatri Spivak, and Homi Bhabha—whom he considers heavily reliant on Western thinkers—Mignolo argues for a shift to 'border thinking or border epistemology' that takes indigenous intellectuals and activists as reference points.[60] In this way, his polemic of 'decolonial options' appears to assume the impossibility of finding an internal vantage point—that there are no lines of escape to be found within Western knowledge.

Interestingly, the challenges in applying postcolonial theories to Thailand seems to lend support to Mignolo's argument for decolonial options. A good example here is Peter Jackson's postcolonial analysis of Thai–Western relations.[61] Jackson's attempt to apply postcolonial theories to Thai studies revolves around the notion of hybridity. He observes that 'hybridity is a defining feature of Siamese/Thai cultural history and of contemporary Thai culture, both elite and popular.'[62] His reflection on Siam's quest for civilisation further illustrates how the hybrid notion of *siwilai* constituted a form of resistance as well as a mode of legitimation.[63] Initially, he argues, the discourse of *siwilai* allowed the ruling elite to appropriate the colonial notion of civilisation to simultaneously negotiate the threat of Western powers and consolidate local authority. However, as Westernisation permeated Siamese society, the discourse of *siwilai* began to escape the control of the ruling elite, posing a threat to their authority.[64]

Thus, Jackson's engagement with postcolonial theories interestingly highlights the ambivalence inherent in pursuing a postcolonial analysis in the Thai context. The agency and dual position of the Siamese ruling elite complicate the colonised/coloniser binary. In postcolonial discourse, Homi Bhabha presents mimicry and hybridity as capable of destabilising colonial representations.[65] But for those in Thailand who aspire to replicate authentic democracy, 'almost the same but not quite' reinforces rather than subverts the totality of Western representations.[66] To speak of hybridity in Thailand signifies an act of simultaneous subversion and domination, depending on the position from which one speaks. At best, hybridity serves as an analytical tool to reveal the persistence of coloniality in Thailand.[67] It is not capable of pointing to a way to escape.

59 'Delinking: The rhetoric of modernity, the logic of coloniality and the grammar of de-coloniality' (2007) 21(2–3) *Cultural Studies* 449, 452.

60 ibid 455.

61 See Peter Jackson, 'Afterword: Postcolonial theories and Thai semicolonial hybridities' in Harrison and Jackson (eds), *The Ambiguous Allure of the West*.

62 ibid 191.

63 ibid 197–198.

64 ibid 200.

65 See Bhabha (n 53).

66 ibid 122. Bhabha argues that the ambivalence in colonial mimicry (i.e. almost the same, but not quite/almost the same, but not white) can be subversive because the colonised subject's mimicking of the coloniser can slip into a mockery of the whole colonial mission.

67 See further discussion on this point in 'Siamese–Western Hybridity' in Chapter 2.

Nevertheless, the postcolonial association of hybridity with cultural repetition and representation of difference complicates the relationship between difference and repetition. Both the imperative of universality and the onus of identity rely on the assumption that things constantly repeat themselves. In other words, the repetition of the same makes perceptible a relationship of before and after that underpins the sense of 'belatedness' in the quest for civilisation. Similarly, the notion that things constantly repeat themselves is necessary for the essentialist assumptions behind the nationalist discourse of 'Thainess,' which persistently dictates what it means to be Thai.

Against this conventional notion of repetition as the return of the same, one could view repetition as the continual act of beginning again.[68] This perspective comes from the work of Gilles Deleuze, whose concepts of difference and repetition suggest that both belatedness and Thainess should be seen as a representation of reality rather than as a reality of repetition itself.[69] And through beginning again and again, repetition creates movement instead of stagnation. This could be a movement out of the binary opposition of tradition and modernity, as well as that of the Thai self and the Western Other. The temptation to go back to pre-modern/pre-colonial life should be resisted. One issue with this nostalgic view of tradition is evident in Thailand, where tradition is constructed as the binary opposite of modernity, and together, they paint the world in black and white and demand that one chooses sides.

Rather than 'delinking' or insisting on a fresh start, understanding repetition as beginning again opens the possibility of engineering an escape from within. Here, it is worth noting that the historian Dipesh Chakrabarty offers a similar perspective on postcolonial India, arguing that the Indian curse of belatedness should be seen as an opportunity.[70] In fact, he proposes a potential dialogue between Indian subaltern history and the history of modern Thailand, noting an unexpected convergence in the fact that both countries came to modernity belatedly.[71] For Chakrabarty, both India and Thailand face the problem of naming and categorising their supposedly derivative modernity, or as he puts it,

> How do we, under such circumstances, deal with the problem of what may be genuinely new about the modern that also seems belated and resembles something that has already happened somewhere else?[72]

68 This concept of repetition is further developed in 'Repetition and Learning' in Chapter 5.

69 See Gilles Deleuze, *Difference and Repetition* (Paul Patton tr, Continuum 1968) 10. 'The theatre of repetition is opposed to the theatre of representation,' says Deleuze. This comparison, along with Deleuze's preference for dramatisation to representation, is further discussed in 'Moral Panic' in Chapter 5.

70 For more detail, see Dipesh Chakrabarty, 'Belatedness as possibility: Subaltern histories, once again' in Elleke Boehmer and Rosinka Chaudhuri (eds), *The Indian Postcolonial: A Critical Reader* (Routledge 2010).

71 Dipesh Chakrabarty, 'The names and repetitions of postcolonial history' in Harrison and Jackson (eds), *The Ambiguous Allure of the West*, x.

72 ibid.

By framing belatedness as opportunity, Chakrabarty highlights the difficulty of recognising newness, which he suggests enters the world through displacement and disguise, drawing on the Deleuzian conception of repetition.[73]

A Question of Learning

Chakrabarty's observation on postcolonial history resonates in intriguing ways with the history and contemporary significance of copyright law in Thailand. But rather than attempting to identify newness—which may regress into a representation of differences as a function of fixed identities (e.g. the 'Thai' way)—this book approaches a decolonial jurisprudence as a way of engineering an escape from that kind of capture, even only a small escape. The goal here is not to escape everything all at once but to start over and over in the middle of things.[74]

The paradox of claiming a vantage point from within can be avoided if learning is understood as distinct from imitation. As Deleuze says, 'We learn nothing from those who say "Do as I do." Our only teachers are those who tell us to "do with me."'[75] Implicit in the second model of learning is the experimentation of learning by doing that generates a proliferation of meaning. This raises the question of whether the experience of copyright protection in Thailand can offer fresh insights into the meaning of copyright in law. Ultimately, this second model of learning lies at the heart of this book, which seeks to explore these ideas in relation to Thailand and its copyright law.

Thus, the task of this book involves two distinct yet intertwined questions. First, can the experience of copyright protection in Thailand offer an alternative conception of copyright in law? Second, how can the Thai experience be properly engaged, considering the country's complicated history of colonialism? To address these questions, some methodological points must be clarified regarding how the study of Thai copyright protection is approached.

Law and Society

This book does not treat copyright law as a field of technical knowledge reserved for lawyers but rather as a regulatory aspect of social life. However, rather than attempting to establish a causal relationship between law and society—often the focus of contemporary scholarship on copyright and creativity[76]—it acknowledges the complexity of such relations, aiming instead to trace the presence of copyright law in society as it is collectively experienced. In doing so, this book not only puts

73 ibid xi.
74 This point is further developed in 'Repetition and Learning' in Chapter 5.
75 Deleuze, *Difference* (n 69) 23.
76 See for instance Christopher Jon Springman, 'Copyright and creative incentives: What do(n't) we know' in Rochelle Cooper Dreyfuss and Elizabeth Siew-Kuan Ng (eds), *Framing Intellectual Property Law in the 21st Century: Integrating Incentives Trade Development Culture and Human Rights* (CUP 2018).

copyright law back into society but also problematises the very notion of society itself, particularly when society is understood as a unified whole.

Throughout the discussions, the notion of community is used, both implicitly and explicitly, to examine the problems, conditions, and consequences of copyright protection in social life. However, this book does not invoke the idea of community in a nostalgic sense. Nor does it use community to denote a social structure or something physical. In this book, 'community' is synonymous with collectivity, and it 'exists as something for people to think with.'[77] In this way, the first half of this book focuses on the political community—the nation—which remains the primary site of copyright regulation.[78] Central to the discussion is the interplay between nation building, colonialism, and law, examining the development of copyright law as the law of the nation-state. But as the attention shifts towards contemporary Thai cinema, the focus expands beyond state law to explore the role of copyright in social interactions.

Central to this book is, therefore, the recognition that copyright is both a social and legal institution. And for the purposes of further inquiry, it draws a working distinction between 'copyright' as a social category making up the field of social experience and 'copyright law' as an institutionalised doctrine comprising a body of rules, principles, concepts, and values. This approach allows the book to move beyond the conventional focus on legal texts and court rulings. Certainly, these legal materials were attentively consulted, so are various non-legal materials and perspectives necessary to understand the social phenomenon of law, particularly in its relationship with an oppressive social order under colonialism, nationalism, and authoritarianism.

However, this conceptual distinction in no way demarcates two separate realms of legal doctrine and social inquiry, as this book views law as an inherently social phenomenon.[79] Ultimately, the book aims to delivers juristic knowledge with an account of copyright law as it is experienced in everyday life. For this reason, the approach taken has to be empirical, moving beyond the black-letter method of doctrinal legal research, and yet interpretative, as opposed to the explanatory approach of mainstream social science.

Law and Film

Films are of interest to this book not only because their narratives can challenge social and political institutions but also because their modes of production and

77 Anthony Cohen, *The Symbolic Construction of Community* (Routledge 1985) 19.

78 Throughout this book, the nation will be referred to as an 'imagined community,' a term coined by Benedict Anderson. It is also important to note that 'imagined' is not the same as 'imaginary.' Anderson makes it clear that any community larger than face-to-face interaction has to be imagined, and so imagining means envisioning, not making things up. See Anderson (n 37) 6.

79 This perspective will become evident in the historical discussion that traces the development of Thai copyright law from its emergence in the early 20th century to its rise to prominence by the century's end. As will be seen in Chapter 1, this copyright historiography does not investigate legal development per se. Legal change offers a site for examining the power structures that emerged in Siam/Thailand following the encounter with Western colonialism.

consumption can be instructive for a re-conception of copyright in law. As seen earlier, film analysis can provide fresh insights into familiar social phenomena. However, the analysis of Chulayarnnon's film also illustrates how this kind of examination does not seek to establish a cause–effect relationship between copyright and creativity. Nor does it go as far as providing a 'thick description' in the style of ethnographic research. Instead, Thai cinema is considered a valuable site of exploration for two reasons.

First, it reflects social change. As a product and a cultural form, film can capture the state of society at a given time. At the same time, films like Chulayarnnon's also highlight the potential of self-reflexivity in this form of cultural expression. Thai cinema, in this regard, not only offers a reflection on the very social change it embodies but also situates Thailand within the global network of film production and distribution. Thus, Thai cinema as an object of study is conducive to examining the particularity of place (Thailand) within the commonality of experience (the globalisation of copyright law).

To define the field of 'Thai cinema,' this book draws on the concept of national cinema, as discussed by the film scholar Andrew Higson. Higson notes four different ways the notion of national cinema has been conceptualised.[80] First, national cinema may be equated with a domestic film industry, where the primary concerns revolve around economic issues related to film production and distribution. Second, national cinema may refer to a body of national film texts, highlighting the issues of common style and national identity. Third, national cinema may focus attention on film consumption, raising questions about Hollywood's dominance and cultural imperialism. And, lastly, national cinema may indicate the cinema 'steeped in the high-cultural and/or modernist heritage of a particular nation-state' as opposed to what is popular with the audiences.[81] This book adopts Higson's multifaceted definition as a practical framework for analysing contemporary film policy and practice in Thailand.

Still, a crucial question remains: Should 'film' be understood in a conventional sense—as shorts and features—or, more broadly, as audiovisual artefacts? Consider Chulayarnnon's works. He describes himself as a filmmaker and an artist, with his audiovisual practice ranging from conventional filmmaking to performance video and video installation.[82] His experimentation in *100 Times Reproduction of a Cock Kills a Child* extends the notion of creativity to mundane activities such as video exporting while challenging the traditional notion of film that is closely tied to authorial expression and theatrical exhibition. Similarly, in *100RTD*, Chulayarnnon draws attention to the vast 'content' created by social media users, who are typically not considered artists and filmmakers. These two instances understandably position Chulayarnnon as an outsider venturing into the established domain of feature films. And yet this very engagement suggests that similar discussions can

80 Andrew Higson, 'The concept of national cinema' (1989) 30(4) *Screen* 36, 36–37.

81 ibid 37.

82 See the information on his website <http://www.chulayarnnon.com/profile.html> accessed 20 February 2025.

also be initiated from within the film industry, where authorship remains significant yet evolving.

Indeed, in hopes of finding success independently of the studios, many Thai filmmakers submit their films to the circuit of international film festivals to build an artistic reputation.[83] This branding exercise has become crucial for Thai independent filmmakers, who need to pursue 'auteur' status for better funding prospects and, ultimately, the ability to continue making films.[84] While fundraising through auteur branding may not be necessary for those working on studio productions, their commercial prospects can certainly benefit from established brand loyalty. In this regard, auteur branding, also brings into view the active role of contemporary audiences, blurring the distinction between a producer and a consumer as well as between investment and mere use. What this means for copyright law is worth considering, particularly as these changes are unfolding right before our eyes.

Some Preliminary Lessons

In his final remarks on the legal history of 'colonial copyright' imposed across the British Empire, Michael Birnhack identifies an area for further research:

> The parallels between the condition of colonial copyright and contemporary globalisation is yet another area for further research, so to better understand how the earlier form of globalisation by colonisation has affected the latter phase.[85]

This book takes up Birnhack's suggestion but begins from a different starting point. Rather than viewing the process of globalisation as a by-product of colonisation, it regards globalisation as characterised by power relations. One might not wish to stop at the notion of globalisation when it is apparent that relations of domination are as much a concern in contemporary times as they were in the colonial era. Accordingly, the book does not approach colonialism simply as historical events but seeks to trace its lasting influence in contemporary power structures.[86] In doing so, it helps move the critique of the international copyright system beyond the anti-colonial rhetoric and sentiments that were particularly prevalent at the height of the intellectual property rights (IPR) globalisation around the turn of the century.

Knowledge, Coloniality, and Intellectual Property

In shifting from a historical to an analytical perspective, the main focus becomes neither the military might of Western colonisers nor the economic power of industrialised countries. Instead, issues surrounding knowledge production form the

83 See further discussion on the relations between international film festivals and contemporary Thai cinema in 'Co-Authoring a Brand' In Chapter 6.

84 See further discussion on the significance of auteur branding in contemporary Thai cinema in 'Brand Agency' in Chapter 6.

85 Michael Birnhack, *Colonial Copyright: Intellectual Property in Mandate Palestine* (OUP 2012) 287.

86 This is the central theme running through the first half of the book.

book's central theme. This theme first emerges in the familiar story of the commodification of knowledge, as seen in the global expansion of IP protection. However, beyond this relationship between knowledge and IP lies the knowledge of IP. Since property relations—especially unequal ones—are sustained by ideology, the problem of knowledge production considered in this regard also encompasses the coloniality of knowledge. This perspective offers interesting insights into recent developments in Thai IP policy and may also shed light on similar developments elsewhere in the Global South.[87]

Indeed, a key issue in a critical examination of Thai-Western relations is the 'in-between' status of Siam/Thailand, based on the 'colonised vs coloniser' model of explanation.[88] This issue also extends to the history of Thai copyright law, which does not neatly follow the conventional narrative of the 'Global North vs Global South.' However, this book does not aim to propose a tripartite taxonomy. It is more concerned with the effect of colonialism on Thailand, where existing power structures can be traced back to the 19th-century encounter with Western colonialism. Notably, the nationalist discourse of Thai identity/Thainess is primarily supported by the royal–nationalist myth of independence, which ironically constitutes the colonial legacy in the Thai context.

Meanwhile, copyright historiography tends to adopt the colonised–coloniser perspective, making countries like Thailand appear exceptional and yet peripheral to global copyright history.[89] Consequently, an attentive engagement with the history and contemporary significance of copyright law in Thailand offers a unique perspective on how relations of domination can persist in the absence of formal colonisation. After all, more than just an account of legal technicality is necessary to explain the continued membership of the Global South in the global IP system following the political process of decolonisation.[90] As for the place of Thailand in the Global South, this book opens a dialogue between academic studies of Thailand (area studies) and the intellectual traditions of postcolonialism and decoloniality.[91] In doing so, it also addresses the politics of resistance in Thailand, often bifurcating between a national liberation from 'domination by the West' and a domestic struggle against nationalist authoritarianism.

87 See further discussion on recent developments in Thai IP policy in 'The politics of creativity' in Chapter 5.

88 See further discussion on this issue in 'A Crypto-Colony' in Chapter 1.

89 See for instance, 'The "extraordinary multiplicity" of intellectual property laws in the British colonies in the nineteenth century' (2011) 12(1) in 162; Uma Suthersanen and Ysolde Gendreau, *A Shifting Empire: 100 Years of the Copyright Act 1911* (Edward Elgar 2013); Birnhack (n 85); Catherine Seville, 'British colonial and imperial copyright' in Isabella Alexander and H. Tomás Gómez-Arostegui (eds), *Research Handbook on the History of Copyright Law* (Elgar Edwards 2016).

90 See for instance Ruth Okediji, 'The international relations of intellectual property: Narratives of developing country participation in the global intellectual property system' (2003) 7(2) *Singapore Journal of International & Comparative Law* 315.

91 Area studies (e.g. Thai studies) are generally dedicated to specific geographical locations and culturally defined areas, such as countries and regions, and are usually multidisciplinary in approach.

Cinema, Society, and Copyright's Community

The choice of Thai cinema as a site of examination is influenced by developments in Southeast Asian studies in the early 2000s.[92] The turn of the century saw an increase in visibility and popularity of films from the region, highlighting the complex relationship between Southeast Asian cinema and its Western counterparts, as well as other influential cinematic traditions such as Hong Kong, Japan, and India.[93] In her assessment of this emerging scholarly direction, Rachel Harrison argues for an academic study of Southeast Asian cinema as 'a mapping of varied cultural influences, inextricably intermeshed, extensively hybridised, and intensely interconnected with networks of global power.'[94] In Thailand, as this book aims to show, cinema embodies the problem of modernity/coloniality. After its introduction in Siam as a modern technology, cinema gradually evolved into a state apparatus in a propaganda war and, more recently, an object of desire in the pursuit of a creative economy as a new path to development.

Regarding the relationship with copyright law, this book follows a line of inquiry in copyright scholarship that examines film protection as a way to reflect on the relationship between copyright protection and creativity.[95] This perspective was already anticipated in the early history of cinema, when the industry sought to obtain copyright protection by recasting film—emerging then as a technology of reproduction—into a work of authorship.[96] And while film authorship remains a source of agitation for legal doctrine, the changing commercial and cultural landscape has dramatically transformed the industry, inviting a broader examination of copyright's relationship to film production and consumption. In this way, a study of Thai cinema offers an instructive perspective, allowing this book to explore an emerging form of social production that produces new meaning and value as much as new goods and services.[97] This development in Thai cinema resonates with

92 See Rachel Harrison, 'Introduction: Cinema as an emerging field in South East Asian studies' (2006) 14(2) *South East Asia Research* 133.

93 ibid 136.

94 ibid 140.

95 See for instance F Jay Dougherty, 'Not a Spike Lee joint? Issues in the authorship of motion pictures under US copyright law' (2001) 49 *UCLA Law Review* 22; Fiona Macmillan, 'The cruel C: Copyright and film' (2002) 24(10) *European Intellectual Property Review* 483; Michael Handler, 'Continuing problems with film copyright' in Fiona Macmillan (ed), *New Directions in Copyright Law, Vol 6* (Edward Elgar 2007); Lionel Bently and Laura Biron, 'The author strikes back: Mutating authorship in the expanded universe' in Kathy Bowrey and Michael Handler (eds), *Law and Creativity in the Age of the Entertainment Franchise* (CUP 2014); Oğulcan Ekiz, 'My film in your pocket: An analysis of user interactions with films and copyright law' (2019) 9(2) *Queen Mary Journal of Intellectual Property* 196; Fiona Macmillan, *Intellectual and Cultural Property: Between Market and Community* (Routledge 2021). See also Bernard Edelman, *Ownership of the Image: Elements for a Marxist Theory of Law* (Elizabeth Kingdom tr, Routledge Kegan and Paul 1979).

96 See Johanna Gibson, 'The man behind the curtain: Developing film's double exposure of intellectual property' in P Sean Morris (ed), *Intellectual Property and the Law of Nations, 1860–1920* (Brill 2022).

97 Indeed, the second half of the book primarily revolves around this theme.

Johanna Gibson's concept of familiar production,[98] and it entices a reorientation of copyright law towards the idea of community.

While drawing attention to practices and norms in creative communities, this book does not seek to make copyright law 'mirror' social practices. Instead, it proposes to realign the law and society relations.[99] Ultimately, this book puts forward a legal concept of community resource for an alternative conception of copyright in law.[100] The concept of community resource shifts the focus from the originality of expression to the repetition of familiar production; it envisions the role of copyright law in facilitating community relations. This new legal concept draws upon and reinterprets Roger Cotterrell's sociological perspective on law, specifically his work on law and community, which accords a central role to the idea of mutual interpersonal trust.[101]

A fundamental aspect of how copyright law may forge a sense of community lies in its ability to cultivate trusting relationships,[102] yet mistrust is also what the law has been facing in the Thai public.[103] Emphasising the idea of trust thus addresses both the particular situation of Thailand and the broader question of what copyright law can be. The point of convergence here is the question of how social relations are imagined and what role the law plays in creating or sustaining particular imageries. Particularly relevant to this issue is the balance notion in copyright law and the territoriality of public–private boundaries that it implies.[104] Community and trust, therefore, present a different paradigm of copyright protection, one in which interpersonal trust as the building block of community becomes the law's primary concern.

Moving Forward

This book is divided into four parts, each consisting of two chapters.

Chapter 1 examines the early development of Thai copyright law in the broader history of Siamese modernisation and the expansion of Western colonialism. It engages with a growing body of scholarship on Thai history that regards the dominant narratives of independence and modernisation as a distraction from the apparent subjugation of Siam to the colonial world order. As law was instrumental to Siam's modernising effort, the chapter looks specifically at three legislative

98 See Johanna Gibson, *The Logic of Innovation: Intellectual Property and What the User Found There* (Routledge 2014) 38–41.

99 For a view along similar lines, see Bently and Biron, 'Discontinuities between legal conceptions of authorship and social practices: What, if anything, is to be done?' in Mireille van Eechoud (ed), *The Work of Authorship* (Amsterdam University Press 2014).

100 The concept of community resource is further developed in Chapter 8.

101 Cotterrell, *Law's Community* (n 58) 329–330; Cotterrell, *Law, Culture, and Society* (n 53) 73–74.

102 See further discussion on this point in 'Mutual Trust' in Chapter 8.

103 See further discussion on public mistrust of copyright law in 'Burning Down the House' in Chapter 7.

104 See further discussion on the legal notion of balance in 'The Public–Private Dichotomy' in Chapter 8.

milestones between the birth of Thai copyright law in 1901 and Siam's accession to the Berne Convention in 1931.

Chapter 2 further explores the historical connections between copyright and colonialism, using Thai copyright history to reflect on Siam's transition into the era of colonial modernity. Informing the discussion in this chapter is recent copyright scholarship on the entangled history of modern authorship and literary ownership in 18th-century Europe. The chapter similarly turns to Thai literary history to examine the changing literary culture of 19th-century Siam and the subsequent emergence of literary property.

Chapter 3 leaps forward to the years of the Cold War. It continues to examine Thai–Western relations but shifts the context to a major revision of Thai copyright law in the wake of US global influence. The chapter seeks to show how relations of domination did not necessarily end with the end of European colonial empires, tracing the persistence of coloniality in Thailand's 'special' relationship with the US amidst the latter's anti-communist campaign in Southeast Asia. It pays particular attention to the American-led process of socio-economic development, beginning in the late 1950s and responsible for an overhaul of Thai copyright law in the 1970s.

Chapter 4 then follows the ramifications of the new law into the troubled 1990s, which saw the breakdown in Thai–US relations playing out against global intellectual property rights harmonisation. It reappraises the cries of neo-colonialism against the Global North, pointing towards Siamese–Western relations to suggest some continuity in contemporary power structures. Notably, it argues that Western narratives around media piracy in Thailand gave a new meaning (and power) to the idea of creativity in Thailand's policy and political landscape.

Chapter 5 examines a deeply ingrained sense of belatedness—specifically that Thailand came to modernity belatedly—that always lurks behind the discussions in previous chapters. The chapter finds its site of examination in contemporary issues surrounding Thai cinema. Specifically, it first looks closely at recent public discussions around the country's film industry. Then, it turns the attention to exploring how Thai cinema has navigated and made sense of digital transformation by repeating and working through the Western language of property and ownership

Chapter 6 shifts the focus to emerging practices in Thai cinema, presenting a cultural analysis of copyright law. It draws on a mix of document research and in-depth interviews with key actors in the film industry. Informed by the scholarship on auteurism in film studies, the chapter examines the related phenomenon of auteur branding and active audience. Both developments challenge the legal distinction between authors and users, pointing to a relational conception of copyright and, thereby, a mediating role for copyright law.

Chapter 7 delves deeper into contemporary Thai cinema, building on the filmmaker–audience analysis in the previous chapter. It broadens the scope to include studios, producers, distributors, and exhibitors, all in order to better understand the changing conditions in Thai cinema, especially concerning copyright. By examining such contemporary practices and perceptions, the chapter highlights the significance and creativity of community relations, as well as the role of copyright law in creating a resourceful community. This then serves as a basis for proposing a new meaning of copyright—one that shifts the focus away from the traditional paradigm of original expression towards fostering trusting relations.

Chapter 8 introduces the legal concept of community resource to reconceptualise copyright in modern legal thought. It first examines the legal notion of balance to uncover the conception of social relations that is deeply embedded in the contemporary copyright framework. The chapter then contrasts this with relations of community, emphasising the importance of shared interests and interpersonal trust in fostering collective involvement, which becomes the function of copyright as a community resource.

Part I

Colonial Modernity

1 The Coloniality of Legal Modernity

Conventional historical accounts often trace the origin of Thailand's first copyright legislation to a royal initiative at the beginning of the 20th century.[1] Occupying a central role in the standard narrative around the Author's Ownership Act 1901 (AOA) was Prince Rabi (1874–1920), a prominent member of the royal family and a revered figure in Siam's legal community.[2] As far as the story goes, Siam enacted its first copyright legislation because Rabi, then Minister of Justice, advocated for copyright protection against rogue book printers who took the liberty of printing and selling his law textbooks without permission.[3] It probably helped that Rabi was the son of King Chulalongkorn (1853–1910), who is now highly regarded as the modernising monarch. And it was Chulalongkorn who sent Rabi along with his many siblings and cousins to Europe for Western education.[4]

Like other Western-educated royals and nobles in their respective fields, Rabi returned home to become a prominent figure in the modernisation of Siam's legal system. This contribution later earned him the title of 'Father of Thai law.'[5] Indeed, this pattern was common among members of the royal family and nobility who assumed various roles and responsibilities during the 'era of reforms' in Thai history.[6] For instance, Prince Damrong Rachanuphap (1862–1943), who was King Chulalongkorn's half-brother and the drafter of the AOA, became known as the

1 See for instance Praya Nitisartpaisarn, ปาฐกถา เรื่องพระราชบัญญัติคุ้มครองวรรณกรรมและศิลปกรรม ('Lecture on the protection of literary and artistic work act') in Luang Lekawichit (ed), รวมปาฐกถา *ซึ่งแสดงที่สามัคยาจารย์สมาคม ตั้งแต่ พ.ศ. 2470 ถึง พ.ศ. 2474 (A Collection of Lectures at Samakayacharn Society, 1927–1935)* (Bumrungnukulkij 1935) 597–598; Chavalit Atthasart, ลิขสิทธิ์ภายในประเทศ ('National copyright') (1984) 9(1) *Chulalongkorn Law Journal* 128, 129; Chaiyot Hemaratchata, *ลักษณะของกฎหมายทรัพย์สิน ทางปัญญา (Characteristics of Intellectual Property Law)* (13th edn, Nititham 2022) 52.

2 ibid.

3 ibid.

4 Ministry of Justice, *100 ปี กระทรวงยุติธรรม (100 Years of the Ministry of Justice)* (1992) 88.

5 See Preedee Kasemsup, 'Reception of law in Thailand–A Buddhist society' in Masaji Chiba (ed), *Asian Indigenous Law: In Interaction With Received Law* (Routledge 1986) 291.

6 Some well-known examples include Adulyadej, 'The father of Thai modern medicine'; Jayakorn, 'The father of Thai railways'; Devawongse, 'The father of Thai diplomacy'; Vongsevoradej, 'The father of the Thai postal service'; and Kiartivongse, 'The father of the Thai navy'.

DOI: 10.4324/9781003592037-3

'Father of Thai history.'[7] Thus, an emerging theme here is the role of the Siamese ruling elite in the modernisation of Siam along Western lines.

Contrasting with these popular narratives of 'royal initiative,' this chapter aims to present an early history of Thai copyright law from a different starting point. Central to this new perspective is the idea that Thai copyright law emerged at the juncture between the threat of Western colonialism and the development of Siam into a modern absolutist state. This critical perspective on the history of Thai copyright law emerges from a growing body of scholarship that seeks to expose the nationalist myth of independence, highlighting the ruling elite's role in Siam's subjugation to the colonial world order.[8] An instructive example is Tamara Loo's work on Siam's imperialistic relationships with the southern Malay states.[9] In this historical study of Malay Muslim settlements that later became the southernmost provinces of Thailand, Loos investigates Siam's conscious competition with encroaching Western powers and essentially argues that Siam shared some of the traits of both an imperial nation and a colonised country but could not be reduced to either.[10] Amplifying Loos' critical appraisal of the Siamese project of modernisation was a remark by the long-time observer of Thai politics, Kasian Tejapira, who describes the Siamese ruling elite as the 'colonial masters with a royal Thai face.'[11]

Contrary to the familiar trope of modernisation in Thai legal historiography, it is the ambiguity in Siamese-Western relations that constitutes a central theme linking the early history of Thai copyright law to the broader history of Western colonialism. So far, there has been limited discussion on colonialism and Thai law, let alone in the specific area of copyright law.[12] And in truth, the current state of research on the history of Thai copyright law is rather insignificant. This topic has received little attention in Thai scholarship. And when it does, the discussion tends to pay more attention to the legal history of copyright in Europe while treating the emergence of Thai copyright law as a mere consequence. Most historical discussions about Thai copyright law usually amount to a reproduction of the same historical fragments narrated into a developmental timeline.[13]

7 See his contribution to the AOA in 'The Emergence of Literary Property' in this chapter.

8 See for instance Chaiyan Rajchagool, *The Rise and Fall of the Thai Absolute Monarchy: Foundations of the Modern Thai State From Feudalism to Peripheral Capitalism* (White Lotus 1994); Winichakul, *Siam Mapped*; Michael Herzfeld, 'The absent presence: Discourses of crypto-colonialism' (2002) 101(4) *The South Atlantic Quarterly* 899; Loos, *Subject Siam*; Harrison and Jackson (eds), *The Ambiguous Allure of the West.*

9 See Loos, *Subject Siam* (n 8).

10 ibid 21.

11 Kasian Tejapira, *Commodifying Marxism: The Formation of Modern Thai Radical Culture, 1927–1958* (Kyoto University Press 2001) 6.

12 This discussion is normally historical in perspective and usually focuses on the modernisation of Siamese law in response to the threat of Western colonisation. See for instance the discussions in Andrew Harding and Munin Pongsapan (eds), *Thai Legal History: From Traditional to Modern Law* (CUP 2021).

13 See for instance Chavalit Atthasart, '**ลิขสิทธิ์ภายในประเทศ**' (n 1) 128–132; Chaiyot (n 1) 51–53.

Outside of the legal history, however, there has been much scholarly discussion aimed at shedding light on the independent yet subjugated status of Siam during the era of colonialism.[14] On one level, there is undoubtedly no contest that Thailand never experienced direct colonial rule despite being caught in the colonial rivalry between Great Britain and France.[15] Yet it is not always straightforward to square the independent status with evidence of pervasive Western influence, not only in the realm of culture but also in economy and law.[16] One emerging argument suggests that the complexity of Siam's situation challenges the postcolonial model of the colonised versus coloniser.[17] This argument further implies that some other countries may well have experienced a similar situation that does not quite fit into the postcolonial binary.[18]

Given that former colonies have so far been the focus of historiography on the globalisation of copyright, the following discussion adds new dimensions to the history of how this Western concept spread globally before the emergence of TRIPS, the Agreement on Trade-Related Aspects of Intellectual Property Rights.[19] Notably, shifting the focus to the in-between, the ambiguous, and the paradoxical can provide a revitalised perspective. For one thing, the Thai example raises the question of whether copyright's emergence outside the colonial West was always a straightforward case of Western domination. The change in Thai law, though Western in form, could also reflect power relations at home. But then again, the external threat of colonialism could very well hold relevance to domestic politics. Ultimately, what becomes clear in the absence of formal colonisation is the fact that even countries like Thailand could not opt out of the colonial world order.

Recognising colonial experiences of this kind means acknowledging that there is no singular colonial history but rather a variety of colonial experiences. Notably, a crucial theme emerging from the early history of Thai copyright law is not the familiar subject of Western concepts being imposed upon a non-Western nation. On the contrary, the birth of Thai copyright law is characterised by the appropriation of

14 See for instance Udom Srisuwan (Aran Phrommachomphu), **ไทยกึ่งเมืองขึ้น** *(Thailand, A Semi-colony)* (Udomatham 1950); Craig Reynolds (ed), *National Identity and Its Defender: Thailand, 1939–1989* (Silkworm 1993); David Streckfuss, 'The mixed colonial legacy in Siam: Origins of Thai racialist thought, 1890–19010' in Laurie Sears (ed), *Autonomous Histories: Particular Truths, Essays in Honour of John Smail* (University of Wisconsin 1993) 123; Chaiyan (n 8); Thongchai, *Siam Mapped* (n 8); Herzfeld, 'Crypto-colonialism' (n 8); Loos, *Subject Siam* (n 8); Harrison and Jackson (n 8).

15 Baker and Phongpaichit, *A History of Thailand*, 62–66.

16 See for instance Francis Bowes Sayre, 'The passing of extraterritoriality in Siam' (1928) 22 *American Journal of International Law* 70.

17 See Peter Jackson, 'The ambiguities of semicolonial power in Thailand' in Harrison and Jackson (eds), *The Ambiguous Allure of the West,* 38.

18 See the discussion in Herzfeld, 'Crypto-colonialism' (n 8), on how the experiences of Greece, Thailand, and, by extension, other countries that were never directly controlled are comparable but marginal in scholarly discourses.

19 For the discussion of copyright law in the colonial era, see for instance Bentley, 'The "extraordinary multiplicity" of intellectual property'; Suthersanen and Gendreau, *A Shifting Empire*; Birnhack, *Colonial Copyright,* 287; Seville, 'British colonial and imperial copyright'.

Western law. For the Siamese ruling elite, who found themselves at the intersection of Western colonialism and Thai absolutism, the West constituted the seductive but dangerous Other—one to learn from yet to keep at a safe distance.

Such is the nature of Siamese–Western relations that provided the impetus and the meaning for the transplanting of copyright law into Siam. Tamara Loos considers the Siamese ruling elite to be actively engaging in the project of colonial modernity.[20] Similarly, the historian Thongchai Winichakul equates the reform era with the arrival of colonial modernity, designating a specific period between the 1880s and 1930s.[21] As for what colonial modernity refers to, this is explored in the next section, where the discussion begins with the mid-19th century story of an English governess who became well-known for her time in the Siamese court.

I. Colonialism and the Making of Thai Copyright Law

The global image of 19th-century Thailand seems to owe much to how the country's past has been portrayed in Western popular culture. Hollywood, in particular, has played a significant role in this context, producing several high-profile films about the adventures of Anna Leonowens in the exotic, faraway land called Siam.[22] However, it is clear that Hollywood's representation of Siam cannot be expected to mirror the experiences of Siamese people or the expectations of contemporary Thais. Yet this view from the outside and the treatment it received within Thailand raise some important questions that cast doubt on the prevailing narratives of Siamese independence.

Most historical accounts of Thailand's encounters with Western colonialism begin during the reign of King Mongkut (1851–1868).[23] Mongkut's attitudes and policies towards Western countries mark a significant change in Siam's relations with the West.[24] His image in Thai historiography is that of a trailblazer for the Westernisation of Thailand in the 19th century,[25] but outside of Thailand, King Mongkut is famously known as 'The King' from *The King and I* (1956)—a Hollywood adaptation of a Broadway musical by Richard Rogers and Oscar Hammerstein that found its way into global popular culture. *The King and I* starred

20 Loos, *Subject Siam* (n 8) 2.

21 Thongchai Winichakul, ***เมื่อสยามพลิกผัน: ว่าด้วยกรอบมโนทัศน์ของสยามยุคใหม่*** *(Siam at a Turning Point: On the Foundational Mentality of Siam in the Modern Era)* (Fah-diew-kan 2019) 6.

22 See for instance John Cromwell (dir), *Anna and the King of Siam* (1946); Walter Lang (dir), *The King and I* (1956); Andy Tennant (dir), *Anna and the King* (1999). See also the animation Richard Rich (dir), *The King and I* (1999).

23 See for instance Thanet Aphornsuwan, 'The West and Siam's quest for modernity: Siamese responses to 19th-century American missionaries' (2009) 17(3) *South East Asia Research* 401; Baker and Pasuk, *History* (n 15); Taweesak Pueksom, ***หยดเลือด จารึก และแท่นพิมพ์: ว่าด้วยความรู้/ความจริงของชนชั้นนำสยาม พ.ศ.*** *2325–2411 (Blood, Inscription, and Printing Press: The Conception of Knowledge/Truth of the Siamese Elite, 1782–1868)* (Illumination 2018); Thongchai, *Turning Point* (n 21).

24 For detailed discussion of King Mongkut and Westernisation, see Thanet (n 23).

25 ibid 402.

the iconic Yul Brenner in the lead role, which not only earned him the Oscar for Best Actor but also rendered his on-screen persona a global representation of the 19th-century Thai King. Furthermore, Yul Brenner's portrayal of Mongkut as a modernising despot ties closely to the film's underlying themes of colonialism and modernisation.[26] Central to the narrative in *The King and I* is the tension between tradition and modernity that animates the relationship between the English governess and the Siamese King.[27]

To long-time observers of Thailand, the ban on *The King and I* should come as no surprise for it was symptomatic of what Thongchai Winichakul famously terms 'royal nationalism.'[28] Thongchai argues that royal nationalism constitutes a long-standing Thai mentality fundamental to the production of knowledge in Thailand since the late 19th century.[29] This foundational mentality, he argues, was a product of Siam's encounter with Western colonialism, an experience that triggered a ripple effect throughout the country's modern history. In particular, it was this encounter that set the Siamese ruling elite on a quest for *siwilai,* a transliterated term meant to encapsulate the Western ethos of civilisation.[30] For historians like Thongchai, as well as Loos, this specific period in Thai history is characterised by a pursuit of colonial modernity—an era that Thongchai associates with the time between the 1880s and 1930s.[31]

Colonial Encounter and Thai Modernity

The arrival of Anna Leonowens in Siam in 1862 not only coincided with the expansion of Western colonialism into Siam but also signified the country's early encounter with Western knowledge. In *The King and I*, this encounter is aptly portrayed in a scene where *the King* and *Anna*, whom he refers to as his 'employee,' find themselves quarrelling about prior contractual arrangements that hinge on *the King*'s acknowledgement of Western-style individual rights. Historically speaking, King Mongkut has been credited with paving the way for the modernisation of the country, which reached its peak after his son, Chulalongkorn, ascended the throne

26 Chistina Klein, *Cold War Orientalism: Asia in the Middlebrow Imagination, 1945–1961* (University of California Press 2003) 149–156.

27 The theme of tradition vs. modernity not only described Siamese-Western relations in the 19th century but also spoke to global cultural politics during the Cold War years when the film was released. For further discussion, see 'Thailand in the cultural cold war' in Chapter 3.

28 Thongchai Winichakul, **ประวัติศาสตร์ไทยแบบราชาชาตินิยม: จากจากยุคอาณานิคมอำพราง สู่ราชาชาตินิยมใหม่หรือลัทธิเสด็จพ่อของกระฎุมพีไทยในปัจจุบัน** (Royal–nationalist historiography: From the age of crypto-colonialism to a new royal nationalism, or the Thai bourgeoisie's cult of the Father-King in the present)' (2001) 23(1) *Silapawattanatham* (Art & Culture) 56.

29 Thongchai, *Turning Point* (n 21) 17–19.

30 ibid 12–13. For a detailed discussion, see Thongchai Winichakul, 'The quest for 'siwilai': A geographical discourse of civilizational thinking in the late nineteenth and early twentieth-century Siam' (2000) 59(3) *Journal of Asian Studies* 528.

31 Loos, *Subject Siam* (n 8) 2; Thongchai, *Turning Point* (n 21) 6.

in 1868.[32] Historians consider the reign of King Mongkut, the fourth king of the reigning royal family, to present a period in Thai history where the ruling elite began shifting their attention westward and away from traditional regional powers such as China.

King Mongkut was indeed a keen student of Western knowledge, and he also desired a Western-style education for his children.[33] However, Yul Brenner's iconic portrayal of *The King* as a sexualised, Oriental despot contrasts sharply with local perceptions of Mongkut, who had spent his life in monkhood from a young age.[34] Furthermore, it was during his time in the monastery that Mongkut became aware of the West through fellow Western missionaries.[35] Mongkut learned of the growing presence of Western powers in the region, particularly following China's defeat in the First Opium War in 1842, and considered interactions with Westerners as 'future eventualities.'[36]

In Thai historiography, it is argued that his strategy in dealing with Western countries was to 'flexibly abide by the storm from the West.'[37] One can see this strategy reflected in a series of treaties that Siam entered into with many Western nations in the second half of the 19th century.[38] Spearheading this development was the signing of a trade treaty between Siam and the British Empire in 1855, which, in hindsight, proved to be a watershed moment in modern Thai history.[39] As discussed later, the Anglo-Siamese Treaty of 1855 (also known as the Bowring Treaty) required Siam to open up to free trade and integrate into the world market. But it was not until Prince Chulalongkorn succeeded his father in 1868 that the country's Western-inspired transformation went into full swing.

Siamese Modernisation Under Colonial Influence

Hollywood portrays Prince Chulalongkorn (1868–1910) as a young Protégé of *Anna Leonowens*. And as far as the official history goes, the transformation of Siam during Chulalongkorn's reign also reflected his admiration for Western civilisation. As the King of Siam, Chulalongkorn surrounded himself with Western advisors and undertook a long and arduous journey to Europe twice during his 42-year reign.[40] His reform initiatives—which ranged from creating a Western-style administration and material infrastructures to introducing formal education and a modern

32 David Wyatt, *Thailand: A Short History* (2nd edn, Yale University Press 2003) 163–164.

33 Baker and Pasuk, *History* (n 15) 40; Wyatt, *Short History* (n 32) 161. For a detailed discussion about Mongkut and Westernization, see Thanet (n 23).

34 Wyatt, *Short History* (n 32) 182.

35 ibid.

36 Executive Committee of the Eighth Congress of Far Eastern Association of Tropical Medicine, *In Siam: General and Medical Features* (Bangkok Times Press 1930) 37.

37 Sulak Sivaraksa, *อำนาจของภาษาและสถาบันวิชาการ: เพื่อใคร (The Power of Language and the Academy: For Whom?)* (Semmasikkhalai 1997) 9.

38 Sayre (n 16) 71–72.

39 ibid 70.

40 Wyatt, *Short History* (n 32) 211.

legal system—all purported to follow Western models.[41] And to ensure that he had a sufficient workforce, Chulalongkorn sent his children and those of the Siamese ruling elite to Europe for Western-style education.[42] Among them were Prince Vajiravudh—a future King who spent his formative years in England before succeeding Chulalongkorn on the throne—and Prince Rabi, who returned to establish himself as a prominent and revered figure in Siam's legal community.[43]

In *The King and I*, the audience also learns that Crown Prince Chulalongkorn will continue to modernise Siam once he succeeds the throne from his father. And indeed, Chulalongkorn's modernisation programme features prominently in mainstream Thai historiography, with his efforts usually discussed in connection with Western colonialism.[44] As far as the official history goes, Siam secured its unique status as an independent country due to Chulalongkorn's shrewd foreign policy and his many reform initiatives.[45] While there is much truth in this popular perception of 19th-century Thailand, the self-congratulatory emphasis on Thai exceptionalism has distracted attention from the true extent of colonial influence in the country. One need not look further than the previously mentioned trade treaties that Siam entered into with Western countries.

These 'unequal treaties'—a term reflecting their one-sided nature, lack of time limit, and limited possibility of revision—obliged the Siamese government to remove trade restrictions, such as by fixing low import tariffs and opening up the country to Western capital.[46] In other words, these obligations did not just deprive the Siamese government of control over foreign trade: Perhaps more importantly, they also opened the door for Western powers to dominate the economy of an otherwise independent country. A notable example is the British economic interests that were so prevalent in Siam, spanning across various industries, from banking and railways to mining and teak trade.[47] This situation leads Chaiyan Rajchagool to argue, interestingly, that Western penetration of Siam was not achieved by politico-military means but 'was consummated directly at the economic level.'[48]

To protect their economic interests in Siam, the Western powers included a clause on extraterritoriality. This aimed to safeguard their subjects from the misfortunes

41 ibid 192–197.

42 Ministry of Justice (n 4) 88.

43 See 'The emergence of literary property' in this chapter.

44 See for instance Baker and Pasuk, *History* (n 15) 51; Wyatt, *Short History* (n 32) 208.

45 See for instance Narong Puangpit and Wuthichai Mulsilp, ***หนังสือเรียน รายวิชาพื้นฐาน ประวัติศาสตร์ไทย ม.4—ม.6: ชั้นมัธยมศึกษาปีที่ 4–6 (Coursebook for the Compulsory Subject of Thai History, Secondary School Year 4–6)*** (Aksorn-charoen-tat 2015) 51–61.

46 For more discussion on the 19th-century phenomenon of 'unequal treaties' between European powers and countries like Siam, Japan, and China, see Matthew Craven, 'What happened to unequal treaties? The continuities of informal empire' (2005) 74 *Nordic Journal of International Law* 335, 342–349. See also Pär Kristoffer Cassel, *Grounds of Judgment: Extraterritoriality and Imperial Power in Nineteenth-Century China and Japan* (OUP 2012).

47 See detailed discussion in Peter Sek Wannamethee, *Anglo-Siamese economic relations: British trade, capital and enterprise in Siam, 1856–1914* (MPhil thesis, University of London (LSE) 1990).

48 Chaiyan (n 142) 82.

of the 'uncivilised' legal and judicial systems in the 'despotic' Kingdom of Siam.[49] The extraterritorial powers of Western consuls—which first appeared in the Bowring Treaty and was later adopted by other Western nations—served to exclude the jurisdiction of Siamese courts and the application of Siamese law over Western subjects; this effectively constituted the attenuation of Siam's judicial sovereignty.[50]

Thus, law played an intermediate role in Siamese-Western relations.[51] As a mark of civilisation, law constituted a strategic domain for Siam to demonstrate its civilised status to Western nations, among whom were Great Britain and France, the two imperial powers competing for influence in Siam.[52] Meanwhile, the modernisation of Siamese law was also very much an exercise in legal borrowing by the Siamese ruling elite for the benefit of governing their own subjects.[53] This multifaceted nature of legal modernity in Siam explains the adoption of Western copyright law at the beginning of the 20th century.

As discussed later, it was indeed the complex interplay between colonial threat, *siwilai*, and print capitalism that underpinned the emergence of Thai copyright law and shaped its development in the early years. The increasing commercial activities around book publishing undoubtedly contributed to the eventual enactment of the Author's Ownership Act 1901 (AOA). However, this novel attempt to regulate the book trade seemed to pursue an objective beyond the commercial realm, resonating more with King Chulalongkorn's state-building project.[54] Similarly, the first and only amendment to the AOA, introduced by King Vajiravudh in 1914, must be understood in the context of his efforts to promote Thai nationalism in the colonial world order.[55] And finally, Siam's accession to the Berne Convention presented the most conspicuous instance of colonial influence for reasons discussed later.[56] Suffice it to say that the early development of Thai copyright law was bound with the country's fraught and complicated relationship with colonialism. But before turning to specific developments in the field of copyright law, some useful pointers can be drawn from the overall history of modern Thai law.

Transplanting Western Law

For legal historians, modern Thai law began to emerge when the Siamese ruling elite embraced the challenge of modernising the country in the second half of the

49 John Bowring, *The Kingdom and People of Siam*, vol 1 (OUP 1969) 171. See also Ntina Tzouvala, 'And the laws are rude . . . crude and uncertain: Extraterritoriality and the emergence of territorialised statehood in Siam' in Daniel Margolies, Umut Özsu, Maïa Pal, and Ntina Tzouvala (eds), *The Extraterritoriality of Law: History, Theory, Politics* (Routledge 2019) 137–138; Roger Cotterrell, *Law, Culture, and Society: Legal Ideas in the Mirror of Social Theory* (Aldershot 2006) 137–138.

50 Sayre (n 16) 73.

51 Loos, *Subject Siam* (n 8) 3; Tzouvala (n 49) 137–138.

52 ibid.

53 ibid; Tejapira, *Commodifying Marxism* (n 11) 5–6.

54 See 'A Modern Solution for a Modern Problem' in this chapter.

55 See 'The Twin Birth of the RSL and the AOA 1914' in this chapter.

56 See 'Integrating Siam into a Global Capitalist System' in this chapter.

19th century.[57] Until then, however, Indian moral ideologies had long influenced the law of the land,[58] where a compilation of traditional law called the 'Three-Seal Code' had been in force since 1805.[59] It is thus quite remarkable that all of this soon underwent a rapid and drastic change following Siam's encounter with European colonialism. Recalling the problem of extraterritoriality, Chulalongkorn and his successors had to initiate a series of judicial and legal reforms to free the country from the shackles of consular jurisdictions that kept Western citizens, subjects, and protégés out of Siamese courts.[60] That said, it is worth noting that Chulalongkorn also considered 'good law, merciful judicial system, and an effective administration of justice' to take priority in his aspiration of turning Siam into a civilised nation.[61]

As the end of the 19th century approached, Chulalongkorn decided to follow recommendations from his European advisors and embark on a comprehensive reform of the Siamese legal system.[62] The process appeared to progress through three stages. The first stage was a reform of the judicial system reform, which was part of Chulalongkorn's broader effort to create a centralised bureaucracy. This was followed by the introduction of formal legal education and, ultimately, the making of continental-style law codes.

Interestingly, the early years of the modernisation of Siamese law saw the growing influence of English law, which in many respects reflected the influence of British imperialism in the country.[63] Students returning from Great Britain, including Prince Rabi, not only facilitated the use of English law in Siamese courts but also promoted the role of English law in training future judges and lawyers.[64] Beginning with the establishment of the country's first law school in 1897, it was English law that the school mainly taught along with some traditional Thai law, which made up the rest of the curriculum.[65] Known as 'the law school of the Ministry of Justice' to the public, this law school was, in fact, privately managed and founded by Prince

57 This is clearly reflected in the discussions by many contributors in Harding and Munin (n 12).

58 Tokichi Masao, 'Researches into indigenous law of siam as a study of comparative jurisprudence' (1905) 2 *Journal of the Siam Society* 14, 15; Sawaeng Boonchalermvipas, ***ประวัติศาสตร์กฎหมายไทย*** *(Thai Legal History)* (Winyouchon 2005) 86–87.

59 Sarasin Viraphol, 'Law in traditional Siam and China: A comparative study' (1977) 65 *Journal of the Siam Society* 81, 1; Sompong Sucharitkul, 'Thai law and Buddhist law' (1998) 46 *American Journal of Comparitive Law* Supp 69, 75.

60 For an overview of this decades-long struggle, see Sayre (n 16).

61 King Chulalongkorn, ***การเสด็จประพาสยุโรปของพระบาทสมเด็จพระจุลจอมเกล้าเจ้าอยู่หัว ร.ศ.*** *116 (King Chulalong-korn's Visit to Europe in 1897)* (Department of Fine Arts 2008) 306–308.

62 See Munin Pongsapan, *The reception of foreign private law in Thailand: The case study of specific performance* (PhD thesis, University of Edinburgh 2013) 74–86.

63 ibid 2, 77–78.

64 The influence of English law can also be observed in legislation as important statutes enacted prior to the codification were also modelled on English law. See Sansern Kraichitti, 'The legal system in Thailand' (1967) 7 *Wahburn Law Journal* 239, 241.

65 Thanin Kraivichien, ***การปฏิรูปประบบกฎหมายและการศาลในรัชสมัยพระบาทสมเด็จฯ พระจุลจอมเกล้าเจ้าหัวพระปิยะมหาราช*** *(The Reforms of Law and Judicial Administration during the Reign of King Chulalongkorn)* (Ministry of Justice 1968) 28.

Rabi, Chulalongkorn's English law-educated son.[66] This formalisation of legal education was Rabi's personal initiative to provide Siam's new judicial system with a much-needed workforce.[67] Graduates from his law school were certified as Siamese barristers, reflecting Rabi's own educational background. And nearly all of them served in the Siamese judiciary, helping to forge a lasting connection between the judiciary and the English law-educated prince that endures to this day.[68]

Legal thought from continental Europe had to wait until well into the first half of the 20th century to gain a foothold in Thailand.[69] Fundamental to this continental shift was the development of the Civil and Commercial Code (TCCC), which today comprises over a thousand provisions, addressing all matters in one's life from birth to death. Thus, it is no surprise that the TCCC project took a considerable amount of time to complete. Part of the difficulty arose from the fact that the TCCC was not just a systematic collection of existing Siamese law. The TCCC is, first and foremost, a product of legal transplantation incorporating influences from various European legal codes.[70] Consequently, the promulgation of the TCCC effectively introduced Siam/Thailand to a plethora of continental rules and concepts and, by extension, the continental-style legal methods that constituted the very text of the European codes from which the TCCC borrowed.[71]

Given the scale of the task, the TCCC was preparaed in several phases over a span of almost three decades.[72] One might think that this long process allowed enough time for the Siamese government to take necessary steps to prepare local practitioners for the new code.[73] Indeed, since the initiation of the TCCC drafting, it was only a matter of time before legal education in Siam began to shift its focus away from English law. Beginning in the 1920s, a shift towards continental-style

66 Luang Saranaiprasas, *พัฒนาการการศึกษากฎหมายในประเทศไทย (The Development of Legal Education in Thailand)* (Thammasat University 1956) 3.

67 Dusadi Leelamien, 'การศึกษากฎหมายในประเทศไทยตั้งแต่การปฏิรูประบบกฎหมายและการศาลในรัชสมัยพระบาทสมเด็จฯ พระจุลจอมเกล้าเจ้าอยู่หัว' ('Legal Education in Thailand since the Reform of Thai Law during the Reign of King Chulalongkorn') in *100 ปี โรงเรียนกฎหมาย (A Hundred Years of the Thai Law School)* (Institute of Legal Education of The Thai Bar 1999) 95–97.

68 ibid 95–97.

69 For more discussion, see Andrew Harding, 'The eclipse of the astrologers: King Mongkut, his successors, and the reformation of law in Thailand' in Pip Nicholson and Sarah Biddulph (eds), *Examining Practice, Interrogating Theory: Comparative Legal Studies in Asia* (Brill 2008).

70 Some notable examples include French codes, German codes, Italian codes, and Swiss codes. The drafters also consulted European-derived law codes, particularly the Japanese Civil Code. See Munin (n 62) 111–112.

71 The fact that the TCCC borrowed considerably from the German Civil Code (BGB) has much to do with the influence of German 'legal science' in contemporary Thai law. For a discussion on the BGB as a product of German legal science, see Stefan Vogenauer, 'An empire of light? Learning and law-making in the history of German law' (2005) 64(2) *Cambridge Law Journal* 481.

72 The work began in 1908, and the last phase finished in 1935.

73 See for instance National Archive of Thailand, 'Georges Padoux's memorandum on the question on legal education in Siam' (20 December 1913) *Kor Tor* 35.10/10, 142. Georges Padoux, a French legislative adviser to the Thai government, proposed a reform of legal education based on a European programme of law.

'legal science' became noticeable, though this was primarily a result of political pressure from European countries than anything else.[74] Even so, English law had already secured its position in Thailand by the time this transformation took place. Today, the lingering influence of English law can still be felt in the judiciary.[75] The same can be said about many other aspects of the Thai legal system,[76] and copyright law is one such instance.

Given that the launch of the TCCC project occurred long after the first copyright legislation was enacted in 1901, it should come as no surprise that the most significant influence came from English law. Nevertheless, this early impact of English copyright law in no way shielded Thailand from the tradition of the author's rights. One example is Siam's accession to the Berne Convention in 1931, as discussed later.[77] It is therefore appropriate to regard the historical development up to this point as very much shaped by the orbital pull of Anglo-Eurocentrism. This observation also suggests that the changing world order following World War II would be reflected in Thailand's legal landscape in some way. As it happens, one may justifiably argue that towards the end of the 20th century, the global harmonisation of IPRs brought about the Americanisation of Thai copyright law.[78] Although the actual outcome was far from a complete transformation of Thai law, this process has added an American layer to the stratification of the Thai legal framework. In this way, the reception of US copyright law presents yet another instance of legal modernisation that, as the following discussion shows, was never a straightforward case of Western domination from the beginning.

Introducing the First Copyright Legislation Proper

In the early 1890s, official correspondence between Siam and the United States indicated that the law of *'kopeerai'* (a transliteration of 'copyright') was locally regarded as unnecessary.[79] The topic of copyright protection came up in the communication between the two nations after the US Congress had passed the Chace Act 1891, which granted protection to citizens of foreign states on a reciprocal basis.[80] This issue was duly raised with the Chulalongkorn government, whose response was unequivocal in declining to legislate copyright law while offering

74 Luang Saranaiprasas (n 200) 43–46.

75 The crucial role of legal precedents in Thai judicial practice is a case in point. See more discussion in Paul Du Plessis and Kongsatja Suwanapech, 'Law and identity: The case of the "common law" of Scotland with comparative insights from Thailand (2021) 1(1) *Thai Legal Studies* 47.

76 Thai trust law and the Thai Bar Association are two existing legal institutions that stand out in this regard.

77 See further discussion later in 'Elevating Siamese Law up to the European Standards.'

78 See 'The Birth of Copyright Scholarship' in Chapter 3.

79 National Archive of Thailand, Department of Royal Private Secretary Doc No Aor 20/1, '**พระราชหัตถเลขากรมหลวงเทวะวงศ์วโรประการกราบบังคมทูลพระบาทสมเด็จพระจุลจอมเกล้าเจ้าอยู่หัว เรื่องกฎหมายกอปีไรต์อเมริกัน**' ('Letter from Prince Devawongse to King Chulalongkorn on US copyright law') (6 July 1893) 2–4.

80 US International Copyright Act (The Chace Act) 1891.

to protect American subjects on an ad hoc and case-by-case basis.[81] The Siamese government cited a lack of domestic need for a general law but also showed appreciation for the Chace Act's scheme.[82] By that time, Siam was no stranger to the issue of unauthorised printing and already had some experience with what could be called printing privileges.

In fact, it was American missionaries who introduced modern print technology to Siam in the first place.[83] In the early 19th century, this new technology was meant for printing Gospels and religious tracts, but the American missionaries later ventured into commercial printing.[84] However, these were just the early days of print technology in Siam, and it was not until the signing of a series of trade treaties—beginning with the Bowring Treaty in 1855—that commercial printing began to flourish.[85] Encouraged by protection from extraterritoriality, more foreign nationals entered the commercial activities of newspaper publication.[86] Two notable figures, Dr Dan Breach Bradley and Reverend Samuel J. Smith, both missionaries, also began to engage in book publishing business.[87] Their enterprises paved the way for Siamese printers to follow suit in the late 1880s and early 1890s, a period considered to be the early boom in Siam's book business.[88]

As for the Siamese ruling elite, their early experience with print technology can be described as a learning process.[89] It was the time to become familiar with the new technology and the new literary forms it made possible.[90] Particularly significant to the history of Thai copyright law was the publication of a weekly journal titled *Wachirayan-wiset*. This journal was circulated among members of the *Wachirayan* Library, which served as sort of an exclusive club. It featured a variety of styles and content ranging from poems and short stories to articles that covered many fields of knowledge.[91] In 1892, Chulalongkorn ordered that reprints of works from *Wachirayan-wiset* would require the library's permission.[92] This decree, issued in 1892, originated from the request by the *Wachirayan* Library, whose motivation was not purely commercial. The idea that such prohibition would restrict the

81 National Archive "US copyright law" (n 79) 3.

82 ibid.

83 The working group on the history of printing in Thailand, *สยามพิมพการ: ประวัติศาสตร์การพิมพ์ในประเทศไทย (Sayam Phimphakan: History of Printing in Thailand)* (Matichon 2006) 5–9.

84 ibid; Thanapol Limapichart, 'The Royal Society of Literature, or, the birth of modern cultural authority in Thailand' in Rachel Harrison (ed), *Disturbing Convention Decentering Thai Literary Cultures* (Rowman & Littlefield International 2014) 39.

85 Thanapol Limapichart, 'The emergence of the Siamese public sphere: Colonial modernity, print culture and the practice of criticism (1860s–1910s)' (2009) 17(3) *South East Asia Research* 361, 372–373.

86 ibid.

87 ibid 389.

88 ibid 392.

89 Thanapol, 'Royal Society of Literature' (n 84) 39. Mongkut, for one, had a printing press set up on the temple premise during his years as a monk, see the Working Group (n 83) 16–17.

90 ibid 89–91, 206–211; Thanapol, 'Siamese public sphere' (n 85) 379.

91 ibid 209.

92 *Government Gazette* (19 August 1892) Book 9, 180–181.

journal's circulation to the library members appeared to be an important consideration alongside potential financial gains that the library might derive from commercial reprints.[93]

The Emergence of Literary Property

A conventional historical account attributes the birth of the AOA to the English law-educated Prince Rabi, who submitted a petition to the King seeking protection against unauthorised printing.[94] Indeed, the drafting of the AOA was set in motion by Rabi's petition, but Rabi did not ask for copyright legislation and was quite wary of having one. Once he learned that a copyright bill was under consideration, Rabi sought to withdraw his petition, partly to avoid complications and partly because he did not regard his request as urgent.[95] Furthermore, it was a different concern than Rabi's that transformed the King's deliberation over his petition into a plan for new legislation.

Available records show that the unauthorised printing of government textbooks had recently become an issue for the Ministry of Public Instruction (MOPI), which cited the absence of 'copyright law' as a contributing factor.[96] Additionally, MOPI had already prepared a draft law to present to Chulalongkorn, who ultimately decided that a new law, rather than the privilege Rabi effectively requested, was the way forward.[97] Once the King set his sights on new legislation, the drafting process moved forward very quickly, taking less than a month before the promulgation of the AOA on 18 August, 1901.[98] Taking charge of the drafting process was Prince Damrong Rajanubhab, the King's trusted half-brother.[99]

According to his account, Prince Damrong consulted the UK Copyright Act of 1842 and appeared to adopt it as a model but then made extensive modifications.[100]

93 ibid 180.

94 See for instance Praya Nitisartpaisarn (n 1) 597–598; Chavalit (n 1) 129; Chaiyot (n 1) 52.

95 National Archive of Thailand, Department of Royal Private Secretary Doc No Aor 20/2, '**พระราชหัตถเลขากรมหมื่นราชบุรีดิเรกฤทธิ์ถวายพระบาทสมเด็จพระจุลจอมเกล้าเจ้าอยู่หัว เรื่องขอพระราชทานอำนาจกอปีไรต์ในหนังสือทรงแต่ง**' ('Prince Rabi's letter to the King to request ad-hoc copyright') (7 July 1901) 2.

96 National Archive of Thailand, Ministry of Public Instruction Doc No Sor Thor 9.2/23, '**หนังสือจากพระยาวุฒิการบดีถึงอธิบดีกรมศึกษาธิการ เรื่องกฎหมายกอปีไรต์**' ('Praya Wutthikarnbordi's letter to the Director of Education on the subject of copyright law') (12 March 1900) 3–4.

97 National Archive of Thailand, Department of Royal Private Secretary Doc No Aor 20/2, '**หนังสือจากเจ้าพระยาภาสกรวงศ์ถวายพระบาทสมเด็จพระจุลจอมเกล้าเจ้าอยู่หัว เรื่องร่างพระราชบัญญัติกอปีไรต์ของกระทรวงธรรมการ**' ('Chao Phraya Pasakorawong's letter to the King on MOPI's draft copyright law') (3 August 1901) 4–7.

98 *Government Gazette* (18 August 1901) Book 18, 286–288.

99 National Archive of Thailand, Department of Royal Private Secretary Doc No Aor 20/2, '**รายงานการประชุมเสนาบดีสภาตั้งแต่วันที่ 18 กรกฎาคม ถึง 5 สิงหาคม ร.ศ.** 120' ('Minutes of the meetings of the Council of State') (18 July–5 August 1901) 59.

100 ibid 57, 59; National Archive of Thailand, Department of Royal Private Secretary Doc No Aor 20/2, '**ร่างพระราชบัญญัติว่าด้วยกรรมสิทธิ์ผู้แต่งหนังสือของกรมพระยาดำรงราชานุภาพ**' ('Damrong's copyright bill') 33–37.

The final result was a piece of legislation that contained only 18 provisions, all of which were relatively short but not necessarily concise. The object of protection was the 'book,' which was not defined anywhere in the Act.[101] The meaning of books, as far as can be gathered from the AOA, suggests an understanding of the subject matter that was closely tied to physical objects.[102] Furthermore, the AOA only offered protection to published books on the condition that they were formally registered.[103] Upon successful registration, the conferred 'ownership' exclusively entitled the author to print, copy, translate, and sell the book.[104] This ownership could change hands,[105] and the protection would last for the lifetime of the author plus an additional seven years or for a total period of 42 years, whichever was longer.[106] Notably, the AOA contained no exceptions to the rights of the author, but an infringement of literary ownership was not punishable under criminal law.

Opinions on Damrong's draft were sought from Rabi, whose comments revealed much about the book business in Siam at the time. Rabi drew attention to a typical relationship between authors and publishers in Siam to raise the question of how to reconcile the new rights with existing contractual relations.[107] He was wary of tipping the existing balance in favour of the authors. This apparent sympathy for publishers, who back then were also printers, may initially seem surprising, but it is actually understandable given that writing was not thought of as a profession in Siam until at least the 1930s.[108] The situation was different at the start of the century, as writing tended to be considered a 'play' for royals and nobles and certainly was not considered a source of livelihood.[109]

In this regard, the issue that Rabi anticipated was not merely a matter of legal technicality but also a socio-economic one. Expanding on point, Rabi flirted with the idea of making the new law not applicable to existing works yet cautioned against this 'easy way.'[110] Regarding this easy solution, he said, 'The government would be stirring a hornet's nest and would be very popular and unfair. Future writers do not yet come forward ready to defend the government, if any will defend the government at all.'[111]

101 Author's Ownership Act RE 120 (1901), s 3.
102 On the development of the concept of work see Jaszi, 'Toward a theory of copyright', 471–480.
103 AOA 1901, s 10.
104 ibid s 4.
105 ibid s 14.
106 ibid s 5.
107 National Archive of Thailand, Department of Royal Private Secretary Doc No Aor 20/2, '**พระราชหัตถเลขากรมหมื่นราชบุรีดิเรกฤทธิ์ถวายพระบาทสมเด็จพระจุลจอมเกล้าเจ้าอยู่หัวทำความเห็นร่างพระราชบัญญัติกรรมสิทธิ์ในหนังสือ**' ('Prince Rabi's letter to the King on his opinion about the copyright bill') (8 August 1901) 29–30.
108 See Chusak Pattarakulvanit, '**ปริศนาข้างหลังภาพ 'คณะสุภาพบุรุษ**'' ('A mystery behind a picture of the "Gentleman Group"') in Chusak Pattarakulvanit (ed), *อ่าน(ไม่)เอาเรื่อง (Read Against the Grain)* (Kobfai 2002) 77–91.
109 ibid. See also Thanapol, 'Royal Society of Literature' (n 84).
110 National Archive, 'Rabi's assessment of the draft AOA' (n 186) 29.
111 ibid.

Rabi's view and reservations paint a picture of the literary landscape in which the right to prohibit copying might indeed been an issue for authors, but not yet an urgent one. Indeed, this was just a view of one individual author—someone in a privileged position. Yet the history of the AOA has been reduced to this individual author who, after all, did not ask for copyright legislation and was not involved in making the decision. One might feel that there is more to the story of the AOA. It is, therefore, time to turn to the government's education policy, which was very important to Chulalongkorn's state-building project.

A Modern Solution for a Modern Problem

When Rabi's petition was presented at the meeting of the Council of State, Chulalongkorn's advisory body for administrative and legislative matters, among the participants was Chaopraya Phatsakorawong, the Minister of Public Instruction.[112] Phatsakorawong seized the opportunity to inform the King and the Council that his ministry had undertaken work to prepare a bill on copyright protection.[113] It appeared that Phatsakorawong's interjection changed the direction of the discussion. The Council agreed to bypass Rabi's request with a plan to introduce Siam's first copyright law.[114] This, of course, raises the question of what lent weight to Phatsakorawong's suggestion that apparently made the King change his stance from the one in the early 1890s. As mentioned earlier, the promulgation of the AOA must be seen in the context of Chulalongkorn's state-building project, which now appeared to be suffering from a serious shortage of human resources.[115] Chulalongkorn himself attributed this issue to the sluggish progress of the education reform aimed at providing Siam's modern bureaucracy with skilled civil servants.[116]

It is worth reiterating that many reform projects during Chulalongkorn's reign were as much a creation of an absolutist state as it was his response to the threat of colonialism. A notable example was the adoption of a Western-style bureaucracy.[117] The establishment of the Ministry of Justice aimed to systematise and centralise the judicial power, which had so far been the source of corruption and dispersedly vested among various government departments and individual princes.[118] Inevitably, the judicial reform created new posts that had to be filled by trained civil servants. Consequently, it became the objective of Chulalongkorn's education policy

112 National Archive, 'The meetings of the Council of State' (n 99) 55–56.

113 ibid.

114 ibid.

115 See David Wyatt, *The Politics of Reform in Thailand: Education in the Reign of King Chulalongkorn* (Yale University Press 1969) 255–256; Kullada Kesboonchoo Mead, *The Rise and Decline of Thai Absolutism* (Routledge 2004) 76.

116 ibid 256–257.

117 See Wyatt, *Short History* (n 32) 200.

118 For a criticism of Siam's judicial system prior to the reform, see NA McDonald, *Siam: Its Government, Manners, Customs, &c* (A Martien 1871) 50; Bowring, *The Kingdom and People of Siam*, 171.

as well as the important task of the MOPI to train future civil services to meet the demands of the modernised bureaucracy. Central to the much-needed education reform was the question of how to finance the enterprise to ensure the availability of quality textbooks for every school across the country.[119]

As it turned out, MOPI had been slow to progress the education reform, which made Chulalongkorn very anxious.[120] In addition, in the few years leading up to the introduction of the AOA, it appeared that MOPI had been embroiled in a dispute with local printers. Chulalongkorn might have prioritised education, but MOPI had been beset by budgetary cuts, which exacerbated the impact of piracy.[121] Thus, MOPI wanted to prohibit private printers from printing and selling government textbooks without permission, but it lacked legal authority and came to the conclusion that copyright law was needed.[122] Given the sense of urgency around the education reform, the link with Chulalongkorn's state-building project provides a clearer explanation for why the King changed his mind. This explanation also falls in line with the history of colonial modernity in Siam, where modern law became a mark of civilisation while offering a potent technology of rule.

Alan Watson is correct in suggesting that legal rules transplant easily among legal professional elites, though he says little about what will become of these rules socially.[123] The Siamese ruling elite conveniently borrowed and adapted Western copyright law for their purposes, but that does not mean the promulgation of the AOA took place in a cultural contact zone devoid of power and hierarchy. On the contrary, the very act of legal borrowing pointed to the logic of power that permeated Siam in the early 20th century. The Siamese quest for *siwilai* meant that the modern problem of print commodities naturally demanded the modern solution of copyright. It may be necessary to add one cautionary note here—it was not typical of the Siamese ruling elite to borrow merely for the sake of imitation. This approach to Western modernity was reflected in the very text of the AOA, as well as in the 1914 amendment that was passed by King Vajiravudh (1910–1925), son of Chulalongkorn.

Keeping Up With the Emerging Public Sphere

The preamble to the 1914 amendment stated that the changes made to the AOA were intended to encourage every literary person 'to put effort into writing for the long-term benefits of the country.' For contemporary readers, this rationale seems to invite a comparison to the well-rehearsed argument that copyright provides incentives for creativity. But there is only so much similarity to be had there, not least because writing as a livelihood was not yet recognised in Siam at the time. And

119 Wyatt, *Politics of Reform* (n 115) 130.
120 ibid 255–256.
121 ibid 149.
122 National Archive, 'Praya Wutthikarnbordi's letter to the Director of Education' (n 96); National Archive, 'MOPI's draft copyright law' (n 97) 5.
123 Alan Watson, 'Comparative law and legal change' (1978) 37 CLJ 313, 315.

while discussions of creativity and innovation characterise contemporary copyright discourse, colonisation and modernisation were predominant in early-20th-century Siam. Reading the 1914 amendment through the lens of Anglo-American utilitarianism would only get one so far. The following discussion shows that the preamble is better understood when seen through the lens of colonial modernity. More specifically, the 1914 amendment should be read in conjunction with Vajiravudh's efforts to promote Thai nationalism within the colonial world order.

One of the most significant developments in Siam in the second half of the 19th century was the emergence of a literary public sphere. Fundamental to this development was the proliferation of newspapers and journals, which provided platforms for views and values that would otherwise have no public outlets. Unsurprisingly, the flourishing print media and the emerging public sphere did not necessarily work in the ruling elite's favour. Newspapers, in particular, became fertile ground for launching public criticism of the government. But the ruling elite neither attempted to suppress, and nor were they just content to remain on the sidelines.[124] Instead, they voluntarily and enthusiastically entered and often excelled in this new space. At least that was the case for Vajiravudh, whom many Thais now regard as a literary genius. The oeuvre of Vajiravudh constitutes a considerable body of work that lends weight to his reputation as an acclaimed essayist, dramatist, and poet, not to mention an accomplished translator.[125] He also wrote for newspapers to share his views on matters of public interest and, perhaps more frequently, to respond to criticism aimed at the government.[126]

In many ways, Vajiravudh's engagement with the world of letters helps paint a picture of the state of literary production and consumption in which the AOA Amendment Act 1914 appeared to fit seamlessly. The 22 provisions of the 1914 amendment primarily aimed to expand the protectable subject matter and to clarify the rules rregarding book registration. Notably, a definition of 'book' was finally provided that covered even a single sheet of paper, so there was a marked expansion in the subject matter.[127] Meanwhile, elsewhere in the amendment also left no doubt about the available protection for certain literary forms, with special mentions given to periodicals, plays, and speeches.[128] Still absent from the amended AOA was a criminal liability for infringement, but the possibility to request an injunction was a new inclusion,[129] as was the rebuttable presumption of fault.[130] Overall, the 1914 amendment was unquestionably an attempt to bring the AOA up

124 On how they engaged with the emerging public sphere, see Thanapol, 'Siamese public sphere' (n 85).

125 An extensive discussion about his literary works can be found in Walter Vella, *Chaiyo! King Vajiravudh and the Development of Thai Nationalism* (University of Hawaii Press 2019).

126 ibid 256; Thanapol, 'Siamese public sphere' (n 85) 397–398.

127 AOA 1914, s 3.

128 ibid s 3, 7, 11.

129 ibid s 20.

130 ibid s 21.

to speed with the literary scene in the early 1910s. What remains a question now is the reason behind this change.

The preamble to the 1914 Act explicitly addressed the thinking behind the amendment, but the rationale provided seems to raise more questions, as noted earlier. Curiously, what exactly is meant by 'for the long-term benefits of the country' may not be as straightforward as it appears. Meanwhile, it is also fair to say that Vajiravudh's English upbringing and literary credentials must have influenced the 1914 amendment, but to suggest that the new law was enacted on a whim would be overly simplistic. There must be something more at play beyond the need to support Thai authors and the long-term benefits to the country. It is argued here that the 1914 amendment should be viewed in the context of Vajiravudh's programme of royal nationalism.

Writing the Nation

The historian Walter Vella describes Vajiravudh as a 'Siamese Victorian prince'—this is an apt description for a paradoxical figure who oscillated between being a 'traditional autocrat and modern nationalist.'[131] As a prince of Siam, Vajiravudh received his education in England from an early age and was well trained in Western etiquette.[132] The effects of this upbringing are evident in Vajiravudh's appreciation for Western arts and culture, as well as his admiration for the Victorian ethos.[133] However, Vajiravudh's time as the King of Siam is generally remembered for his programme of royal nationalism. Notably, he promoted the notion of Thainess that emphasised cultural heritage and, thereby, purported to be a prescription against Westernisation.

Arguably, the paradox in Vajiravudh's persona can be explained by the growing challenge that Westernisation came to pose to absolute monarchy. By the time Vajiravudh ascended to the throne, Chulalongkorn's strong desire for a modern and civilised Siam meant that his policy of Westernisation had changed local outlook and attitudes towards Western knowledge and culture.[134] Exemplifying this transformation is the term '*Lak-witthaya*' ('stealing knowledge'), which emerged as a title for one of the earliest literary magazines in Siam.[135]

Lak-witthaya (1900–1902) was founded by a group of intellectual royals and nobles who made no pretence of imitating the West in their pursuit of publishing translations and adaptations of European literature.[136] When Vajiravudh returned to Siam, he became a prolific writer. He famously targeted the kind of writing practices

131 Vella (n 125) 1.
132 ibid 2.
133 ibid 9.
134 See more discussion on the Siamese conception of knowledge in 'The Spiritual–Material Bifurcation' in Chapter 2.
135 Thanapol, 'Siamese public sphere' (n 85) 382–383.
136 Thak Chaloemtiarana, *Read Till It Shatters: Nationalism and Identity in Modern Thai Literature* (ANU Press 2018) 465.

typified by the journal *Lak-witthaya* as he undertook his nationalist projects through his writings.[137] Vajiravudh coined the phrase *'latthi-ao-yang'* ('the cult of imitation') to refer to those who followed European models in arguing for social and political changes against absolutism.[138] Such propositions were, he deemed, excessive Westernisation, and he denounced them as a sacrifice of Thainess.[139]

It is important to note that Vajiravudh's notion of Thainess is best encapsulated in his still-influential slogan, '*Chart, Sart, Kasat*' ('Nation, Religion, and King'), which he adapted from the British phrase 'God, King, and Country.'[140] It is fair to say that his nationalism was an apparent 'anxiety of influence' that was symptomatic of a more implicit condition. Try as one might, it is impossible to reconcile his cult of imitation critique with the common practice of *lak-witthaya* among the Siamese ruling elite. The real issue here is not the contradiction on the surface. Arguably, it was the concern for the monarchical authority, which had benefitted from appropriating the West but now faced a growing rejection of absolutism.[141] In other words, Vajiravudh realised that the fruit of Chulalongkorn's Westernisation policy—previously instrumental in the birth of Thai absolutism—began to turn against him. Therefore, the monarch turned his attention inward, in purported rejection of the West, to construct proper Thainess as the source of his authority.

To cultivate a sense of national pride among the Siamese population, Vajiravudh engaged in various nationalist projects to instil the idea of distinct Thainess, which assumed an invariable link between the nation and monarch. This association was also a recurring theme in his writings, where he sought to redefine the Siamese institution of monarchy in terms that were reminiscent of Hobbesian thought.[142] A case in point is his analogy of the state as a human body, with every part (every Thai) carrying a function, while the King represented the brain.[143] In this way, the issue of monarchical authority was central to Vajiravudh's nationalism, and in a typical fashion of colonial modernity, Vajiravudh's nationalist programme revolved around presenting Siamese culture and traditions as equal to Western civilisation.[144]

Vajiravudh identified literary heritage as a hallmark of civilisation. It may have been his father who recognised the significance of literacy to the nation; he also came to regard books as national possessions and symbols of civilisation late in his life.[145] However, it was Vajiravudh who drew attention to the very act of writing through his literary talent and how he used it to bring the civilisation of the Thai

137 Thanapol, 'Royal Society of Literature' (n 84) 43–44.

138 Matthew Phillip Copeland, *Contested nationalism and the 1932 overthrow of the absolute monarchy in Siam* (PhD thesis, Australian National University 1993) 36.

139 ibid.

140 Baker and Pasuk, (n 15) 118.

141 See more detail of the public criticism in Baker and Pasuk, (n 15) 121–124.

142 Vella (n 125) 63. See also Thomas Hobbes, *Leviathan* (J C A Gaskin ed, OUP 2008).

143 Baker and Pasuk, (n 15) 117.

144 See an extensive discussion in Vella (n 125).

145 Patrick Jory, 'Books and the nation: The making of Thailand's national library' (2000) 31(2) *Journal of Southeast Asian Studies* 351, 357–358.

nation into existence. In one well-known instance, he made use of his interest in antiquity to narrate a story of past Thai achievements, presenting them as national marvels and evidence against claims that the country was uncivilised.[146] In short, the oeuvre of his work suggests how well Vajiravudh understood the potential of literature and the power of writing. It thus comes as no surprise that writing was among the social practices that saw a significant impact from the King's nationalist impulse.

The Twin Birth of the RSL and the AOA 1914

In 1914, Vajiravudh sought to promote 'literary writing of high quality' by establishing *Wannakhadi-samoson*, the Royal Society of Literature (RSL).[147] By his own account, the mission of the RSL was to rescue the Thai literary language from being corrupted by Western influence.[148] The RSL's primary responsibility was to select and present literary works of exemplary quality for an award.[149] This has been interpreted by some scholars as a nationalist attempt to proclaim the country's literary heritage and achievements.[150] Recognising a nationalist project in the RSL, historian Thanapol Limapichart adds an interesting dimension to this interpretation by highlighting the significance of the RSL to the cultural authority of the Siamese ruling elite.[151]

In many ways, Vajiravudh appeared to criticise Western elements in the vernacular Thai language (e.g. words and syntax) in order to render the knowledge of the 'proper' Thai language exclusive to the ruling elite.[152] This implicit agenda made another appearance when Vajiravudh followed the establishment of the RSL with a plan to revive his father's *Samakom-kaephasa*, the Society for Language Correction, intending 'to protect and rectify the Thai Language' from rapid and deplorable change.[153] Although nothing of note appeared to follow from this idea, the same cannot be said of the RSL's work over the next decade. While the term success would make a contested description, the RSL did present awards to 11 works which, Thanapol argues, equated 'the court's act of self-congratulation' and rendered the RSL award 'a rite of consecration.'[154] This demonstrates how Vajiravudh's construction of Thainess in the literary field was more than a nationalist call

146 King Vajiravudh, *เที่ยวเมืองพระร่วง (Travels in Phra Ruang Country)* (Ministry of the Interior 1954) preface.

147 Royal Decree to establish the Royal Society of Literature BE 2457 (1914), preamble.

148 ibid.

149 ibid.

150 See for instance Vella (n 125) 250.

151 Thanapol, 'Royal Society of Literature' (n 84) 38.

152 ibid.

153 National Archive of Thailand, Miscellaneous documents of the sixth reign, Doc No Bor 10/10, 'ร่างประกาศตั้งนิรุกติสมาคม' ('Draft announcement to establish the society of language') (31 August 1916) 30.

154 Thanapol, 'Royal Society of Literature' (n 84) 49.

to action; it represented an attempt to reassert monarchical authority in the literary public sphere.

Several months after the unveiling of the RSL, the AOA Amendment Act was enacted and came into effect. While the timing alone does not necessarily warrant a historical link, they were connected in practical aspects. Under the rules, a nomination for the RSL award could not contradict the wishes of the authors and literary owners.[155] If all went well, winners of the RSL award could have the royal seal affixed to the book manuscripts for the purpose of ownership registration, presumably to facilitate the process under the AOA.[156] Meanwhile, the broadened definition of a book and the clarified rules on registration, as brought about by the 1914 amendment,[157] should have been beneficial to authors of the award-winning works. For one thing, works of a relatively short length, such as poems and essays that were eligible for the RSL award, would have no trouble seeking protection under the amended AOA.[158]

More strikingly, both the RSL and the 1914 amendment arose out of the idea that Siamese authors should be rewarded for their contributions to the nation. Again, it is important to emphasise that these were the days of Vajiravudh's nationalist programme, where the people of Siam were urged to become civilised and yet remain truly Thai. This paradoxical blend was fundamental to Vajiravudh's royal nationalism, which began to permeate Siamese life in the early 20th century. As discussed earlier, the realm of literary production was essential to this development as literature served as Vajiravudh's tool of choice for building a proud Thai nation.[159] And by the logic of his brand of nationalism, national achievements and nationalistic pride went hand in hand with royal power and monarchical loyalty. So, by establishing the RSL, the monarch stood to gain cultural authority by acting as the nation's literary heritage guardian. By the same token, the proliferation of books and knowledge that was expected to flow from the 1914 amendment, corresponded to the power/responsibility of the monarch to guide the nation towards civilisation. Ultimately, it is important to remember that the 1914 amendment was enacted in the era of colonialism and at a time when the modern notion of the nation influenced the country's policy climate.

Accession to the Berne Convention

Perhaps Vajiravudh's plan to revive the Society for Language Correction did not come to fruition because a much more significant matter demanded his attention. In July 1917, Siam departed from its initial neutrality in WWI as Vajiravudh declared

155 See 'Statute of the Royal Society of Literature' (*Government Gazette*, 29 April 1917) Book 34, 68–71.

156 Royal Decree to establish the Royal Society of Literature BE 2457 (1914), s 9(1).

157 AOA 1914, s 3–4.

158 ibid.

159 See also Vella (n 125) 246–254.

a state of war against Germany and Austria-Hungary.[160] In the following year, Siam deployed an expeditionary force to support the Allies in the occupation of German territories and consequently became an original member of the League of Nations in 1920.[161] The timing and manner of Siam's participation in the European war suggest that this was a strategic move in Siam's own anti-colonial struggles.[162] But as far as Thai copyright law is concerned, it also marked the beginning of a pivotal yet unexplored series of events that culminated in Siam's accession to the Berne Convention in 1931.[163]

As discussed earlier, extraterritoriality had been a thorny issue in Siamese–Western relations since the late 19th century, and it was only a matter of time before this issue caught up with Thai copyright law. However, the remarkable manner in which this development unfolded may still surprise scholars. As discussed shortly, Siam's involvement in WWI and the subsequent membership to the Berne Convention were both part of the same journey that Siam undertook with a strong desire to end extraterritoriality. This means that joining the Convention was yet another result of the country's encounter with colonialism, and this was perhaps the most conspicuous instance since the promulgation of the AOA.

It is worth noting here that the Berne Convention is no stranger to colonialism. The link between European colonialism and its extended reach is a well-trodden path in copyright scholarship.[164] Notably, it has been pointed out that the Convention's early impact on non-European countries came primarily from the fact that these were colonies and colonial dependencies of the European powers that made up the initially small membership of the Union.[165] Indeed, Siam became a member of the Berne Union relatively early and long before many other non-European countries, including the large and economically significant ones, namely, the US, China, and Russia.[166] This alone seems to suggest the possible influence of colonialism on Siam's early participation in the Union.

160 Stefen Hell, *Siam in the League of Nation: Modernisation, Sovereignty and Multilateral Diplomacy, 1920–1940* (River Books 2010) 25–28.

161 ibid.

162 Worachart Meechoobot, 'สยามกับสงครามโลกครั้งที่ 1' ('Siam and the First World War') (2017) 39(1) Silapawattanatham 104–105.

163 The Convention came into existence when a handful of countries, mostly European, signed the Berne text of 1886 to constitute the Berne Union with a view to securing the same level of legal protection for foreign and local authors in member states. See further discussion in Sam Ricketson, 'The birth of the Berne Union' (1986) 11 *Columbia-VLA Journal of Law and the Arts* 9.

164 See for instance Ricketson (n 163); Okediji, 'The international relations of intellectual property'; Alpana Roy, 'Copyright: A colonial doctrine in a postcolonial age' (2008) 26(4) *Copyright Reporter* 112; Alexander Peukert, 'The colonial legacy of international copyright system' in Ute Röschenthaler and Mamadou Diawara (eds), *Copyright Africa: How Intellectual Property, Media and Markets Transform Immaterial Cultural Goods* (Sean Kingston Publishing 2016).

165 Ricketson (n 163) 29–30.

166 These countries joined the Berne Convention in 1988, 1992, and 1994, respectively.

Elevating Siamese Law to European Standards

Regarding the consequences for the AOA, it was the Berlin Act of 1908 and the Berne Additional Protocol of 1914 that Siam initially signed in June 1931. The Siamese government chose to fulfil its obligations with an entirely new Act to ensure compliance with the Berne Convention.[167] The result was the Protection of Literary and Artistic Works Act 1931 (PLAWA), which superseded the AOA and resembled its contemporary counterparts more than its predecessors. The title of the new law clearly indicated a very important change: Non-literary works were now recognised and protected. The 1931 Act replaced the concept of 'book' with that of 'literary and artistic work,' defined so broadly as to include 'every production in the literary department, scientific department, and artistic department.'[168] Also noticeably absent from the PLAWA was the requirement of registration, which was no longer a condition for protection under Thai law.

Meanwhile, making an appearance in Thai law for the first time was the word 'copyright.' The PLAWA conferred not 'ownership' but 'copyright' to the author—or the employer where the work was created for the latter.[169] The exclusivity conferred by copyright was not limited to copying and translation, previously recognised under the rubric of author's ownership, but also included public performance and the first publication.[170] Furthermore, the general term of protection also extended quite considerably from 7 to 30 years after the author's death.[171] Finally, copyright infringement could result in criminal liability, a consequence that was absent under the AOA.[172] In light of these positive changes for authors under Thai law, the 1931 Act also aimed to balance the level of protection with several copyright exceptions (e.g. personal use, criticism, and quotation), which, again, had never been a feature of the AOA.[173]

Apart from the extensive changes to the object and scope of protection, another new component of the PLAWA was the regime of 'International Copyright.'[174] Under the heading of International Copyright, the 1931 Act introduced specific rules for foreign authors to adhere to the principle of national treatment, which required Siam to provide authors from other Berne countries with the same protection as its own citizens. These rules were arguably the most revealing aspect of the PLAWA with respect to why Siam decided to join the Berne Convention. Interestingly, it was not the promise of a thriving cross-border trade that underpinned

167 National Archive of Thailand, The Ministry of Education Doc No Sor Tor 0701.35, '**รายงานประชุมกรรมการพิจารณาการออกกฎหมายคุ้มครองวรรณคดีและศิลปกรรม ครั้งที่** 1' ('Minutes of the first meeting of the committee to consider the promulgation of the law to protect literary and artistic works') (31 May 1928) 73–75.

168 The Protection of Literary and Artistic Works Act BE 2474 (1931), s 4.

169 ibid.

170 ibid.

171 ibid s 14.

172 ibid s 25–27.

173 ibid s 20(1)–(4).

174 ibid s 28–31.

the decision of the Siamese government. Instead, this was a duty that Siam had assumed towards foreign powers in exchange for abolishing their extraterritorial rights on Siamese soil.[175]

As discussed earlier, a series of commercial treaties that Siam entered into with foreign powers ushered in a regime of consular jurisdictions. This regime first appeared in the Bowring Treaty of 1855 before being replicated in a series of Western–Siamese treaties over the following two decades. Siam's acceptance of these extraterritorial clauses ended up creating a patchwork of multiple jurisdictions within its territory. This overlaid regime of consular jurisdictions threw Siam's administration of justice into disarray, bringing uncertainty, arbitrariness, and lawlessness to the country.[176] Furthermore, the Siamese ruling elite also came to recognise the one-sided nature of this problematic regime as unfair and, more crucially, a mark of Siam's inferior status in the eyes of the great nations of the world.[177]

Towards the end of the 19th century, Chulalongkorn began the work to abolish extraterritorial rights and regain the integrity and autonomy of Siam's judicial system.[178] This task proved to be a significant challenge, and he did not live to see the outcome. It was only after Siam's participation in WWI that his son, Vajiravudh, began to see the momentum swing in Siam's favour. Following the formation of the League of Nations, Siam called on Western powers to rectify injustice faced by smaller nations and to restore full sovereignty to Siam.[179] Responding to Siam's plea for justice was American President Woodrow Wilson, who made a promise to give Siam a new treaty to address the injustice of extraterritoriality.[180]

The signing of the Siamese-US treaty of 1920 was a crucial step in Siam's liberation from extraterritoriality.[181] Although the subsequent attempts to replicate the American treaty with European powers proved difficult, France and Britain eventually agreed in 1925 to give up their extraterritorial rights.[182] However, these European nations were not willing to do so without setting their conditions. Notably, Siam was required to establish laws concerning IP protection and ensure that their subjects received the same treatment as Siamese nationals.[183] Here, France went even further by demanding that Siam join several international conventions on IP protection.[184] The list unsurprisingly included the latest Berne text (up to 1925),

175 See the Japanese-Siamese Treaty of 1924, art 16; The Franco-Siamese Treaty of 1925, art 24; The Anglo-Siamese Treaty of 1925, art 30–31.
176 Hong Lysa, 'Extraterritoriality in Bangkok in the reign of King Chulalongkorn, 1868–1910: The cacophonies of semi-colonial cosmopolitanism' (2003) 27(1) *Itinerario* 125, 128–133.
177 ibid 132.
178 Sayre (n 16) 74.
179 ibid 81–82.
180 ibid.
181 Treaty of Amity and Commerce, 16 December 1920.
182 See the Franco-Siamese Treaty of 1925 and the Anglo-Siamese Treaty of 1925.
183 The Franco-Siamese Treaty of 1925, art 24; The Anglo-Siamese Treaty of 1925, art 30–31.
184 The Franco-Siamese Treaty of 1925, art 24.

namely, the Berne Convention as revised at Berlin in 1908 and complemented by the additional protocol signed at Berne in 1914.

Integrating Siam Into a Global Capitalist System

The preceding historical account seems to reveal a picture of noticeable contrasts. Whereas Siam invoked the restoration of full sovereignty in its appeal to the League of Nations, France and Great Britain sought to impose IP law on Siam by making it a condition for giving up their exterritorial rights. While it seems Siam only used the legal language of sovereignty to pursue recognition of equal status in the international community, France and Great Britain's demands for national treatment were not just a matter of equality.

As discussed in relation to the Bowring Treaty, the purpose of consular jurisdiction under the unequal treaties was to facilitate the expansion of Western capital into Siam.[185] Similarly, the discussion on the birth of the AOA also highlighted the role of extraterritoriality in the Western-led development of Siam's print capitalism in the late 19th century.[186] Furthermore, the penetration of Western capital—as evident from the extent of British economic interests in Siam—was so great that in 1914, Siam enacted a new law to protect trademarks and trade names only to discover that the law was almost ineffective since those engaging in illegal acts were mainly foreigners who were under consular jurisdiction.[187] Considering these economic implications, the fact that France made no demands on Siam regarding moral rights protection appeared less puzzling. Siam's accession to the Berne Convention mattered as a guarantee of 'business as usual' for European economic interests in this Southeast Asian nation.[188]

Interestingly, the obligation to protect foreign authors did not seem to concern the Siamese government despite the potential impact on the domestic market. Arguably, this air of nonchalance can be explained by the reservation that Siam made under Berne regarding translation, where Siam opted to abide by Article 1 of the Paris Additional Act of 1896.[189] The corresponding provision in the PLAWA thus required foreign authors to authorise the translation of their literary and dramatic works within ten years from publication or risk seeing their rights limited to that period.[190] On this particular issue, the Siamese drafters were unequivocal in their view that 'The market for foreign works translated into Siamese is so limited

185 See 'Siamese Modernisation Under Colonial Influence' in this chapter.

186 See 'The Emergence of Literary Property' in this chapter.

187 Sayre (n 16) 74.

188 That said, it is worth nothing that moral rights were not expressly recognised by the Berne Convention until it was revised by the Rome Act in 1928. This could have another factor in the absence of moral rights in the Franco-Siamese Treaty of 1925.

189 For the reservations Siam made upon accession to the Berlin Act in 1931, see WIPO, 'Treaties and contracting parties' <https://www.wipo.int/wipolex/en/treaties/parties/remarks/TH/15> accessed 20 February 2025.

190 The Protection of Literary and Artistic Works Act BE 2474 (1931), s 28–29.

that few authors will of their own motion arrange for such translations.'[191] Perhaps lending support to the drafters' conviction was the sympathy shown by the British government when Siam first communicated its intention to reserve its right regarding translation to the Berne Union.[192] The British representative even suggested a modification of the Berne text to allow countries like Siam to translate foreign works without permission, albeit for reasonable fees.[193]

The circumstances surrounding the translation right seem to reflect the kind of colonial arrangements typical in the governed territories. Western powers expanded IPRs into their colonies and dependencies to regulate the commercial relations among themselves rather than to benefit local people.[194] When colonialism came to a formal end, international law played an important role in the transition to ensure the continuity of IP protection in former colonies and dependencies.[195] When viewed in this light, it is unsurprising that Thailand did not join any other Berne revisions for a long time after freeing itself from the colonial shackles of extraterritoriality. In fact, it was not until 1980 that Thailand acceded to another Berne text.[196]

II. A Problem of Categorisation: Naming the In-Between

In the year following Siam's accession to the Berne Convention, a bloodless revolution brought an end to the age of absolute monarchy.[197] The last monarch of Siamese absolutism was King Prajadhipok (1925–1935), who succeeded his half-brother Vajiravudh on the throne from amidst the anti-absolutist sentiments coming from various groups in society.[198] The absolutist framework struggled to meet the demands that arose from new imagination and expectations of life, progress, and nation.[199] The impact of the Great Depression, beginning in 1929, only added to Prajadhipok's already precarious position. On the morning of 24 June 1932, a coalition of military officers, bureaucrats, and civilians who called themselves the 'People's Party' assumed and completed the task of bringing the monarch under a constitution.[200]

In some way, it is possible to say Thai absolutism had simply run its course when the People's Party came onto the political stage. The political scientist Kullada Kesboonchoo Mead considers Thai absolutism to be a transitional stage in the

191 National Archive of Thailand, The Ministry of Education Doc No Sor Tor 0701.35, 'Memorandum on draft copyright law' (5 April 1930) 214.

192 National Archive of Thailand, The Ministry of Education Doc No Sor Tor 0701.35, 'Prince Varnvaidya's report on the Copyright Conference' (25 June 1929) 267–268.

193 ibid.

194 Okediji (n 164) 320–325.

195 ibid 326–327.

196 See more detail in 'Modernising Thai Copyright Law' in Chapter 3.

197 Baker and Pasuk, *History* (n 15) 115–120.

198 ibid 109–111.

199 ibid.

200 ibid 115–120; Wyatt, *Short History* (n 32) 245–246.

development of pre-modern Siam into a capitalist nation-state.[201] For the historian David Wyatt, what transpired on the morning of 24 June 1932 was not so much a revolution but 'the political working out of the social consequences of the reforms of Chulalongkorn's reign.'[202] These two commentators may talk from different disciplines and focus on different issues, but they seem to agree that the 1932 revolution did not mark a historic break. Instead, it flowed directly from Siam's encounter with Western colonialism, suggesting that the historic victory of the People's Party might have turned out to be a false dawn for Thai democracy. Indeed, many military coups throughout the 20th century have put Thailand on the world map as a country with an entrenched history of authoritarianism.[203] This is not to mention the revival of the monarchy during the Cold War years, which saw a political alignment between the palace and the military, facilitated by the US and its counterinsurgency operations.[204]

At this point, it is worth revisiting *The King and I* and the thematic clash between tradition and modernity. The pertinent question now is whether the diffusion of modernity had really been all that happened when the West brought its modern knowledge to Siam in the mid-19th century. The fact that this film was banned—and remains so—suggests that the transition to modernity is yet to be complete, even after a century. Perhaps this is true considering the contemporary sense of dissatisfaction among many in Thailand who lament that the country still has a long way to go to catch up with Western nations. But then again, even if one disputes the perception that fixes Euro-American experiences as the standard and the centre, it is important to consider the postcolonial critique of modernity in the Western imagination. Notably, Gurminder Bhambra argues that

> [c]olonisation was not simply an outcome of modernity, or shaped by modernity, but rather, modernity itself developed out of colonial encounters, encounters which are hardly captured by the idea of 'diffusion' and continue to shape our world to this day.[205]

In contrast, the early development of Thai copyright law shows that the era of colonial modernity was more than simply a transition to modernity; that Siam's situation defies a simplistic distinction between colonisation and independence. Economically, the Bowring Treaty marked the annexing of Siam into Pax Britannica under the British empire, indicating the European capitalist expansion into Siam and the rest of Southeast Asia,[206] but in political terms, Siam's participation

201 Kullada (n 115) 10.
202 Wyatt, *Short History* (n 32) 234.
203 For a historical overview of Thai authoritarianism, see Bamrungsuk, 'The development of the hybrid regime'.
204 See 'The era of development' in Chapter 3.
205 Gurminder Bhambra, *Rethinking Modernity: Postcolonialism and the Sociological Imagination* (Palgrave Macmillan 2007) 77.
206 Kullada (n 115) 8–9.

in Pax Britannica was not equal to the British occupation of Burma or the British control over the Malay peninsula. Furthermore, the admiration for Western imperialists among the Siamese ruling elite has long been acknowledged in scholarship, which criticises the 'Siam vs the West' mode of analysis for obscuring the ruling elite's own hegemonic aspirations.[207] These aspirations are otherwise observable in many projects of Siamese monarchs, who borrowed and adapted Western models and modes of rule. As Kasian Tejapira argues, it was from the colonial West that Chulalongkorn borrowed the techniques and technologies of rule that enabled him to consolidate the monarchical power.[208]

A Crypto-Colony

Contrary to the pervasive influence of Western colonialism, the popular assertion that 'we Thai have never been anyone's colony' persists. This prevailing notion illustrates how the myth of Siamese independence has obscured the true legacy of colonialism in Thailand. In Thai legal discourse, for instance, the dominant narratives of independence have translated into the idea of a clean break that resulted in 'traditional' Thai law being replaced by a 'modern' legal system. As seen earlier, the main focus of Thai legal historiography is Chulalongkorn's programme of legal reforms, regarded as a key strategy in how Siam negotiated the threat of colonisation.[209] With the discussion revolving around how legal change contributed to a struggle to maintain independence, little attention has been spared for the 'external' legal culture or what a Westernised legal system actually meant in the broader Siamese society.[210] Notably, a crucial question remains regarding the changes that the legal reform brought about in the dynamics between the ruling elites and other classes within society.

Considering the Siamese–West relations as reflected in the early development of Thai copyright law, one may ask what has been lost or concealed by the invocation of the independence myth. Related to this question, a family of concepts Peter Jackson collectively refers to as 'semicolonialism' have been devised to challenge the dominant narratives of independence and highlight the ambiguity in Siamese–Western relations.[211] As Jackson explains, the prefix 'semi' alludes to a sense of indeterminacy, while 'colonialism' explicitly calls attention to the unequal/unbalanced relations between Siam and Western powers.[212] In addition, the deep sense of indeterminacy in this term alerts one to how the model of a postcolonial state is

207 See the survey of Thai scholarship in Jackson, 'Semicolonial power' (n 17) 37–41.

208 Kasian Tejapira, *Commodifying Marxism* (n 11) 5–6. A case in point is the legal reform programme, which was given high priority: Its first step was the judicial reform via the establishment of a modern, Western-based system of government; see King Chulalongkorn, *Visit to Europe* (n 61) 306–308.

209 See for instance Sawaeng (n 192).

210 See a critique of Thai legal historiography in Thongchai, *Turning Point* (n 21) 177.

211 Jackson, 'Semicolonial power' (n 17) 39.

212 ibid 49.

incomplete, as vividly exemplified by its inability to account for the agency of the Siamese ruling elite.

Among the related concepts within the 'semicolonial' family is Michael Herzfeld's notion of 'crypto-colonialism.' According to Herzfeld, this concept is heuristic rather than typological, and he uses it to create a provocation instead of a solution.[213] For this reason, the defining features of crypto-colonialism are set out in the following description:

> I shall . . . define [crypto-colonialism] the curious alchemy whereby certain countries, buffer zones between the colonised lands and those as yet untamed, were compelled to acquire their political independence at the expense of massive economic dependence, this relationship being articulated in the iconic guise of aggressively national culture fashioned to suit foreign models.[214]

When one looks at the penetration of European capital into Siam, one finds Herzfeld's 'aggressively national culture' reflected in the term *siwilai,* which was newly coined by the Siamese ruling elite. As noted earlier, *siwilai* was a local attempt at transliteration designed to capture the Western ethos of civilisation.[215] This term thus represented a new consciousness among the Siamese ruling elite, who made it their mission to keep pace with the times they saw embodied in Western modernity.[216] In other words, *siwilai* represented the ruling elite's effort to refashion the country in the image of the West, and so it presents the instance of national culture that is 'fashioned to suit a foreign model.'

As Thongchai observes, the meaning of *siwilai* 'ranged from etiquette to material progress, including new roads, electricity, new bureaucracy, courts and judicial system, law codes, dress codes, and white teeth.'[217] Nevertheless, the history of Thai copyright law already demonstrates how *siwilai* was not merely an imitation but highly hybridised. Western ideas and practices were localised through selective appropriation and assimilation by the local elite, who took up the role of a civilising agent.[218] Once localised, the notion of *siwilai* became so embedded in the domestic culture that it transformed into a site of political contests, where different meanings were put forward by various local groups.[219]

This brief survey of the historical significance of *siwilai* illustrates how crypto-colonialism is less about the traces and operations of direct colonial rule

213 Michael Herzfeld, 'The conceptual allure of the West: Dilemmas and ambiguities of crypto-colonialism in Thailand' in Harrison and Jackson (eds), *The Ambiguous Allure of the West*, 174.

214 Herzfeld, 'Crypto-colonialism' (n 8) 900–901.

215 Thongchai, 'Siwilai' (n 30) 529.

216 ibid 531.

217 ibid 529.

218 ibid 532, 538.

219 ibid 530.

and more about capitalist expansion and cultural imperialism.[220] In the case of Thailand, recognising the crypto-colonial conditions in Siam means understanding how Western powers economically and culturally subjugated Siam within a global hierarchy, and how this dynamic was deeply intertwined with domestic struggles over power, identity, and sensibility.

Modernity/Coloniality

As Herzfeld suggests, the history of crypto-colonial conditions has left a legacy that runs far deeper than the apparent Western-derived social etiquette and institutions.[221] By the late 1930s, Hollywood was immensely popular among Thai audiences, to the extent that one observer made this remark.

> Many Siamese young men yearn to go to Hollywood and fail to understand why any American should miss the opportunity. . . . Standards of living shown in [Hollywood] movies, patterns of behaviour which are acted out, and styles of clothing that are shown, are all observed and often are copied.[222]

The colonial encounter has embedded Thailand with a logic of cultural imperialism that the film scholar Adadol Ingawanij aptly describes as 'the historically ingrained mode of imagining modernity as Western.'[223] This observation resonates with the work of scholars such as Aníbal Quijano and Walter Mignolo, whose names have become synonymous with the 'decoloniality' school of thought that emerged from the colonial experiences of Latin America.[224] Among decolonial scholars, a common theoretical premise is the idea that modernity/coloniality are inseparable, as two sides of the same coin.[225] This theoretical duality was first posited by the sociologist Quijano, whose critique of the contemporary world order is inextricably linked with a history of colonialism that traces back to the 15th-century conquest of Latin America.[226]

Despite its geographical specificity, Quijano's theoretical framework aims at a global phenomenon, culminating in a call for epistemological decolonisation.[227] His theoretical formulation of modernity/coloniality serves to highlight the necessity of bringing histories of capitalism and colonialism to bear on the history of the

220 Herzfeld, 'The crypto-colonial dilemmas of Rattanakosin island' (2012) 100 *Journal of the Siam Society* 209, 216.

221 See Herzfeld, 'Dilemmas and ambiguities' (n 213) for a discussion on Thai etiquette from an anthropological perspective.

222 Kenneth Perry Landon, *Siam in Transition* (University of Chicago Press 1938) 176.

223 Adadol Ingawanij, *Hyperbolic heritage: Bourgeois spectatorship and contemporary Thai cinema* (PhD Thesis, University of London (Birkbeck) 2006) 262.

224 Bhambra, 'Postcolonial and decolonial' (n 205) 115.

225 See for instance Walter Mignolo, 'Introduction: Coloniality of power and de-colonial thinking' (2007) 21(2–3) *Cultural Studies* 155.

226 Quijano and Ennis, 'Coloniality of power, eurocentrism, and Latin America'.

227 Quijano, 'Coloniality and modernity/rationality'.

modern world.[228] Perhaps more importantly, modernity/coloniality also signifies enduring structures of power that did not cease with the formal process of decolonisation. The coloniality of power, as Quijano calls it, has outlasted historical colonialism because it cannot merely be reduced to political domination.[229] Rather, coloniality consists of a Eurocentric paradigm of knowledge that emerged alongside the historical formation of Western modernity.[230]

Quijano identifies the initial alignment of colonial power with knowledge production in the European discovery of America.[231] He explains that this encounter produced the concept of race that later justified slavery and colonial domination in the establishment of a global capitalist system,[232] but race is merely one example of social categories that endure in 'a colonisation of the imagination' under the hegemonic Eurocentric paradigm of knowledge.[233] This is why knowledge production is central to Quijano's decolonial critique of the global order, which he contends has continued since the colonisation of America.

By considering modernity within the broader histories of capitalism and colonial exploitation, the concept of modernity/coloniality has inspired the neologism 'colonial modernity,' which helps to explain Asian histories of modernisation beyond the classic case of India.[234] Loos and Thongchai, as noted earlier, view the period in Thai history between the late 19th and early 20th centuries as characterised by the pursuit of colonial modernity, which Thongchai attributes to a specific period between the 1880s and 1930s.[235] For both historians, King Chulalongkorn's legal modernisation programme provides a good illustration. In her study of Siam's relations with Malay Muslim states, Loos discusses the notion of competitive colonialisms, where she draws attention to Siam's own imperial ambitions and how, in response to Western colonialism, the Siamese ruling elite appropriated modern/Western law for that purpose in the Malay Muslim states.[236]

Arguments along similar lines are central to Thongchai's critique of the development of the rule of law in Thailand. Like Loos, Thongchai contends that the Siamese ruling elite appropriated modern/Western legal science for their purposes, hence the derogatory 'Thai-style' rule of law—or the 'rule by law' as Thongchai describes it.[237] But unlike Loos, Thongchai does not confine himself to producing

228 Quijano and Ennis (n 226) 533–534.

229 Quijano (n 227) 169.

230 ibid 171.

231 ibid; Quijano and Ennis (n 226) 534–535.

232 ibid.

233 Quijano (n 227) 169.

234 Hyunjung Lee and Younghan Cho, 'Introduction: Colonial modernity and beyond in East Asian contexts' (2012) 26(5) *Cultural Studies* 601, 604.

235 See Loos, *Subject Siam* (n 8) 2; Thongchai, *Turning Point* (n 21) 6.

236 Tamara Loos, 'Competitive colonialisms: Siam and Malay Muslim South' in Harrison and Jackson (eds), *The Ambiguous Allure of the West*, 75.

237 Thongchai Winichakul, ***นิติรัฐอภิสิทธิ์และราชานิติธรรม ประวัติศาสตร์ภูมิปัญญาของ*** *Rule by Law* ***แบบไทย*** *(Legal-Privileged-State and Royalist Rule of Law: The Intellectual History of Thai-Style Rule by Law)* (Thammasat University 2020) 78.

a historical account. His true ambition is to demonstrate a continuity between the strategies of the Siamese ruling elite and the contemporary practices and discursive frame of Thai officials.[238] In this regard, his study aligns closely with the inquiry pursued in this book. Additionally, his observations of legal development in Siam strongly resonate with the early development of Thai copyright law, as discussed throughout this chapter.

Considering that this historical trajectory began from the 19th-century encounter with Western colonialism, it raises the question of how the Siamese ruling elite came to consider and respond to the West and its knowledge the way they did. To answer this question, attention must now turn to the cultural and intellectual processes that helped usher in the era of colonial modernity.

238 ibid 79.

2 The Quest for Civilisation

The promulgation of the AOA 1901 provides a snapshot of late-19th-century Siam as a country in transition. As discussed in Chapter 1, Siam's reception of Western law should not be understood as a diffusion of modernity in the teleological conception of history as a march of progress emanating from Europe. Rather, what one can see in the emergence of 'author's ownership' is a transformation of the Siamese worldview. The impact of the encounter with Western colonialism was so profound that it produced a significant change in Siamese mentality, ushering in the era of colonial modernity.[1] Perhaps even more fascinating is how this transformation was articulated in the cultural field. Chapter 1 touched on this aspect, particularly when discussing Vajiravudh and his specific brand of nationalism,[2] but the overall discussion was geared towards explaining the legal product of colonial modernity rather than the cultural process that defined it.

That is why the discussion to follow aims to shift the emphasis from the history of law to the history of ideas and cultural history. This change in perspective moves away from viewing copyright history primarily as a story about legal change. Instead, it seeks to explain social change through copyright historiography.[3] Regarding the subject of reflection, this means shifting attention from the diffusion of copyright law (or legal transplantation) to focusing on the emergence of literary property as a social category and the ideology it carried.

Two landmark texts in copyright historiography have blazed a trail for a study that seeks to explain a society in transition, measured through a change in literary culture. Martha Woodmansee's *The Genius and the Copyright* (1984) and Mark Rose's *The Author as Proprietor* (1988) trace the modern conception of authorship back to 18th-century Europe, specifically to the thoughts and writings of German

1 Thongchai refers to this as a shift in Siam's 'foundational mentality', the epistemic aspect of which is discussed in this chapter. For an exploration of what constitutes Siam's foundational mentality, see Thongchai Winichakul, *เมื่อสยามพลิกผัน: ว่าด้วยกรอบมโนทัศน์ของสยามยุคใหม่ (Siam at a Turning Point: On the Foundational Mentality of Siam in the Modern Era)* (Fah-diew-kan 2019) 3–27.

2 See 'Writing the Nation' in Chapter 1.

3 In contrast, see Martin Kretschmer, Lionel Bently, and Ronan Deazley, 'Introduction' in Ronan Deazley, Martin Kretschmer, and Lionel Bently (eds), *Privilege and Property: Essay on the History of Copyright* (Open Book Publishers 2010) 5–6.

DOI: 10.4324/9781003592037-4

thinkers and the litigation of a famous copyright case under English law.[4] Evident in the work of both scholars is the entangled history of authorship and ownership within Western copyright traditions.

As discussed later, Woodmansee and Rose go back to the 18th century to examine the link between the emergence of literary property and the romantic construction of authorship. This relationship was contingent upon the presence of specific historical conditions, notably the emerging mass production of books. In the 18th century, Woodmansee notes, 'Germany found itself in a transitional phase between the limited patronage of aristocratic age and the democratic patronage of the marketplace.'[5] Similarly, Rose situates the landmark case of *Donaldson v. Becket (1774)* within the broader history of a transition from the patronage system to the mass market for books.[6]

In 19th-century Siam, book trade began to emerge following the signing of the unequal treaties in the second half of the century.[7] Modern printing technology, however, had arrived earlier, bringing with it Western literary forms and practices that set off a chain of transformations, ultimately leading to the birth of modern Thai literature.[8] In this regard, the twin birth of the 1914 Amendment Act and Vajiravudh's RSL was a testament to the eventual status of the literary field as a site for the ruling elite to negotiate Western influence and construct their version of Thai identity.[9] What remains tantalisingly open is the question of what intellectual and cultural strategies had been devised to carry out such a task; one can say these strategies signified the arrival of colonial modernity.

As discussed later, viewing the historiography of modern authorship from the perspective of Siamese–Western relations raises many puzzling questions. Certainly, this chapter is not an appropriate place to inquire into the practices and myths that constituted the literary field in Siam/Thailand.[10] And yet it is relevant to ask what the 'romantic' turn in Western copyright scholarship really means for Thailand, especially regarding how the country should engage with its own history. Fundamentally, one is confronted with the broader epistemic question of whether there can be a commonality of experience that also allows for the particularity of place. This conundrum begs to be addressed through the lens of modernity/coloniality.[11]

4 See Woodmansee, 'The genius and the copyright'; Mark Rose, 'The author as proprietor: *Donaldson* v. *Becket* and the genealogy of modern authorship' (1988) 23 *Representations* 51.

5 Woodmansee, *The Author, Art, and the Market: Rereading the History of Aesthetics* (Columbia University Press 1994) 41–42.

6 Rose (n 4) 55–56.

7 The working group on the history of printing in Thailand, *สยามพิมพการ: ประวัติศาสตร์การพิมพ์ในประเทศไทย (Sayam Phimphakan: History of Printing in Thailand)* (Matichon 2006) 5–9.

8 See 'The Cultural Life of Literature' in this chapter.

9 See 'Writing the Nation' in Chapter 1.

10 For an interesting discussion of this subject, see Thanapol Limapichart, *Prescription of good books: The formation of the discourse and cultural authority of literature in modern Thailand (1860s–1950s)* (PhD thesis, University of Wisconsin-Madison 2008).

11 See 'Modernity/Coloniality' in Chapter 1.

The shift in the Siamese worldview not only ushered in the era of colonial modernity but also demonstrated the coloniality of power. The history of Thai copyright law, as a story of legal transplants, has drawn attention to the active role of Siamese agents, and this perspective will be extended to the domain of literature. Specifically, shifting the focus to literature means paying attention to the intellectual strategies that allowed the Siamese ruling elite to embrace the allure of the West while asserting the essence of Thainess.[12] This preliminary observation already suggests that romantic authorship might have played a part in the emergence of Thai copyright law—but only insofar as it was allowed by local actors, either through their selective appropriation or the limits of their comprehension.[13] The caveat here is crucial as it raises the question of how one can be certain that the belated arrival of modernity simply delayed the inevitable birth of Thai copyright law, which would just be equivalent, albeit belated, to Western experiences.[14] To begin to address this issue, one needs to start with the emergence of literary property in Europe—in a transformation that was supposed to place the figure of the author at the centre of the history of copyright law.

I. The Birth of Literary Property

'What is an author?' Michel Foucault asked in a lecture he delivered to the Société française de philosophie in 1969. Foucault argues that the significance of identifying the author of a given text goes beyond designating an actual individual.[15] He claims that the name of an author is indicative as much as descriptive in that an author's name also functions to classify and establish relationships among texts.[16] In this regard, the significance of an author's name, which is to be contrasted with the flesh-and-blood author, comes from the role it plays in classifying and organising knowledge in a broad sense. Foucault claims that this function of the author figure, or the 'author-function' as he calls it, has long characterised literary production and consumption in Western culture and perhaps elsewhere.[17] Indeed, he came to address this question because of his observation that 'the coming into being of the notion of the author constitutes the privileged moment of individualisation in the history of ideas, knowledge, literature, philosophy, and the sciences.'[18]

Two decades after his 1969 lecture, Foucault's genealogy of the author inspired literary and legal scholars in the Anglo-American world to pose the same question. This time, however, copyright law moved to the forefront, and the inquiry gave rise to a body of literature that presents a critique of what is now known as romantic

12 See 'The Spiritual/Material Bifurcation' in this chapter.

13 See 'Authorship and Ownership in the Emergence of Thai Copyright Law' in this chapter.

14 See 'Belated Modernity and the Repetition of History' in this chapter.

15 Michel Foucault, 'What is an author?' in Josué Harari (ed), *Textual Strategies: Perspectives in Post-Structuralist Criticism* (Cornell University Press 1979) 146.

16 ibid 147.

17 ibid 149.

18 ibid 141.

authorship.[19] Many scholars in the 1990s attributed copyright's expansive impulses and the excesses of copyright's substantive expansion to the romantic author.[20] But the romantic author critique also comes with its own excesses, drawing criticism from within the academia that called for qualifications and clarifications.[21] Nevertheless, the counter-critiques and the responses they created do not take away from the significant subject of authorship, which remains intertwined with such notions as self, creativity, and property in Western thought.

Authorship and Ownership

Citing Foucault's observation, as quoted earlier, two landmark texts by literary scholars set out to demystify authorship in the Anglo-American context, creating significant repercussions in legal scholarship.[22] Martha Woodmansee's *The Genius and the Copyright'* and Mark Rose's *The Author as Proprietor* take the readers back to the 18th century to trace the modern conception of authorship in Western culture.[23] For her part, Woodmansee's work sheds light on how 18th-century German writers contributed to the development of literary property as part of their broader social and cultural project, which saw the author in the modern sense emerge as a function of aesthetic discourse.[24]

In writings by figures such as Johann Gottlieb Fichte, Woodmansee identified the romantic turn in the conception of writing that constituted a departure from prior notions of writing as derivative and collaborative. These German theorists developed the idea of an author as 'an individual who is solely responsible—and

19 See for instance Jaszi, 'Toward a theory of copyright' (n 236); Jaszi, 'On the author effect'; Jaszi and Woodmansee, 'Introduction' in Woodmansee and Jaszi (eds), *The Construction of Authorship* (Duke University Press 1994); Boyle, *Shamans, Software, and Spleens.*

20 ibid.

21 See for instance Lionel Bently, 'Copyright and the death of the author in literature and law' (1994) 57 *Modern Law Review* 973; Mark Lemley, 'Romantic authorship and the rhetoric of property' (1997) 75 *Texas Law Review* 873; Lionel Bently, 'R v the author: From death penalty to community service' (2008) 32 *Columbia Journal of Law and Arts* 1; Oren Bracha, 'The ideology of authorship revisited: Authors, markets, and liberal values in early American copyright' (2008) 118 *Yale Law Journal* 186.

22 Not only did his work inspire literary scholars to inquire into the relationship between authorship and ownership, but '*What is an author'* also appeared to rejuvenate general interest in the history of copyright law among legal scholars too. Kretschmer et al. observe a 'historical turn' in copyright scholarship and attribute this trend to the English translation of Foucault's 1969 essay. See Kretschmer, Bently, and Deazley (n 3) 2.

23 Woodmansee, 'The genius' (n 4); Rose (n 4).

24 Although her 1984 article, well-known among legal scholars, looks at the question of authorship and ownership, Kathy Bowrey observes that the main goal of Woodmansee's historical inquiry is to be found in her 1994 book *The Author, Art, and the Market*, in which the 1984 article appears a chapter. See Kathy Bowrey, 'Law, aesthetics and copyright historiography: A critical reading of the genealogies of Martha Woodmansee and Mark Rose' in Isabella Alexander and Tomás Gómez-Arostegui (eds), *Research Handbook on the History of Copyright Law* (Edward Elgar 2016) 28–37.

therefore exclusively deserving of credit—for the production of a unique work.'[25] Perhaps more importantly, Woodmansee shows how the romantic conception of authorship arose from the interplay between philosophy, economy, and law. With a view to improving material conditions, these 18th-century writers presented writing as a solitary originary process whereby 'ideas'—free to everyone as raw materials—were given 'form' by the author who created something distinctly his—his own property—that could not be reduced to either the physical book or the ideas it presented.[26]

Acknowledging Woodmansee's contributions as far as the Anglo idea of the author is concerned, Mark Rose locates the genesis of modern authorship in the English courtrooms.[27] His response to Foucault's question offers a historical account of a 'twin birth' of modern authorship and literary proprietorship, which is marked by the emergence of the idea that equates authorship with proprietorship.[28] Through a close reading of old tracts generated by 18th-century debates on literary property, Rose draws attention to the rhetoric and arguments surrounding the 'battle of the booksellers,'[29] a series of legal disputes between London booksellers and their pirate Scottish counterparts that culminated in the decision of the House of Lords in *Donaldson v. Becket*[30] and ultimately, as Rose argues, gave rise to the legal-cultural conception of the author as a proprietor.[31] Central to Rose's historical account of 'the author as proprietor' is a cross-fertilisation between philosophical and aesthetic ideas that played out in the legal arguments put forth by the advocates of literary property. Rose describes how their propositions blended the Lockean discourse of property with an abstract conception of literary composition (i.e., the notion of style and sentiment),[32] which, according to Rose, helped clear the ground for the English romantic movement in the early 19th century.[33]

Romantic Authorship and Copyright Law

Because the aim of historicising the notion of authorship is to de-naturalise it, the genealogical analysis by these two literary scholars prompted legal scholars to investigate the myth of romantic authorship in copyright law. However, such efforts sometimes produced an exaggerated account of romantic authorship that

25 Woodmansee 'The genius' (n 4) 426.

26 ibid 444–445.

27 Rose (n 4) 58.

28 ibid 65.

29 For detailed discussion on the battle of the book sellers, see Ronan Deazley, *On the Origin of the Right to Copy: Charting the Movement of Copyright Law in Eighteenth-Century Britain, 1695–1775* (Hart 2004).

30 *Donaldson* v. *Becket* (1774) *Hansard, 1st ser.*, 17 (1774) 953–1003.

31 Rose (n 4) 58.

32 ibid 62–64. See also John Locke, *The Second Treatise on Government; and a Letter Concerning Toleration* (Mark Goldie ed, OUP 2016) 15–16.

33 ibid 69–70, 76.

overlooked socio-economic factors.[34] More controversially, the romantic author often turned into a strawman in arguments aimed at critiquing the development of copyright law from the past to the present.[35] Critical as they were, what became lost in these narratives was the contingency and complexity in the historical construction of modern authorship, which appealed to legal scholars in the first place.[36] Thus, inasmuch as they attempted to bring down the author-king, the work of these commentators also helped to inaugurate the romantic author as the sovereign of meanings in the history of copyright law, as well as contemporary legal doctrine.[37]

Problematic though they may be, these shortcomings do not justify neglecting this line of inquiry. Instead, they call for a more nuanced perspective to capture the finer aspects of the authorship–copyright nexus. In this regard, Oren Bracha's studies of US copyright law in the 19th century are instructive for how this relationship can be reconsidered.[38] According to Bracha, it is not that aesthetic ideals never had a significant bearing on law, and nor did the late 18th century usher in the 'golden age' of authorship, which faded into insignificance over the next century.[39] The romantic conception of authorship, he argues, supplied the modern copyright framework with rudimentary concepts as well as the ideology that 'constructed a new representation of the creative process.'[40] These elements then constituted a conceptual field in which US legal actors had to operate over the course of the 19th century.[41]

On one level, Bracha's close reading of 19th-century US case law shows how the lexicon of authorship constituted the language of legal doctrine that legal

34 In the American context in particular, an influential body of literature, as seen in n 391, developed in the 1990s on the assumption that the myth of romantic authorship still plays a central role in modern copyright law.

35 This observation is central to Lionel Bently's critical reflection on the romantic authorship critique in 'R v The Author' (n 21).

36 The prism of romantic authorship appears to presume certain relations between law and society as well as legal doctrine and humanities that restrict the vision of the viewers. Anne Barron, for instance, repels the charge of 'romantic determinism' by shifting the focus from the subject of copyright law (the author) to its object (the work) to show that 'it is the manner in which copyright law defines the work, rather than the manner in which it defines the author, that exposes the affinities between the discourses of copyright law and aesthetic theory most vividly'. See Barron 'Copyright and the claims of art' (2002) 4 IPQ 368, 369–370. Similarly, the limiting effect of authorship on the recognition of a new subject matter (and so the expansion of capitalism) is central to Bernard Edelman's work on French law and authorship in films, whereas the legal recognition of collective authorship in films also presents a clear deviation from the romantic idea of the lone genius. See Edelman, *Ownership of the Image.*

37 Erlend Lavik contends that a lack of interpretative constraints in the romantic author metaphor offers a good explanation, for which he points towards the challenge in bringing the insights from humanities to bear on legal scholarship. See Lavik, 'Romantic authorship in copyright law and the uses of aesthetics' in Mireille van Eechoud (ed), *The Work of Authorship* (Amsterdam University Press 2014) 59–63.

38 Bracha (n 21).

39 ibid 196.

40 ibid 191–192.

41 ibid 201.

professionals and commentators—those who participated in what Lawrence Friedman calls 'internal' legal culture[42]—would speak even when dealing with the external forces of political and economic change. Consequently, this situation produced 'the modern copyright framework, which simultaneously is pervaded by the ideology of authorship and has little to do with it.'[43] Furthermore, Bracha's law-in-context analysis also suggests that the ideology of authorship had similarly formed part of the 'external' legal culture or 'the legal culture of the general population.'[44] This indicates that romantic authorship vocabulary had come to provide legal arguments to social and economic actors, enabling them to articulate their economic interests and ideological commitments through legal reasoning.[45] In this respect, Bracha's contextual analysis of the originality concept shows how commercial and political agents, in pursuing their own interests not necessarily align with romantic authorship, played a significant role in establishing originality as the foundation of US copyright law by the end of the 19th century.[46]

By injecting contingency and complexity into an account of legal change, critics of romantic author scholarship resist the tautology of copyright and authorship, which allowed romantic determinism to take a leap of causality from the twin birth in the 18th century.[47] Furthermore, historical accounts such as Bracha's also call into question the implicit presumption of law as a 'mirror image' of society.[48] While later chapters provide further discussion on this point, it is worth noting here that Bracha's history of copyright serves as a good reminder that the relationship between law and society is far more complex—it cannot be reduced to a mere reflection of society or an instrument for social order.[49] Therefore, it is prudent not to assume a direct correspondence between legal change and social reality in the context of crypto-colonial Siam.

Person, Property, and Empire

From the discussion so far, what has emerged as closely connected to the birth of modern authorship and the spectre of the romantic author is an economic conception of 'the person.' Fundamentally, the romantic view of authorship presupposes

42 Lawrence Friedman, *The Legal System: A Social Science Perspective* (Russell Sage Foundation 1975) 223–224.
43 Bracha (n 21) 197.
44 Friedman (n 42) 223–224.
45 ibid.
46 Bracha (n 21) 209–224.
47 Responding to what he terms romantic–historicist accounts by authors such as Woodmansee and Rose, David Saunders in his history of copyright argues that the relations between the legal and the literary are contingent rather than integral. See Saunders, *Authorship and Copyright* (Routledge 1992) 212.
48 See 'Law and development' in Chapter 3.
49 Brian Tamanaha identifies a common supposition among different Western theories of law to consist of two separated but closely connected ideas, namely, law is a reflection of society, and law maintains social order. See Tamanaha, *A General Jurisprudence of Law and Society* (OUP 2001) 25–38.

that individuals are 'self-possessed and self-contained,' so they are the proprietors of themselves.[50] To put this another way, the idea that people own their minds and bodies not only makes themselves the authors of their own actions,[51] but it also renders self-ownership the foundation of literary property. This perspective exemplifies what Marilyn Strathern calls 'Western proprietism,' which posits two complementary propositions about the relations between persons and things.[52]

Strathern observes that within the Western system of thinking, the person is conceived as the 'possessive individual'—a unitary self either capable of freely exchanging things external to it while identified by things in its possession or otherwise indissolubly linked to its own activities such that its identity is fragmented when alienated from the products of its actions.[53] In this regard, selfhood and self-expression are inextricable from property, whereby the self is not only unitary but also manifests in the person's relations with property.[54] Consequently, to say like Strathern does that 'persons *are* what they *have* or *do*'[55] resonates with the fixed identities in the author–user polarity that copyright law, with its possessory model of creativity, presents through the language of authorship. This division between authors and users constitutes a cultural frame of reference that posits the user as an indebted consumer of the author's unique and proprietary self,[56] creating an asymmetrical relationship that renders the notion of balance a necessary yet elusive task for copyright law.[57]

Interestingly, the Western model of proprietary personhood is also implicated in the history of Western colonialism. John Locke's labour theory—which posits that each person has a property right in their body and, thus, the fruits of their labour—became a theoretical justification for the expropriation of indigenous peoples by the circuits of empire in the late 18th and 19th centuries.[58] Colonial powers often employed the Lockean argument to assert that indigenous peoples, deemed primitive and uncivilised, had failed to improve their land with their labour and thus had no legitimate claim to it.[59] This logic underpinned widespread dispossession across the world, including the expansion of Western colonialism into Southeast Asia.

50 John Frow, *Time and Commodity Culture: Essays in Cultural Theory and Postmodernity* (Clarendon 1997) 126.

51 Marilyn Strathern, *The Gender of the Gift: Problems with Women and Problems with Society in Melanesia Studies in Melanesian Anthropology* (University of California Press 1988) 135.

52 ibid 157–158.

53 ibid. See also Frow (n 50) 126.

54 Johanna Gibson, *Creating Selves: Intellectual Property and the Narration of Culture* (Routledge 2006) 124–127.

55 Strathern (n 51) 158.

56 Gibson (n 54) 127.

57 For a more detailed discussion of the concept of balance, see 'The Public-Private Dichotomy' in Chapter 8.

58 David Armitage, 'John Locke: Theorist of empire?' in Sankar Muthu (ed), *Empire and Modern Political Thought* (CUP 2012) 100–101.

59 ibid. For further discussion on Locke's view of property and its implications for the idea of territory, see Uday Singh Mehta, *Liberalism and Empire: A Study in Nineteenth-Century Political Thought and Practice* (University of Chicago Press 1999) 123–132.

While Siam managed to avoid direct control, the European colonisation of its former tributary states—such as Cambodia, Laos, and the Malay Peninsula—exemplified the persistent colonial threat facing the Siamese ruling elite.[60] This pressure, however, was not restricted to territorial encroachment. Siam's judicial authority was also affected, as demonstrated by the system of extraterritoriality, which the British Empire was the first to impose on Siam through the Bowring Treaty.[61] As discussed earlier, extraterritoriality became a contentious issue, particularly because the patchwork of consular jurisdictions had left the country's administration of justice in disarray.[62] Siam's desire for judicial autonomy also highlighted the extent of Western dominance, as extraterritoriality was produced by the Western standard of civilisation. This 19th-century perception of law and civilisation is succinctly expressed by John Bowring, who negotiated and signed the Bowring Treaty on behalf of the British Empire, when he wrote that 'The laws of a country are among the most practical and prominent evidences of its civilisation and advancement.'[63]

In addition to the country's legal system, literature was another social domain in Siam that experienced a transformation following the encounter with the West. Just as law was mobilised by the ruling elite in their interactions with both Western powers and local populations, the field of literature also underwent a strategic shift in thinking and practice, not only with regard to the literary form and language but also the very notion of knowledge.[64] Central to this transition from the practice of traditional Thai literature to the emergence of modern Thai literature was the intellectual strategy of spiritual–aterial bifurcation. This strategy allowed the Siamese ruling elite to negotiate the influx of Western influence both within and beyond the literary field.

Literature in Siam: Authors, Readers, and the Promise of Nirvana

Indeed, one would assume that the transplanting of Western law into Siam was influenced by the local conception of truth and justice,[65] personhood and

60 Under colonial pressure, the modern borders of Siam were drawn between the late 19th and early 20th centuries, conceding some former tributaries to European powers in the process. For illustration, see the map in Baker and Phongpaichit, *A History of Thailand*, 65. For an interesting discussion highlighting the complexity surrounding claims of 'territorial' losses, see Winichakul, *Siam Mapped*, 150–152.

61 Article III of the supplementary agreement (1856) stipulated that 'British subjects, their persons, houses, premises, land, ships or property of any kind, shall not be seized, injured, or in any way interfered with by the Siamese.' See also Sayre, 'The passing of extraterritoriality in Siam', 70, 71, and 73.

62 See 'Elevating Siamese Law to European Standards' in Chapter 1.

63 Bowring, *The Kingdom and People of Siam*, 171.

64 See 'When Print Capitalism Met Siamese Absolutism' in this chapter.

65 For the notion of truth in Siam's traditional justice system, see Taweesak Pueksom, ***หยดเลือด จารึก และแท่นพิมพ์: ว่าด้วยความรู้/ความจริงของชนชั้นนำสยาม พ.ศ.*** *2325–2411 (Blood, Inscription, and Printing Press: The Conception of Knowledge/Truth of the Siamese Elite, 1782–1868)* (Illumination 2018).

community,[66] time and space,[67] materiality and spirituality[68]—this list goes on. Consequently, it is difficult to imagine that Siam's adoption of copyright law was not furnished or constrained by local thoughts and beliefs in any way. At least, that does not seem to be how translation works, and it is also unwise to overlook the political and ideological projects that permeated the early history of Thai copyright law. In the Western context, Bracha describes authorship as the ghost in the copyright machine.[69] The pertinent question here is how the people of Siam may have related to this ghost when Chulalongkorn brought in copyright law at the beginning of the 20th century. One way to answer this question is to draw a parallel to another ghost, as it were—one that was transported from the fictional world of Victorian Gothic into the writings of a Siamese author.

Just as Thai law was influenced by the West, so, too was literature. Marking the birth of modern Thai literature was the emergence of novels as one of the new literary forms.[70] Available records show that *Nang-neramit* (1916), or *The Divine Nymphs*, was one of the first Thai novels to be published.[71] It was written by a Western-educated Thai author known as Khru Liam and was published to cater to the growing Siamese readership.[72] The story, though written in Thai, follows the adventures of the English hero James Billford, whose pyramid expedition in exotic Egypt leads him to discover mysterious female mummies, sending him on a dangerous journey full of lust and magic.

If this summary strikes one as odd, given that the story was written by a Siamese author for Siamese readers, it is safe to conclude that Khru Liam succeeded in what he wanted to achieve. Resembling the 'mummy fiction' of the Victorian period,[73] *The Divine Nymphs* was written as if it had been translated from an English original when in fact there was none.[74] By his own admission, this was Khru Liam's deliberate attempt to appeal to the taste of the Siamese readers to make up for the commercial failure of his previous work.[75] Certainly, the country's quest for *siwilai* was reflected in local demand for Western fiction that Khru Liam had identified in

66 For the interactions between modern law and the indigenous conception of personhood and community in northern Thailand, see David Engel and Jaruwan Engel, *Tort and Karma: Globalisation and Legal Consciousness in Thailand* (Stanford University Press 2010). See also Loos, *Subject Siam* (n 24).

67 David and Jaruwan (n 66) also shed light on how the indigenous conception of time and space in northern Thailand does not neatly align with modern law and the concept of the nation-state.

68 See the Siamese distinction of the material/the spiritual in Taweesak (n 65).

69 Bracha (n 21) 188.

70 For the genesis and historical development of Thai novels, see Supannee Varathorn, *ประวัติศาสตร์การประพันธ์นวนิยายไทย (The History of Thai Novel)* (Chareonwitkarnpim 1976).

71 See Chaloemtiarana, *Read Till It Shatters,* 50; Thak goes so far as to say that *The Divine Nymphs* was the second novel in Thai literary history that was composed originally in Thai by a Thai author.

72 ibid.

73 Rachel Harrison, 'Mummies, sex and sand: Bangkok gothic and the adventure fiction of 'Victorian' Siam' in Harrison (ed), *Disturbing Convention Decentering Thai Literary Cultures*, 89.

74 Sombat Phlainoi, 'ครูเหลี่ยม ผู้เขียนนวนิยายไทยคนแรก' ('Khru Liam: The First Thai Novelist') in Nai Samran (ed), *ความไม่พยาบาท (non-vendetta)* (Dokya 2002) 92–93.

75 ibid.

the Siamese readership at the time.[76] But what is more striking about Khru Liam's candid admission is the way it reflected on literary conventions in Siam.

Khru Liam's 'forgery,' as it were, was not born out of the cult of originality. Quite the contrary, *The Divine Nymphs* aimed to tap into the desire for Western modernity among Siamese aristocrats, whose quest for *siwilai* meant they 'envisaged themselves through the eyes of, and on a par with, the British colonial elite.'[77] What these crypto-colonial subjects sought from Western fiction was a quasi-colonial fantasy where the notion of originality—which ironically demarcates 'fiction' as a mode of literature in Western conventions—did not appear to be a relevant frame of reference.[78] This point is evident in the fact that Khru Liam was mindful of the Western flavours in his work and tried to adapt them to the Thai palate by casually inserting many unmistakable Thai elements into the supposedly Western fiction.[79]

Indeed, Thai translations of Western literature between the late 19th and early 20th centuries generally shared this characteristic.[80] These Siamese translators did not draw a clear distinction between writing and translating and were willing to let the otherwise demarcated territories shade into one another. In her study of Thai literary cultures, Rachel Harrison observes that Khru Liam and many of his contemporaries not only engaged in Western borrowing and intertextual composition but also took pride in how they went about it.[81] This practice understandably rendered the notion of original authenticity marginal in literary categorisation in Siam. In fact, to say otherwise would be difficult to reconcile with the collective and collaborative practices that characterised Siamese literature of the 19th century.

The Cultural Life of Literature

Unlike the romantic conception of authorship, literature in 19th-century Siam was rooted in social relations (tradition) rather than attributed to a unitary subject (the author). This may be the effect of the oral culture that continued to prevail, despite the emerging book trade resulting from the growing presence of Westerners.[82]

Nevertheless, the development of the book trade signalled the arrival of Western knowledge, which proved to be all-encompassing and transformative later in the

76 See Harrison (n 73) 95–96.

77 ibid 96.

78 'Novel' implies novelty/originality in the sense that the stories are not based on tales or mythologies.

79 See the textual analysis of *The Divine Nymphs* in Thak (n 71) 46–56.

80 Wibha Senanan notes that Western literature that was imported into 19th-century Siam was the kind that provided immediate entertainment, so the stories were normally adapted or rewritten by the Siamese authors at their liberty. See Senanan, *The Genesis of the Novel in Thailand* (Thai-Watana-Panich 1975).

81 Harrison (n 73) 94–95. On the subject of cultural borrowing, Thak similarly notes that 'appropriating the novel from the West was in fact seen as a 'clever' mastery of the West, and not as the bankruptcy of indigenous genius.' See Thak (n 71) 16.

82 For a view that emphasises the oral tradition in Thai literature, see Chetana Nagavajara, 'Literature in Thai Life: Reflections of a Native' (1994) 2(1) *South East Asia Research* 12.

19th century. After all, Thai literature was not shielded from the transformation taking place in the country, and the publication of novels is but one instance. Consequently, a comparison tends to be made between the early and late 19th centuries. The former belonged to the era of cultural restoration following the devastation of dynastic warfare with the old foe Burma (Myanmar) and the latter to the era of modernisation in the face of Western colonialism.[83] That said, one would rightly expect some continuity despite the temptation to equate the arrival of colonial modernity with a clean historical break. Indeed, Thai literature of the 19th century presented a form of enjoyment that was anchored in Buddhist cosmology and typically characterised by a distributed or composite form of authorship.

It is by no means unusual that the people of Siam derived pleasure from literature, but to equate literature with pleasure and play is a different matter. Literary historians argue that entertainment was the primary function of literature in traditional Siam, and this was particularly so with folk literature.[84] The fact that mass education was not yet available—at least until the late 19th century when Chulalongkorn pushed for educational reforms—meant orality was possibly the reality of the general populace who recited and sang poetry for enjoyment and socialisation.[85] Meanwhile, literacy was already prevalent among the Siamese aristocracy, whose status and authority meant their written culture had to fulfil stately and ceremonious functions.[86] Yet scholars argue that even court literature possessed an aesthetic quality and evolved over time to resemble folk literature, thereby becoming more entertaining.[87] In many ways, this Siamese conception of literature as enjoyment highlights the important role of oral tradition in Siamese literary culture,[88] and this helps explain the prevailing modes of authorship in 19th-century Siam.

Weaving Self in the Flow of Tradition

Identifying an author in traditional Thai literature is undoubtedly a challenging task. However, this is not to say that authorship was an alien concept in 19th-century Siam. On the contrary, it is well documented that the Siamese poets of the early

83 See for instance Chonlada Reungraklikid, Reunrutai Sajjaphun, and Duangmon Jitjamnong, ***ทอไหมในสายน้ำ 200 ปีวรรณคดีวิจารณ์ไทย*** *(Weaving Silk in Flowing Water: 200 Years of Thai Literary Criticism)* (2nd edn, A.N. Publishing 1998).

84 See for instance Duangmon Jitjamnong, ***คุณค่าและคุณลักษณะเด่นของวรรณคดีไทยสมัยรัตนโกสินทร์ตอนต้น*** *(The Value and Characteristics of Thai Literature in the Early Rattanakosin Period)* (Thammasat University Press 1997) 40–41; Niti Eoseewong, *Pen and Sail: Literature and History in Early Bangkok* (Silkworm 2005) 15, 21, 25.

85 Niti Eoseewong, however, notes a rise in literature for reading in the early nineteenth century, although entertainment was still the primary function of literature. See Niti (n 84) 50.

86 ibid 11.

87 ibid 25.

88 ibid 25–50: Niti separates folk/court literature along the oral/written line, which means the adoption of folk literature by the Siamese court also signifies the influence of the oral tradition on the development of Thai written culture. See also Chetana (n 82) 32–35.

19th century were on a mission to emulate the old masters, whose works had been passed down through previous centuries.[89] For those who adhere to the modern concept of authorship, the Siamese literary tradition may appear to have a limited concept of authorship. This, however, is precisely where Siamese literature defies a simple individualism–collectivism dichotomy that goes hand in hand with the East–West binary.

Siamese poets were avid readers of classical works and keen learners of tradition. Poetry thus commanded cultural prestige in traditional Siam, and it was not uncommon for a work of Siamese poetry to demand to be read by a learned person who understood the tradition.[90] However, it would be a mistake to think that Siamese poets simply threw themselves into the pit of sameness by following convention and tradition. Quite the contrary, a work of Siamese poetry would begin with a tribute to the teacher and conclude with an utterance of self-assertion and self-aggrandisement.[91] Such confidence is described as '*ahangan,*' which translates to arrogance in English but perhaps carries a connotation of transgression.[92] A good illustration of a poet's *ahangan* is the longing for immortality that Siamese poets often expressed in their wish that their works would endure until the end of time.[93] This commitment to poetry—the desire to leave behind immortal works—brings into discussion another convention that reminds us that their self-expression (*ahangan*) was always situated within the flow of tradition.

It was not unusual for a Siamese poet to invite the readers to improve the work to ensure its eternal legacy. Certainly, such a request thinly disguised the poet's self-confidence, for one would have to believe in one's work to expose it to criticism in that manner. However, this literary practice did not necessarily boil down to the poet's ego. Duangmon Jitjamnong, a scholar of Thai literature, argues in her seminal work that it was part of the convention of '*klao-klon,*' which she traces back to the Siamese tradition of orality.[94] The phrase *klao-klon* may roughly translate as 'poetry refining,' which implies the idea of a gradual improvement in the use of language and versification. As a literary convention, Duangmon argues, *klao-klon* refers to a collective and collaborative process of gradually improving a piece of poetry to attain immortality.[95] This also means that authorship of a particular poem could be distributed temporarily and spatially across a group of people who were both readers and authors and could not be reduced to either.

89 See for instance Chonlada et al. (n 83) 47–48.

90 ibid 56–59. See also Suchitra Chongstitvatana, *The nature of modern Thai poetry considered with reference to the works of Angkhan Kalayanaphong, Naaowarat Phongphaibun, and Suchit Wongthet* (PhD thesis, University of London (SOAS) 1984) 255–356: Suchitra makes the same observation when she discusses *Chindamani,* a seventeenth-century text on Thai versification as well as the first Thai textbook on language.

91 Chetana (n 82) 14–15; Duangmon (n 84) 27–28.

92 ibid.

93 ibid.

94 Duangmon (n 84) 27.

95 ibid 28, 47.

Furthermore, the practice and meaning of *klao-klon* suggest a view of poetry, or for that matter a conception of literature, that did not yield to the supremacy of the text. Leading the charge against a text-based appraisal of Thai literary heritage is the literary scholar Chetana Nagavajara, who argues that

> [m]uch of our great 'literature' is improvised, never recorded, is appreciated and assimilated by the living public. . . . It transfers its riches through human experience and contact, each generation seeking to perpetuate what it has inherited and to add to it something of its own. It is thus self-perpetuating and self-renewing. . . . Embedded in this tradition is the extreme confidence in the creative power of man which is not the exclusive property of any particular moment in history, or any particular generation.[96]

Weaving self in the flow of tradition seems an apt statement to summarise the ethos of Thai literary heritage that Chetana seeks to highlight. It is understandable if one is wary of tradition, considering the history of how individual life and freedom have been taken away in its name. Especially in the Thai context, to speak of tradition tends to evoke the essentialist notion of 'Thainess' that has long been assimilated into the royalist–nationalist mythology.[97] In this respect, tradition presents an inextricable relationship between power and knowledge, and like other forms of power/knowledge, tradition too can be productive. The productivity of tradition is evident in the early 19th century in the state project of cultural restoration.[98] This was the time when the Siamese ruling elite elevated old literature from previous centuries into an exemplary status.[99]

Revisiting and restoring the literature of the glorious past was the dominant theme in the early 19th century, resulting in numerous works of composite authorship.[100] The ruling elite of this period presented their regime as a restoration of the glorious literary tradition of a once-powerful Siamese state—the Ayutthaya Kingdom—which flourished in the region between the 14th and 18th centuries.[101] Since most things were destroyed in the sack of Ayutthaya at the hand of Burmese armies in 1767, written records of Ayutthaya literature did not survive the fall of the Kingdom.[102] The revival of the Ayutthaya tradition was thus a tall task where the King sometimes required a collective effort of the court poets, who had to rely on unwritten works that survived through the oral tradition.[103] Whether it be a

96 Chetana (n 82) 35.

97 See 'Writing the Nation' in Chapter 1.

98 Duangmon Jitjamnong, Suchitra Jongsathitwattana, Kusuma Raksamanee, and Maneepin Phromsuttirak, ***พัฒนาการวรรณคดีไทย*** *(Development of Thai Literature)* (Sukhothai Thammathirat Open University Press 1990) 637–638. See also Chonlada et al. (n 83) 45–49.

99 ibid.

100 See Chonlada et al. (n 83) 47–49.

101 Duangmon et al. (n 98) 637; Chonlada et al. (n 83) 45.

102 ibid.

103 Duangmon et al. (n 98) 637–638; Chonlada et al. (n 83) 46–49.

collective project ordered by the King or an initiative of an individual poet, these literary connoisseurs regarded the Ayutthaya masters as the teachers they had to emulate while seeing their own creative endeavours through the lens of *klao-klon*. Thus, it was not unusual for Siamese literature of the early 19th century to be a composite of many individual elements whose authors may not have belonged to the same era.[104]

While the production of this traditional literature continued, the second half of the 19th century also witnessed the emergence of new literary forms influenced by the growing impact of the West.[105] Western-style fiction was introduced to the small yet expanding Siamese readership through Western-educated aristocrats, who brought back not only Western knowledge but also Western culture.[106] Another effect of Western influence, taking the form of print technology and commercial printing, also contributed to the proliferation of Western-style fiction among the literate Siamese aristocracy. The translations and adaptations of Western literature, which all began in a small circle of royals and nobles, eventually abounded in the early 20th century.[107]

The watershed moment arrived with the landmark publication of early Thai literary magazines such as *Lak-witthaya* (*Stealing knowledge*), *Thalok-witthaya* (*Exposing knowledge*), and *Thawee-panya* (*Increasing wisdom*), beginning around the turn of the century.[108] The forerunner of this trend was *Lak-witthaya,* whose title nicely foregrounded the newfound role of Siamese authors as an agent of *siwilai*.[109] As discussed in Chapter 1, *Lak-witthaya* (1900–1902) made no excuses for drawing on the West as it published translations and adaptations of Western literature, which laid the foundation for modern Thai literature to emerge subsequently.[110]

In terms of the reception of Western literature, the Siamese act of appropriating and absorbing external culture was never short of precedents if one looks across the pre-Western history of mainland Southeast Asia.[111] Similarly, scholarship on Thai literary history has long recognised foreign roots of the Ayutthaya literary convention in the ancient civilisations of Ceylon (now Sri Lanka) and Khmer (now Cambodia).[112] From this perspective, the 19th-century reception of Western literature appeared to continue this long-standing cultural pattern, but generalisations can only go so far in offering an explanation. Insofar as the mechanics of Siamese–Western relations are concerned, one must also pay attention to the mediating role of Buddhism.

104 ibid.
105 Supannee (n 70) 38–39.
106 Limapichart, 'The emergence of the Siamese public sphere', 361, 382–383.
107 ibid.
108 ibid; Supannee (n 70) 53–54. See also the working group (n 7) 211–214.
109 See 'Writing the Nation' in Chapter 1.
110 See also Supannee (n 70) 54–57.
111 Winichakul, 'Coming to terms with the West', 138.
112 See for instance Suchitra (n 90) 247–249.

The Spiritual–Material Bifurcation

Siamese literature's relationship to Buddhism was not as simple as one of servitude. In fact, the identification of literature with pleasure and poets with *ahangarn* already signals a departure from Buddhist thinking, which equates desire with suffering and emphasises the idea that all in life is impermanent. Nevertheless, it was Buddhism that provided the intellectual framework within which literary production and consumption took place in 19th-century Siam.

Some interesting attempts to resolve this puzzle have linked weak didacticism in classical Thai literature back to Buddhism itself. Among those pursuing this line of argument is Duangmon Jitjamnong, who examines the literary tradition of the Ayutthaya period to uncover what might be called a Siamese–Buddhist conception of authorship.[113] Duangmon argues that the poets of this period, despite showing no interest in didacticism, saw writing as a path to (Buddhist) enlightenment.[114]

In the Ayutthaya tradition, Duangmon contends, there existed the notion of writing as a good deed—for, like most things in that era, the process of writing was perceived through a Buddhist lens.[115] For instance, the fact that writing required an endeavour of the mind rendered the act of writing equivalent to spiritual training in *Panya* (the ability to perceive the true nature of reality) that Buddhism posits as a prerequisite to nirvana.[116] So while literature, with all its power to delight and entertain, was considered a worldly matter belonging to the material realm, the act of writing could help the author cross over to the spiritual one.[117] Duangmon argues that the notion of writing as a good deed persisted into the early 19th century.[118] This may not come as a surprise given the royal project to restore the Ayutthaya tradition, as discussed earlier, but consideration should also be given to the arrival of Western culture and its implications for Siamese literature. It is, therefore, important to look closer at the role of Buddhism in the Siamese–Western relations.

There has been much discussion around the intellectual strategy employed by the Siamese ruling elite to selectively appropriate and reject Western knowledge. Notably, the historian Taweesak Pueksom highlights the operation of an intellectual framework that, he argues, continued the long tradition of Buddhist influence in Siamese thinking.[119] Taweesak identifies the crucial distinction between body and soul as fundamental to the way the Siamese ruling elite of the early 19th century approached all the important questions in life, including who we are, where we

113 Duangmon (n 84) 27–31. For another example, see Bunlua Thepayasuwan, '**หัวเลี้ยวของวรรณคดีไทย**' (The turning point in Thai literature') in Social Science Association of Thailand (ed), ***วรรณไวทยากรณ์ ชุมนุมบทความทางวิชาการ*** *(Wanwaithayakon: A Collection of Academic Essays)* (Thaiwattana-panich 1971) 65–66, 69.

114 ibid 28–29.

115 ibid.

116 ibid.

117 ibid 29.

118 ibid 49–50.

119 Taweesak (n 65) 69–71.

come from, and where we are going.[120] More significance was attached to the soul because of its transcendental potential (i.e. nirvana), but the body was not neglected because of its function as a vehicle for the soul.[121] This body–soul distinction also divided the world and the knowledge about it along the lines of the material and the spiritual.[122] Unsurprisingly, the knowledge that belonged to the spiritual realm was considered superior to the knowledge about the material world,[123] and it was this conceptual bifurcation that later provided the Siamese ruling elite with an effective intellectual tool as contact with the West began to increase around the mid-19th century.

Historians like Thongchai and Loos probably agree with Taweesak's claim that the Siamese quest for *siwilai* did not presuppose a clean break from Siam's own intellectual tradition.[124] The real question seems to be that of manner and degree, where the spiritual–material bifurcation presents another point of convergence.[125] Like Taweesak, Thongchai identifies the conceptual distinction between spirituality and materiality as a crucial element in the arrival of colonial modernity in Siam.[126] But unlike Taweesak, Thongchai puts an emphasis on the unique dynamic between this epistemological frame and the rise of Western colonialism, noting that this bifurcation never occurred prior to the arrival of the imperial West and has since evolved into a Thai cultural logic for with the West.[127]

For Thongchai, this all began when the Siamese ruling elite employed the spiritual–material distinction as an intellectual strategy 'to negotiate between the power of the modern West and the persistent strength of local culture and identity.'[128] More specifically, the spiritual–material bifurcation allowed the ruling elite to navigate between Western knowledge as the 'outer' material world and Buddhism as the 'inner' spiritual self.[129] In arriving at this conclusion, Thongchai draws a comparison to a similar way of thinking found in the Indian experience and considers a strategy of this kind to be specific to a colonial and postcolonial experience.[130] Here, whether one perceives the continuity of an intellectual tradition (like Taweesak) or a disruption by the colonial discourse (like Thongchai), this conceptual dichotomy operated to allow Siam to absorb Western influence while subjecting it to the higher spiritual realm of Buddhism.

The reception of Western literature in Siam fit seamlessly into this framework. The worldly affairs of literature were one cultural sphere that experienced an

120 ibid 84–91.
121 ibid 91.
122 ibid 94–95.
123 ibid 102.
124 See Loos, *Subject Siam*; Thongchai, 'Coming to terms' (n 111).
125 See Thongchai, 'Coming to terms' (n 111) 136–141.
126 ibid 137.
127 ibid 136.
128 ibid 139.
129 ibid 139–140.
130 ibid 139.

influx of Western influence that was embraced by royalty and nobility before the trend permeated the general public. In terms of the innovations that appealed to the Siamese, not only did Western literature introduce a new form of narrative, but the translation of foreign languages also had the effect of revolutionising the Thai language.[131] However, on the spiritual level, it is unclear whether the notion of writing as a good deed still persisted once books began to assume the status of commodity, with authors being compensated for their manuscripts. In contrast, there is evidence suggesting that the growing book market produced an economic conception of authorship, where literary accomplishment came to be measured by book sales.[132]

So where does this leave Buddhism? Thongchai's observation is instructive here. The spiritual/material bifurcation presented Western culture as an outer appearance of the Thai essence, which remained religious and moral.[133] This idea succinctly describes *Non-Vendetta* (1915), a seminal work by Khru Liam that is regarded as the first Thai novel by scholars. In his discussion of Western modernity and the Thai literary canon, Thak Chaloemtiarana perhaps articulates it best when he states that 'this novel is a fascinating example of appropriating a Western cultural form in order to enunciate an anti-Western position.'[134] And of course, Buddhism played a vital role in the author's negation of Western values.

Siamese–Western Hybridity

Khwam-mai-phayabat, or *Non-vendetta,* was not only one of the earliest Thai novels but also the first by Khru Liam, who published his second novel, *The Divine Nymphs,* a year later.[135] In fact, it was due to the commercial failure of *Non-vendetta* that Khru Liam resolved to write *The Divine Nymphs* in such a manner that presented contrasting attitudes towards the influx of Western culture in his two successive novels.[136] In his 1916 work, Khru Liam adopted the perspective of 'the mimic-man par excellence' as he set out to trick readers into thinking that *The Divine Nymphs* was a translated work.[137] This practice of mimicry contrasted sharply with his first novel, which opened with the famous quote—'non-revenge is sweet'—as a deliberate subversion of the Western proverb 'revenge is sweet.'[138]

Indeed, it is understood that Khru Liam made the Buddhist notion of forgiveness central to *Non-vendetta* to counter the theme of revenge in Marie Corelli's

131 Thak (n 71) 19–20.
132 In the verse that she composed around the late-19th century, the Siamese poet called Khun Pum alluded to the success of her previous work as she mentioned how well it sold in the market. See Chonlada et al. (n 83) 75.
133 Thongchai, 'Coming to terms' (n 111) 139.
134 Thak (n 71) 24.
135 ibid 23–24.
136 ibid 39–40.
137 Harrison (n 73) 95.
138 Thak (n 71) 28.

novel *Vendetta.*[139] Perhaps more importantly, the fact that *Non-vendetta* and *The Divine Nymphs* were written by the same author and published only one year apart seems to reflect the Siamese society in the late 19th and early 20th centuries. With the arrival of colonial modernity, authors like Khru Liam found themselves in a liminal space where different ideas and practices coexisted, coalesced, and clashed, giving rise to Thai–Western cultural hybridities.

The issue of hybridity is particularly relevant for understanding Thai society under the Siamese ruling elite, who came to regard the imperial West as 'a seductive but dangerous Other.'[140] King Chulalongkorn, for his part, responded to the rising status of Western countries by embarking on the pursuit of *siwilai,* ushering in an era of reforms.[141] When his son, King Vajiravudh, ascended the throne, the quest for *siwilai* redirected its course from overt Westernisation towards self-assertion. And even so, Vajiravudh's programme of nationalism ironically borrowed many ideas from the West, not least the very concept of nationalism.[142] As discussed in the first chapter, the hybrid construct of *siwilai* typified the cultural dynamics of crypto-colonialism—a condition that calls attention to 'a symbolic as well as material dependency on intrusive colonial power.'[143]

At one level, the hybrid construct of *siwilai* represented the elite's resistance to the colonial West by projecting an image of a civilised nation for foreign consumption. Peter Jackson highlights this point in his insightful attempt to apply postcolonial analysis to Siamese/Thai–Western relations.[144] However, Jackson also argues that the elite's construction of *siwilai* simultaneously indicates 'another dimension of hybridity in modern Thailand, namely, subaltern cultural assimilation of the foreign as resistance to internal colonialism.'[145] The popularity of works such Kru Liam's *The Divine Nymphs*—which led King Vajiravudh's to intervene against what he called the cult of imitation—reveals the elite's anxiety over cultural imitation. Jackson observes that Thai subaltern hybridity 'emerges both as a consequence of and a resistance to the politico-cultural hegemony of the semicolonial state.'[146] Thus, it functioned as resistance to internal colonisation by the ruling elite rather than a direct response to Western colonialism.[147]

Following Jackson's analysis, to speak of Thai cultural hybridity is to reinforce the crypto-colonial dynamics of domination and submission.[148] The elite's discourse of *siwilai* was as much a project to centralise domestic power as it was a response to intrusive colonial power. A similar form of symbolic dependence also

139 ibid 23.
140 Thongchai, 'Coming to terms' (n 111) 135.
141 See 'Siamese Modernisation Under Colonial Influence' in Chapter 1.
142 See 'Writing the Nation' in Chapter 1.
143 Herzfeld, 'The conceptual allure of the West', 173.
144 Jackson, 'Afterword', 198–200.
145 ibid 201.
146 ibid 202.
147 ibid.
148 See 'A Crypto-Colony' in Chapter 1.

pervaded popular borrowings, where 'excessive' Westernisation became a means of contesting the ruling elite's hegemony. Crucially, both forms of hybridity were anchored in the West's global dominance, which imbued Western forms with local prestige. As Quijano argues, what characterised the modernity that emanated from Europe was a global model of power that was truly global.[149]

Ultimately, what Jackson discovers in the postcolonial theories of hybridity is a means to articulate persistent patterns of power rather than a means of escape.[150] In his analysis, hybridity is not inherently subversive to Western dominance but is instead coextensive with the domestic hierarchies of power.[151] Jackson predicts that the enduring allure of the West will eventually wane, citing the economic and political ascendancy of China and East Asia, which may shift the Thai cultural gaze towards a new centre of power.[152]

While this seems to be a valid observation, it is important to add a caveat that 'de-Westernisation' must be distinguished from decolonisation. A process of de-Westernisation may be contingent on a claim of authentic non-Western identities and amenable to existing dynamics of global capitalism. The Thai experiences discussed so far should illustrate how these dynamics characterise the coloniality of power. Siam's integration into the colonial world order was driven by the universality–identity paradox, which combined the universal standard of civilisation with the assertion of an essential Thai identity.

This is why modernisation in Siam should not be taken at face value. Another mistake would be to overlook local agency and equate Western influence with outright domination by the West. Reflecting these observations is Siam's reception of Western copyright law. Far from replicating notions such as the genius author and original authorship, the birth of Thai copyright law was not so romantic. As will be discussed, the introduction of the AOA 1901 was not bound in any meaningful way with the original genius, which in any case was foreign to Siamese literary thought. On the contrary, it is worth noting again that the introduction of copyright protection in Siam was primarily a product of the quest for *siwilai*.

II. Copyright on a Civilising Mission

The second half of the 19th century saw the development of print capitalism, courtesy of American missionaries who ventured from printing Gospels and religious tracts into newspapers and book publishing.[153] The last decade marked a boom time for commercial printing, with a rising number of Siamese printers who followed in the footsteps of the American pioneers.[154] That said, this period was relatively the early days of the book trade in Siam, where the division of labour was still in

149 Quijano and Ennis (n 85) 544–545.
150 Jackson (n 144) 198.
151 ibid 203.
152 ibid 204.
153 The working group (n 7) 5–9.
154 ibid 28.

its nascent. It was common for Siamese printers to be their own publishers and sellers.[155] While there are records of writing commissions and new titles, it is well documented that much of the commercial printing was based on classic works, folk literature, and translations.[156] Relatively unexplored is, unfortunately, the dynamics of competition among various commercial actors in the flourishing book market. And yet, one can say with some confidence that the emergence of literary property—or the author's ownership as referred to in the AOA—was not a significant event for Siamese authors and printers in general.

Records of copyright registration indicate that only 13 copyright requests were submitted in the first year, eight of which related to law (i.e. legal text, cases, and commentary) and instructional materials (i.e. textbooks and handbooks).[157] Furthermore, out of the total of 13 requests, only one involved a fictional work despite recreational reading being the primary reason behind the late-19th-century boom in the book trade.[158] When one looks across the following five years, the trend in copyright registration did not appear to change much. At least two-thirds of the 65 copyright requests submitted between 1901 and 1906 were made in relation to informational and instructional works.[159] In contrast, requests for copyright in fictional works remained few and far between. This paints a contrasting picture to the trend in Siam's book trade, where the popularity of *reung-pralom-lok* (possibly translated as 'fiction for pleasure reading') is well-documented.[160]

In some ways, this statistic on copyright registration is not particularly surprising when viewed within the socio-political context of Siam in the early 20th century. The discussion of the AOA has shown that Thailand's initial reception of Western copyright law must be understood in relation to Chulalongkorn's education reforms, which gained momentum in the last decade of the 19th century.[161] Similarly, Prince Rabi—whose copyright petition inadvertently set the legislative machine in motion—was primarily concerned with something as practical as the publication of legislation and court decisions.[162] As a law graduate from England, Rabi was also an important figure in the modernisation of Thai law in his capacity as the Justice Minister and the founder of Thailand's first law school.[163] Given

155 ibid 278.

156 Supannee (n 70) 33–37; Thanapol, 'Siamese public sphere' (n 106) 392–393.

157 National Archive of Thailand, Department of Royal Private Secretary Doc No Aor 20/4, '**บาญชีรายชื่อผู้ขอกรรมสิทธิ์จดทเบียนกอปีไรต์**' ('Copyright applicants register') (22 August 1901–6 October 1910) 2–3.

158 ibid.

159 ibid 2–7.

160 For the rise of *reung-pralom-lok* in the second half of the 19th century, see Duangmon et al. (n 470) 641–642.

161 See 'A Modern Solution for a Modern Problem' in Chapter 1.

162 In the first year since the AOA had come into effect, Rabi submitted three copyright requests, and all of them were made for law-related materials. See National Archive, 'Copyright applicants register' (n 157) 2.

163 Rabi is now widely regarded as the 'Father of (modern) Thai law', whose death has been commemorated by the recognition of 'Rabi Day' on the 7th of October each year.

this socio-political background, it is fitting to regard the AOA as an elitist project insofar as it stemmed from the ruling elite's concern for the modernisation of Siam.

When Print Capitalism Met Siamese Absolutism

Once embedded, the notion of *siwilai* became a site of political contests where various local groups put forward different meanings.[164] In the late 19th century, one thing that *siwilai* was closely associated with was knowledge. The spiritual–material bifurcation had redefined knowledge into an understanding of the material world—distinct from the final and finite nature of the Buddha's teachings—fostering the desire to collect and accumulate knowledge.[165]

The establishment of the *Wachirayan* Library in the early 1880s represented this shift.[166] The historian Patrick Jory notes that the royal court regarded *Wachirayan* Library as an aristocratic club, and its role as a book repository signalled the changing perceptions among the ruling elite regarding the formation and possession of knowledge.[167] In this context, the initial collection of the library also indicated the growing interest in all books, both Thai and foreign, for books had come to represent the wide-ranging and limitless knowledge of the material world.[168] Given this evolving conception of books, it was to be expected that books would play a key role in the modernisation of Siam. However, few could have anticipated that a library—as a repository of books—would itself become a symbol of *siwilai*.[169]

This is mainly because books occupied a central place in Chulalongkorn's vision for modern education.[170] Early in his pursuit of education reforms, Chulalongkorn once remarked that 'The study of books is the greatest form of study' when giving a speech to school students in 1884.[171] Indeed, from the mid-1880s onwards, 'the study of books' would shape the core of his education policies, where attention was always on the production and distribution of government textbooks.[172] Understandably, providing schools across the country with government textbooks was a means of promoting uniformity and quality, ultimately producing a workforce of sufficiently trained young men to staff government offices.[173] In this context, books represented a new mode of knowledge production closely linked to the new conception of

164 Winichakul, 'The quest for 'siwilai'', 528, 530.

165 Jory, 'Books and the nation', 351, 354–356.

166 ibid 354; Prince Damrong Rachanuphap, *ตำนานหอพระสมุด หอพระมณเฑียรธรรม หอวชิรญาณ หอพุทธสาสนสังคหะ แลหอสมุดสำหรับพระนคร (History of the Book Hall, the Palace Dhamma Library, the Buddhist Collection and the State Library)* (Cremation volume for Phra Inthabenya (Sarakham Wattha) 1969) 21–22.

167 Jory (n 165) 352.

168 The collection, when the library opened in 1884, consisted of 125 Thai printed books and 144 Western books. See Prince Damrong (n 166) 27.

169 Jory (n 165) 357–358.

170 See Wyatt, *The Politics of Reform in Thailand,* 68.

171 Quoted in Prapai Ekun, *Thai Education* (Suan Sunandha Rajabhat Institute 1999) 83–84.

172 Wyatt, *Politics of Reform* (n 170) 130.

173 ibid. See also Mead, *The Rise and Decline of Thai Absolutism*, 74.

knowledge itself. In addition, implicit in the study of books was the perception of books as a mode of knowledge transfer between the centre and periphery.

By the late 19th century, books had come to be regarded as a modern vehicle for transferring knowledge—from the West to Siam and from Bangkok to the rest of the country.[174] It was no coincidence that this direction of flow alludes to Siam's conditions of crypto-colonialism.[175] After all, Chulalongkorn's education reform efforts were part of his response to Western colonialism as much as they contributed to his state-building project.[176]

The Book as a Commodity

Initially, the government intended to provide all schools with textbooks free of charge.[177] In Chulalongkorn's education policy, the production and dissemination of knowledge remained outside the commercial sphere.[178] This conception of knowledge as a 'gift' was not limited to the domain of government policy but resonated with broader social practices. The publication of funeral books or cremation volumes is a case in point; as a way of mourning the deceased, family members commissioned a printing of books to be given away as gifts. This practice was considered a form of good deeds—acts of merit-making on behalf of the deceased—that could be found in the late 19th century and became quite common in the early 20th century.[179] However, both the provision of government textbooks and the publishing of cremation volumes took place amidst the booming book trade. In fact, the histories of government textbooks and funeral books were closely intertwined with the development of the Siamese book trade, where books were, first and foremost, a commodity.

The Siamese government owed much to foreign and local printers for their entrepreneurial acumen, as this helped elevate the technology and craft of printing to a level where books could be produced in good quality and significant volume. Furthermore, these book entrepreneurs, whether by offering their services or directly investing in the enterprise, often played a role in the publication of official and public documents. The government's first publication came from the American missionary Dr Dan Breach Bradley, who received a royal commission in 1839 to print the royal

174 In 1898, Phraya Wisut, who later took charge of MOPI, advocated for the translation of English-language books instead of sending students abroad as a way to learn from the West. See Wyatt (n 170) 202. Similarly, a series of government textbooks titled *Thammachariya* was produced and distributed to all schools as a means for the foreign-educated elite to bring Western knowledge to the Siamese people throughout the country. See Kullada (n 173) 86.

175 See 'A Crypto-Colony' in Chapter 1.

176 See 'A Modern Solution for a Modern Problem' in Chapter 1.

177 Wyatt (n 170) 130; Kullada (n 173) 74.

178 Education at many schools was free, and some schools even paid students a stipend. See Wyatt (n 170) 114, 150–151; Kullada (n 173) 78. In one instance, a policy on an annual tuition fee was introduced, with the intention to exclude common people from entry. See Wyatt (n 170) 150–151; Kullada (n 173) 74.

179 So much so that cremation volumes are now regarded as a valuable source of insight for historians as well as a distinct publication genre in their own right.

decree on the opium ban.[180] Another milestone occurred between 1862 and 1863 when Dr Bradley published two volumes of Siamese law that later became important references for lawyers in Siam, particularly during the transition into modern law.[181] This trend continued towards the end of the century, as it became common for individuals and enterprises to accept commissions from the Education Department for printing government textbooks.[182] In some cases, these commercial actors even financed the printing on behalf of the government and recouped their investment from sales, with evidence suggesting that they turned a good profit in this way.[183]

Naturally, the commodity status of books influenced how Siamese authors viewed their literary activities to the extent that their intellectual labour may not been understood as a good deed or a gift to the reader. It is in this regard that Prince Rabi's petition for ad hoc copyright makes for an interesting read. One would assume that financial gains were not the main appeal to Rabi, not least because of his royal status and the technical subject of his writing, which is law. Yet he asked King Chulalongkorn for legal entitlements against unauthorised reprinting of his law books, which, by his own account, were not always for sale but sometimes given away.[184] Why, then, did he need to make such a request to the King? Rabi himself addressed this point as he pleaded to Chulalongkorn:

> Since I have put so much effort into writing, I do not wish to see other people copy and reprint [my books] for sale as if these were their property and make the one who has taken up book-writing feel disheartened.[185]

Although the notion of 'writing as a good deed' might still hold relevance, and 'living by the pen' had yet to become a literary ethos, Rabi's resentment reveals the kind of subjectivity emerging from the commodification of books in Siam. It is interesting that even a prince like him, who likely had little to worry about in terms of financial returns, could feel aggrieved by book entrepreneurs seeking more printing materials to satisfy the growing book market. Even more interesting

180 The working group (n 7) 12.

181 Yoneo Ishii, 'The Thai Thammasat (with a Note on the Lao texts)' in M B Hooker (ed), *Laws of South-East Asia, Vol. 1, The Pre-Modern Texts* (Butterworth 1986) 152. See also Loos (n 124) 39.

182 See National Archive of Thailand, Ministry of Public Instruction Doc No Sor Thor 9.2/23, '**หนังสือจากหลวงชำนิบรรณาคมถึงขุนประพนธ์เนติประวัติ เรื่องการพิมพ์หนังสือแบบเรียนของกรมศึกษาธิการ**' ('Luang Chamni-bannakom's letter to Khun Praponniprawat on printing government textbooks') (30 March 1900) 8–11.

183 ibid 8–9: In respond to MOPI's move to prohibit reprinting of government textbooks, the printer Luang Chamnibannakom made a business proposition to the ministry that would see him become the sole publisher of the government textbooks. For a similar response from a private printer, see National Archive of Thailand, Ministry of Public Instruction Doc No Sor Thor 9.2/23, '**หนังสือจากหลวงดำรงสารถึงพระเจ้าลูกยาเธอ พระองค์เจ้ากิติยากรวรลักษณ์ อธิบดีกรมศึกษาธิการ**' ('Luang Damrongsan's letter to the Director of Education') (23 March 1900) 13–14.

184 National Archive of Thailand, Department of Royal Private Secretary Doc No Aor 20/2, '**พระราชหัตถเลขากรมหมื่นราชบุรีดิเรกฤทธิ์ถวายพระบาทสมเด็จพระจุลจอมเกล้าเจ้าอยู่หัวเรื่องขอพระราชทานอำนาจกอปีไรต์ในหนังสือทรงแต่ง**' ('Prince Rabi's letter to the King to request ad-hoc copyright') (7 July 1901) 2.

185 ibid.

is how Rabi's sentiment rested on the idea of writing as labour, as reflected in his emphasis on effort, which indicated a conception of authorship in economic terms. Here, one can reasonably expect Rabi's resentment to find some resonance in a broader group of his contemporaries, for whom the idea of remuneration for literary labour was probably quite familiar, if not an expectation.[186]

Book Trade and Siamese Aristocracy

Rabi's petition was by no means a protest against the commodification of books. His criticism was directed at those who had printed his works without authorisation. In fact, Rabi later appeared to sympathise with commercial printers as he reflected on the penitential impact of Prince Damrong's draft AOA provisions on the state of Siam's book trade.[187] After all, the benefits of the book trade were not lost on the Siamese ruling elite, as many of whom were active participants in the emerging literary public sphere.[188] King Mongkut, for one, recognised the value of the book trade, particularly the circulation of newspapers.[189] He acknowledged that newspapers played a crucial role in disseminating information, which was useful for both commerce and state administration.[190]

However, this appreciation did not mean that Mongkut and his fellow elites refrained from asserting their authority over the book trade. Indeed, records of book censorship activities emerged as soon as modern printing technology became available in Siam.[191] A well-known incident occurred in 1850 when a young Siamese noble saw a profitable opportunity to market printed copies of Siamese law.[192] The King at the time did not entertain the idea that these printed copies would enable everyone to get their hands on the law of the land, so he ordered all the copies to be confiscated and buried.[193] In this respect, King Mongkut was more modern than his predecessor, for he allowed Dr Bradley to publish the two historic volumes of Siamese law.[194]

186 Regarding the relationship between printers and writers, Rabi remarked that 'writers permit their works to be printed and published by [printers] by goodwill only, by receiving percentages of gain, or by selling their works out right.' See National Archive of Thailand, Department of Royal Private Secretary Doc No Aor 20/2, '**พระราชหัตถเลขากรมหมื่นราชบุรีดิเรกฤทธิ์ ถวายพระบาทสมเด็จพระจุลจอมเกล้าเจ้าอยู่หัวทำความเห็นร่างพระราชบัญญัติกรรมสิทธิ์ในหนังสือ**' ('Prince Rabi's letter to the King on his opinion about the copyright bill') (8 August 1901) 28–29.

187 ibid.

188 See Thanapol, 'Siamese public sphere' (n 106); Limapichart, 'The Royal Society of Literature'.

189 Mongkut's letter to Dr Bradley as quoted in Amphai Chanchira, '**พระบามสมเด็จพระจอมเกล้าเจ้าอยู่หัวกับการพิมพ์หนังสือ**' (King Mongkut and Publishing) (Cremation Volume for Nai Banleu Chanchira 1972) 56–57.

190 ibid.

191 American missionaries in the early 19th century had to be cautious about printing Christian texts because they did not want to violate the Siamese authority.

192 Loos (n 124) 39–40; Thanapol, 'Siamese public sphere' (n 106) 370–372.

193 ibid.

194 ibid.

As books rapidly became an elitist mode of knowledge production in the late 19th century, Siamese aristocrats also ventured into the newspaper and magazine publishing business.[195] For his part, King Chulalongkorn decided to revive the publication of *Ratchakitchanubeksa* in 1874, but this time, the government gazette would be distributed free of charge.[196] His brother, Prince Phromwaranurak, also made a significant entry into the world of print business with the first issue of *Darunowat* in 1874.[197] Regarded as the first Siamese-owned newspaper[198] and a precursor to Siamese magazines,[199] *Darunowat* was an experiment with print media by young and progressive members of Siam. Leading the group was Prince Phromwaranurak, who regarded *Darunowat* a venture into commercial publications.[200] *Darunowat* could continue for only a year, but it was only the beginning.

The next notable project by the royal court was the publication of the *Wachirayan* journals, starting with *Nangsu-Wachirayan* in 1884 and followed by *Wachirayan-wiset* in 1886.[201] Similar to *Daranuwat*, the *Wachirayan* journals featured a variety of content, ranging from official and informative to cultural and entertaining.[202] Initially, these journals were meant to circulate among members of the *Wachirayan* Library, before the library began to allow commercial reprints aimed at a members of the general public.[203]

By 1892, unauthorised reprinting had become a concern for those managing the *Wachirayan* journals. That year, the *Wachirayan* Library issued a historic decree to prohibit all reprinting of its journals without permission, citing unauthorised commercial reprints as the reason.[204] This prohibition against reprints was sanctioned by King Chulalongkorn and is now regarded as Thailand's first copyright law. Understandably, this designation might unsettle copyright scholars who associate the foundation of copyright law with concepts such as property and authorship or with the vesting of rights in the author.[205]

Regardless of what it should be called, the 1892 decree was a crucial step in the evolution of market intervention by the Siamese state. The purpose of the *Wachirayan* Library's prohibition was to exclude certain texts from market circulation, much like the royal order to confiscate printed legal texts in 1850. While these two measures were far from identical, they can be understood as part of the same state regulatory toolkit—one that would include the promulgation of the AOA 1901, which followed a decade later.

195 The Working Group (n 7) 207.
196 *Government Gazette* (17 May 1847) Book 1, 1–2.
197 The Working Group (n 7) 207–208.
198 See for instance Wyatt (n 170) 45; Thanapol, 'Siamese public sphere' (n 85) 380.
199 See for instance The Working Group (n 7) 207–208.
200 ibid 207.
201 ibid 209–210.
202 Thanapol, 'Siamese public sphere' (n 106) 382.
203 The Working Group (n 7) 277.
204 *Government Gazette* (19 August 1892) Book 9, 180–181.
205 The 1892 decree would probably count as a printing privilege in Western copyright historiography.

When considered together, the *Wachirayan* Library's prohibition not only emerged chronologically between the 1850 confiscation order and the AOA 1901 but also appeared to be conceptually in between. More specifically, the aim of the 1892 decree was to keep the *Wachirayan* journals circulating among library members while ensuring that profits would accrue to the library should financial gains be made in the market.[206] The first part of this two-pronged objective resonated with the confiscation of printed legal texts, as both legal and literary knowledge was to be kept beyond the reach of the market, preserving them as exclusive possessions of the aristocracy.[207] However, unlike outright censorship, the prohibition against reprints was also expected to enable the *Wachirayan* Library to assert market exclusivity, should it wish to treat the knowledge in its possession as a commodity.[208] This dual, somewhat transitional objective of the 1892 decree indicated an evolution in the way the Siamese ruling elite dealt with the development of the book trade. It is from this perspective that the *Wachirayan* Library decree of 1892 can be seen as a precursor to the AOA 1901 as a full-fledged trade regulation.

Not So Romantic and Not Much of a Twin Birth

Contrasting with how the 1892 decree conceived of knowledge, the term 'book' that appeared in the AOA 1901 referred primarily to the commodities circulated in Siam's book market.[209] Textbook piracy was the primary issue that led the government to introduce the AOA as a full-fledged trade regulation targeting printers and book entrepreneurs.[210] As discussed earlier, Chulalongkorn's approach to education reforms emphasised the importance of textbooks. MOPI experienced this first-hand as the responsible agency and understood the costs involved at every stage in the production of government textbooks. Yet MOPI had been beset by budgetary cuts just as the pressure to deliver results was mounting.[211] This challenging situation brought the issue of textbook piracy to a critical point.

Internal correspondence from MOPI reveals that while the Ministry acknowledged the public benefits of unauthorised reprinting—namely, greater availability

206 The decree began with a remark that stories published in the *Wachiranyan* journals were written for the library members; then it said that if these stories were to have commercial potential, the benefits should also accrue to the library. See *Government Gazette* (19 August 1892) Book 9, 180–181.

207 Regarding the censored text of Siamese law, Loos notes that 'the text served a sacred function as part of the royal regalia. From the 1780s until the 1880s, Siam's Buddhist kings dispensed justice, or *dhamma,* as a function of their position as monarch. Justice . . . sprang from the laws of universal, moral truth to which the king, judges, and other representatives of the king had access by virtue of their position rather than by virtue of their application of legal codes to case 'facts'. See Loos (n 124) 34.

208 See *Government Gazette* (19 August 1892) Book 9, 180.

209 See 'The Emergence of Literary Property' in Chapter 1.

210 See 'A modern solution for a modern problem' in Chapter 1.

211 But the budget cuts appeared to be a problem of its own making. See Wyatt (n 170) 214–215.

of textbooks—it still had to prioritise its own financial interests.[212] Concerned that it could lack the authority to stop rogue printers, MOPI appealed to Chulalongkorn for the introduction of a Western-style regulation, which the Ministry referred to as *kopeerai* (copyright) law.[213]

Authorship and the Emergence of Thai Copyright Law

Fundamentally, the promulgation of the AOA 1901 represented an attempt to address the modern problem of book piracy with a modern solution from Western law. However, the discussion on 19th-century Siamese literature already shows how modernity, as understood and practised in Siam, was not necessarily an exact imitation of the Western model. The ambiguity of Western influence in Siam was evident in Chulalongkorn's educational reform ambitions, and the same is true for the reception of Western copyright law in the early 20th century. The Siamese concept of 'author's ownership' did not draw its legitimacy from the myth of the romantic author or any philosophical ideas that put individual authors before all else.

Perhaps it did not need to do so, given that it came from the highest authority of the land. Or maybe it could not have done so, given how the notion of an original genius would have rung hollow in the context of Siam's literary conventions and intellectual tradition.[214] Either way, what stood out in the discussions leading to the enactment of the AOA 1901 was the issue of commercial misappropriation. So, after all, it was the commodification of books that conditioned the emergence of literary property in Siam, as it had been the case in Western countries in the 18th century.[215] And yet, as the discussion so far should make clear, Siam's adoption of Western copyright law had little to do with aesthetic discourse and much to do with the quest for *siwilai*.

Unlike the intertwined development of law and authorship in Western copyright traditions, Siam's experiences did not indicate a 'twin birth' that Mark Rose observes in the British context.[216] Certainly, this is not to suggest that the AOA emerged in isolation, detached from norms and practices in Siamese literature. To posit books as the object of authors' ownership necessarily made a reference to the book as a cultural artefact, as seen in King Chulalongkorn's emphasis on 'the study

212 National Archive of Thailand, Ministry of Public Instruction Doc No Sor Thor 9.2/23, '**หนังสือจากกรมศึกษาธิการถึงกระทรวงธรรมการ**' ('Memo from the Department of Education to the Ministry of Public Instruction') (17 January 1901) 6.

213 National Archive of Thailand, Department of Royal Private Secretary Doc No Aor 20/2, '**หนังสือจากเจ้าพระยาภาสกรวงศ์ถวายพระบาทสมเด็จพระจุลจอมเกล้าเจ้าอยู่หัว เรื่องร่างพระราชบัญญัติกอปีไรต์ของกระทรวงธรรมการ**' ('Chao Phraya Pasakorawong's letter to the King on MOPI's draft copyright law') (3 August 1901) 4–7. *Government Gazette* (18 August 1901) Book 18, 5.

214 See 'Weaving Self in the Flow of Tradition' in this chapter.

215 See 'The Genius and Literary Property' in this chapter.

216 Rose (n 4) 65.

of books.'[217] However, the recognition of literary property in Siamese law did not appeal to a valorisation of some metaphysical link between the author and their work. The concept of author's ownership did not arise from attempts by publishers and authors to support their proprietary claims through the alchemy of philosophical, aesthetic, and legal ideas that was otherwise observed by Woodmansee and Rose.

On the contrary, the AOA 1901 was technically a product of legal transplantation and historically a function of the quest for *siwilai*. There is no doubt that the arrival of colonial modernity profoundly affected both fields of Siamese law and literature. However, this did not produce a conceptual convergence that would have transformed ownership and authorship into mutually defined concepts. Unlike the genealogies of Woodmansee and Rose, a historical reflection on Thai copyright law does not lead one back to the emergence of modern authorship in Siam but to the modernisation of Siam under colonial influence.

Belated Modernity and the Repetition of History

What is significant about the ambiguity around Western influence reveals itself when we focus our attention on the Siamese agents. Their intellectual strategy of material–spiritual bifurcation highlights the colonial structures of power, while the Thai forms of hybridity suggest the challenge of seeing and naming the differences in what seems to be a mere repetition. Dipesh Chakrabarty raises this crucial issue—which is relevant to early Thai copyright law as much as to the history of Thai modernity—when he asks the following:

> How do we, under such circumstances, deal with what may be genuinely new about the modern that also seems belated and resembles something that has already happened somewhere else?[218]

Chakrabarty then draws on Gilles Deleuze's concepts on difference and repetition to argue that newness enters the world through a continual process of working through existing categories, meaning it does so in the disguise of the old categories.[219]

This theoretical conjecture provides a valuable perspective on the changes in Thai law following the promulgation of the 1901 Act. Despite the specific circumstances that brought Thai copyright law into existence, the peculiar birth of the AOA did not prevent the language of romantic authorship from permeating Thai law. The transplantation of Western law continued throughout the 20th century; a notable example is the requirement of originality.

217 Prapai (n 171) 83–84.
218 Chakrabarty, 'The names and repetitions of postcolonial history'.
219 ibid xvi.

The concept of originality was absent from Thai law from the start of the 20th century until its final decade.[220] This *sine qua non* of copyright law was only introduced in Thai law in the early 1990s when the Supreme Court began to adopt the English law language of labour, skill, and judgement.[221] In fact, there was a notable rise in the number of copyright cases in the Thai Supreme Court in the late 20th century, in contrast to the limited number of copyright judgements up until the late 1970s.[222] This shift in the legal landscape coincided with the growing phenomenon of media piracy, which escalated into a serious trade dispute between Thailand and the US by the end of the 1980s.[223] What occurred between Thailand and the US was just part of the globalisation of IPRs that swept across the developing world. This worldwide trend culminated in the global harmonisation of IPRs, which established Western protection standards as the new world order.[224] The end of the 20th century thus saw the spectre of Western colonialism in the global expansion of IPRs.[225]

In this way, and in the way colonial modernity also complicated the birth of the AOA, one should resist the temptation to view the late 20th century as the 'coming of age' of Thai copyright law. It is true that copyright protection began to capture the attention of Thai lawyers as much as policymakers, and there were even signs

220 Prior to Siam's accession to the Berne Convention in 1931, Thai copyright law only covered the publication, distribution, and translation of books as an item of commercial value. As already discussed in Chapter 1, the AOA 1901, as well as the 1914 amendment, conceived of its subject matter (the 'book') in terms of the latter's physical embodiment rather than its abstract quality in the expression of the author's thoughts. Furthermore, the AOA only conferred literary ownership over a book that had already been published and had its first public distribution in Siam. Consequently, the system of copyright registration under the AOA regime did not require that a book be original. It rather emphasised the newfound appreciation for commercial publication (and its political implications) as the basis of protection. In terms of originality, no substantive change was evident in the introduction of the PLAWA 1931 to align Thai law with the Berne Convention, which itself did not explicitly state that a work must be original. The real pressing issue for the Siamese government was to free the country from the colonial shackles of extraterritorial jurisdictions, of which Siam's accession to international IP conventions was a part of the trade-off.

221 See, in particular, the Supreme Court decision No 2750/2537. Delivered in 1994, the Supreme Court was called upon to decide a copyright case concerning a dictionary, where the defendants argued that the claimant's dictionary was essentially not new. The Supreme Court clarified that a work need not be new to qualify for copyright protection. The Court also introduced the notion of industriousness and asserted that a work must not be copied from others, which shifted the ensuing analysis of the claimants' work into an exposition of the long and laborious process of dictionary production, during which process the Court had no trouble in finding the work original. As for the long-term consequences, the Court's two-part formula constituted what would later become the two components of the Thai originality doctrine.

222 See more details in 'Modernity/Piracy' in Chapter 3.

223 See 'In the Name of Free Trade' in Chapter 3.

224 See Peter Drahos, 'Global property rights in information: The story of TRIPS at the GATT' (1995) 13(1) *Prometheus* 6; Peter Drahos and John Braithwaite, *Information Feudalism: Who Owns the Knowledge Economy?* (Earthscan, 2002); Daniel Gervais, *The TRIPS Agreement: Drafting History and Analysis* (5th edn, Sweet & Maxwell 2021). See also Roy (n 163).

225 See 'Modernity/Piracy' in Chapter 3.

of Thai copyright scholarship, as discussed in Chapter 3.[226] The issue lies in the tendency to view 'progress' in Thai law as a belated repetition of what already happened in the West. Although tempting, this is problematic as it overlooks the particularity of the encounters between each and every individual thing that constitutes the change in question.[227] Moreover, the role of authorship in the historical development of Thai law may not be the most relevant question, especially if authorship itself is just another old category disguising newness in what seems like a repetition. Just as Bracha describes authorship as the ideology in Western copyright traditions, perhaps the more important and challenging question in Thailand is how even to begin to name this new 'ghost' in the copyright machine.

The impact of colonial modernity on knowledge production in Siam extends well beyond the 19th century. For one thing, and for what happened to the global IP system a century later, modernity/coloniality provides a more effective analytical framework than the anti-colonial rhetoric and sentiments prevalent during the globalisation of IPRs. Notably, the signing of TRIPS did not necessitate significant substantive changes in Thai law. This was all because a major legislative overhaul had already occurred two decades earlier in the modernisation of the Thai copyright law following the Cold War era of 'development.' It is fair to say that parallels can be drawn between this period in Thai history—the 'American era,' as Benedict Anderson calls it—and Siam's experiences of European colonialism. It is thus to the second half of the 20th century that the attention now turns.

226 See 'The Birth of Copyright Scholarship' in Chapter 3.
227 The problems of belatedness and repetition are central to the discussion in Chapter 4.

Part II

The Persistence of Coloniality

3 Thai Copyright in the Cultural Cold War

Shot over eight years on every operating railway route in Thailand, *Railway Sleepers* (2016) is a documentary that explores the connection between the Thai people and the Thai railway. The film's director, Sompot Chidgasornpongse, wants to immerse viewers in a 'fly-on-the-wall' perspective of rail travel while prompting personal reflection. Scenes featuring passengers from different service classes interweave with the broader social stratifications, while the relentless passage of time alludes to the country's uncertain future.[1] But despite this rich backdrop, *Railway Sleepers* is largely uneventful. The film is held together by a linear passage of time, or as Sompot says,

> In the film, you're on the train the whole time and almost always on the move. Moving signifies changes, the passing of time, and, most importantly, progress. But the Thai railway doesn't really move anywhere, figuratively. It's 'frozen in time'. The history, 'the past', is trapped in the vehicle. If the Thai railway were a person, he or she would have a lot of stories from the past to tell.[2]

Indeed, the journey of the Thai railway through time tells interesting stories about the country's past, one of which is the persistence of coloniality in Thailand.

Let us begin with the passage of time since the introduction of the railway system in Siam. *Railway Sleepers* opens with the royal order inaugurating Siam's first railway route in 1893. 'This grand aspiration has finally come to fruition,' announced King Chulalongkorn. He later emphasised, 'You will see this country flourish beyond what has come before.' The King's message was clearly optimistic and underscored a commitment to the country's prosperous future. However, what follows the opening scene are mundane shots of train passengers that reveal the

1 *Railway Sleepers* (2016), dir Sompot Chidgasornpongse. See also Rachel Harrison, 'Traveling in Siamese time and space' (*Docalogue*, November 2020) <https://docalogue.com/railway-sleepers/> accessed 20 February 2025.

2 Annette Lingg, 'Mon rot fai/Railway Sleepers' (Berlin International Film Festival, 2017) <https://www.berlinale.de/en/2017/programme/201716963.html> accessed 20 February 2025.

DOI: 10.4324/9781003592037-6

reality of the railway system long after his modernisation project. The slow-running carriages are now in a deteriorating state, while the stark division of passenger classes serves as a reminder of the harsh economic divides. This material reality suggests that not enough has changed since the inauguration of the first train line. In fact, four decades after Chulalongkorn's death in 1910, Thailand emerged from World War II with an agrarian economy. The railway is indeed a metaphor for the country.

While opening with the introduction of the railway as a mark of modernisation, time flows aimlessly in *Railway Sleepers* and gives no clear sense of direction or destination. The film does not dwell on feelings of regret. Nor does it lament why progress has yet to come. Instead, it lingers over the uncertainty of the unknown destination, alluding to the country's unclear future under authoritarian rule. Clearly, *Railway Sleepers* is under no illusion that the pursuit of modernisation simply embodied a natural unfolding of human progress. The exploration of the Thai railway towards the end of the film links the construction of the first railway route to both the encroaching threat of Western colonialism and the consolidation of power by the Bangkok elite. As it turns out, rail infrastructure allowed Bangkok to physically and administratively reach out to areas on the frontiers of the French and British holdings.[3] The birth of the Thai railway was, therefore, a modernising effort under colonial influence: It was a hallmark of colonial modernity.[4]

Thus, it is quite fitting that one important reason for the decline of Thailand's railway system began amidst the post-war decline of European powers and the emergence of the US as the new axis mundi. Thailand in the second half of the 20th century saw a rapid expansion of roads and highways along with the rise of the auto industry, which almost brought railway expansion to a standstill.[5] In Thai historiography, the Cold War period is synonymous with the pursuit of economic liberalism and the construction of basic infrastructure.[6] This was all courtesy of financial aid and technical assistance from the US, which regarded Thailand as a strategic player in its anti-communist campaign.[7] And courtesy of the US-led economic and infrastructure development, Thailand during the Cold War years also witnessed an upsurge in local film production.[8]

The technology of cinema arrived in Siam during the same period as the railway technology. It was not long before cinema going became a popular activity for

3 Ichiro Kakizaki, *Rise of the Kingdom: The History of Thai Railways* (White Lotus 2012) 29.

4 See 'Modernity/Coloniality' in Chapter 1.

5 Kakizaki (n 3) 139. For details of the policy shift, see Office of the National Economic and Social Development Board (NESDB), 'แผนพัฒนาเศรษฐกิจและสังคมแห่งชาติ ฉบับที่ 1 พ.ศ. 2504–2506' ('First National Economic and Social Development Plan, 2017–2012') 53–54 <https://www.nesdc.go.th/ewt_dl_link.php?nid=3776> accessed 20 February 2025 (1st NESD Plan).

6 Baker and Phongpaichit, *A History of Thailand*, 167–168.

7 See 'Rural Development' in this chapter.

8 See Boonrak Boonyaketmala, 'The rise and fall of the film industry in Thailand, 1897–1992' 6(2) *East-West Film Journal* 62, 78–79. See also Mary Ainslie, 'Post-war Thai cinema: Audiences and film style in a divided nation' in Daniela Treveri Gennari, Danielle Hipkins, and Catherine O'Rawe (eds), *Rural Cinema Exhibition and Audiences in a Global Context* (Palgrave Mcmillon 2018).

people of all social strata, much like what poetry was to the Siamese people of the 19th century.[9] However, it was long after the cinema came to Siam in the early 20th century that local production by commoners like Sompot began to thrive. Thai film production up until the end of WWII was almost an exclusive enterprise of those who came from the royal and noble families.[10] In contrast, the growth of film exhibitions in the post-war period saw the domination of film production by the growing middle class who ventured into the sector in search of fortune.[11]

The emergence of these new filmmakers partly explains why the style of Thai films during this period—known as 'the 16mm film era'—was disparaged for lacking in artistic value and production quality.[12] The benchmark was set by the overflow of Hollywood films that occupied cinema screens in Bangkok and major cities, and here lies another explanation for the infamous film style.[13] For while audiences in the capital went to a picture palace to enjoy the spectacle of expensive Hollywood production, the low-budget, plebian Thai films rather catered to viewers in the provincial and rural areas that had just become accessible to itinerant projectionists travelling along the newly paved roads.[14]

In Thailand, the change from rail to road is embedded in the collective memory of the Cold War. Locally known as the era of *kanphattana* ('development'), which bears an ominous resemblance to the quest for *siwilai*, the 'special' Thai–American relations during the Cold War years brought about an intensive economic and infrastructure development that stimulated urbanisation and revitalised consumerism.[15] This wave of socio-economic transformation eventually led to the first revision of Thai copyright law after nearly 50 years without amendments since joining the Berne Convention in 1931.[16] The result was a modernisation of Thai copyright law that opted for a high standard of protection such that only a few substantive changes were needed when TRIPS came along in the mid-1990s.[17]

One thing that made Thai–American relations 'special' was the close tie between the US government and the Thai authoritarian regime, which came to power in post-WWII Thailand. A key figure of this period was Field Marshal Sarit Thanarat, a former prime minister of Thailand whose name is now synonymous

9 See Scot Barmé, *Women, Man, Bangkok: Love, Sex, and Popular Culture in Thailand* (Rowman & Littlefield 2002) 69–70. See also Palita Chunsaengchan, *Ruling aesthetics: Intermediality, media modernity and early Thai cinema (1868–1942)* (PhD thesis, University of Oregon 2020).

10 Boonrak (n 8) 69.

11 ibid 79.

12 ibid 81; Ainslie (n 8) 314–315.

13 ibid.

14 For further discussion, see Adadol Ingawanij, 'Itinerant cinematic practices in and around Thailand during the Cold War' (2018) 2(2) *Southeast of Now: Directions in Contemporary and Modern Art in Asia* 9.

15 See Baker and Pasuk, *History* (n 6) 155, 167–168, 180–181.

16 See 'Legislative Overhaul' in this chapter.

17 See 'In the Name of Free Trade' in Chapter 4.

with a Thai-style military dictatorship (the 'Sarit regime').[18] Much like the Siamese ruling elite, Sarit adopted and adapted a Western model to his advantage.[19] The emphasis he placed on *kanphattana* is comparable with the Siamese discourse of *siwilai*, and the 'era of development' was indeed a relation of domination in disguise. Colonialism was over, but coloniality was all over. Hence, lurking behind the modernisation of Thai law was the coloniality of power that would become concentrated in the system of IPRs by the end of the 20th century.[20]

Curiously, as the century drew to a close, the controversy around the global war on media piracy casts a different light on Thailand's modern copyright law.[21] The statutory text and the international standard it espoused appeared irreconcilable with the country's situation of rampant piracy.[22] This apparent dissonance between law and society raises questions over the 'success' of copyright law transplantation, dating to the era of absolute monarchy. While the law was not rejected—it stuck—it also did not seem to have deeply penetrated Thai society. Framing the discussion solely in terms of success or failure can only take one so far; more attention should be given to the nature of law's relations to society, exploring how a foreign rule ties itself to a new social context.[23]

This perspective not only offers a more nuanced understanding of copyright law but also positions copyright historiography as a site for exploring broader socio-political transformations. Attention must now turn to a major reform in Thai copyright law in the 1970s. This development highlights the complex interplay between legal modernisation, economic transformation, and evolving Thai–Western relations. To fully grasp the significance of these changes that unfolded during what Benedict Anderson termed the American era, we must ask, What really happened in Thailand during the Cold War?

I. The Era of Development

A recent revival of outdoor screenings amidst cinema's recovery from the COVID-19 pandemic is a good reminder of a distinct historical mode of cinema going that had been pushed to the margin.[24] Itinerant film projection played an important role in the development of the Thai film industry in the second half

18 See for instance Chaloemtiarana, *Thailand*; Federico Ferrara, 'The logic of Thailand's royalist coup d'état' in Pavin Chachavalpongpun (ed), *Routledge Handbook of Contemporary Thailand* (Routledge 2020).
19 See further discussion in 'Identity Politics' in this chapter.
20 See further discussion in 'The Coloniality of Knowledge' in Chapter 4.
21 See further discussion in 'Contested Modernity' in Chapter 4.
22 See further discussion in 'Inauthentic Self' in Chapter 4.
23 See further discussion in 'A Logic of Legal Transplants' in this chapter.
24 See for instance 'Bangkok organises outdoor cinema festival to boost local economy' (Thai PBS World, 8 July 2022) <https://www.thaipbsworld.com/bangkok-organises-outdoor-cinema-festival-to-boost-local-economy/> accessed 20 February 2025; Pattarawadee Saengmanee, 'Outdoor cinema is exercise in soft power' (*Bangkok Post*, 25 July 2022) <https://www.bangkokpost.com/opinion/opinion/2353281/outdoor-cinema-is-exercise-in-soft-power> accessed 20 February 2025.

of the 20th century,[25] and even so, discussions about digital transformation since the turn of the century tend to focus on the change and challenge facing theatrical exhibitions.[26] Far less has been made of the now-marginal practice of itinerant exhibitions, which has nonetheless persisted since its heyday in the 1970s.[27] Those were the years when itinerant projectionists travelled to the most rural and inaccessible parts of Thailand to bring films to the far-flung populations.[28] In the time when cinemas in Bangkok competed to be the most lavish and cutting edge, the presence of itinerant film troupes around the country seemed like a belated arrival of modernity.

The flourishing business of film exhibitions was closely connected with the growing influence of the US in Thailand.[29] Hollywood films began to dominate Thai cinemas as soon as the exhibition sector began its recovery in the immediate post-WWII period.[30] Also established around this period was the Motion Pictures Export Association of America and its network of representatives in Bangkok, who would play a crucial role in the war on media piracy when the 20th century drew to a close.[31] Meanwhile, in the 1960s, film exhibition quickly developed into a lucrative sector as Thai–American relations began to tighten. During the decade following Sarit's coup d'état in 1957, the number of cinemas in Bangkok almost doubled, while the rest of the country saw a nearly tripled increase—this occurred as Sarit embraced the growing American influence in Southeast Asia.[32] The spectacular, brand-new cinemas in Bangkok offered concrete manifestations of the development ethos espoused by the Sarit regime; material progress became synonymous with the decade of development. The government followed the US prescription of economic liberalism by retreating from meddling with the economy to concentrate on improving the country's infrastructure.[33]

25 See Unaloam Chanrungmaneekul, *120 ปี ธุรกิจภาพยนตร์ไทย ในมิติประวัติศาสตร์เศรษฐกิจและสังคมไทย (120 years of Thai film business from the historical perspective of Thai economy and society)* (Thailand Research Fund 2018) 171–174.

26 See for instance Ministry of Culture, '**ยุทธศาสตร์การส่งเสริมอุตสาหกรรมภาพยนตร์และวีดีทัศน์ ระยะที่** 3 **พ.ศ.** 2560–2564') ('Strategies for film and video promotion, phase 3, 2017–2021') <https://filmcommittee.m-culture.go.th/th/db_63_filmcommittee_9/8579> accessed 20 February 2025.

27 For discussion of contemporary practices, see for instance Thitiya Pojanapitak, '**การปรับตัวของหนังกลางแปลงในประเทศไทยต่อการฉายภาพยนตร์ในระบบดิจิทัล**' ('The adaptation of Thai outdoor cinema to a digital cinema system') (2017) 35(2) *Journal of Communication Arts* 19; Richard MacDonald, 'Film projection and the sacred geography of site-specific cinema in contemporary Thailand' in Gabriel Menotti and Virginia Crisp (eds), *Practices of Projection: Histories and Technologies* (OUP 2020).

28 See Adadol, 'Itinerant cinematic practices' (n 14).

29 Unaloam, *Thai Film Business* (n 25) 160.

30 For more details, see Patipat Sathaporn, '**การฟื้นคืนชีพของกิจการฉายภาพยนตร์กับวัฒนธรรมการชมภาพยนตร์ในกรุงเทพฯ ทศวรรษ** 2490' ('The revival of film screenings and film culture in Bangkok, 1947–1956') (2016) 3(2) *Thammasat Journal of History* 69, 100–107.

31 Boonrak (n 8) 71.

32 See National Statistical Office, '**สมุดสถิติรายปี บรรพ** 29 (**พ.ศ.** 2512–2513)' ('Statistical Yearbook, Chapter 29 (1969–1970)') (Bangkok 1970).

33 Thak, *Despotic Paternalism* (n 18) 152.

In 1958, Sarit inaugurated the high-standard *Mittraphap* ('Friendship') Highway, which was a watershed in the Thai history of national transport policy.[34] The name Friendship referred to the financial and technical support from the US, which made possible the construction of this state-of-the-art highway to improve the connection between Bangkok and the rural provinces in the northeast.[35] And with US aid continuing to pour into Thailand over the next decade, the inauguration of the Friendship Highway foreshadowed the expansion of Thailand's road network during the Cold War period. Notably, this upward trend in motor transport was pronounced in the Northeastern region (*Isan*).[36] Because of Thailand's proximity to insurgency-stricken Laos and Cambodia, its natural terrain, and the level of poverty, the Thai government and the US considered this region to be most susceptible to the communist insurgency.[37] In Cold War Thailand, the expansion of the road network epitomised the close link between rural development and the suppression of communist insurgency.

Rural Development

Thus, the road to the Free World's victory began with the construction of roads. And these were the roads that allowed the film unit of the United States Information Service to spread its anti-communist propaganda to remote villages in rural areas.[38] In this way, the Thai history of itinerant cinema is partly a story of modernity/coloniality—the waging of imperial psychological warfare came in the disguise of modern entertainment that became possible because of modern roads.[39] But these roads also brought material changes to the rural areas of Thailand. Road construction was initially a priority for the Thai–American cooperation in the Accelerated Rural Development (ARD) programme, launched in 1964.[40] Development activities under ARD spanned various areas (e.g. irrigation, occupational promotion, health services) as they depended on the needs of each selected province of sensitive security.[41] The ARD programme originated from growing concern in the Thai government over 'the increased communist activity in the Northeast.'[42] It thus became the ARD's objectives 'to increase the income of the rural population,

34 For further discussion, see Kakizaki (n 3) 119–124.
35 See 1st NESD Plan 3, 127.
36 In the 1st Plan, the total distance of planned road construction and improvements in the Northeast was the highest among all regions across the country. See 1st NESD 126–128.
37 See the summary by the US government in Department of State, 'Mobile development unit PROP, 22 May 1969' (USAID) 2 <http://pdf.usaid.gov/pdf_docs/pdaad616b1.pdf> accessed 20 February 2025.
38 ibid 10. The ARD programme had recorded '136 film showings a month on the average to villagers near ARD construction projects'.
39 See also Adadol, 'Itinerant cinematic practices' (n 14) 19–20.
40 USOM, 'A brief history of USOM support to the office of accelerated rural development, September 1969' (USAID) 1 <http://pdf.usaid.gov/pdf_docs/Pdacr645.pdf> accessed 1 March 2023.
41 ibid 6–8.
42 ibid 2.

to improve ties between the Royal Thai Government and rural people, and to strengthen local self-government,'[43] though the last objective seemed to be no more than lip service.[44]

As rural development and national security went hand in hand, a development programme like ARD epitomised 'a drive to tighten Bangkok's administrative grip on the country's overwhelmingly agricultural population,'[45] but development did not just mean better infrastructure. The Friendship Highway, for instance, transformed the province of Khorat into a gateway to *Isan* and the economic hub of the region. Clearly, economic growth—or the expansion of capitalist production—was high on the agenda of the Sarit regime, and nowhere can this be better seen than in the creation of the country's first National Economic and Social Development (NESD) Plan that essentially launched the American-led programme of economic liberalism.[46]

'Work Is Money. Money Is Work. This Brings Happiness'

Kanphattana ('development') was Sarit's policy watchword and his source of political legitimacy.[47] During his time in power between 1958 and 1963, Sarit stated time and again that he saw national development as the main task of his government. Thak Chaloemtiarana argues in his well-known work that Sarit placed great emphasis on the idea of progress and modernisation and conceived of development in terms of making 'a Thai way of life no less civilised than the life in the West.'[48] So rather like the Siamese ruling elite and *siwilai*, Sarit's view of development was also a Thai-ised one in that it did not necessarily conform to the Western models.[49]

However, when it comes to economic development, considered to be of high priority, Sarit was more than willing to listen to Western experts and Western-trained technocrats.[50] Clearly, following the US's lead was very much Thailand's approach to economic development under the Sarit regime.[51] In the first NESD Plan, announced in 1961, the Thai government followed recommendations from the

43 ibid 1.

44 After all, the US knowingly recruited and supported a Thai authoritarian regime to suppress communist insurgency in Indochina. For more details, see Nattapon Jaijing, *ขุนศึก ศักดินา และพญาอินทรี การเมืองไทยภายใต้ระเบียบโลกของสหรัฐอเมริกา 2491–2500 (Warlord, Sakdina, and the Bald Eagle: Thai Politics in the American World Order, 1948–1958)* (Fah-diew-kan 2020).

45 Benedict Anderson, 'Introduction' in Benedict Anderson (ed) and Ruchira Mendiones (tr), *In the Mirror: Literature and Politics in Siam in the American Era* (Duangkamol 1985) 20–21.

46 Baker and Pasuk, *History* (n 6) 167–168. See also 1st NESD Plan 3.

47 Thak, *Despotic Paternalism* (n 18) 147–150.

48 ibid 149.

49 ibid 147–150.

50 Baker and Pasuk, *History* (n 6) 167–168.

51 Ukrit Pattamanun, *การศึกษาเปรียบเทียบบทบาทต่างประเทศต่อการเปลี่ยนแปลงทางเศรษฐกิจไทย: ทศวรรษ 1960 และ 1990 (A Comparative Study of the Role of Foreign Countries in the Change in the Thai Economy: 1960s and 1990s)* (Institute of Asian Studies, Chulalongkorn University 2001) 12–13.

World Bank, which essentially required the state to limit its role to providing infrastructure in order to create a favourable environment for private capital.[52]

With economic growth at the forefront of the national agenda, the notion of *kanphattana* operated to engage more people in capitalist production, clearly targeting those in rural areas reliant on subsistence agriculture.[53] Encapsulating this aspect of Sarit's notion of *kanphattana* was his famous slogan, 'Work is money. Money is work. This brings happiness.'[54] Implicit in this slogan was not only the intention to transform rural communities and their subsistence practices into capitalist relations but also an underlying assumption about the importance of consumption in achieving happiness. During the era of development, intensive economic development fuelled the returning consumption in the post-war period to go from strength to strength, ultimately bringing the issue of obsolete copyright law to a head.[55]

Modernising Thai Copyright Law

The post-WWII development of Thai copyright law differed significantly from the enactment of the PLAWA 1931, which arguably anticipated the political and legal manoeuvring of Western powers over former colonies during post-war decolonisation.[56] Unlike the struggle for judicial autonomy that gave rise to the 1931 Act, a major reform of Thai copyright law in the 1970s was not engineered by Western powers but rather stemmed from the Cold War-era ethos of *kanphattana*. Becoming the bastion of the Free World brought in technological advances and US-style consumerism. This change ultimately necessitated a review of the PLAWA 1931, culminating in Thailand's accession to the Paris Act (1971) in 1980. The new Thai Copyright Act of 1978 (TCA 1978) set a high standard of protection, so much so that small adjustments were required to fulfil the country's obligations under TRIPS.[57]

The death of Sarit in 1963 did not mark the end of the *kanphattana* era, which persisted into the early 1970s under the leadership of his successor, Field Marshal Thanom Kittikachorn.[58] The commencing of the PLAWA review came late in Thanom's tenure,[59] but this initiative should be understood as a legal extension of the transformation process set in motion by his predecessor. The infrastructure investment that went into improving communication facilities became instrumental in

52 ibid 13–14.
53 For more details, see Baker and Pasuk, *History* (n 6) 177–180.
54 Surachart Bamrungsuk, *United States Foreign Policy and Thai Military Rule, 1947–1977* (Duangkamol 1988) 114.
55 See 'Modernising Thai Copyright Law' in this chapter.
56 See 'Integrating Siam into a Global Capitalist System' in Chapter 1. See also Okediji, 'The international relations of intellectual property', 315, 325–326.
57 See further discussion in 'In the Name of Free Trade' in Chapter 4.
58 Baker and Pasuk, *History* (n 6) 167–168.
59 National Archive of Thailand, The Ministry of Education Doc No Sor Tor 0701.5.1/6, '*รายงานการประชุมคณะกรรมการพิจารณาแก้ไขพระราชบัญญัติคุ้มครองวรรณกรรมและศิลปกรรมฯ ครั้งที่* 1/2516' ('Minutes of the first meeting of the committee to amend the PLAWA') (30 March 1973) 50.

the upward trajectories of the music business.[60] The increasing number of radio stations combined with the household ubiquity of radios provided public exposure to new music and a new marketing tool for entrepreneurs.[61] The popularity of radio transformed the business and consumption of music, which led to an early boom in recorded music sales.[62] This development inevitably brought the issue of unauthorised reproduction to a head.

The problem in the music sector is central to a widely held belief that attributes the TCA 1978 to the changing music business landscape and credits the law reform to the Music of Association of Thailand (MAT), which called on the government to tackle music piracy.[63] While the MAT's anti-piracy campaign undoubtedly had an impact, the changes introduced in the TCA 1978 were so significant. It is clear that the new Act aimed to do much more than simply strengthen the position of songwriters and composers.

Legislative Overhaul

Among the many changes introduced by the TCA 1978, some notable ones included new categories of subject matter, a broader scope of protection, a considerable increase in penalties, and a fair number of new exceptions. On the face of it, the extent of the copyright system revamps seemed to come from the absence of legislative amendments for over four decades, but when more attention is given to individual provisions of the 1978 Act, it appears that this law was intended to achieve something greater than making up for the lost time.

Many of the changes in the TCA 1978 came in the form of definitions and redefinitions. Notably, the concept of 'work' finally appeared in the meaning of copyright to refer to the object of protection.[64] Meanwhile, the definitions of protectable works also spelt out the availability of protection for such new media as film, audiovisual, and broadcast.[65] And owing to the explicit diversity in the subject matter, the term '*phu-sarngsun*' ('creator') was preferred over the conventional '*phu-phraphun*' ('author') to signify the initial bearer of the rights conferred, which also saw an expansion in scope.[66] Owners of copyright under the TCA 1978

60 Baker and Pasuk, *History* (n 6) 181. See also Chakarj Ratchaburi, 'ประวัติศาสตร์ธุรกิจเพลงลูกทุ่งไทย พ.ศ. 2507–2535' ('The history of Thai *luk-tung* music, 1964–1992') (Master's thesis, Thammasat University 1994) 48–50.

61 Chakarj (n 60) 48–50.

62 ibid 53; Sakamol Limpichai, 'บทบาทของธุรกิจเทปเพลงไทยสากลต่อการสร้างสรรค์ผลงานเพลง' ('The role of cassette tape business in music production') (Master's thesis, Chulalongkorn University 1989) 88–89.

63 This line of argument usually references observations by Sakamol (n 62) 88–89 and Charkaj (n 60) 109. See for instance Suphontat Techaburana, 'การเปลี่ยนแปลงและการขยายตัวของธุรกิจเพลงไทยสากลในทศวรรษที่ 2520' ('The change and expansion of Thai pop music business in the 1980s') (2016) 3(2) *Thammasat Journal of History* 115, 128.

64 Copyright Act BE 2521 (1978), s 4.

65 ibid.

66 ibid.

enjoyed broader-scope protection than before thanks to the broad wording of the reproduction right and the expanded right of publication, which now covered any act of making available to the public.[67]

Under the TCA 1978, the protection of copyright was markedly reinforced in three respects. First, an increase of 20 years brought the general term of protection under Thai law to the lifetime of the author plus 50 additional years.[68] Meanwhile, the penalties for copyright infringement saw an even sharper rise with an increase in the maximum fines up to four times higher than before.[69] This remarkable rise in the penalties not only showed how outdated the previous law had been but also reflected the perceived seriousness of copyright infringement, which explains why sentences of imprisonment also became possible for the first time under Thai law.[70] That said, the strengthened protection was also met with improvements in limitations and exceptions. Notably, copyright exceptions grew from one section in the PLAWA into one chapter in the TCA 1978.[71]

Interestingly, despite the extensive changes, the TCA 1978 has received little recognition for laying the foundation that all subsequent copyright legislation has built upon. Instead, far greater historical significance has been attributed to the Thai Copyright Act of 1994 (TCA 1994), which superseded the TCA 1978 while incorporating only a few significant amendments to its provisions. One explanation could be that interest in the 1994 Act stemmed from a series of high-profile political controversies set against the backdrop of global IP politics in the early 1990s. Furthermore, it is fair to say that much attention was drawn to the TCA 1994 because of the government's increased efforts in law enforcement and awareness campaigns, suggesting that the 1978 Act may have failed to create a significant impact on Thai consciousness. Indeed, this observation is reinforced by the reservations expressed by Marut Boonak, a distinguished member of the TCA 1978 drafters, who also served as president of the Lawyers' Association and later became the country's Minister of Education.

Marut viewed the expansion of the Thai copyright system as extensive and potentially disruptive, believing that it would lead to confusion and misunderstandings.[72] Given his involvement in the drafting process, his candid comment raises questions about how the drafters understood and approached the task at hand. Furthermore, Marut's caution interestingly suggests the public's lack of familiarity and prior knowledge regarding copyright law, inviting comparisons to some of the views expressed in the debate of the bill before the National Legislative Assembly (NLA).[73] One notable instance occurred during a legislative session when a speaker

67 ibid.
68 ibid s 16.
69 ibid s 43–44.
70 ibid.
71 ibid s 30–41.
72 Marut Boonnak, 'วิจารณ์ พรบ ลิขสิทธิ์ พศ 2521' ('A review of the Copyright Act 1978') (1979) 4(14) *Journal of Business Administration* 44, 46, 52–53.
73 National Legislative Assembly Deb 16 June 1978, no 30, 144, 198–199.

interrupted the discussion on the copyright bill to voice his frustration with the NLA's prioritisation of issues. He argued that addressing the 'more urgent' problems of livelihoods should take precedence over copyright law. Understandably, the president of the NLA had to intervene to maintain the focus of the discussion, though the president also stated that he concurred with the speaker.

As such, it is fair to say that the circumstances surrounding the enactment of the TCA 1978 are somewhat perplexing. Many decades had passed since the AOA 1901, and copyright law still seemed foreign to Thai society. But to say the law was irrelevant would be difficult to reconcile with MAT's anti-piracy campaign, let alone the extent of the legislative overhaul, which ultimately aligned Thai law with Western standards. Indeed, economic and technological changes following the country's economic transformation offer some explanation, but these aspects of *kanphattana* do not tell the whole story of Thailand during the Cold War. Rather like the notion of *siwilai*, *kanphattana* is both material and aspirational, and once again, it raised the question of what it meant to be Thai.

II. Thailand in the Cultural Cold War

Analyses of Thai society that aim to portray the country under Sarit and his immediate successor, Field Marshal Thanom Kittikachorn, often feature the trope of Americanisation.[74] Indeed, the socio-cultural impact of US military bases and personnel—not to mention the influx of US expatriates and tourists—has developed into a subject of study in its own right.[75] Among the topics of discussion is the gravitational pull of US consumer culture and its effect on local production and consumption. Here, the music tastes brought by US soldiers to Thailand offer insight into how immediate the US presence must have felt to the local population. In the 1960s, the nightlife that sprang up in Bangkok and provincial Thailand to cater to off-duty military personnel almost single-handedly introduced heavy metal to Thailand's music scene.[76] Similarly, famous rock and roll artists such as Elvis Presley and Cliff Richard were pivotal to the emergence of '*pleng-string*,' a new music genre and the predecessor of Thai pop music.[77]

To the Thai public, the growing US presence in the aftermath of WWII already signalled the moving of the world axis across the Atlantic Ocean. This shift in the global cultural hierarchy—the dawn of the 'American era' in Benedict Anderson's

74 See Rungchai Yensabai, *Competing narratives in cold war Thailand: Identity politics and the construction of foreign others* (PhD thesis, University of London (SOAS) 2019) 34–37.

75 See for instance Anderson, *In the Mirror* (n 45); Matthew Phillips, *Thailand in the Cold War* (Routledge 2016). See also Rungchai (n 74).

76 Athip Jittareuk, 'จาก 'เฮฟวี่' ถึง 'เมทัล': นักดนตรีเฮฟวี่เมทัลไทยจาก 'วัยรุ่นมืออาชีพ' สู่ 'ผู้ใหญ่มือสมัครเล่น 1970–2010' ('From "heavy" to "metal": Thai heavy metal musicians, from "young professionals" to "adult amateurs," 1970–2010') (2010) 22(1) *Journal of Social Sciences*, Chiang Mai University 231, 235–241.

77 Nalin Wuttipong, *The Thai popular music industry: Industrial form and musical design* (PhD thesis, University of Nottingham 2011) 49–50.

terminology—was evident when a controversy erupted over the screening of *The King and I* in 1956. As discussed in Chapter 1, this musical adaptation of the Anna Leonowens story has been noted for directly engaging with the issue of modernisation.[78] The narrative is propelled by the tension between tradition and modernity, presenting a perennial theme that begs to be read in conjunction with 'the increased geopolitical importance of Thailand to the United States' after WWII.[79] Because Thailand was free from European colonisation and not troubled by nationalist and communist-led revolutions, the country appeared in the American imagination as 'an oasis on the troubled continent' that may be traditional and backward but also eager to learn and modernise.[80]

Meanwhile, the plan to release *The King and I* in Thailand was met with a banning order that was mired in local politics.[81] *The King and I* was released in the same year that America's military presence became a subject of fierce criticism in the Thai press.[82] With a general election looming, *The King and I* constituted a prime target for the press and the opposition, whose anti-imperialist narratives had fuelled public antagonism against the government and its relationship with the US.[83] In addition, rumours of Hollywood's contemptuous portrayal of King Mongkut ran rife in public and were played up as a humiliation inflicted upon the country by US neo-imperialism.[84] All this goes to show how Thailand, before the Satir regime, was already intertwined with the emergence of the US as the new axis mundi.

From the perspective of Cold War Thailand, the US had surpassed Europe to be the embodiment of modernity and—as Benedict Anderson argues—the metropolis to the provincial Bangkok.[85] This, however, does not mean Thai people were passively Americanised, and nor does it mean the so-called Americanisation of Thailand necessarily precluded the agency of Thai actors. Quite the opposite. Take, for instance, the Cold War history of development. Sarit's notion of *kanphattana* was never a mere imitation but a localised version of the American/Western model. Thak Chaloemtiarana argues that Sarit selectively constructed his own notion of development from both Thai and Western elements, drawing legitimacy from

78 See 'Colonial Encounter and Thai Modernity' in Chapter 1. See also Klein, *Cold War Orientalism,* 194–202.

79 ibid 197.

80 Phillips (n 75) 65.

81 Panu Aree, 'จากแอนนากับพระเจ้ากรุงสยาม ถึง *The King and I* ภาพสะท้อนแนวคิดเสรีนิยมและชาตินิยมแบบไทยๆ' ('From "Anna and the King of Siam" to *The King and I*: A reflection of Thao-style liberalism and nationalism') (1999) 2 *Thai Film Journal* 3, 7–9.

82 Nattapon (n 44) 203–204.

83 Panu (n 81) 8.

84 ibid 8–9; Police Department, 'คำชี้แจงของกรมตำรวจเกี่ยวกับภาพยนตร์ เรื่อง 'เดอะ คิง แอนด์ ไอ' (Police Department Clarification Regarding the Film *The King and I*) *Sayamnikorn* (Bangkok, 19 August 1956), republished in full in Panu (n 81).

85 Anderson, *In the Mirror* (n 45) 42.

its association with Western modernity.[86] In this regard, Sarit's strategy certainly appears reminiscent of the quest for *siwilai*—and the similarity does not end there.

The pursuit of development was also a nationalist project aimed at consolidating state power. In this context, *kanphattana* was presented as essential for national progress, which, in turn, would foster a sense of national pride. In this way, the pursuit of *kanphattana* provided legitimacy to the authoritarian regime, which not only positioned itself as the promoter of development—exemplified by rural development—but also as the guardian of Thainess, as discussed below. This is how the era of development can be best understood, and it helps to make sense of the TCA 1978.

Identity Politics

The encounters with American imperialism prompted a re-imagining of what it meant to be Thai. Matthew Phillips interestingly argues that the Thai-US relations of this period fostered a trans-Pacific symbiosis between US consumerism and Thai identity.[87] In this relationship, Phillips explains, Americans could demonstrate their non-imperialist internationalism by consuming and supporting products from the developing world.[88] Phillips provides the example of Thai silk, which became a coveted fashion item following the success of *The King and I,* as it came to signify 'a morally commendable investment in the future of Thai society' while also being a luxury item that enhanced the status of US consumers.[89] Meanwhile, Phillips contends, this US portrayal of Thailand as traditional yet fast-developing returned to inform Sarit's construction of Thainess and, by extension, his unabashed assertion of 'Thai-style democracy' despite glaring evidence of dictatorship.[90]

Writing on the same subject but with a different emphasis, Rungchai Yensabai recognises the cultural power of the US/Western model of development but calls for more attention to the agency of the Thai actors.[91] She highlights how the Thai ruling elite managed to keep *kanphattana* in check with a cultural strategy that created 'an identity dichotomy between American/Western materialistic development and the spiritual virtues of Thai traditions and culture.'[92] Rungchai argues that the strategy of cultural relativism justified a selective adoption of US development in the preservation of the Thai core. In this way, her argument is reminiscent of Thongchai's material/spiritual bifurcation model, suggesting another similarity between the era of *kanphattana* and the quest for *siwilai*.[93]

86 Thak, *Despotic Paternalism* (n 18) 147–150.
87 Phillips (n 75) 34.
88 ibid 47–48.
89 ibid 66–73.
90 ibid 209.
91 Rungchai (n 74) 32.
92 ibid 54.
93 For a comparison, see 'The Spiritual–Material Bifurcation' in Chapter 2.

Despite their differences, both Philips and Rungchai help uncover further traces of coloniality in Cold War Thailand. Persistent in the notion of *kanphattana* was the imperative of universality that once characterised the Siamese quest for *siwilai*. And much like the Siamese ruling elite, Sarit drew on the construction of national identity to carve out a space for local hegemony while conceding the country to the US sphere of influence. Such complex relations of domination were encapsulated in the association of rural development with national security, a hallmark of Cold War mentality that played out strikingly—and violently—in *Isan*.

Along with the physical violence of brute force, the violence in the state's response to communist insurgency in *Isan* also came in the form of knowledge production. One legacy of the US anti-communist psychological warfare is the revival of royal hegemony. The US enlisted the monarchy as a bulwark against communist insurgency and reciprocated the Thai institution with a rejuvenated public image and popularity.[94] This effort to promote loyalty to the King reinforced the crypto-colonial conception of Thainess—the tripartite of Nation, Religion, and King—that the Thai government employed in depicting the rural populace of *Isan* as 'the Others within' as distinct from the US/Western Others.[95]

In portraying *Isan* villagers 'as more Lao than Thai, uneducated, and poor, and thus as communist targets,' official narratives were imbued with 'the dichotomy between Bangkok (us) and *Isan* (them), which depicted the latter as 'inferior' to the former.'[96] Even today, this kind of representation of *Isan* still remains a site of contestation, as discussed later.[97] In Cold War Thailand, *Isan*'s Otherness reflected the persistence of coloniality. The state's depiction of *Isan* as 'the Other within' not only reinforced its Cold War security agenda but also shaped broader narratives of national development. In this context, the pursuit of *kanphattana* encompassed more than material progress: It was also an ideological project that sought to define Thai identity and Thailand's place in the world.

Law and Development

From this perspective, *kanphattana*—much like the quest for *siwilai*—was a transcultural process that 'transferred, localised, and hybridised' Western ideas and practices, so much so that *kanphattana* itself may lack a fixed meaning.[98] During the debate on the draft TCA 1978, discussed earlier, the disgruntled NLA member

94 Nattapon (n 44) 155–156.

95 Before *kanpatthana* and the *Isan* Others, there were *siwilai* and the 'Wild' Others, where people in the *Isan* region were perceived as barbaric and uncivilised by the Siamese ruling elites. See Thongchai Winichakul, 'The others within: Travel and ethno-spatial differentiation of Siamese subjects, 1885–1910' in Andrew Turton (ed), *Civility and Savagery: Social Identity in Tai States* (Routledge 2000).

96 Rungchai (n 74) 79.

97 See further discussion on this issue in 'Let Me Entertain You' in Chapter 6.

98 See Winichakul, 'The quest for 'siwilai'', 528, 529.

cited the rise in pork prices to emphasise his point about priority and urgency.[99] In this context, pork prices as material concerns signified the material objects of development (e.g. prosperity and quality of life), which was similar to how a transformation in the transport of pigs between Bangkok and *Isan* came to signify a measure of success for the opening of the Friendship Highway.[100] In contrast, the drafters of the TCA 1978 justified the need for revision by invoking Thai cultural heritage as a marker of national progress.[101] In this regard, development was expressed more through cultural expression than economic production.

Despite the variations, these interpretations of *kanphattana* presupposed an image of society as territorially defined and politically unified—a society of the nation-state, as it were. This contrasts with a more nuanced view of social relations as a diverse and intricate network of interests and values, as discussed in detail later. Moreover, equating society with the nation-state reinforces the conception of law and society as mutually defined, assuming a perspective on legal change that finds phenomena such as the TCA 1978 perplexing.[102]

Legal change is often understood through the lens of the nation-state, which provides law with conceptual stability as national law while defining the outer limits of society through its jurisdictional reach. This perspective shapes conventional understandings of how law changes. Notably, legal development is often seen as a process of borrowing—an idea central to Alan Watson's theory of legal transplants.[103] Through his observation of legal change in ancient and modern societies, Watson argues that legal development is always a result of legal transplants and receptions.[104] He claims that this process is driven by the borrowing of ideas among lawyers and lawmakers, so much so that one does not need to seek 'external' explanations in society.[105] In other words, what is important to Watson is the 'legal culture' of those professional elites who make or practice law.[106]

Granted that these actors do play a crucial role, a significant issue with his theory of legal transplants is its formalistic understanding of law. As Watson appears more interested in refuting the notion that law necessarily mirrors society, his claim that law develops through transplantation says little about what will become of a

99 National Legislative Assembly (n 73) 198–199.

100 Kakizaki (n 3) 123.

101 Office of the Minister, Ministry of Education Doc No Sor Ror 0203/19130, '**คำชี้แจงประกอบร่างพระราชบัญญัติลิขสิทธิ์ พ.ศ.**' ('Explanatory notes on a draft Copyright Act') (9 September 1977) 8.

102 For further discussion on this conception of law, society, and nation, see Cotterrell, *Law, Culture, and Society*, 66–67.

103 Alan Watson, *Legal Transplants: An Approach to Comparative Law* (2nd edn, UGA Press 1993) 95–96.

104 ibid 95. See also Alan Watson, 'Legal change: Sources of law and legal culture' (1983) 131 *The University of Pennsylvania Law Review* 1121, 1146; Alan Watson, *Society and Legal Change* (2nd edn, TU Press 2001) 98.

105 Watson, *Society and Legal Change* (n 104) 7–8; Alan Watson, *The Evolution of Law* (Blackwell 1985) 72ff.

106 Watson, *Legal Origins and Legal Change* (Hambledon Press 1991) 102.

transplanted rule in the broader social context.[107] Yet it is precisely this question that makes the reception of Western law an important area of inquiry in the Thai context. With Watson's emphasis on borrowing, however, every change in law simply becomes another instance of the supposedly common phenomenon of legal transplants. It is unsurprising, then, that Watson's simple yet appealing claims have faced strong criticism.[108]

Notable among Watson's critics is Pierre Legrand, who strongly contends that the meaning of law is always embedded in the culture of its place, that is, the society as a whole.[109] It is worth pointing out that Legrand's cultural critique took aim at the Europeanisation of law, which would lead to the convergence of legal systems from civil law and common law traditions.[110] Here, Legrand strongly opposed this idea, even claiming that transplanting law from one society to another is 'impossible' as a rule will have different meanings in different cultural settings.[111] This explains why Legrand's strong culturalist stance collides head-on with Watson's theory of legal transplants, and the two perspectives appear difficult to reconcile.[112]

Thus, the formalist–culturalist perspectives present a conceptual impasse, but this can be avoided by adopting a different way of thinking about society and its relations to law. Here is where insights from legal sociology can be helpful, with Roger Cotterrell's law-and-community approach serving as a good starting point.[113] Roger Cotterrell advocates for viewing law as part of social life, promoting a particular conception of law and society. Briefly put, Cotterrell recasts social life into a myriad of community relations that extend from family and neighbourhood to business organisations and professional associations.[114] As such, the idea of community represents a form of collective involvement that can be transnational or intranational, thus providing an alternative to the notion of society as necessarily

107 See also Andrew Harding, 'Global doctrine and local knowledge: Law in South East Asia' (2002) 15(1) *International Comparative Law Quarterly* 35, 45.

108 See for instance Pierre Legrand, 'The impossibility of legal transplants' (1997) 4 *Maastricht Journal of European and Comparative Law* 111.

109 ibid 114. This contention is likely to resonate with copyright scholars, who must be familiar with the perennial East–West dichotomy that often frames discussions about the development of copyright law outside of Europe and North America. See for instance Willian Alford, *To Steal a Book is an Elegant Offense: Intellectual Property Law in Chinese Civilization* (Stanford University Press 1995). Furthermore, this culturalist perspective does not seem to be far off the mark when considered within the Western context. Different traditions and schools of thought also animate Western copyright discourse. See for instance Peter Baldwin, *The Copyright Wars: Three Centuries of Trans-Atlantic Battle* (Princeton University Press 2004).

110 See Pierre Legrand, 'European legal systems are not converging' (1996) 45(1) *International Comparative Law Quarterly* 52.

111 Legrand, 'The impossibility' (n 108) 120.

112 For further discussion, see Andrew Harding, 'The legal transplants debate: Getting beyond the impasse?' in Vito Breda (ed.), *Legal Transplants in East Asia and Oceania* (CUP 2019).

113 See Roger Cotterrell, *Law's Community: Legal Theory in Sociological Perspective* (Clarendon Press 1997); Cotterrell, *Law, Culture, and Society* (n 102).

114 Cotterrell, *Law, Culture, and Society* (n 102) 68–70.

the nation-state.[115] Indeed, the nation constitutes one form of community, an imagined community in Benedict Anderson's terminology, but a variety of community relations with different regulatory needs now appear to make up the fabric of social life—and all of this can be studied empirically using Cotterrell's schema of community types (instrumental, traditional, affective, etc.).[116]

A Logic of Legal Transplants

It is worth noting that Cotterrell considers his community concept to be of use in a study of legal transplants.[117] The law-and-community approach offers 'a framework for examining the borrowing of law in particular contexts,' he contends, while also recognising the relative insulation of the internal legal culture.[118] To Cotterrell, the legal profession only constitutes one type of community, which is why he argues against a simplistic understanding of legal transplantation as a borrowing of legal ideas among legal professional elites.[119] Regarding the problem of culture, or the idea that law mirrors society, viewing social life through the community lens also means recognising that state law has many types of relationships with different forms of community.[120] Here, it is worth pointing out that this aspect of Cotterrell's sociological perspective is instructive for analysing the contemporary experience of copyright law in Thailand, a subject of discussion in later chapters.[121] As for the history of the TCA 1978, the community concept is stimulating but offers limited explanatory power, with it being a tool for empirical studies.

Presenting a more abstract approach, or a set of postulates in Cotterrell's assessment,[122] is Gunther Teubner's concept of 'legal irritants.'[123] Teubner considers legal transplants as a source of irritation whose effect on the recipient is not as straightforward as the 'transplant' metaphor suggests.[124] In many ways, Teubner shares Cotterrell's position against the notion that law necessarily mirrors society,[125] and where Cotterrell sees a myriad of community relations, Teubner sees diverse social fragments.[126] The main point of divergence comes from Teubner's thesis regarding the impact of legal irritants. Teubner posits a dynamic process of parallel

115 ibid 65–66.
116 ibid 76–77.
117 ibid 119.
118 ibid 125.
119 See his critique of Watson's arguments in Roger Cotterrell, 'Is there a logic of legal transplants' in David Nelken and Johannes Feest (eds), *Adapting Legal Culture* (Hart Publishing 2001).
120 Cotterrell, *Law, Culture, and Society* (n 102) 76–77.
121 Particularly, his concept of community is fundamental to developing the legal concept of community resource, to be discussed in Chapter 8.
122 Roger Cotterrell, *The Sociology of Law* (2nd edn, Butterworths 1992) 66.
123 Gunther Teubner, 'Legal irritants: Good faith in British law or how unifying law ends up in new divergences' (1998) 61(1) *Modern Law Review* 11.
124 ibid 12.
125 ibid 18.
126 ibid.

transformations, wherein a foreign rule 'irritates' the new context by setting off a chain of transformations in the recipient's legal and social systems.[127]

Central to Teubner's concept of legal irritants—and this is where his idea resonates with the current discussion—is his view on the binding arrangements between law and society.[128] For Teubner, the social ties of contemporary law are not comprehensive but selective and varying.[129] He contends that law does not bind itself to society as a whole but to diverse fragments of society.[130] And in this way, law is not an expression of society *tout court*; 'it ties up closely with some of its areas, only on specific occasions and only to different fragments of society.'[131] From the perspective of Thai copyright law history, Teubner's notion of law's binding arrangements appears particularly illuminating. A good place to observe these binding arrangements is King Vajiravudh's amendments to the AOA 1901.

Recalling Vajiravudh's nationalist programme, the AOA (Amendment) of 1914 was his attempt to employ the commodity status of books in promoting the country's literary heritage and, thus, national pride.[132] Considering that the 1914 Act was an amendment, one can discern that there must have been a particular alignment between legal and literary discourses following Chulalongkorn's promulgation of the AOA in 1901. In this regard, it is worth noting again that the crypto-colonial discourse of Thai literary standards neither legitimised nor challenged the idea of property rights in knowledge. Rather, the commodification of books and the corresponding legal categories (e.g. author's ownership, the author, the book) were presupposed by Vajiravudh's promotion of 'good books,' which awarded a royal seal of excellence that simultaneously acted as royal approval for copyright registration.[133] In other words, the aim of the elitist discourse of literary standards was to stratify the literary public sphere (already over-coded by market relations and law) with an aesthetic order that valorised the notion of literary heritage.[134] As such, one could argue that the binding agent between copyright law and Thai society in this instance was not the ideology of romantic authorship but rather one of nationalism.

Many decades later and the same dynamics appeared to underpin the development of the TCA 1978. Just as Vajiravudh's nationalist programme represented an attempt to redirect the quest for *siwilai* from Westernisation towards self-assertion, Sarit's hybridised notion of *kanphattana* projected an image of 'a Thai way of life no less civilised than life in the West.'[135] Both the ruling elite of crypto-colonial Siam and the authoritarian government of Cold War Thailand found themselves in

127 ibid 27–28.
128 ibid 18–19.
129 ibid 18.
130 ibid.
131 ibid 22.
132 See 'The Twin Birth of the RSL and the AOA 1914' in Chapter 1.
133 For otherwise, there would not have existed a literary public sphere in Siam, and nor would there be a need for a project like the RSL that represented Vajiravudh's attempt to reassert monarchical authority in the country's literary public sphere.
134 See 'Writing the Nation' in Chapter 1.
135 Thak, *Despotic Paternalism* (n 18) 149.

the cultural contact zone ‘where they gazed outward at the West and inward upon “the Others within” at the same time.’[136] And for what the notion of literary heritage meant in crypto-colonial Siam and how it was connected to the 1914 Act, one can see something similar in the link between consumerism and identity construction that the notion of cultural heritage came to signify to the drafters of the 1978 Act.

A Life No Less Civilised

For the drafters of the 1978 Act, several aspects of the PLAWA warranted a comprehensive review of the 1931 Act.[137] Substantively, the drafters cited a lack of clarity around new forms of work, inappropriately low penalties, and a discrepancy with international terms of protection.[138] A broad parameter was thus drawn for the review of the PLAWA that extended far beyond merely addressing issues facing songwriters.[139] To this end, foreign materials from both copyright and authors' rights jurisdictions were heavily consulted, and assistance was also sought from WIPO.[140] However, when it came to the preparation of the bill, selecting and adapting from the texts of foreign laws seemed to be the primary and sole method employed. The drafters appeared to make minimal efforts to understand the circumstances in relevant creative sectors and cultural practices, sometimes showing no interest at all. A pertinent example is the inclusion of works of applied art.

Previously, the PLAWA did not protect works of applied art, and Thailand made a corresponding reservation upon joining the Berne Convention in 1931.[141] It is understandable that the drafters of the TCA 1978 wanted to reconsider the exclusion, particularly given that a considerable period of time had passed. However, the reason given for the inclusion did not indicate that stakeholders had been consulted or that there was a great understanding of the situation on the ground. It seemed that the drafters merely agreed among themselves that Thailand had great artists, and, so the logic goes, offering protection would encourage Thai artists to create new works of applied art with higher quality.[142]

136 Rungchai (n 74) 60–61.

137 National Archive, ‘Minutes of the first meeting to amend the PLAWA’ (n 59) 51–52.

138 ibid.

139 Ibid. Four preliminary issues were identified including an outdated list of protected works, ineffective criminal penalty, inadequate terms of protection, and deficiencies in the language used.

140 The drafters consulted a wide variety of sources that include WIPO draft model law and the law of various nations, including Australia, the UK, the US, France, Germany, Sweden, Japan, India, and Pakistan.

141 Consequently, Article 8 of the Berlin Act 1908 was replaced with Article 5 of the Berne Convention 1886 as modified by the Paris Additional Act 1896 in respect of the exclusive right of authors to make or to authorize the translation of their works. See <https://www.wipo.int/wipolex/en/treaties/parties/remarks/TH/15> accessed 20 February 2025.

142 Office of the Minister, Ministry of Education Doc No Sor Ror 0601/585, ‘รายงานการประชุมคณะกรรมการพิจารณาแก้ไข พรบ คุ้มครองวรรณกรรมและศิลปกรรม พุทธศักราช 2474 ครั้งที่ 4/2519’ (‘Minutes of the meeting of the committee to amend the PLAWA 1931, No 4/1976’) (9 November 1976) 32.

This style of reasoning points to the self-referential, relatively autonomous nature of the legal discourse that when considered in relation to the transfer of rules can lend support to the idea of legal transplants as an exclusive enterprise of legal professional elites. Indeed, as just discussed, records of the drafting process suggest a picture of insulation and internal communications where the distinction between inside and outside was drawn not nationally but professionally. Notably, the drafters actively sought technical assistance from WIPO. On one occasion, Marut was sent to Japan to attend a copyright seminar that WIPO helped organise to bring together countries in Asia for the purpose of information sharing.[143] All of this demands that the internal logic and dynamics of legal communities be observed, but this observation alone does not quite explain what logic underpinned the embrace of high protection standards. Surely, the drafting did not occur in a social vacuum, not least because it began as a response to social change in the first place.

Interestingly, the notion of national cultural heritage loomed large in the rationale behind the overhaul of Thai copyright law.[144] It is also worth noting that the review of the PLAWA began as an initiative of the Department of Fine Arts. This is a government agency whose primary responsibility was to restore and conserve national cultural heritage. Therefore, it is pertinent to ask how copyright law came to be considered relevant to cultural heritage. The answer to this question lies in the unexpected connection between national identity and cultural commodities, or as the drafters put it,

> Literary and artistic works are . . . cultural heritage that dignifies the nation as well as signifies the progress and civilisation achieved by the population . . . the committee abide by the conviction that creators of literary and artistic works must be supported in reaping the benefits of their industry so that they will expend their talents on creating intellectual property that will become national treasures.[145]

Implicit in this statement is the recognition that market exchange plays a crucial role in cultural production and that cultural commodities must be protected in the marketplace to benefit Thai culture. This marriage of convenience between national identity construction and cultural commodification may otherwise be perplexing but made perfect sense in the early 1970s.

While the question concerning the extent to which the social context influenced the final outcome remains, this does not negate the observation that the TCA 1978 was symptomatic of the post-war capitalist expansion and indicated

143 Office of the Minister, Ministry of Education Doc No Sor Ror 0601/585, 'รายงานการประชุมคณะกรรมการพิจารณาแก้ไข พรบ คุ้มครองวรรณกรรมและศิลปกรรม พุทธศักราช 2474 ครั้งที่ 1/2517' ('Minutes of the meeting of the committee to amend the PLAWA 1931, No 1/1974') (11 February 1974) 2.

144 Office of the Minister, 'Explanatory notes' (n 101) 8.

145 ibid.

the corresponding growth of consumerism. Indeed, such changes were effectively captured in the views expressed by one member of the NLA during the debate over the 1978 copyright bill.[146] The nationally renowned author Wimol Chiemcharoen—commonly known by the pen name Tomyantee—praised the government's initiative to review and update Thai copyright law. Wimol lamented the inadequate remuneration for those who 'worked with the brain,' whose 'products' were imitated and exploited by others in the marketplace.

She highlighted several types of creative and artisanal goods, but her example of Thai silk exports is particularly illustrative of the state of Thai capitalism: already expanding inward into the artisanal countryside and outward into the international marketplace.[147] Equally telling was when she shared her experience as a fiction writer dealing with the all-too-common unauthorised use in film adaptations: a personal anecdote that offered a broader snapshot of Thailand's emerging cultural industry.[148]

In this way, the introduction of the TCA 1978 can be seen as a harbinger of the shifts and changes that would unfold over the next two decades.

146 National Legislative Assembly (n 73) 194–195.

147 ibid 195. For further discussion on the internationalisation of Thai silk through the well-known figure of Jim Thompson, see Phillips (n 75).

148 National Legislative Assembly (n 73) 195.

4 The War on Piracy

Thailand's moderate economic growth since the 1960s took a remarkable turn when the decade of an economic boom took off in the second half of the 1980s.[1] Just as the economy started to surge, local media also began to pick up on the ubiquity of piracy in the country.[2] The growing media attention on piracy signalled the changing dynamics of global trade, which saw developed countries give in to protectionism. Members of the Global North, particularly the United States, began to exert pressure on Thailand to recognise new forms of IP, raise protection standards, and tighten law enforcement.[3] The same also happened to other developing countries as the waves of IP globalisation swept across the developing world.[4] The peak of this globalising tide came when TRIPS was concluded in 1994 to establish a global regime of minimum protection standards. It now perhaps goes without saying that TRIPS represents the global harmonisation of IP protection that instituted Western protection standards as the new world order.[5]

Arguably, the issue with the global harmonisation of IPRs was not so much that it represented a process of neo-colonialism or the domination of less-developed countries through indirect forms of control.[6] As exemplified by TRIPS itself, one such way is through economic means, with government agencies backing multicultural corporations in a bid to maintain developing countries' dependence

1 Baker and Phongpaichit, *A History of Thailand*, 221.

2 Annette Hamilton, 'Video crackdown or the sacrificial pirate: Censorship and cultural consequences in Thailand' (1993) 5 *Public Culture* 515, 522–523; Hamilton claimed that piracy accounted for 90–95 per cent of foreign music cassettes in Thailand, and the local circulation of foreign films was made up mainly of pirated videotapes.

3 Bundit Limsakul, *ผลการเจรจาแกตต์รอบอุรุกวัยต่อระบบการคุ้มครองทรัพย์สินทางปัญญาของไทย: รายงานการสัมมนาเชิงปฏิบัติการ (The Impact of The Uruguay Round of GATT Negotiations on Thailand's IP Protection System: The Workshop Report)* (Thailand Research Fund 1994) 8.

4 Okediji, 'The international relations of intellectual property', 315, 336–337.

5 See Drahos, 'Global property rights in information'; Drahos and Braithwaite, *Information Feudalism*; Gervais, *The TRIPS Agreement*.

6 For a critique of the global IP system from this perspective, see Andreas Rahmatian, 'Neo-colonial aspects of global intellectual property protection' (2009) 12(1) *Journal of World Intellectual Property* 40.

DOI: 10.4324/9781003592037-7

on the developed world.[7] However, as contentious as TRIPS was, one could say that a similar form of domination can already be found in the Thai experience of 19th-century colonialism.[8]

As discussed in Chapter 1, Western penetration of Siam was not achieved through politico-military means but 'was consummated directly at the economic level.'[9] In this regard, and as far as Thailand is concerned, what was particularly poignant about the global harmonisation of IPRs was not so much the neo-colonial aspects of the global IP system but the persistence of coloniality. In fact, one does not need to look far for traces of coloniality in contemporary Thailand. The self-image of a 'developing country' not only indicates a hierarchical order in Thai–Western relations but also implies a specific pattern of power relations between the Thai state and its citizens.

The fact that ideas such as development have become a Thai idiom of power highlights the persistence of the coloniality of power and its relations to knowledge production. Since the late 20th century, however, one can argue that the coloniality of knowledge has taken on a new meaning in addition to 'a colonisation of the imagination,' which once allowed the colonial masters, equipped with the notions of race and civilisation, to subject the dominated to economic exploitation.[10] Now that knowledge has become inextricable from the comparative advantage of the world's advanced economies, ownership of knowledge has emerged as a tool for economic domination.[11] However, the notion of property is always animated by the issues of exclusion and distribution, suggesting that some form of ideology is always at work in the organisation and structuring of property relations.[12] In this regard, what inevitably becomes crucial to the propertisation of knowledge is the knowledge of IP—the latter encompasses not only the rules and their interpretations but also the taken-for-granted understanding and common sense that are narrated through these rules.

Crucially, it was the Western narratives surrounding media piracy that breathed new life into the well-worn cliché 'knowledge is power,' which ultimately came to characterise the introduction of Thailand's Creative Economy policy in the late 2000s.[13] Presented as a solution to the country's lack of competitiveness in the global economy, this policy initiative aimed to bolster the legitimacy of a military-backed government that claimed to steer Thailand down the same path as countries in the developed world. As discussed in detail later, the adoption of the Creative Economy imagery embodied the fact that the pursuit of Western-style development continued into the 21st century—as did the country's military authoritarianism.

7 ibid 41–42.
8 See also 'Siamese Modernisation Under Colonial Influence' in Chapter 1.
9 Rajchagool, *The Rise and Fall of the Thai Absolute Monarchy,* 82.
10 See 'Modernity/Coloniality' in Chapter 1.
11 See 'In the Name of Free Trade' in this chapter.
12 See 'Modernity/Piracy' in this chapter.
13 See 'The Pirate King Dreaming of a Creative Economy' later in this chapter.

Marking a break from the era of *kanphattana* was, nonetheless, the role and image of copyright law. The following discussion briefly recounts the socio-economic changes that by the late 1980s had placed the issue of copyright protection at the centre of the decline in the once-special Thai–American relations.

I. Globalisation and Its Discontents

Post-war Thailand enjoyed steady economic growth following the America-led process of economic development.[14] This transformation only took a few decades to change Thailand's post-war agrarian-based economy beyond recognition. Notably, the country's economic transformation accelerated during a decade of an economic boom that began around the mid-1980s.[15] The decision to shift to export-oriented industrialisation to benefit from economic globalisation yielded substantial benefits during the boom years, in which the Thai economy was recorded as the world's fastest-growing.[16] By the turn of the millennium, Thailand had developed into an upper-middle-income economy, an astonishing achievement given its place among the poorest nations after WWII.[17] This remarkable rise in fortune enveloped the country with a sense of euphoria, fostering the belief that Thailand was on course to perform another 'Asian Miracle' and become the 'Fifth Asian Tiger' following the examples of Singapore, South Korea, Hong Kong, and Taiwan.[18]

Contrasting with the economic performance was the post-Cold War relationship with the US. While many socio-political factors are considered to have contributed to the dramatic shift in Thai–American relations,[19] one area where the unravelling of the special relationship made itself strongly felt was IP protection. The divergence over the protection of American interests in IPRs created so much tension in Thai–American relations that it escalated into contentious disputes by the late 1980s. Prominent among the points of tension was the widespread infringement of American-owned copyright in media products. The American discontent over Thai piracy reveals a great deal about the socio-economic transformation that Thailand was going through.

The Birth of Copyright Scholarship

In the early 1980s, the ripple effect of the 1978 revision became evident when academic discussions were ignited by the gaps and ambiguities in the new copyright act. Initially, the discussions were mostly a cursory examination of the new

14 Peter Warr, 'Economic development of post-war Thailand' in Pavin Chachavalpongpun (ed), *Routledge Handbook of Contemporary Thailand* (Routledge 2020) 37.
15 ibid 37–38.
16 ibid 38.
17 ibid 36.
18 Pasuk Phongpaichit and Chris Baker, *Thailand's Boom and Bust* (Silkworm Books 1998) 22–23.
19 For more details, see Pongphisoot Busbarat, 'Thai–US relations in the post-Cold War era: Untying the special relationship' (2017) 13(3) *Asian Security* 256.

law, albeit with a particular focus on the uncertainty surrounding foreign works that raised a question about compliance with the Berne Convention.[20] Before long, the breadth and depth of the topics started to expand.[21] More legal commentators began to join in, and together, they produced a modest but growing body of literature that transformed the previously inert area in Thai law.[22] Indeed, one can see in retrospect that the 1980s was a formative period for Thai copyright scholarship; not only were there more copyright-related publications in this period than over many decades prior, but most of the prominent authors in Thai copyright scholarship began their trade around this time.[23] These authors, along with the others who published on copyright law in the 1980s, belonged to a new generation of Thai lawyers, many of whom had American legal education and most of whom extrapolated Anglo-American materials to Thai legal text.[24]

The influence of the US was thus evident, and this is significant. The growing presence of US copyright law represented the legacy of the American era, on the one hand, while also anticipating the impending American war on piracy, suggesting that the emergence of Thai copyright scholarship was not purely internal to the legal communities but was also connected to Thai society at large. A good illustration of this point is the discussion on the protection of foreign works, which initially attracted Thai lawyers' attention for reasons that were primarily legal

20 The implementing legislation came out in 1983 and dealt primarily with the protection of foreign works in reference to Thailand's obligations under the Berne Convention. For an example of the academic response, see Jarun Pakdeethanakul, '**ลิขสิทธิ์ระหว่างประเทศ**' ('International copyright') (1984) 13(4) *Thammasat Journal of Law* 39.

21 In retrospect, Jarun's commentary on the new copyright act signalled the growing academic interest in copyright law regarding basic legal concepts (e.g. originality, fixation, moral right, fair use) and contemporary issues (e.g. rights in videos, protection for US materials, software protection). Clearly, this development was caught up in, and stimulated by, the IP-related controversy around the Thai–US trade disputes that began in the mid-1980s.

22 Following Jarun's foray into commenting on the new copyright act, *Chulalongkorn Law Journal* dedicated a special section to copyright law that featured three articles by three different authors. See Chavalit Atthasart, '**ลิขสิทธิ์ภายในประเทศ**' ('National copyright') (1984) 9(1) *Chulalongkorn Law Journal* 128; Thatchai Supapolsiri, '**องค์ประกอบมูลฐานของงานอันมีลิขสิทธิ์**' ('A fundamental element of a protected work') (1984) 9(1) *Chulalongkorn Law Journal* 173; Sampan Hoonpayon, '**กฎหมายลิขสิทธิ์กับธุรกิจวีดีโอ**' ('Copyright law and the VHS business') (1984) 9(1) *Chulalongkorn Law Journal* 191.In that same year, Thai legal scholarship also saw the publication of one of the earliest Thai copyright law textbooks, which has remained a much-consulted book to date. See Chaiyot Hemaratchata, ***คำอธิบายกฎหมายลิขสิทธิ์*** *(A commentary on copyright law)* (1st edn, Nitibunnakarn 1984).

23 Prior to the 1980s, available records show that publications on copyright law were few and far between. By contrast, just the decade of the 1980s saw an emergence of authors such as Chaiyot Hemaratchata, Thatchai Supapolsiri, Pisawat Sukonthapan, and Vichai Ariyanuntaka, whose names and work have become highly familiar to those currently working in the field.

24 By way of illustration, authors such as Jarun Pakdeethanakul, Chaiyot Hemaratchata, Thatchai Supapolsiri and Chavalit Atthasart—all of whom are now well-known academics/practitioners—were at one point educated at a prestigious university in either England or the US.

but later transformed into socio-political concerns when the protection of foreign works assumed central importance in the Thai–American disputes.[25]

More fundamentally still, the emergence of Thai copyright scholarship might not have happened in the way it did if it had not been for the growing phenomenon of media piracy. New media technology, notably cassette tapes, began to create new forms of consumption and new business practices in the late 1970s,[26] and by the early 1980s, basic copyright questions were being raised with direct implications for the new businesses, both legitimate and otherwise, that had sprung around VHS and video recorders.[27] Then, soon enough, the emerging software industry would begin to infiltrate legal discussions, and software piracy would quickly become a highly contentious topic by the late 1980s. Suffice it to say that the reception of US copyright law in Thai legal scholarship did not just coincide with the booming of the new media. Rather, they were part of the same social processes that also produced the consumer culture that was thriving during the decade of the economic boom.

Culture of Consumption/Consumption of Culture

The continued liberalisation of the Thai economy into the 1980s also carried forward the development of the consumer culture that had been revitalised during the Cold War years. Thailand's embrace of the free market economy not only opened the Thai market to global trade and investment but also exposed Thai consumers to global tastes and values.[28] As such, when came the decade of the economic boom, which began in the late 1980s, a new agent of change also emerged in modern Thai history. The sudden expansion of the urban, white-collar middle class went hand in hand with their increasing influence in the political and cultural spheres.[29] No longer the passive followers of modernising kings and autocrats, this urban middle class began staking their claim to cultural authority through their purchasing power.

That consumerism was labelled 'the new religion' by Sulak Sivaraksa, a prominent Thai thinker, attesting to the state of Thai consumer culture in the early 1990s.[30] However, Kasian Tejapira finds it more analytically useful to focus on the underlying

25 For a comparison, see Jarun (n 20); Boonlart Eimwattana, '**ลิขสิทธิ์กับซอร์ฟแวร์ของสหรัฐอเมริกา**' (Copyright and US Software) (1987) 17(4) *Thammasat Journal of Law* 202.

26 The birth of the Thai music industry in the early 1980s was largely due to the proliferation of cassette tapes and the promulgation of the TCA 1978. For more details, see Suphontat Techaburana, '**การเปลี่ยนแปลงและการขยายตัวของธุรกิจเพลงไทยสากลในทศวรรษที่** 2520' ('The change and expansion of Thai pop music business in the 1980s') (2016) 3(2) *Thammasat Journal of History* 115.

27 See for instance Ian Buruma, 'Thailand's film-makers sink in a morass of money vs artistry' (1983) 122(43) *Far Eastern Economic Review* 53; Hamilton, 'Video crackdown or the sacrificial pirate', 515.

28 Baker and Pasuk, *History* (n 1) 230–231.

29 Ingawanij, 'Hyperbolic heritage', 27.

30 Sulak Sivaraksa, '**ศาสนาและวัฒนธรรม: วิกฤตและแนวโน้ม**' ('Religion and culture: Crisis and tendency') (1994) 16(1) *Silapawattanatham* 103.

'consumption of culture' behind the deplored 'culture of consumption.'[31] Kasian points to the fact that Thai people had come to associate consumption with freedom and cultural consumption with identity construction.[32] The latter point finds ample expression in the social imagery that Adadol Ingawanij encapsulates in the concept of '*Thai-sakon.*'[33] This oxymoron evokes the idea of being *Thai* yet *sakon*—or Thai but universal (Western)—which seemed to permeate Thai public discourse towards the end of the millennium. This *Thai-sakon* imagery was symptomatic of what Kasian calls the 'cultural schizophrenia' that characterised the urban middle class during the economic boom.[34]

In her study of Thai cinema at the turn of the century, Adadol observes the embodiment of *Thai-sakon* in the marketing and public reception of *Suriyothai* (2001), then the most expensive and highly anticipated Thai film, whose theatrical release became nothing short of a national event.[35] As a patriotic biopic, *Suriyothai* tells an epic, royal–nationalist story of a 16th-century warrior queen who fought to her death to defend the Kingdom of Ayutthaya, an ancient capital of Siam, from an invasion by the Burmese, Siam's pre-colonial archenemy.[36] As a big-budget film project, *Suriyothai* was a conscious attempt to make a Thai film on the scale of Hollywood blockbusters.[37] The marketing of the film deliberately played on the imagery of *Thai-sakon* by circulating marketing materials that lent international credibility to the film, thereby creating a sense of Thai prestige on a global stage.[38]

As the epitome of *Thai-sakon*, *Suriyothai* set an example of cultural modernity against the lowbrow 'plebian' modernity of the 16 mm film era.[39] As discussed in relation to post-war Thailand, 16 mm film denotes the infamous period in Thai cinema history when films were produced in great numbers but were often deemed lacking in value and quality, falling short of the *sakon* standard that many perceived in Hollywood.[40] The contrast between the contempt for past 16 mm films and the jubilant reception of *Suriyothai* illustrates how Thai cinema 'aspires to connote Thai difference from the West, while also attaining an accepted 'universal' (*sakon*)

31 Pracha Suveeranon and Kasian Tejapira, *อัตลักษณ์ไทย: จากไทยสู่ไทยๆ และบริโภคความเป็นไทย (Thai Identity: From Thai to Thai-Thai and the Consumption of Thainess)* (Fah-diew-kan 2011) 110.
32 ibid 112–113.
33 Adadol, 'Hyperbolic heritage' (n 29) 29.
34 Pracha and Kasian (n 31) 135.
35 Adadol, 'Hyperbolic heritage' (n 29) 15, 193.
36 *Suriyothai* (2001), dir Prince Chatrichalerm Yukol.
37 See David Rooney, 'The Legend of Suriyothai' (*Variety*, 29 September 2002) <https://variety.com/2002/film/reviews/the-legend-of-suriyothai-1200545836/> accessed 20 February 2025.
38 This included a projection of international sales, a speculation on Oscar contention, and the employment of the West's elite professionals (e.g. Francis Ford Coppola). In this way, the media promotion of this Thai film is revealing of the changing face of Thai sensibility in the IMF era. See Adadol, 'Hyperbolic heritage' (n 29) 194–198.
39 See the discussion on Thai cinema history at the beginning of this chapter.
40 See also Ainslie, 'Post-war Thai cinema', 305–306, 314–315.

standard of filmic quality.'[41] In this way, the imagery of *Thai-sakon* also testified to the persistence of coloniality in the field of cultural production.

In the Name of Free Trade

Meanwhile, the late 20th century also saw a new kind of *sakon* standard emerging at the intersections of law and culture. Beginning in the 1980s, Western industrialised countries—the major IP exporters—began demanding that Thailand raise the standards of IP protection and tackle the widespread piracy of media products. The most active and insistent among these countries was the US, which placed the Thai government under enormous pressure with the Special 301 Report that posed the threat of trade sanctions.[42] The troubled relations with the US sent reverberations through the country, not least because the US market was crucial to Thailand's export-dependent economy.[43]

Just how much the Thai–US relations had deteriorated can be seen in the shifting perceptions among Thai policymakers, who had gone from calling the US '*maha-mitr*' ('great friend') to labelling US trade policy as bullying and insincere.[44] Adding fuel to this antagonistic view was the way in which the US government pursued its interests in media copyright and the protection of software and pharmaceutical products by making demands to Thailand in ultimatum-like terms.[45] Ultimately, the tension between the two nations escalated into full-blown trade disputes with the arrival of the Special 301 Report, which posed a serious threat to Thailand's export sector that had played a crucial role in the country's economic boom.[46]

Beginning in 1989, the US Trade Representative (USTR) designated Thailand as a Priority Watch List country in the Special 301 Report.[47] Essentially, this signified that Thailand was found to have 'serious intellectual property rights deficiencies,' which meant the US could withdraw the trade privileges that Thai exports

41 Adadol, 'Hyperbolic heritage' (n 29) 3.

42 See Office of the US Trade Representative (USTR), 'Special 301' on intellectual property' (25 May 1989) <https://ustr.gov/sites/default/files/1989%20Special%20301%20Report.pdf> accessed 20 February 2025. See also Thomas N O'Neill III, 'Intellectual property protection in Thailand: Asia's young tiger and America's growing concern' (1990) 11 *University of Pennsylvania Journal of International Law* 603.

43 See for instance 'Thai cabinet resigns over US copyrights' (*New York Times*, 30 April 1988) <https://www.nytimes.com/1988/04/30/world/thai-cabinet-resigns-over-us-coprights.html> accessed 20 February 2025. This incident is discussed later in this chapter.

44 Pongphisoot (n 19) 261.

45 Wiwat Mungkandi, 'Changing perceptions of Thai-US relations' in Clark Neher and Wiwat Mungkandi (eds), *US-Thailand Relations in A New International Era* (University of California 1990) 71–72.

46 See Niphon Puapongsakorn and Peter Mytri Ungpakorn, *เอกสารประกอบการสัมมนาเรื่องผลกระทบของการเจรจารอบอุรุกวัยต่อประเทศไทย (Materials for the Seminar on the Impact of the Uruguay Round on Thailand)* (Thailand Research Fund and Thailand Development Research Institute 1996) 19.

47 USTR, 'Special 301' (n 42) 1.

had benefited under the US Generalised System of Preferences (GSP).[48] The US government insisted that Thailand, among other things, implement accelerated action plans to address issues concerning IP protection.[49] Failing to improve the situation would put Thailand at risk of not only losing the GSP but also facing other trade sanctions.[50]

Access to the US market and the GSP were crucial to the Thai economy of that time, to the extent that American demands for software protection were central to the country's political controversy.[51] In 1988, the then-Prime Minister, Prem Tinsulanonda, had to dissolve the Parliament following a dispute over a copyright bill that would have ensured copyright protection for software.[52] This political setback came as a result of the government's hasty attempt to push through a copyright amendment bill to address the lack of legal protection for US software.[53] Controversial as it was, software was eventually recognised as a literary work in the subsequent enactment of the TCA 1994.[54]

The promulgation of the TCA 1994 occurred amidst serious concerns about Thailand's declining status in the Special 301 Report.[55] In addition to addressing the issue of software copyright, the TCA 1994 introduced two more important changes to the TCA 1978, namely the introduction of the rental right and performers' rights. In fact, much of the parliamentary debate revolved around the question of whether and to what extent the government should concede to the US demand for software protection. In the end, software copyright was considered a necessary concession in a trade-off that would secure the GSP for Thai exports and guarantee the continued inflow of foreign direct investment.[56] In this way, the rupture in Thai–US relations reflected the global trend of protectionist policies that were on the rise in the 1980s and subsided by the mid-1990s with the establishment of the WTO and the signing of the TRIPS Agreement.

Understandably, the narratives surrounding the Thai-US disputes often focus on the enactment of the TCA 1994, but the most important legacy of this controversy arguably lies in the broader socio-political impact of global IP politics.[57] Crucially, the strong pressure from the US brought about institutional readjustments within the Thai government, which led to the two notable additions of the Department of Intellectual Property (DIP) and the Central Intellectual Property and International

48 ibid. For the suspension of the GSP, see 19 US Code § 2411(c)(1)(a) (1988).

49 USTR, 'Special 301' (n 42) 8.

50 For the scope of the retaliation actions, see 19 US Code § 2411 (1988).

51 On the political impasse see '**วิเคราะห์ปัญหาพระราชบัญญัติลิขสิทธิ์ ฤาจะปิดประตูตีกันเอง**' ('Analysing the problem with the Copyright Act, Will this turn into a domestic fight?') *Siamrath Weekly* (Bangkok, 9–15 October 1988) 15, 15–17.

52 ibid.

53 ibid.

54 Copyright Act BE 2537 (1994), s 6.

55 House of Representatives Deb 29 September 1993, vol 18, year 2 (first session), no 3, 7, 13–15, 57, 65.

56 ibid 46, 68, 74, 104.

57 This legacy includes the changing idea of the Thai self, as discussed later in 'Inauthentic self'.

Trade Court (CIPIT). The introduction of these two specialised agencies proved critical in promoting the awareness and expertise of IP within the state apparatuses.

The setting up of the CIPIT has contributed to the development of specialised judges and legal practitioners, as well as a growing body of IP decisions.[58] Similarly, the consolidation of the government's IP-related responsibilities into the mandate of the DIP, a new agency under the Ministry of Commerce, has created a focal point within the Thai bureaucracy for developing and promoting IP law and policy. Furthermore, the DIP has been acting as an active agent for legal transplantation and functioning as the institutional factor in the increasing visibility of IP in the public sphere.[59]

Contested Modernity

The arrival of the CIPIT and the DIP signified the changing perceptions towards IP law within the government. Perhaps unsurprisingly, the protracted bilateral disputes with the US had forged a close association between IP and international trade in the minds of Thai politicians and policymakers. Following the difficulties they had experienced with the Special 301 Report, these local actors came to view IP law primarily as a matter of global trade and competition.[60] Indeed, the issue with software protection had brought to their attention the economic power of IP, which they now regarded as the comparative advantage of Western industrial countries but lacking in Thailand.[61] Thus, when the US government returned in the early 2000s to negotiate a Free Trade Agreement (FTA) that would contain TRIPS-plus obligations, the Thai government appeared prepared to make a necessary concession on IPRs to secure the best possible deal for the country's export-oriented economy.[62]

Unsurprisingly, the government's position did not go down well with local non-governmental organisations (NGOs) and civil society organisations (CSOs).[63]

58 Notably, the establishment of a specialised IP court was followed by an emphasis on IP law knowledge in the judicial recruitment policy, which explains the popularity of a master's degree programme in IP among Thai LLM students at Western universities.

59 Perhaps the most visible of the DIP's promotion efforts is the yearly IP fair, which is usually held in a big conference hall and lasts for a few days. In its 2022 edition, the IP fair programme included seminars, art and technology exhibitions, performances, and business consultations. See <https://www.thailandipfair.com/> accessed 20 February 2025.

60 In an inauguration speech before the parliament on 23 March 2005, re-elected Prime Minister Thaksin Shinawatra identified the role of IP in the global production chains, in which Thais 'worked more but earned less' because they worked for' foreign IP owners' or had to rely on them for imported technology. See Thaksin Shinawatra, '**คำแถลงนโยบายของคณะรัฐมนตรี**' ('Cabinet's policy statement') (Royal Thai Government) <https://www.thaigov.go.th/aboutus/history/policy/11> accessed 20 February 2025.

61 Chayun Tantivasadakarn, ***นโยบายการค้าระหว่างประเทศของไทยในช่วงปี*** *2543–2549* (*Thailand's International Trade Policy between 2000 and 2006*) (Thailand Research Fund 2006) 6–8.

62 Rungrawee Pinyorat, 'Civil groups want IP off trade-talks agenda with US' (*The Nation*, Bangkok, 12 October 2014).

63 See for instance '**ต้าน** FTA **ไทย-สหรัฐ**!' ('No to Thai-US FTA') (Manager Online, 18 January 2006) <https://m.mgronline.com/politics/detail/9490000006951> accessed 20 February 2025.

In what the Thai government considered a significant trade deal with the US, they saw neo-colonialism and mobilised strong resistance on the contentious issues of access to medicine, seed monopoly, and consumer welfare.[64] One of their key battlegrounds since the early 1990s had been the expansion of inequalities in the wake of the economic boom.[65] After the turn of the century, the concerns of these NGOs and CSOs were extended to include the apparent injustice of the global IP system, which added to the problems of urban–rural inequalities and the adverse impact of development on local livelihoods and the environment.[66] The transition from domestic to global did not take place overnight. It is worth noting that these local actors had been calling for a different engagement with globalisation in the aftermath of the 1997 Asian Financial Crisis (AFC).[67]

Also known as the 'Tom Yum Kung' crisis, which refers to its beginning in the collapse of Thailand's bubble economy, the AFC put an end to the premature celebration of 'the Fifth Asian Tiger' with a financial collapse that reportedly left a million Thais unemployed.[68] This crisis necessitated an intervention by the International Monetary Fund (IMF), which put the country under harsh austerity conditions.[69] The IMF bailout package offered Thailand a road to recovery but heavily barricaded it with humiliating austerity measures and reforms.[70] Many Thai companies went out of business or were acquired by foreign institutions at fire-sale prices.

The trajectory of the idea of globalisation, or '*loka-phiwat*' in Thai usage, aptly summarises Thailand between the early 1990s and the early 2000s. Kasian notes that prior to the AFC, the popular notion of *loka-phiwat,* which literally translates as 'to turn the globe,' embodied confidence in the national project of Thai capitalism.[71] On a more individual level, *loka-phiwat* indicated a progressive and outward-looking worldview, the embodiment of which was the figure of '*khon-roon-mai*' ('the new generation') who, as Kasian observes, predominantly stood for the urban, white-collar middle-class.[72] However, after the country was turned upside down by the burst of the financial bubble in 1997, nationalist

64 ibid.

65 See Kanokwan Manorom, 'NGOs and civil society in Thailand' in Pavin Chachavalpongpun (ed), *Routledge Handbook of Contemporary Thailand* (Routledge 2020) 367–370.

66 For instance, a coalition of academics, NGOs, and CSOs called '**กลุ่มศึกษาข้อตกลงเขตการค้าเสรีภาคประชาชน**' or 'FTA Watch' began their activities in 2003 to campaign against the US-Thai FTA negotiations, and they are still active. For more details, see '**เกี่ยวกับเรา**' ('About us') (FTA Watch) <http://www.ftawatch.org/about> accessed 20 February 2025.

67 See for instance Kasian Tejapira, 'Post-crisis economic impasse and political recovery in Thailand: The resurgence of economic nationalism' (2002) 34(3) *Critical Asian Studies* 323, 334; Kanokwan (n 816) 369.

68 Pasuk Phongpaichit and Chris Baker, *Thailand's Crisis* (Silkworm Books 2000) 86.

69 ibid 38.

70 ibid 38–42.

71 Kasian, 'Post-crisis economic impasse' (n 67) 331.

72 Kasian Tejapira, '**ความเป็นไทยที่เปลี่ยนแปลง ตอน สาธารณกรรม**' ('Thainess in a state of change: Profanation') (*Manager Daily*, Bangkok, 5 November 1992) 16.

sentiments and anti-globalisation movements went hand in hand to demand an engagement with globalisation on different terms. Here, the frustration and humiliation were acutely captured in the popular comparison of the IMF loan repayment, which was completed in 2003, to the idea of regaining independence.[73]

Arguably, it was no coincidence that the field of popular culture also saw the rise of the independence motif among Thai films that were released in the IMF years.[74] As evident in the case of *Suriyothai* (2001), which offers a striking example, the period between the late 1990s and early 2000s saw the release of many high-budget, historical dramas that share the common theme of 'national pride in the face of adversity.'[75] Be it a story of a pre-colonial war with a neighbouring country or an encounter with European colonialism, Thai films of the IMF years offered Thai audiences a cultural means of articulating the urge to counter the perceived danger of globalisation. This urge eventually found its real-world expression in the anti-neoliberal globalisation movements that gained political traction in various social groups that coalesced around the post-AFC drive towards economic nationalism.[76] These movements generated significant social forces that carried through into the first decade of the new millennium, where IP protection emerged as a new battlefront.[77]

II. The Coloniality of Knowledge

This energy was soon channelled into deeper political struggles in Thailand. The mobilisation of a royal nationalist, anti-government coalition resulted in months of demonstrations and political deadlocks that in the end led to the country's 12th military coup in 2006.[78] So perhaps, one could say that Thai NGOs and CSOs effectively managed to keep the FTA talks at bay, as the coup brought the negotiations to a halt. However, it is also evident that the globalisation of IPRs had already let the genie out of the bottle. Especially for the Thai government in 2008, 'the power of knowledge' visibly took on a new resonance.

No longer was IP a mere bargaining chip in a trade deal with developed nations. The government's promotion of the 'Creative Economy' as the country's new economic engine famously envisaged a new path towards development closely tied

73 A celebration of the 'Independence Day' was organised after the Thai government managed to repay the IMF loans two years ahead of schedule. For more details, see Pasuk Phongpaichit and Chris Baker, *Thaksin: The Business of Politics in Thailand* (Silkworm Books 2005) 142.

74 Rachel Harrison, 'Mind the gap: (En)countering the West and the making of Thai identities on film' in Harrison and Jackson (eds), *The Ambiguous Allure of the West,* 108–111.

75 ibid 109.

76 Kasian, 'Post-crisis economic impasse' (n 67) 333–335.

77 The emergence of FTA Watch (n 66) in 2003 provides a case in point.

78 For further discussion on the role of NGOs and CSOs in the 2006 coup, see Giles Ji Ungpakorn, 'Why have most Thai NGOs chosen to side with the conservative royalists, against democracy and the poor?' (2009) 1(2) *Interface* 233. See also Erik Martinez Kuhonta and Aim Sinpeng, 'Democratic regression in Thailand: The ambivalent role of civil society and political institutions' (2014) 36(3) *Contemporary Southeast Asia* 333.

to the expansion of the copyright system.[79] As discussed later, the embrace of the creative economy imagery reflected not only the economic power of knowledge but also the coloniality of global power, which had become concentrated in the IP system. But first, the following discussion begins by situating the globalisation of copyright protection—and the challenges it faced—with the broader history of Thai–Western relations.

Modernity/Piracy

In November 1990, a *New York Times* article sternly called Thailand 'the capital of piracy.'[80] Its author, Steven Erlanger, began his observation of IP infringements in Thailand as follows:

> A stroll in any direction from any Bangkok hotel brings one face to face with the souk-like world of commercial piracy: cheap copies of Benetton, Lacoste, (. . .) and, most especially, thousands upon thousands of videotapes and pop-rock and jazz cassettes.[81]

Later, the author returned to repeat the same message, quoting piracy figures from the International Federation of Phonograms and Video Producers.

> In Bangkok alone, 2,500 shops sell pirated tapes, and 95.5 per cent of all tapes sold in Bangkok are pirated, according to federation figures. Outside Bangkok, legitimate tapes represent less than 1 per cent of sales.[82]

Indeed, Thailand saw a significant increase in the number of copyright cases that reached the Supreme Court. Between 1990 and 1993 alone, the Court delivered more copyright judgments than it had the entire decade prior.[83] Furthermore, the questions that the Court had to address in many of these decisions revolved around

79 See '**เปิดโมเดล** Creative Economy **อัด** 2 **หมื่น ล. ดัน** 15 **อุตสาหกรรมสร้างสรรค์**' ('Unveiling the Creative Economy model: Injecting 20,000 million (THB) to push 15 creative industries forward') (*Manager Online*, 5 December 2009) <https://mgronline.com/smes/detail/9520000146841> accessed 20 February 2025; NESDB and Thailand Creative & Design Centre (TCDC), ***รายงานการศึกษาเบื้องต้นเศรษฐกิจสร้างสรรค์*** (*A preliminary study on creative economy*) (Office of the National Economic and Social Development Council, May 2009) <https://www.nesdc.go.th/article_attach/CreativeEconomy.pdf> accessed 20 February 2025.

80 Steven Erlanger, 'Thailand is the capital of pirated tapes' (*New York Times*, 27 November 1990) 15.

81 ibid.

82 ibid.

83 Based on the search through the official database for Thai Supreme Court decisions, the Court delivered 23 copyright decisions between 1990 and 1993 compared with 15 decisions in the 1980s. However, these figures do not represent the trend of copyright lawsuits in the 1990s in comparison with the 1980s because those copyright cases that were decided in the early 1990s could have been started many years earlier. The point being made here is just that there was an evident upsurge in the copyright decisions corresponding to the apparent socio-economic change of the late 20th century.

the phenomena of media piracy, which had escalated into a full-blown trade dispute between Thailand and the US by the end of the previous decade.[84] In this context, it was probably no coincidence that this article was published amidst the rising tensions in Thai–US trade relations.[85] So naturally, the politico-economic backdrop of the US war on media piracy casts reasonable doubt on the reported numbers, which must be taken with a pinch of salt.[86] That said, this article is still worth the attention for its portrayal of Thai piracy.

Perhaps unsurprisingly, the author of the New York Times article attributed the issue of piracy in Thailand to a lack of law enforcement.[87] Although linking piracy to law enforcement in this way was by no means new, what is interesting about this instance is the portrayal of Thai pirates. The author claimed that one of the article's informants insisted his name not appear in the piece because he had already received 'four bullets in the mail from pirate businessmen.'[88] This idea of a rogue trader was later repeated when the author cited Western diplomats and business representatives to assert that 'Thai pirate companies are waging a concerted campaign against enforcement, including threats of violence.'[89] Connecting these anecdotes was the depiction of lawlessness: The author portrayed the phenomenon of piracy in Thailand as wild and dangerous, alluding to the idea of a backward society.

Self-Consumption

Meanwhile, as perplexing as *Thai-sakon* was in the early 1990s, the issue of Thai identity became even more complicated in the aftermath of the 1997 economic crisis. The post-AFC ideal of *sakon* took on a new connotation; it was no longer merely an allusion to Western modernity. As Adadol argues, *sakon* now signified a desire for global recognition that imbued the imagery of *Thai-sakon* with the illusion of Thai prestige on a global stage.[90] In other words, *Thai-sakon* became a refuge for the Thai middle class after the devastating crushing of their confidence in the national project of Thai capitalism. This also suggests that the upsurge of Thai nationalism in the heritage films of the IMF years was, in fact, a prime symptom of the socio-political condition it sought to deny.[91] And indeed, the claim of Thai exceptionalism was ironically presented in the *sakon*/Hollywoodized aesthetics.

84 Of the 23 decisions, 12 involved a VHS containing a foreign film and a Thai defendant accused of infringing audiovisual copyright.
85 For the timing of the publication, see 'In the name of free trade' in this chapter.
86 For discussions about the validity of piracy figures produced by industry-backed research, see Joe Karaganis, 'Rethinking piracy' in Joe Karaganis (ed), *Media Piracy in Emerging Economies* (Social Science Research Council 2011) 8–13.
87 Erlanger (n 80). The author cited Western diplomats and business representatives who claimed that the Thai government did not make its best effort in acting against local pirates.
88 ibid.
89 ibid.
90 Adadol, 'Hyperbolic heritage' (n 29) 262.
91 Harrison, 'Mind the gap' (n 74) 111.

Similarly, the on-screen fight for independence paradoxically marked the reality of off-screen dependence on intrusive foreign powers. This kind of contradiction is reminiscent of the crypto-colonial conditions that characterised Siam during the era of colonial modernity.[92]

As the discussion on Siamese-Western relations already demonstrated, the heuristic concept of crypto-colonialism does not partake in typology and classification.[93] Rather, it examines the relations of domination underlying 'the constant reiteration of national claims of independence by countries whose continuing dependency on more powerful states is manifest and enduring.'[94] This understanding highlights the similarities between 19th-century Siam and post-AFC Thailand regarding the complex nature of Western influence. Notably, some parallels can be drawn between on the one hand, the relationship between the quest for *siwilai* and the emergence of Thai nationalism and on the other, the way in which the *sakon* standards allowed royal–nationalist history to circulate 'as mass commercial products but are nevertheless endowed with an upscale, uplifting veneer.'[95] The possibility of this comparison highlights Siam/Thailand's deep entanglement in a global nexus of cultural hierarchies—one that imbued Western models with cultural authority. Ultimately, this came to encompass the IP system.

Inauthentic Self

With copyright protection emerging as the new *sakon* standard, maintaining 'respect for copyright' also assumed priority in the self-display of externally imposed values. Striving for international respectability, the public exhibition of copyright culture was performed by the Thai government through the occasional public destruction of illegal media goods.[96] However, these actions were often performative,[97] while media piracy remained widespread.

It was common knowledge that located in the heart of Bangkok was Pantip Plaza, a premier electronics mall with a reputation for counterfeit and pirated

92 See 'A Crypto-Colony' in Chapter 1.

93 Herzfeld, 'The conceptual allure of the west,' 174.

94 ibid.

95 Adadol, 'Hyperbolic heritage' (n 29) 77–78.

96 As with the continued inclusion of Thailand in the annual review of the Special 301 Report, this public gesture by the Thai government has continued to date. For a recent example, see Phusadee Arunmas, 'B173m fake goods destroyed' (*Bangkok Post*, 27 August 2022) <https://www.bangkokpost.com/thailand/general/2378000/b173m-in-fake-goods-destroyed> accessed 20 February 2025.

97 Especially with the public destruction of infringing goods, the word 'ceremony' is an appropriate description of such official events, which was even once held online due to the COVID-19 pandemic. See Sukontip Jitmongkolthong, 'First virtual broadcast of a counterfeit-goods destruction ceremony in Thailand' (Tilleke & Gibbins, 7 December 2020) <https://www.tilleke.com/insights/first-virtual-broadcast-of-a-counterfeit-goods-destruction-ceremony-in-thailand/> accessed 20 February 2025.

goods.[98] At the famous Pantip Plaza, a wide array of pirated media were on display and available for purchase over the counter.[99] It is hard to believe that Pantip Plaza's reputation really slipped through the sieve of official knowledge.[100] More likely and commonly believed was the corruption in law enforcement agencies,[101] but corruption is not an explanation; rather, it needs one. Unless one assumes the state of lawlessness in which the corrupted government simply rules by brute force, where does this leave us?

This paradox—where piracy was widespread yet officially disavowed—reflects Herzfeld's cultural intimacy. An interesting aspect of his crypto-colonial analysis is the connection to his concept of cultural intimacy,[102] for this is where the public performance of law enforcement and the everyday experience of piracy can be understood side by side in an anthropological account of nationalism. Here, nationalism is not a formal abstraction imposed by the state but rather a sense of identity that emerges from within the zone of cultural intimacy.[103] Herzfeld describes cultural intimacy as

> the recognition of those aspects of an officially shared identity that are considered a source of external embarrassment, but that nevertheless provide insiders with their assurance of common sociality.[104]

Alleged national traits and self-stereotypes fall within this description, which directly concerns a nation-state because 'the formal operations of national-states depend on coexistence—usually inconvenient, always uneasy—with various realisations of cultural intimacy.'[105] Especially under crypto-colonial conditions, Herzfeld argues, cultural intimacy is observable in a social domain where the state

98 This reputation caught the attention of foreign media, with a BBC report branding Pantip Plaza a 'notorious' market for pirate software. See Larry Jagan, 'Thailand's struggle with goods piracy' (BBC News, 13 December 2001) <http://news.bbc.co.uk/1/hi/world/asia-pacific/1709267.stm> accessed 20 February 2025.

99 For a detailed description, see Duncan McDuie-Ra and Daniel Robinson, 'Pirate places in Bangkok IPRs, vendors and urban order' in Martin Fredriksson and James Arvanitakis, *Property, Place, and Piracy* (Routledge 2007).

100 This is not least because Pantip Plaza was named in the USTR list of Notorious Markets in 2013. See USTR, '2013 out-of-cycle review of notorious markets' (USTR, 12 February 2014) 18 <https://ustr.gov/sites/default/files/FINAL-PUBLISHED%202013_Notorious_Markets_List–02122014.pdf> accessed 20 February 2025.

101 A comparable picture of corruption in law enforcement is offered in one sociological study of media piracy in the neighbouring countries of the Philippines and Vietnam. See Vivencio Ballano, *Sociological Perspectives on Media Piracy in the Philippines and Vietnam* (Springer 2016) 195–198.

102 Herzfeld, 'Dilemmas and ambiguities' (n 93) 182.

103 Michael Herzfeld, *Cultural Intimacy: Social Poetics in the Nation-State* (3rd edn, Routledge 2016) 10.

104 ibid 7.

105 ibid 8.

represses due to externally imposed values while covertly accepting local practices to maintain the citizens' loyalty.[106]

Regarded as shameful and embarrassing, media piracy was a common aspect of everyday life in Thailand. Contrary to the outward display of self-calibration towards the new *sakon* standard, the state–citizen relations were characterised by a tolerance for illegal activities related to media piracy. The high cost of 'authentic' copies was often raised in public discourse as a justification, but the need to justify these actions also indicates public awareness that the ubiquity of pirated copies was a source of shame and embarrassment. As Herzfeld suggests, this rueful self-recognition constitutes the collective representation of intimacy in an 'imagined community' where—unlike the classical notion of *Gemeinschaft* or a community defined by personal social ties—sociality is not based on face-to-face relations.[107] In this way, it is worth noting again that Herzfeld also warns of the 'usually inconvenient, always uneasy' coexistence between a nation-state and cultural intimacy.[108] In the case of media piracy and the Thai state, the rift in their coexistence became more evident with the arrival of the Creative Economy policy.

The Pirate King Dreaming of a Creative Economy

Contentious as it was, the global IP politics of the late 20th century taught Thai policymakers a valuable lesson about the economic value of knowledge and information. In hindsight, it becomes clear that it was only a matter of time before they finally turned to creativity in search of a new path to development. Thus, it came as no surprise when the Thai government announced its vision of the 'Creative Economy' in 2008, aiming to equip the country with a new engine for economic growth.[109] The government located the main thrust of the Creative Economy in the creation of economic value through creativity and the commercial exploitation of IP.[110] The close association between the Creative Economy and the IP system was evident from the start, and the development of both was deemed to go hand in hand.[111] And in this way, the introduction of the Creative Economy policy in 2008 appeared to pick up on a thread that had run through the 1990s.

As discussed, once Thai policymakers were alerted to a new source of economic power in the form of knowledge and information, this awareness formed

106 Herzfeld, 'Dilemmas and ambiguities' (n 93) 176.

107 Herzfeld, *Cultural Intimacy* (n 103) 11.

108 ibid 8.

109 For more details, see Alongkorn Parivudhiphongs, 'Creative industry policy in Thailand: A story of rise and demise' in Lorraine Lim and Hye-Kyung Lee (eds), *Routledge Handbook of Cultural and Creative Industries in Asia* (Routledge 2018).

110 NESDB and TCDC (n 79) 24.

111 Alongkorn (n 109) 74–75.

part of the domestic policy landscape, which allowed their imagination to be captured by the rapid rise of global creative economy discourse in the 2000s.[112] In other words, it was the recognition that the advanced economies of the West had already shifted their focus to knowledge and information—as opposed to material objects—that drew Thai policymakers' attention to the idea of creativity as an economic resource. In this way, the Creative Economy presented Thailand with the opportunity to emulate what many had seen since the 1990s as constituting the comparative advantage of the West. Nevertheless, the government's adoption of the creative economy imagery is not noteworthy solely because it represented a changing perception of IP in Thai policymaking. Perhaps more implicitly, the announcement of the Creative Economy policy in 2008 also pointed to a shift in the political discourse around the notion of development that would later prove enduring.[113]

The 2008 policy initiative was a deliberate attempt by the newly formed government to capitalise on the global rise of the Creative Economy.[114] Indeed, the new idea was relentlessly promoted as a tried and tested one that had been borrowed from developed countries.[115] Despite being promoted as the 'new economy,' the Creative Economy was no less capitalistic and precarious than the one that hadcollapsed in the 1997 financial crisis, albeit with an apparent shift towards cultural resources. Therefore, it is fair to say the pursuit of development continued into the 21st century, and one might be excused for thinking that the Creative Economy was merely a policy fad that primarily served a political purpose.[116]

Arguably, to think otherwise could even be seen as turning a blind eye to the political conflicts that were unfolding. After all, the Creative Economy was a flagship policy of the new government that had been formed contentiously 'inside a military base,' as the media liked to describe it.[117] Following the coup of 2006 that marked the return of military authoritarianism, the political fallout immediately plunged Thailand into protracted political conflicts that in 2008 produced the military-backed government of Prime Minister Abhisit Vejjajiva, who in 2010 oversaw a military crackdown on anti-government protesters that ended in violence

112 ibid. This awareness was embodied in the Department of Intellectual Property, which also played a leading role in the implementation of the Creative Economy policy.

113 This refers to the subsequent 'Thailand 4.0' Policy, to be discussed in Chapter 5.

114 NESDB and TCDC (n 79) 10–12.

115 ibid.

116 See also Alongkorn (n 109) 77–79.

117 See for instance '**นายกไม่รับข้อเสนอยุบสภา 15 วัน**' ('Prime Minister rejects the suggestion to dissolve the parliament') (*Post Today*, 23 March 2010) <https://www.posttoday.com/politics/19545> accessed 20 February 2025. See also Rachel Harvey, 'Thai prime minister defends rise to power on Facebook' (BBC, 7 June 2011) <https://www.bbc.co.uk/news/world-asia-pacific-13685253> accessed 20 February 2025.

and the deaths of 94 people[118] This occurred less than a year after he unveiled the 'Creative Thailand' campaign.[119]

With the arrival of the creative economy imagery, what was once a zone of cultural intimacy began to transform into a set of cultural assumptions, which are now expressed in the familiar, self-deprecating phrase 'We Thais like to copy.' Furthermore, these cultural assumptions have become pervasive in the public discourse on the production and consumption of creative products and will therefore be the focus of the discussion in Chapter 5.

118 The People's Information Centre, April–May 2010 crackdown, *Truth to justice: A fact-finding report on the April–May 2010 crackdowns in Thailand* (July 2012) 5 <http://www.pic2010.org/en-report/> accessed 20 February 2025.

119 See '**อภิสิทธิ์เน้นศก.สร้างสรรค์เพื่อพัฒนาปท.ให้เข้มแข็ง**' ('Abhisit focuses on a creative economy to strengthen the country') (*Komchadluek*, 31 August 2009) <https://www.komchadluek.net/news/26619> accessed 20 February 2025.

Part III

A Line of Escape

5 On Belatedness

'Nation branding' has become a prevalent term for branding practices among national governments aimed at improving their image in the global marketplace,[1] but for Thailand's military junta, which came to power in 2014, the interest of international audiences appeared to be secondary when the junta government unveiled an economic development initiative known as 'Thailand 4.0.'[2] It is fair to say that the official fanfare and subsequent media campaigns that followed were primarily directed at the Thai people.[3]

Thailand 4.0 presented a vision of future Thailand as an innovative and prosperous nation.[4] The term 'Thailand 4.0' represented a specific model of socio-economic development, illustrating a chronological series of developmental stages that culminated in the desired phase 4 characteristic of advanced economies worldwide.[5] The official campaign reiterated a timeline of developmental models that began with agriculture, progressed through various levels of industrialisation, and ascended towards innovation.[6] This is indeed a self-fulfilling prophecy for the future of Thailand that yet again engaged in the politics of development. Furthermore, IP was intended to be integral to the envisaged future.

1 For more discussion, see Melissa Aronczyk, *Branding the Nation: The Global Business of National Identity* (OUP 2013).

2 See a similar assessment in Petra Desatova, 'Thailand 4.0 and the internal focus of nation branding' (2018) 42(4) *Asian Studies Review* 682.

3 See for instance '**รัฐบาลเร่งสร้าง "คนไทย 4.0" รองรับโลกยุคใหม่**' ('Government to develop "Thai 4.0" in preparation for the new age') (BBC Thai, 2 January 2017) <https://www.bbc.com/thai/thailand-38487137?ocid=socialflow_facebook> accessed 20 February 2025.

4 See Secretariat of the Prime Minister, ***วารสารไทยคู่ฟ้า*** (*Thai-khu-fah Journal*) (issue 33, 2017) 2 <https://www.thaigov.go.th/ebook/contents/detail/74#book/> accessed 20 February 2025 (*Thai-khu-fah* 2017).

5 See Secretariat of the Prime Minister, ***วารสารไทยคู่ฟ้า*** (*Thai-khu-fah Journal*) (issue 31, 2016) 20–21 <https://www.thaigov.go.th/ebook/contents/detail/18#book/> accessed 20 February 2025 (*Thai-khu-fah* 2016).

6 ibid. See also Apornrath Phoonphongphiphat, 'Thailand 4.0: Are we ready?' (*Bangkok Post*, 2 January 2017) <https://www.bangkokpost.com/business/1173133/thailand-4–0-are-weready-> accessed 20 February 2025.

DOI: 10.4324/9781003592037-9

To realise this future, Thailand 4.0 placed creativity and innovation at the heart of the nation's economic development strategies.[7] This inevitably brought IP to the forefront of planning and implementation by government agencies. However, the predominant concern shifted from the familiar issue of inadequate and ineffective enforcement to one of ownership and commercialisation.[8] In the government's vision for an innovation-driven economy, more IP signified higher competitiveness in the global marketplace.[9] Thus, the unveiling of Thailand 4.0 pointed to an interesting development in Thailand's economic development discourse. Since the introduction of the Creative Economy policy in 2008, one can observe an upward trajectory of a combative narrative of IP that valorises ownership and exploitation through the politics of having to 'catch up.'

A national report on the reform of the IP system presented to the Prime Minister in 2016 is typical of the emerging narrative.[10] In line with the Thailand 4.0 initiative, the report primarily discussed the economic role of IP and proposed strategies for improving the situation of the country's IP system.[11] Central to the report's analysis and recommendations was the 'IP value chain,' which depicted the economic life of IP as a cycle of creation, protection, commercialisation, enforcement, and repeat.[12] The focus on the so-called value chain also explains the absence of any discussion regarding 'balance' in the proposed reform, which is characterised by a drive towards ownership and exploitation.[13]

Indeed, the very absence of the notion of balance is significant as it highlights the belatedness of this report and the broader discourse of Thailand 4.0. This is not to suggest that the omission of the balance notion—an otherwise integral concept to contemporary IP discourse—constitutes a major flaw that would lead to the failure of Thailand 4.0. Rather, the fact that the proposed reform itself lagged behind the global IP discourse resonates with the idea of a 'belated' national project that the junta government leveraged to mobilise public support. While belatedness is a legitimate concern, the following discussion examines it as the problem of how change is perceived through the lens of development.

7 ibid. See also NESDC, ***แผนพัฒนาเศรษฐกิจและสังคมแห่งชาติ ฉบับที่** 12 **พ.ศ.** 2560–2564* (*12th National Economic and Social Development Plan, 2017–2012*) 3 <https://www.nesdc.go.th/ewt_dl_link.php?nid =6422> accessed 1 March 2023. (12th NESD Plan).

8 12th NESD Plan (n 877) 12.

9 ibid 6.

10 Economic Reform Committee, ***รายงานของคณะกรรมาธิการขับเคลื่อนการปฏิรูปประเทศด้านเศรษฐกิจสภาปฏิรูปแห่งชาติ เรื่อง การปฏิรูประบบทรัพย์สินทางปัญญา*** (*Report by the ERC on the reform of intellectual property system*) (National Reform Council, June 2016) <https://dl.parliament.go.th/handle/20.500. 13072/478808> accessed 20 February 2025.

11 ibid.

12 ibid 4.

13 See further discussion of the balance notion in 'The Social in Copyright Law' in Chapter 6.

I. The Politics of Creativity

While a search for 'the new economy' had been a concern for Thai economists since the devastation of the AFC in 1997,[14] Thailand 4.0 should not be mistaken for serious economic discussions. Contrary to the media fanfare that turned the unveiling of Thailand 4.0 into a national event, the initiative suffered from a lack of clarity and cohesion, which are crucial for a cross-sector and nationwide implementation.[15] The valorisation of innovation as a silver bullet for social and economic progress quickly blew up the meaning of creativity. In the end, Thailand 4.0 became a discourse about everything and nothing, encompassing various topics from digitisation and start-ups to traditional culture and tourist attractions.[16] In this respect, the campaigning for Thailand 4.0 served as a self-branding strategy for the military government, which sought to reinforce its legitimacy through a self-fulfilling prophecy of innovation.[17]

One indication that the branding of Thailand 4.0 was designed for Thai audiences is the government's attempt to tap into public sentiments regarding the country's experience of colonialism.[18] A case in point is the following quote from Suvit Maesincee, then Minister of Higher Education, Science, Research and Innovation, who led the charge and was arguably the face of the Thailand 4.0 campaign.[19] In his public communications as the de facto spokesperson for Thailand 4.0 and the driving force behind this campaign, Suvit used social media to alert the public to the urgency of what he called 'the Second Great Reform,'[20] for which he had the following to say:

> Every country aspires to be a First World country that is secure, prosperous and sustainable.
>
> Many countries in Asia, such as Japan, South Korea, Singapore, and Taiwan, have all been successful in their transition from being a country in 'The Second World,' classified as developing countries, to 'The First World,' recognised as developed countries, over the past century.

14 See the 'The Pirate King Dreaming of a Creative Economy' in Chapter 4.

15 See for instance Pongphiphat Banchanon, '**วิเคราะห์ไทยแลนด์** 4.0: **วิสัยทัศน์ชาติที่ยังขาดรายละเอียด**' ('Analyse Thailand 4.0: A vision lacking in detail') (BBC Thai, 6 January 2017) <https://www.bbc.com/thai/thailand-38527250> accessed 20 February 2025.

16 See for instance *Thai-khu-fah* 2017 (n 874) 13–14.

17 See also Desatova (n 2) 9–11.

18 For example, see an interview in Anucha Thongterm, '**รายงานพิเศษ: สุวิทย์ เมษินทรีย์ สานความฝันเป็นความเชื่อ แล้วลงมือทำ**' ('Special report: Suvit Maesincee, turn a dream into belief and make it happen') (*Matichon*, 1 February 2017) <https://www.matichonweekly.com/column/article_23242> accessed 20 February 2025.

19 Before the ministerial appointment, Suvit wrote a PhD at the Kellog School of Management as well as many books on business management and marketing. Suvit also holds a bachelor's degree in pharmacy.

20 Suvit, like many other Thai public figures, uses Facebook as his main public communication channel.

> This successful transition resulted from a 'systemic Great Reform,' which encompassed economic, social, political, and administrative dimensions.
>
> Thailand is no different. The threats of colonialism during the reigns of Rama IV and Rama V led to the decision of His Majesty King Rama V [King Chulalongkorn] to undertake a major reform initiative, which involved the construction of the Thai nation-state alongside reforms that structured administration at the central, regional, and local levels; social reforms, including the abolition of slavery education and the *prhai*[21] system; educational reforms; transportation reforms, and more—all aimed at modernising the country to be on par with other civilised countries.
>
> The systematic Great Reform during the reign of Rama V resulted in a structural transformation of Thailand's economy, society, and politics over the following century.
>
> However, following the Great Reform during the era of King Chulalongkorn, Thailand lacked systematic and continuous reforms . . . until now.[22]

Here Suvit, who holds a PhD in marketing and co-authored the book *The Marketing of Nations* (1997),[23] is attempting to mobilise public support by appropriating and manipulating the geopolitics of the late 19th century and the Cold War language of development. As seen in earlier discussions, the clever diplomacy of King Chulalongkorn and his numerous modernisation projects were credited with the independence of Siam even as the rest of Southeast Asia was colonised by Western powers.[24] In this way, and in the way that IP globalisation has been framed as a form of imperialism, the shift in Thai IP policy towards ownership and exploitation, as discussed earlier, presents a local repercussion of the global IP politics that echoes the dynamic between Western colonialism and the modernisation of Siam.

Thus, what is significant about the use of national history in the 4.0 campaign is the allusion to the pervasive sense of Thai exceptionalism and the grand narrative of the Thai nation, which centres on the King's ability to fend off external threats and preserve the nation's independence. This myth is made even more significant by the fact that it was the Siamese ruling elite who invented this grand narrative in response to the threat of Western colonisation.[25] In this way, the independence myth does not hide Siam's encounter with Western colonialism. Rather, it serves

21 This term refers to a free commoner who was subjected to unpaid forced labour in the traditional order.

22 Suvit Maesincee, '**ถึงเวลาปฏิรูปขนานใหญ่รอบที่สอง**' ('It is time for the second great reform') (Facebook, 20 April 2006) <https://www.facebook.com/drsuvitpage/posts/1399691550337571:0> accessed 20 February 2025.

23 Philip Kotler, Somkid Jatusripitak, and Suvit Maesincee, *The Marketing of Nations: Strategic Approach to Building National Wealth* (Simon & Schuster 1997).

24 See 'Colonial Encounter and Thai Modernity' in Chapter 1.

25 Winichakul, '**ประวัติศาสตร์ไทยแบบราชาชาตินิยม: จากจากยุคอาณานิคมอำพราง สู่ราชาชาตินิยมใหม่หรือลัทธิเสด็จพ่อของกระฎุมพีไทยในปัจจุบัน**', 58.

to distort the coloniality of power—or the patterns of power that came to dominate Thai society—with the narratives of Thai exceptionalism.[26]

This is why it seemed to make historical and cultural sense for Suvit to reproduce the myth of independence while promoting the '5Fs'—another marketing strategy of the 4.0 campaign—that stand for food, fashion, film, fighting, and festival.[27] The 5Fs represented the application of Thailand 4.0 to the cultural domain, supposedly embodying the exceptional identity of Thai people and their traditions.[28] In an interview published in a state media outlet, Suvit evoked the idea of exemplar Thainess when linking the 5Fs to cultural elements such as *Muay Thai* (traditional Thai boxing) and *Songkran* (traditional Thai New Year).[29] This certainly evokes the desire for *Thai-sakon* in Thai cinema, as discussed in Chapter 4, and as seen next, narrowing the focus of the present discussion to the 'film' in 5F helps to re-situate the issue of belated modernity and repetition in history, discussed in Chapter 2, within the present discussion.

The Thai State and the State of Thai Cinema

Since the late 2000s, the film industry has increasingly attracted interest from the Thai government and policymakers.[30] A recent government report on the national strategies for film and video promotion announced the ambition to establish Thailand as the centre of the film industry in Southeast Asia and a significant player in the global market.[31] Regarding copyright law, the report viewed copyright protection as a key area of consideration and a strategic domain for government action. It identified law enforcement and individual conscience as the primary challenges facing the film industry. Odd though it may sound, it set the elusive objective of raising the moral consciousness among Thai citizens by 50 per cent.[32] Other than that, however, no copyright-related issues appeared to have received the government's attention. Not a mention was made of the overall balance of interests, which is otherwise a constant feature of contemporary copyright discourse. While the national strategy did address the circumstances of individual creators and artists, it primarily focused on developing creative professionals to meet the demands of the nation's new knowledge-based economy.[33] Suffice it to say, the priorities of the national strategy lay in standardising the film product and building the nation brand.

26 See 'Modernity/Coloniality' in Chapter 1.

27 *Thai-khu-fah* 2017 (n 874) 14.

28 ibid.

29 ibid.

30 Ministry of Culture, '**ยุทธศาตร์การส่งเสริมอุตสาหกรรมภาพยนตร์และวีดีทัศน์ ระยะที่** 3 (พ.ศ. 2560–2564)' ('Strategies for film and video promotion, phase 3, 2017–2021') 4 <https://filmcommittee.m-culture.go.th/th/db_63_filmcommittee_9/8579> accessed 20 February 2025 (national strategy).

31 ibid 17.

32 ibid 18.

33 ibid 19.

A brief survey of Thailand's film industry reveals a picture of an uncertain future that undermines the optimism of the national strategy.[34] For instance, the production of Thai feature films has been in a steady decline, with local productions struggling to establish a foothold in a market dominated by Hollywood.[35] In its home country, Thai films have been stigmatised as over-repeating a formula and cutting corners, often being judged against the spectacles and visceral thrill of expensive Hollywood blockbusters.[36] The diminished confidence among Thai audiences is also reflected in the idea that a Hollywood film is worth a trip to the cinema, whereas many would prefer not to pay to watch a Thai film in a theatre—still the main source of revenue for Thai films—since a pirated version is usually available online.[37] The trend also suggests that the popularity of illegal online access has indeed been detrimental to Thai film, albeit in a more specific way than the broad and simple claim that those responsible are stealing from the film industry.[38]

For Thai filmmakers, these troubling trends are exacerbated by the monopoly in the exhibition sector; two major cinema chains effectively hold the power to determine what Thai audiences can watch and which films will be produced.[39] Although the national strategy may signal a turning point for the film industry, several caveats exist regarding issues surrounding film exhibition and working conditions as well as the fact that the relationship between film censorship and the Thai state goes back a long way.[40]

An ongoing history of controversial censorship decisions suggests that the Thai state has yet to separate national film policy from national security.[41] Even the national strategy acknowledged that film censorship had long been the paradigm of Thailand's film policy.[42] This was certainly the case under the Sarit-Thanom regime, which took a notable interest in film regulation following the flourishing

34 For an extensive examination, see Thanayod Lopattananont, Voraluk Klasukon, and Saksit Thaweekul, '**ความสอดคล้องของโครงสร้างอุตสาหกรรมการผลิตภาพยนตร์ไทยกับยุทธศาสตร์การส่งเสริมภาพยนตร์และวีดิทัศน์ ระยะที่** 3 (พ.ศ. 2560–2564)' ('Coherence of Thai film industry and Thailand's strategies for film and video promotion, phase 3, 2017–2021') (Dhurakij Pandit University research paper, DPU 2020).

35 Perhaps one sign of a struggling film industry is a lack of systematic data collection, including statistics on film production and distribution. To get a sense of the struggle facing Thai filmmakers, see for instance 'Thai film industry in crisis' (*The Nation*, 15 March 2023) <https://www.nationthailand.com/lifestyle/30284197> accessed 20 February 2025.

36 Thanayod, Voraluk, and Saksit (n 34) 77–78.

37 ibid.

38 See further discussion on piracy and Thai film in 'Creativity at Risk' in Chapter 6.

39 Unaloam Chanrungmaneekul, ***โรงหนัง สายหนัง ความ(ไร้)อำนาจของคนดูและศิลปิน ธุรกิจการฉายภาพยนตร์และสังคมไทย*** *พ.ศ. 2440–2561 (Cinemas, Distributors, and the (Absent) Power of Audiences and Artists: The Business of Film Exhibition and Thai Society 1897–2018)* (Thailand Research Fund 2020) 148.

40 Even the government acknowledges this; see n 30 3.

41 For more discussion, see Sudarat Musikawong and Malinee Khumsupa, 'Film is dangerous: Ten years of censorship in Thailand's cinema, 2010–2020' (2022) 30(1) *South East Asia Research* 377. See also Matthew Hunt, *Thai Cinema Uncensored* (Silkworm Books 2021).

42 National strategy (n 30) 3.

of film production and consumption in post-war Thailand.[43] Consider the decade between 1962 and 1972 alone: The number of state personnel involved in film censorship rose to an estimated 177, and this number does not include members of the Film Censoring Council that Sarit established as an appellate body.[44] What this means for the present discussion is the fact that cinema embodies the internal dynamics of modernity/coloniality. So while the wait continues for the changing policy direction to produce meaningful results, Thai filmmakers and the viewing public will probably continue to be perplexed by controversial film censorship.[45] On the whole, therefore, any Thai filmmaker would be justified in not sharing the optimism of the government.

An Idiom of Power

In fact, one could even argue that it is wise to exercise a degree of scepticism when it comes to Thailand's film policy. This cautious attitude is particularly relevant in the wake of Korean cinema's global success, a phenomenon that is epitomised by the international success of *Parasite* (2019), which became the first non-English speaking film to win the Academy Award (Oscar) for Best Picture in 2020.[46] The news that *Parasite* had won the prestigious award sparked widespread debates in Thailand, particularly due to the perception that the two countries began to break into the global film market around the same time.[47]

However, the question that seemed to attract the most attention was how Thai film could emulate South Korea's success in exercising 'soft power' on the global stage.[48] This sudden yet belated interest in what is otherwise an old concept in foreign policy discussions struck a dissonant note.[49] The Thai usage of 'soft power' stretched this English term to the extent that this concept from international politics lost its diplomatic dimension. Ultimately, soft power became associated with

43 See Boonyaketmala, 'The rise and fall of the film industry in Thailand', 73–74.

44 Sathian Janthimathorn, '**กรรมการเซ็นเซ่อร์กับหนังต้องห้ามในเมืองไทย**' ('Censorship Board and the films banned in Thailand') (1972) 3 *Social Sciences Review* 26, 27–28.

45 For a recent censorship controversy, see Patrick Frater, 'Thailand's censors get heavy with horror film "Hoon Payon"' (*The Variety*, 10 March 2023) <https://variety.com/2023/film/news/thailand-censorship-horror-film-hoon-payon-1235549168/> accessed 20 February 2025.

46 See for instance 'Oscars 2020: South Korea's Parasite makes history by winning best picture' (BBC, 10 February 2020) <https://www.bbc.co.uk/news/entertainment-arts-51440241> accessed 20 February 2025.

47 See for instance Chanchana Homsab, '**อุตสาหกรรมหนังเกาหลี: สตาร์ทพร้อมไทย 15 ปีผ่านไปถึงฝั่งออสการ์**' ('Korean film industry: Started off at the same time with its Thai counterpart and reached the Oscar 15 years later') (*Way Magazine*, 30 July 2020) <https://waymagazine.org/the-cinema-of-south-korea/> accessed 20 February 2025.

48 ibid. See also Arusa Pisuthipan, 'Lessons from Korea on soft power' (*Bangkok Post*, 28 March 2022) <https://www.bangkokpost.com/opinion/opinion/2286226/lessons-from-korea-on-soft-power> accessed 20 February 2025.

49 The term 'soft power' was coined in the late 1980s by the political scientist Joseph Nye to refer to a country's ability to attract and persuade rather than the hard power of military coercion. For more discussion, see *Soft Power: The Means to Success in World Politics* (Public Affairs 2004).

a variety of cultural exports from Thai food and fashion to Thai boxing and Thai film.[50]

Arguably, the interesting issue here is not what meaning has been lost in translation but how the term could captivate the public's imagination.[51] Furthermore, the ease with which the Thai government has assimilated soft power into its political campaigns and rhetoric draws attention to the cultural politics behind the Thai fascination with soft power. By yoking the notion of soft power to the existing discourse of an IP-driven economy, the government's endorsement of Thai film as soft power reiterated its crypto-colonial commitment to national development.[52] It was therefore a matter of local legitimacy rather than foreign diplomacy that animated the official discourse of Thai soft power.[53] This shows that soft power has become part of the language that signifies the perennial politics of having to catch up with developed nations.

True to the powerful notion of development, a sense of belatedness permeated public discussions on the role of Thai film in promoting Thai soft power. At the heart of these discussions is the perception of Thai film as backward in comparison with the polished modern offerings from Hollywood, reflecting the relentless pursuit of the *sakon* standard out of fear of falling even further behind. But this sense of helplessness ultimately presents a false dilemma, which exposes the problem with framing legal development through the politics of having to catch up. Nevertheless, is there really another way than to carry on chasing? How can one escape the dilemma when the very field of experience is structured by relations of before and after?

II. Global Doctrine and Local Knowledge

In 2014, the release of a nostalgic yet reflective documentary by Nawapol Thamrongrattanarit offered Thai cinephiles a chance to reminisce about life in the late 1990s.[54] Titled in English, *The Master* weaves together various personal accounts about the legendary Van Video, a bootleg VHS shop that was pivotal to Thailand's alternative cinema scene in that era. Mysterious yet familiar, Van Video became somewhat of an urban legend before Mr Van closed his business in the early 2000s.[55]

50 See for instance 'Government eyes soft power as revenue source' (National News Bureau of Thailand, 13 March 2022) <https://thainews.prd.go.th/en/news/detail/TCATG220313171829419> accessed 20 February 2025.

51 By contrast, see Peera Charoenvattananukul, 'Window-dressing policy: Thailand's misuse of soft power as cursory practice' (2023) *Asian Politics and Policy* 1.

52 See 'PM trumpets "soft power" of Thai delights' (*Bangkok Post*, 11 April 2022) <https://www.bangkokpost.com/thailand/general/2293202/pm-trumpets-soft-power-of-thai-delights> accessed 20 February 2025.

53 ibid.

54 Nawapol Thamrongrattanarit (dir), *The Master* (2014).

55 Pimrapee Thungkasemvathana, 'Masterly delve into the video age' (*Bangkok Post,* 5 December 2014) <https://www.bangkokpost.com/life/arts-and-entertainment/447358/masterly-delve-into-the-video -age> accessed 20 February 2025.

To the former clients who appear in Nawapol's film, Mr Van is also a mysterious character and understandably so. After all, his small but profitable enterprise was anything but legal, and Mr Van himself was undeniably a criminal under Thai law,[56] but none of this seemed to bother his clientele, for whom Van Video was like an oasis in the desert. One of the interviewees used to make a weekly 500-mile journey to Bangkok by overnight bus just to visit Van Video.[57]

Nawapol intentionally named his film *The Master* to evoke the idea of a teacher.[58] He explained that Mr Van emerged at a time when alternatives to Hollywood films were very limited.[59] Thus, Van Video helped him discover the world of alternative cinema, where he realised that filmmaking need not be a large-scale and expensive enterprise, and even he could dream of becoming a filmmaker.[60] As viewers will learn from *The Master*, Nawapol is not alone in treasuring these fond memories of the small video shop that seemed to be a lifeline for many Thai film enthusiasts in the late 1990s. Echoing similar sentiments are the cast of well-known filmmakers, critics, and scholars, who joyfully recount their numerous trips to Van Video and their encounters with its owner.

However, it is worth noting that the film neither idolises Mr Van nor romanticises media piracy. The happy trip down memory lane ends midway through when the questions shift to the copyright issues surrounding Mr Van and his illegal enterprise. As it turns out, all the interviewees acknowledge the illegality and profitability of Van Video, although some admit they did not feel guilty when purchasing the pirate videos. Several of the interviewees, who are now filmmakers themselves, also talk about the negative impact of media piracy on their work and the people they are working with. Yet not all the interviewed filmmakers reflect negatively on their own experiences of being pirated, and as for Nawapol himself, this section of *The Master* makes it clear that he is under no illusions about the impact of media piracy.

When all is said and done, however, *The Master* neither passes judgement on piracy nor contemplates a possible way forward. Overall, this is a film that tells a personal story narrated through the memories of those who lived through those same moments between the late 1990s and early 2000s. As such, *The Master* is not

56 An intentional infringement of copyright constitutes a criminal offence under the TCA 1994, which was in force at the time. See TCA 1994, s 69–70.

57 The story is predominantly told from the perspective of those who lived in Bangkok, which further highlights how much more difficult it must have been for non-Bangkok residents to access alternative and arthouse films.

58 See Nattakorn Wiengin, 'คุยกับ เต๋อ-นวพล จดหมายรักถึง 'ร้านแว่นวิดีโอ" ('A conversation with Ter-Nawapol: A love letter to "Van Video"') (*Matichon TV,* 4 December 2014) <https://www.youtube.com/watch?v=_eYj9lOrBF0> accessed 20 February 2025.

59 ibid.

60 ibid. Nawapol's experience resonates with many of his contemporaries throughout Southeast Asia. Tilman Baumgärtel observes that the digital boom in cinema technology has empowered filmmakers in this region to produce alternative and personal works. See Baumgärtel, 'Imagined communities, imagined worlds: Independent film from Southeast Asia in the global mediascape' in Tilman Baumgärtel (ed), *Southeast Asian Independent Cinema* (Hong Kong University Press 2012) 30–31.

only a nostalgic journey for Thai cinephiles but also an attempt to document these hazy moments in the recent history of Thai cinema.[61] Nawapol manages to capture the nuances and specificities that are normally glossed over in the anti-piracy discourse, which tends to be reductive and polarising.[62] But this alone is not the reason why *The Master* has arguably made a significant intervention in contemporary copyright debates.

The fact that *The Master* was produced in the early 2010s means that the interviewees do not just recall historical facts but also reflect on the past from their present perspective. This reflexive process is evident in the above-mentioned sequence, where the exploration of the copyright issues veers into a personal reflection from a buyer-turned-filmmaker. Piracy did not disappear with pirated videos and Van Video; it multiplied and moved online.[63] Nawapol says little about the internet other than suggesting that it was one of the reasons for Mr Van to call time on his shop,[64] but those who watched this film in 2014 must have found the subject of video piracy surprisingly relevant.[65]

The era of videotapes and VHS players is gone, but the moral questions facing these Thai cinephiles also resonated with the growing number of Thai internet users in the early 2010s.[66] Scarcity quickly became a thing of the past, although the ability to watch anything at any time and wherever one wanted also brought into focus the moral implications around personal use of infringing materials.[67] In this context, the story of Mr Van's enterprise raises the question of what to make of the unease felt among the film cast. Is it appropriate to infer that the legal concept of copyright has finally penetrated Thai society? Although tempting, this view risks oversimplifying the relationship between law and society, contradicting the

61 Nawapol made the same point in an interview with Wiengin (n 58).

62 For more discussion, see Debora Halbert, 'Intellectual property piracy: The narrative construction of deviance' (1997) 10(28) *International Journal for the Semiotics of Law* 55.

63 For a brief discussion on the trajectory of media piracy in Thailand after the video era, see Raviwan Rakthinkamnerd, '**ย้อนรอยยุคทองของ "ซีดีเถื่อน" จากเฟื่องฟูสู่ต่ำสุดหลังรัฐประหาร**' ('Tracing the golden age of "illegal CDs": From its ascendancy to the demise after the 2009 Coup') (Thai-Journal Citation Index Centre, 24 April 2016) <https://www.tcijthai.com/news/2016/04/scoop/6167> accessed 20 February 2025.

64 Pimrapee (n 55) notes with a sense of disappointment that Nawapol stops short of making a more meaningful connection between the historical subject of video piracy and the more recent phenomena of Youtube, iTunes, and Pirate Bay.

65 For an indication of this possibility, see Sithikorn Wongwudthianan, 'Copyright and what's right' (*Bangkok Post*, 11 December 2013) <https://www.bangkokpost.com/opinion/opinion/384200/copyright-and-what-right> accessed 20 February 2025. The author gives a personal account of the abundance of choice, both offline and online, when it comes to pirated materials and ponders the moral implications of buying/downloading them.

66 According to the National Electronics and Computer Technology Centre, the total number of internet users in 2014 was approximately 25 million, compared to 2.3 million users in 2000. See 'Internet User' <http://internet.nectec.or.th/webstats/internetuser.iir?Sec=internetuser> accessed 20 February 2025.

67 Sithikorn (n 65) is a good example. See also Pimrapee (n 55).

insights from legal sociology in Chapter 4.[68] Furthermore, to reach such a conclusion suggests that Thailand had just caught up with the global IP discourse, reinforcing the sense that the country always lags and will never be truly contemporary with the West.

This curse of belatedness highlights a fundamental issue in conceptualising a situation where something resembles something else that has gone before.[69] A recurring theme in earlier discussions is the difficulty in seeing and naming differences in what seems like repetition. The following discussion further examines this issue of repetition, reassessing the relationship between repetition and learning. As will be seen, it is more productive to think of repetition as 'beginning and beginning again' than equating it with a recurrence of something that has gone before.

In *The Master*, the particularity of Van Video's rise and decline raises broader questions concerning who, how, when, and where that get underneath the apparent belatedness of legal development in Thailand.[70] It is unfortunate that *The Master* barely explores these questions, but this is not the only film by Nawapol that directly addresses the issues surrounding copyright and the governance of knowledge and information. Two years prior to releasing *The Master*, Nawapol created a short film titled 'Sorry'; in this film, the issue of copying takes centre stage.

What Is Wrong With Copying?

In 2012, Thai television channels aired a short film, which credits Nawapol as both the director and screenwriter.[71] At a length of about 18 minutes, 'Sorry' opens with what seems to be a routine and innocuous meeting at a film production house. The staff members gather to watch a new music video by Sun, who appears to be an established director in the industry. Tensions soon arise as the young intern Imm raises suspicions of theft when asked to share her opinion. Initially, she begins with general questions, asking Sun about his inspiration and working process. These questions are then met with a self-adulation disguised as a humble reply: Sun claims that the idea only came to him in a dream one night before the deadline. In response, Imm decides to confront him with a straightforward question regarding whether he has copied others' work. The senior members quickly leap to Sun's defence and become increasingly hostile towards the young intern. These

68 See 'A Logic of Legal Transplants' in Chapter 3.

69 See 'Belated Modernity and the Repetition of History' in Chapter 2.

70 This raises the question of what really gets repeated, which is central to Gilles Deleuze's concept of repetition, which will be discussed in 'Repetition and Learning' later in this chapter.

71 Nawapol Thamrongrattanarit (dir), *Sorry* (2012). An authorised full-length film is available online: '"Sorry", A film by **นวพล ธำรงรัตนฤทธิ์** (Nawapol Thamrongrattanarit)' (YouTube, 4 January 2013) <https://www.youtube.com/watch?v=XRhPZM9lKyk> accessed 20 February 2025. See also Seksan Rojmethakul, '**กทม เปิดตัวการ์ตูน-หนังสั้นรณรงค์หลักสูตรโตไปไม่โกง**' ('Bangkok Metropolitan Authority unveils animation and short films for the "Growing Good" school curriculum') (Isranews, 2 November 2012) <https://www.isranews.org/investigative/278-thaireform/thaireform-slide/17441> accessed 20 February 2025.

senior members do not let up even when the striking similarities with a music video from a Western indie band appear undeniable. One of them suggests that copying benefits everyone as it gives exposure to the original work. Another believes that there is no such thing as an original idea, insisting that copying is normal and even necessary for development. Eventually, however, Sun gives in to the evidence and admits to stealing. Yet in the final shot of the film, he asks Imm whether the software on her laptop is an authorised version.[72]

Moral Panic

'Sorry' was one of the 15 short films produced by a well-known Thai film studio in collaboration with civil society and government agencies.[73] This joint project was part of the larger initiative by the Thai government to address the issue of corruption—understood as corrupt practices not limited to the political sphere.[74] Nevertheless, this nationwide campaign simply linked the notion of corrupt practices to moral failures, suggesting that they should be addressed through moral education, specifically by cultivating the right set of beliefs and values in the younger generations.[75] Consequently, film and animation studios were enlisted to create media content for theatrical screenings and TV broadcasts, primarily targeting young members of society.[76] For this reason, Nawapol's film was supposed to convey a simple moral lesson: that copying is theft.

For all the short films in this campaign, the producers entrusted the task of delivering the moral of the story to the celebrity monk Wor Wachirametee, whose appearance lends moral credibility to the campaign but goes beyond that.[77] As it turned out, Wor Wachirametee also appeared fluent in the language of Western copyright discourse. To begin with, he referred to Sun's misdeed using the English word 'copy.' He then compared it to stealing, distinguished it from inspiration, and called it a crime. The inclusion of Wor Wachirametee and his moral prescription thus illustrated a local repercussion of the global anti-piracy campaign, suggesting a legacy of the globalisation of IPRs.[78] In this way, his appearance in 'Sorry' also brings back the problem of belatedness discussed in Chapter 2.[79]

72 Most Thai viewers will likely interpret this scene as an allusion to the prevalence of software piracy in Thailand. See 'Inauthentic Self' in Chapter 4.

73 Seksan (n 940).

74 See 'กทม. ร่วมกับนิด้าและองค์กรเพื่อความโปร่งใสในประเทศไทย เดินหน้ารณรงค์โครงการ กรุงเทพเมืองสีขาว 'หลักสูตรโตไปไม่โกง'' ('Bangkok Metropolitan Authority together with NIDA and FACT seek to promote the Bangkok White City Project: The "Growing Good" school curriculum') (*RYT9*, 7 November 2012) <https://www.ryt9.com/s/prg/1524871> accessed 20 February 2025.

75 ibid.

76 ibid.

77 Wor Wachirametee is a well-known author of books about practical and applied Buddhism and, perhaps more crucially, a media personality who preaches Dhamma (the teachings of Buddha).

78 See 'Inauthentic Self' in Chapter 3.

79 See 'Belated Modernity and the Repetition of History' in Chapter 2.

Given the fluency of Wor Wachirametee's moral expressions, it may appear that the global doctrine was beginning to catch on simply because Thai people were trying to catch up.[80] Such is the curse of belatedness that seems to never have been lifted from Thailand. Having come to modernity belatedly, the country's pursuit of *kanphattana* remains characterised by an enduring sense of belatedness that reflects the persistent logic of coloniality.[81] Whether it be the belated arrival of modernity or the belated development of copyright law, the country seems trapped in curious relations of before and after, where any change that occurs always seems belated and resembles something that has happened elsewhere.[82] In this regard, the problem of belatedness is also a problem of how change is understood through the process of naming and categorising.

Through naming and categorising, one conceptualises a situation in which something resembles something else that has come before, and here lies the source of belatedness.[83] As Deleuze suggests, this conceptualisation is undertaken to answer the 'what' question, which gravitates towards a 'representation' of identity and resemblance,[84] just as the event invites a broader set of questions regarding who, how, when, and where that pertain to the particularity of the thing under observation—in other words, it needs 'dramatisation.'[85] Naming and categorising thus constitutes a system of representation that assumes things to be alike through concepts.[86] Anything that falls outside the purview of these concepts may cease to be thought, or as Deleuze says, dissipated into non-being.'[87] Meanwhile, the generality of such concepts also creates the illusion of repetition as a cyclical reproduction or the repetition of the same.[88] Earlier discussions on the problem of naming and categorising Thai modernity point correspondingly to a process of displacement and disguise that, as Deleuze explains, underlies the apparent recurrence of something from before.[89]

Consider the Westernisation of Thai law, for instance. Whether Thailand is classified as a common law or civil law country is a persistent question closely tied to debates around legal methodology and institutional legitimacy.[90] As seen in Chapter 1, this question dates to the late 19th century when common law

80 See also Chakrabarty, 'Belatedness as possibility', 163.
81 See 'The Era of Development' in Chapter 3.
82 See also Chakrabarty, 'Belatedness as possibility' (n 80) 165–166.
83 Chakrabarty, 'The names and repetitions of postcolonial history'.
84 See Deleuze, *Difference and Repetition*, 15.
85 ibid 218. See also Melissa McMahon, 'Difference, repetition' in Charles J Stivale (ed), *Gilles Deleuze: Key Concepts* (McGill-Queen's University Press 2005) 46–47.
86 See Deleuze, *Difference* (n 84) 3, 11. See also James Williams, *Gilles Deleuze's Difference and Repetition: A Critical Introduction and Guide* (Edinburgh University Press 2003) 33–34, 39.
87 Deleuze, *Difference* (n 84) 262.
88 ibid 220.
89 ibid 105.
90 Du Plessis and Kongsatja interestingly note that the insistence on the civil law identity of modern Thai law in Thai legal scholarship does little to critique the actual practice of precedents in the Thai judiciary. They thus raise concerns about the integrity of the Thai legal system and suggest a

influence cannot be easily denied, although the civil law-style codifications often carry considerable weight.[91] Some have suggested that Thailand is indeed a mixed or hybrid legal system.[92] However, this is still classification based on fixing identities and seeking resemblances, whereby anything creative and innovative will fail to be recognised amidst what appears to be merely a diffusion of Western laws.[93]

Lurking behind what Wor Wachirametee presented as the moral lesson of 'Sorry' is a sign of displacement and disguise. As discussed earlier, abstraction and generality characterise his moral judgement of Sun's conduct, and this explains his neglect of the film's ambiguous stance, which is far from condemning copying as theft. As will be seen, 'Sorry' does not appear as interested in passing judgement as in dramatising. The film takes great care to portray the Thai problem of copying in a nuanced and complex way.

Ethical Choice[94]

Contrary to what Wor Wachirametee would have one think, 'Sorry' does not assume a simple distinction between imitation and inspiration. Nor does it argue that stealing can be unproblematically demarcated from everything else that should be considered acceptable. If anything, this film seems to suggest otherwise. A series of ethical choices made by the film's characters as the story unfolds invite critical reflection on the concept of theft. By the final scene, the ambit and validity of this concept seem even more elusive than before, and the only way to understand this is to consider the term 'theft' as a shorthand for ideas and feelings that are yet to be articulated.

It is fair to say that the film's title refers to the feeling of guilt that one develops upon recognising one's own immoral conduct.[95] In the moral discourse of piracy, the crime of copying signifies a disrespect for ownership of knowledge and

problem of unwarranted judicial independence, whereby courts' reasoning can escape scrutiny. For detailed discussion, see Plessis and Suwanapech, 'Law and identity'.

91 See 'Transplanting Western Law' in Chapter 1. See also Andrew Harding, 'Introduction' in Harding and Pongsapan (eds), *Thai Legal History*.

92 See for instance Korrasut Khopuangklang, '**ระบบกฎหมายผสม**' ('Mixed legal system') (2007) 36 *Thammasat Law Journal* 568.

93 By contrast, see an interesting study of Thai trust law that prefers the dramatizing approach of American legal pragmatism to the naming and categorising of legal families in Surutchada Reekie and Narun Popattanachai, 'Thai trust law' in Harding and Pongsapan (eds), *Thai Legal History*.

94 The notion of the 'ethical' as used here refers to the distinction between ethics and morality found in Deleuze's work. In particular, Deleuze explains that 'The difference is that morality presents us with a set of constraining rules of a special sort, ones that judge actions and intentions by considering them in relation to *transcendent values* (this is good, that's bad . . .); ethics is a set of optional rules that assess what we do, what we say, in relation to the ways of existing involved.' See Gilles Deleuze, *Negotiations* (Martin Joughin tr, Columbia University Press 1997) 100.

95 Arguably, it is Sun's refusal to admit his action that constitutes the primary conflict from which the film builds up the tension.

information.[96] Certainly, much has been discussed regarding how the comparison of copying to theft spread globally as a rhetorical strategy of the copyright industry.[97] But the notion of ownership alone does not seem to fully account for the way in which the characters in 'Sorry' use the language of theft. The young Imm does not ask Sun to confess to stealing, only that he has used someone else's property without permission. Similarly, the senior members do not jump to Sun's defence only because they believe he has not trespassed on anyone's IP; stealing does not necessarily refer to a violation of ownership in the tense exchanges among these people. Certainly, their argument revolves around the fact that some objects have been used in a certain way. But the tensions rather arise from the human relations created through these objects, more so than their relations with the objects.[98] A case in point is the senior members' protective stance towards Sun.

As discussed earlier, they respond to the unmistakable similarities and moral implications of theft by shifting the argument to the social aspects of copying. One senior member argues that copying a foreign work is akin to importing that work from abroad, which benefits both the creator of the original work and the Thai audiences. However, viewers may in fact consider this argument a poor excuse, not least because misrepresentation is the primary issue. Nevertheless, many Thais can likely sympathise with the sentiments of giving exposure and gaining access—the cast of Thai cinephiles in *The Master* would probably agree.[99]

The same applies to the subsequent claim that there is no such thing as an original idea. A senior member argues that 'if it weren't for copying, Thai people would still be playing a *kim* or a *ranat* [both are traditional musical instruments]. Anyone picking up a guitar would be copying because they originate from Westerners.' This argument may seem like a blatant attempt to deflect the blame, but it undeniably resonates with the history of Thai cinema—whether in the emergence of film projection as a Western form of spectacle or the perennial drive in the Thai film industry to attain *sakon* standards.[100]

Interestingly, when Sun finally confesses, it is a confession to lying as much as copying, as he acknowledges that he has taken other people's work and presented it as his own. Sun has thus been dishonest about the creative process and taken credit from those who deserve it. Indeed, one can distinguish between the act of taking others' ideas and that of misrepresentation, thereby confining Imm's accusation of

96 Laikwan Pang, *Creativity and Its Discontents: China's Creative Industries and Intellectual Property Rights Offenses* (Duke University Press 2012) 74.

97 See Joe Karaganis, 'Rethinking piracy' in Joe Karaganis (ed), *Media Piracy in Emerging Economies* (Social Science Research Council 2011) 2. See also Lars Eckstein and Anja Schwarz, 'Introduction: Towards a postcolonial critique of modern piracy' in Lars Eckstein and Anja Schwarz (eds), *Postcolonial Piracy: Media Distribution and Cultural Production in the Global South* (Bloomsbury 2014) 13–14.

98 This is similar to the theme of ownership in Chulayarnnon's film, as discussed in 'Life imitating art' in Introduction.

99 See 'What Is Wrong with Copying?' in this chapter.

100 For more information, see the discussion of the film *Railway Sleeper* at the beginning of Chapter 3.

theft to the strictest sense of the term. However, had Sun been honest about using others' work and not taken all credit for himself, the situation may have been different.[101] Surely, his work would have been perceived differently, and understandably so, because the senior members were full of praise for its originality. Nevertheless, what the reactions would have been remains an open question, and the answer will not be found in the moral precept that copying is theft but rather in the ethical choices of taking and using.

In the space of 18 minutes, 'Sorry' adeptly uncovers various ethical dimensions of the otherwise clear-cut morality of theft; in doing so, it reminds the viewers of the complexity of a social phenomenon that tends to be treated as black and white.[102] The film drives this point home in the final scene, where Sun implies that Imm also uses pirated software. This tacit criticism cleverly taps into the collective experience of media piracy, which provides a space of 'cultural intimacy' for many Thais.[103] It is this self-reflexive approach to the issue of copying and theft that makes 'Sorry' not just a social observation but, arguably, a subtle intervention in the debate. It is well-known that the landscape of creative production has been transformed by changes in law, technology, and economy since the late 20th century, but in 'Sorry,' Nawapol offers a glimpse into how Thais have navigated the changing socioeconomic and institutional landscapes by repeating and working through the familiar concept of theft.[104]

Repetition and Learning

At this point, it is pertinent to revisit the issue of Western influence. The notion of cultural imperialism is helpful in highlighting the asymmetrical relations between Thailand and powerful Western countries such as the United States.[105] However, a one-way model of imposition cannot account for Thai actors' ability, if not practice, of riding the waves of homogenisation.[106]

No more satisfactory than imperialism is perceiving Western influence as 'learning from the West.' For one reason, this perspective suggests a temporal lag that reinforces the assumption of belatedness. As discussed previously, Nawapol's *The Master* may be appreciated for its nostalgic depiction of Van Video as the old time. This yearning for the bygone era supports a narrative that portrays the phenomenon

101 Again, deception and shame arguably constitute the main conflict in this film.

102 For an interesting discussion that seeks to shift the perception of piracy from simply being a deviant behaviour, see Ramon Lobato, 'The six faces of piracy: Global media distribution from below' in Robert Sickels (ed), *The Business of Entertainment (Vol. 1): Movies* (Greenwood Publishing 2008) 15–36.

103 See 'Inauthentic Self' in Chapter 3. See also Pimrapee (n 55); Sithikorn (n 65).

104 Chakrabarty makes a similar point regarding the development of socio-political thought outside of the West. See Chakrabarty, 'Postcolonial history' (n 83) 46.

105 See 'Modernity/Piracy' in Chapter 4.

106 For further discussion of such indeterminacy of cultural influence in Thai society, see Herzfeld, 'The conceptual allure of the West'.

of piracy as a transitional phase in the trajectory of modern society towards knowledge ownership.[107] Likewise, an affirmation of such narratives is also evident in his other film, 'Sorry,' particularly in the use of the language of theft and the moral lessons presented at the end.

Furthermore, saying 'learn from the West' also entails the assumption that adopting Western forms and signifiers implies accepting Western meanings and values.[108] This perspective only affirms Euro-American experiences as central and universal, thereby reinforcing the one-way model of cultural influence. Additionally, it suggests a model of learning that has fixed knowledge as the ultimate goal. Here, one learns known solutions to known problems, thereby reiterating pre-determined problems that are otherwise specific to economic, political, or cultural contexts.[109] Consequently, to learn is to follow instructions on how to progress from one stage to another, whether that next stage is referred to as civilisation or development.[110]

In this way, the issue of piracy and the problem with the theft metaphor equally represent a 'learning problem' that can be addressed by simply seeking true modernity through Western knowledge. But so much for Westernisation, or as Deleuze says, 'We learn nothing from those who say: "Do as I do." Our only teachers are those who tell us to "do with me."'[111] For Deleuze, learning should be understood as an experiment; it is a creative process that transcends what is known to discover 'what a body or mind can do, in a given encounter.'[112] If this suggests that instead of assuming the causality of the incentives arguments or readily submitting to the moral claims of the author's personality the Thai experiences should be taken seriously, the question is how one can even begin to do that.

Learning Is Beginning Again and Again

One thing that should be obvious by now is the indeterminacy of cultural influence. When what appears to be a Western influence is critically assessed, it may indeed turn out to be Western-derived rather than an imitation of a Western model. The discussions on *siwilai* and *kanphattana* make it clear that the adoption of Western forms and signifiers does not necessarily mean that the original meanings and underlying values are also accepted.[113] A Western concept may be merged with local ideas or even given a new meaning, making it impossible to determine what is

107 For further discussion, see Eckstein and Schwarz (n 97) 7.

108 By contrast, see Herzfeld, 'Dilemmas and ambiguities' (n 106). For a similar perspective, see also Rachel Harrison, 'Somewhere over the rainbow': Global projections/local allusions in Tears of the Black Tiger/Fa thalai jone' (2007) 8(2) *Inter-Asia Cultural Studies* 194.

109 See the discussion about belatedness and repetition in 'Moral Panic' in this chapter.

110 This model of learning resonates with Thailand's experience with European colonialism in the late 19th century, as discussed in Chapter 2, and US imperialism in the second half of the 20th century, as seen in Chapter 3.

111 Deleuze, *Difference* (n 84) 23.

112 Gilles Deleuze, *Spinoza: Practical Philosophy* (Robert Hurley tr, City Light Books 1988) 125. See also Williams (n 86) 135–136.

113 See 'Siamese-Western Hybridity' in Chapter 2 and 'Identity Politics' in Chapter 3.

homegrown, what is borrowed, and what used to be Western in origin but has been so effectively appropriated that it now forms part of local identity.[114] A similar situation can also be observed in 'Sorry' in the argument about copying and theft. It is far from clear which of the reasons are borrowed, which come from local frames of reference, and which are Western-derived but now follow a more local style of rationality.[115] All of this goes to show how the indeterminacy of cultural influence is a valid point, but to accept this point does not mean whatever lies behind it is necessarily undesirable.

Inasmuch as the coloniality of Thai cultural hybridity can be described in terms of cultural appropriation, as explained in Chapter 2, lying at the heart of the resulting indeterminacy is a process of translation and transliteration that is both ingenious and experimental. Perhaps the quality of being experimental might be unexpected, even though a good example has already been presented in Chapter 2 in the curious case of Khru Liam's *The Divine Nymphs*.[116] Khru Liam's deliberate effort to appeal to the Siamese readers is remarkable for how his strategy to write a story as if it was a translation, while also mindful of too strong a Western flavour, casually blurred the dividing line between writing and translating.[117]

In this way, experimentation also offers a fitting description of how the characters in 'Sorry' navigate the issues of copying and stealing. These characters do not just act out the moral prescription of 'thou shalt not steal' but engage in an ethical dialogue that presents both an examination of and a response to the problem of copying. In this way, what 'Sorry' portrays is quite literally a situation of learning by doing. And indeed, it is through the act of having dialogues and engaging with ideas that new things come to light,[118] or as Deleuze says, 'To repeat is to behave in a certain manner, but in relation to something unique or singular that has no equal or equivalent.'[119] According to Deleuze, one should understand that repeating is to continually start over, for repetition means 'beginning and beginning again.'[120]

Learning to Escape

Let us reconsider the problem of belatedness. The earlier discussion cautioned against taking apparent repetition of something that has gone before at face value—merely considering them as imitations. Instead, it is more productive to

114 Harrison, 'Tears of the Black Tiger' (n 108) 203.

115 See a similar discussion about Western influence in Herzfeld, 'Dilemmas and ambiguities' (n 106).

116 See 'Weaving Self in the Flow of Tradition' in Chapter 2.

117 See Harrison, Rachel Harrison, 'Mummies, sex and sand: Bangkok gothic and the adventure fiction of 'Victorian' Siam' in Harrison (ed), *Disturbing Convention Decentering Thai Literary Cultures*, 94.

118 This is comparable with Deleuze's example of how we learn to swim. In his explanation, a teacher or a swimming instructor may explain swimming facts and techniques, but students actually learn something new when they take these things into the sea and start engaging with the waves. See Deleuze, *Difference* (n 84) 23, 165, 192.

119 ibid 1.

120 ibid 136.

regard repetition as a mode of learning, and this perspective should inform our understanding of development. Inasmuch as development encapsulates the Thai response to belatedness, to develop is the same as to repeat, as what is reproduced is the teleological assumption of belatedness, not just the foreign model being adopted. Such is the curse of belatedness, as seen in the history of Thai copyright law, and one way to overcome this is to think of repetition as beginning and beginning again.

But where do we begin? How do we not get caught up in the problem of belatedness and, for that matter, the logic of coloniality? Here, as Deleuze and Guattari might say, the answer is to begin in the middle[121]: One should neither go back to the essence of Thainess nor work their way back from the ideal of Western modernity. However, this is not to say that one can simply disregard Western influence and begin with a clean slate, as Deleuze and Guattari would caution.[122] Consider the development of copyright law, for example. One will always come to this field as already stratified by a long history of legal transplantation; this means that one will always have to begin in the middle of things, learning and experimenting as one goes. In this way, the image of repetition becomes that of a 'rhizome,' always multiplying in various directions, making new relations and connections between things.[123]

Such multiplicity is embodied in films like Nawapol's, which emerge from an assemblage of diverse elements known as Thai cinema—or Thai cinema perceived as 'a hybrid of people, texts, elements, social practices, discourses, and technologies with all manner of relations between them.'[124] As explored in Chapter 6, the assemblage of Thai cinema is the abode of ethics, where learning takes place. Thus, by examining Thai cinema, one may find a line of escape in the middle of things.

121 'It is never the beginning or the end that are interesting; the beginning and the end are points. What is interesting is the middle,' said Deleuze. See Gilles Deleuze and Claire Parnet, *Dialogues II* (Hugh Tomilson and Barbara Habberjam trs, Continuum 1987) 39. This statement calls attention to the concept of rhizome in his work with Félix Guattari. See Gilles Deleuze and Félix Guattari, *A Thousand Plateaus: Capitalism and Schizophrenia* (Brian Massumi tr, University of Minnesota Press 1987).

122 Deleuze and Guattari, *Thousand Plateaus* (n 121) 25.

123 ibid 6–7.

124 As discussed earlier, the term 'Thai cinema' does not merely refer to a body of films that express homogeneous national culture. The discussions so far have proceeded on a working definition based on the multifaceted meanings of national cinema observed in Higson (n 131), And through these discussions, what has emerged is the picture of a constellation of heterogeneous elements (e.g. stories, objects, bodies, institutions, territories) that combine to create what is generally known as Thai cinema. Therefore, it becomes appropriate to introduce the idea of national cinema as an 'unprincipled assemblage' as explained in Tom O'Regan, *Australian National Cinema* (3rd edn, Taylor & Francis 2005) 36.

6 The Cinema of Interactions

In the digital era, a critical understanding of the creative process increasingly recognises collaboration as the norm rather than the exception.[1] Yet the figure of the auteur continues to loom large in contemporary film culture, with Thai cinema being no exception.[2] This contradiction invites reflection on what authorship means in an industry where filmmaking has always been a collaborative process. It also raises crucial questions about the implications for copyright law. Notably, has legal recognition long been overdue for many contributors who have so far been overlooked by copyright law? If so, what about the audiences who otherwise give meaning to the projected sights and sounds? Does this suggest that they, too, can be considered authors? And if so, how far can the concept of authorship be stretched before the author function becomes dysfunctional? If the author–user distinction were to disappear, what could replace the author function in organising property relations in film production and consumption?

Not only are these questions timely and worthwhile, but they also suggest how practices of authorship may reflect the ever-changing cultural and economic landscapes of creative production, such as filmmaking.[3] From this perspective, it is also fair to say that authorship provides a fertile ground for mapping discrepancies and

1 See for instance Henry Jenkins, *Convergence Culture: Where Old and New Media Collide* (NYU Press 2006); Yochai Benkler, *The Wealth of Networks: How Social Production Transforms Markets and Freedom* (Yale University Press 2006); Henry Jenkins, Ravi Purushotma, Margaret Weigel, Katie Clinton, and Alice Robison, *Confronting the Challenges of Participatory Culture: Media Education for the 21st Century* (MIT Press 2009). For an analysis of how the popular models of creativity are constructed through the IP system, see Gibson, *Creating Selves*. For an attempt to reconceptualise creativity, see Rob Pope, *Creativity: Theory, History, Practice* (Routledge 2010).

2 See for instance Timothy Corrigan, 'The commerce of auteurism: A voice without authority' [1990] *New German Critique* 43; Wikanda Promkhuntong, '"Why so Wong": Transnational Asian cinema through the lens of cinephiles and transmedia fans' in Aaron Han Joon Magnan-Park, Gina Marchetti, and See Kam Tan (eds), *The Palgrave Handbook of Asian Cinema* (Palgrave 2018); Johanna Gibson, '"Gimme the prize": The author dysfunction' (2019) 9 *Queen Mary Journal of Intellectual Property* 127. See also Bently and Biron, 'The author strikes back.'

3 See Corrigan, 'The commerce of auteurism' (n 2); Wikanda, 'Why so Wong?' (n 2).

DOI: 10.4324/9781003592037-10

discontinuities between legal concepts and social practices.[4] Attempts can therefore be made to bridge the gap, by either making law mirror society, moulding society in the image of law, or otherwise reconfiguring their relationship, which is indeed the objective of this chapter.[5] To this end, a good place to begin to think about this issue in the context of Thai cinema is the branding of a director as a film auteur. This is a cultural and commercial practice that is beginning to receive broad recognition.

The phenomenon of auteur branding is significant for the way it calls attention to the contemporary link between authorship and agency. Branding is an exercise of individual agency, for it is a process of identity construction aimed at creating a public perception of individual filmmakers. Even from this perspective, one can already observe the nature of branding as a social practice that individual filmmakers may undertake with a view to acquiring creative agency. As discussed in detail later, Thai filmmakers have been leveraging the auteur brand to negotiate their positions in the changing cultural and business landscapes. 'Agency' is thus a key issue that must be distinguished from 'autonomy' for the purposes of this discussion. The notion of autonomy likely evokes the image of a creative genius in the tradition of romantic authorship.[6] Agency, by contrast, is adopted here to refer to the capacity to act, which always hinges on the interactions between the agent and its environment. In this way, thinking about authorship and agency helps to foreground the role of the audience, whose contributions to contemporary Thai cinema promise to shed a different light on the function of copyright law.

To complement documentary research, empirical work was conducted between August and September 2021. The focus was particularly on the life cycle of a film, tracing its journey from production to public reception. The aim was to shed light on the network of social relations that underpin the system of film production and distribution, as well as the role of copyright as practised and understood by the parties involved. This perspective reflects the broader view taken in this book that copyright law is not merely institutionalised doctrine but rather a regulatory aspect of social life.[7]

The empirical work involved interviews with key actors in Thai cinema, including directors, producers, screenwriters, distributors, critics, and cinephiles. A total of 13 separate interviews were carried out with a total of thirteen interviewees between August and September 2021. Each interview lasted between 60 and 90 minutes, and each was an in-depth, semi-structured interview. Interviewees were

4 See for instance Bently and Biron, 'Discontinuities between legal conceptions of authorship and social practices'.

5 The relationships between law and society are far more complex and reducible to neither a reflection of society nor an instrument for social order. Brian Tamanaha identifies a common supposition among various Western theories of law, which consist of two closely related yet distinct ideas: that law is a reflection of society, and that law maintains social order. See Tamanaha, *A General Jurisprudence of Law and Society*.

6 See 'Authorship and Ownership' in Chapter 2.

7 See 'A Question of Learning' in Introduction.

selected using non-random purposive sampling to ensure that the chosen group of participants possessed the characteristics and information relevant to the research questions. The small sample size of 13 simply reflects the small size of the Thai film industry.

To maintain confidentiality, all interviewees remain anonymous. All quotes and statements are attributed using the letters A-M following the chronological order of the interviews, all of which were recorded and transcribed for analysis.

I. Authorship as Agency

In his home country, the name Apichatpong does not attract a large audience to the cinema. A senior official at the Ministry of Culture went so far as to say, 'Nobody goes to see films by Apichatpong. Thai people want to see comedy. We like to laugh.'[8] Controversial though it may be—and it is understandable why this infamous remark caused outrage among serious filmmakers and filmgoers—there is some truth in the damning comment, as it is fair to say Apichatpong's films are challenging for mainstream audiences to understand.[9] For one thing, his filmmaking style has been described as 'uniquely combining Western avant-garde traditions and documentary filmmaking with stories of working-class people across Thailand and the fantasy worlds they construct.'[10] Surely, this combination of style and substance does not make for casual viewing. Furthermore, Apichatpong's films were often set in the mystical jungle of Thailand's rural northeast and usually finds its subject in life at the border, i.e., the people and non-people who traverse the geographical, national, and ontological boundaries.[11]

Yet, Apichatpong has become one of the most renowned filmmakers in the country and arguably the only Thai filmmaker whose international status could possibly allow the country to finally lay claim to achieving the ideal of *Thai-sakon*.[12] However, describing Apichatpong as the epitome of *Thai-sakon* shifts the focus from the coloniality of domestic power to a neo-colonial tendency within Western cultural institutions. The branding of Apichatpong as 'the Thai auteur' occurred in a network of European film festivals whose international funding programmes were

8 Ladda Tangsupachai, head of the Cultural Surveillance Department at the Ministry of Culture, made this comment to Time magazine in 2007 in reference to the controversy surrounding the Thai Censorship Board's decision to ban Apichatpong's *Syndromes and A Century* that was due to be released in that year. See Simon Montlake, 'Making the cut' (*TIME*, 11 October 2007) <https://content.time.com/time/subscriber/article/0,33009,1670261,00.html> accessed 20 February 2025.

9 Apichatpong himself appears to be well aware of the enthusiastic reception of his work in Thailand. See Tilman Baumgärtel, '"I make films for myself:" Interview with Apichatpong Weerasethakul' in Tilman Baumgärtel (ed), *Southeast Asian Independent Cinema* (Hong Kong University Press 2012).

10 Wikanda Promkhuntong, 'Apichatpong Weerasethakul' in Mary Ainslie and Katarzyna Ancuta (eds), *Thai Cinema: The Complete Guide* (I B Tauris 2018) 21.

11 This has profound implications for Thai historiography on the violence committed by the authoritarian Thai state during the Cold War years. By contrast, see 'What It Meant to Be Thai' in Chapter 3 for dominant narratives in official Thai historiography.

12 For the discussion of *Thai-sakon*, see 'Culture of consumption/consumption of culture' in Chapter 3.

implicated in Eurocentrism and the exotic representation of non-Western cultures.[13] Nevertheless, with his auteur status, Apichatpong also managed to negotiate and exercise his creative agency.[14]

Co-Authoring a Brand

In 2010, Apichatpong became a national hero overnight after winning the Palme d'Or at the Cannes Film Festival.[15] But for Thai filmmakers, this prestigious award serves as a testament to Apichatpong's greater achievement, which has established him as a trailblazer in Thai independent cinema. It is fair to say that his engagement with the international network of film festivals has opened an alternative path for fellow Thai filmmakers, who may find it difficult to secure local investment for projects that lack commercial viability.[16] In this respect, his auteurist status suggests that making films for an international festival circuit is a path worth exploring. Indeed, winning awards is rewarding, but what is arguably most important about international festivals is the potential for a sustainable career in filmmaking.[17] In this regard, participation in international festival circuits serves as an exercise in branding.

Implicit in the celebration of Apichatpong as a film auteur is a social process that could be termed co-branding.[18] Before the affirmation of his auteur-star status at top-tier festivals, Apichatpong emerged on the international film festivals scene after being 'discovered' by the International Film Festival Rotterdam (IFFR), with the support from the Hubert Bals Fund (HBF).[19] Promoting emerging talents and

13 For more discussion of neo-colonialism in international film funding, see Randall Halle, 'Offering tale they want to hear: Transnational European film funding as neo-orientalism' in Rosalind Galt and Karl Schoonover (eds), *Global Art Cinema: New Theories and Histories* (OUP 2010).

14 For further discussion on his auteur brand and creative agency, see Wikanda Promkhuntong, *Film Authorship in Contemporary Transmedia Culture: The Paratextual Lives of Asian Auteurs* (Amsterdam University Press 2023).

15 The Palme d'Or was awarded to **ลุงบุญมีระลึกชาติ** (*Uncle Boonmee who can Recall his Past Lives*). See 'Retrospective' (Festival-Cannes) <https://www.festival-cannes.com/en/f/lung-boonmee-raluek-chat/> accessed 20 February 2025.

16 'Independent' thus refers to working outside the film studio system by becoming dependent on international film festivals and their funding programmes. For further discussion on the relationship between Thai independent cinema and international film festivals, see Sonthaya Subyen and Teekadech Watcharathanin, ***ปฏิบัติการหนังทุนข้ามชาติ*** *(Operation Transnationally Funded Films)* (Openbooks 2010); Peerachai Kerdsint, 'The dependence on international film festivals of Thai independent cinema' (EuroMedia2017, Brighton, July 2017).

17 See 'Why So Serious?' in this chapter for more discussion on the importance of international film festivals to Thai independent filmmakers.

18 Wikanda argues for the notion of co-branding as an alternative way of looking at a symbiosis relationship akin to 'corporate partnerships between consumer brands and celebrities,' but with film directors such as Apichatpong 'considered as celebrities and endorsers of film festivals' who, on their part, help to promote the auteur-star statuses of these directors. See Wikanda, 'Asian auteurs' (n 14) 58–62.

19 ibid 75.

established auteurs has long been part of festival branding, especially at the IFFR, where the aim is to discover emerging international talents to promote its international reputation as a site of discovery.[20] That said, it has not been just the festivals that have engaged in branding exercises. For his part, the name Apichatpong has also become a distinct brand thanks to the process of cultural consecration within the festival network.[21] Apichatpong's dedication to art cinema has garnered him festival awards and critical acclaim, which have elevated him to the status of an auteur.[22] Although he won the Palme d'Or in 2010, his films remain largely unknown to the general public, and unsurprisingly so—but his auteur status is not.

Consumer Brand

Recent developments in local film productions suggest that other Thai filmmakers have drawn inspiration from Apichatpong's journey. In particular, the name Nawapol has even been referred to as a brand, and understandably so given the publicity surrounding his films and the allure of his presence in the Thai media. It is fair to say that his work bears a signature style recognised even by those who do not profess to be his fans. Nawapol's preference for experimenting with concepts combines cleverly with his keen eye for detail, while his use of arthouse cinematographic techniques (e.g. a long take) also mixes interestingly with a deadpan yet punchy dialogue.[23] However, what really sets him apart from the Thai filmmakers of his generation is not simply the arthouse sensibility or deadpan humour. Arguably, the key to his unique position in Thai cinema lies in the active role of Thai audiences in shaping his brand.

If Apichatpong has an international network of film festivals and art institutions to thank for his auteur status, a similar relationship exists between Nawapol and the local cinephile and filmmaking communities. Nawapol's first audiences were the Thai cinephiles and independent filmmakers who were active in the Thai

20 The IFFR's PR materials make it clear that 'the festival's focus is on recent work by talented new filmmakers' and that 'the HBF focuses on supporting filmmakers from Africa, Asia, Latin America, the Middle East and parts of Eastern Europe.' See 'Mission & Vision' (IFFR) <https://iffr.com/en/about-us/mission-vision> accessed 7 May 2025. For a critical perspective on the IFFR and its funding programme, see Tamara Falicov, 'Migrating from South to North: The role of film festivals in funding and shaping Global South film and video' in Greg Elmer, Charles Davis, Janine Marchessault, and John McCullough (eds), *Locating Migrating Media* (Lexington Books 2010).

21 Wikanda explains that 'the process of cultural consecration can be found through various practices that distinguish certain directors as "auteurs" based on agreed norms set by agents involved in the film festival context' (n 14) 40.

22 As a result of co-branding, the Western notion of art cinema—emphasising the role of the director—has been negotiated by the geographical and aesthetic foreignness present in Apichatpong's films. This process has given rise to an auteurist persona steeped in the realism of Thailand's socio-political histories as much as the Western tradition of auteurism, which emphasises self-expression.

23 For a more extensive discussion of his auteurist style, see Anchalee Chaiwaraporn, ***ภาพยนตร์ในชีวิตไทย มุมมองของภาพยนตร์ศึกษา*** *(Cinema in Thai Life: A Perspective of Film Studies)* (Varaporn Publishing 2016) 150–155.

independent cinema scene around the late 2000s.[24] Nawapol himself was part of the scene, and it was these people who provided him with support and recognition as an emerging talent.[25] When his debut feature film won an international award in 2012, his authorial status began to grow at home, as did the public attention.[26] At this point, Nawapol was openly determined to pursue filmmaking as a career.[27] This ambition was audacious for a Thai filmmaker, even more so for an independent one.

When his reputation as an 'indie' director began to gain wider recognition, Nawapol publicly sought to counter the 'mass–indie' dichotomy.[28] Although his efforts to bridge the mass–indie divide proved futile, the act of resistance has been successful as an exercise in cross-branding. With his early films, Nawapol gained many fans through an arthouse sensibility that resonated with growing urban sub-cultures identifying with the 'alternative' label of independent cinema.[29] It was not until he made the first crossover to the domain of 'mass' cinema that the general public started to recognise his name. By collaborating with the local film studio GTH, he gained exposure to wider audiences and a better marketing platform.[30] It is also worth noting that GTH was probably the most recognisable brand, if not the most successful, in the Thai film market at the time. Nawapol's first studio production did not meet the level of commercial success that the studio had hoped for. Even so, the collaboration has brought his style and aesthetic to the general public and, thereby, established his authorial status.

While Apichatpong's auteurist reputation emerged from the physical spaces of festival venues and art galleries, it is rather the online space of social media that is home to Nawapol's ardent supporters. Recalling the digital boom of the late 1990s and early 2000s, discussed in Chapter 5, Nawapol belongs to a generation of Thai filmmakers who grew up through the digital transformation—one could even argue that the digital boom produced his generation of Thai filmmakers.[31] However, the

24 Interviewee L.

25 ibid.

26 Nawapol's first feature film '36' won the New Currents award at the 17th Busan International Film Festival (2012). See 'Archive' (BIFF) <https://www.biff.kr/eng/html/archive/arc_history.asp?pyear=2012&page_name=award> accessed 7 May 2025.

27 In one interview following the award at Busan, Nawapol discussed his strategies for self-distributing and, thus, commercialising and sustaining his not-so-mainstream practice of filmmaking. See Tuchchai Wongkitrungrueng, '**นวพล ธำรงรัตนฤทธิ์ ผู้กำกับ 36–กับยุค ๓๖ ช็อต ที่ผ่านพ้นไป**' ('Nawapol Thamrongrattanarit, the director of 36, and the bygone era of 36 shots') (*Sarakadee*) <https://www.sarakadee.com/magazine/338-issue/> accessed 20 February 2025.

28 ibid. Nawapol took film marketing seriously, contrary to the highbrow disposition in Thai independent cinema at the time. For his first feature film, Nawapol self-organised film promotion campaigns with the hopes to draw potential audiences to the screening locations that were carefully chosen to suit the film's profile.

29 Interviewee L.

30 This was his third feature film. It was tilted ***ฟรีแลนซ์ ห้ามป่วย ห้ามพัก ห้ามรักหมอ*** */Heart Attack* and released in 2015 to much publicity.

31 Baumgärtel interestingly observes a similar development across Southeast Asia due to the changing technological and media landscape. See Baumgärtel, 'Imagined communities, imagined worlds,' 26–31.

proliferation of digital media offered gave Nawapol more than just increased access to foreign films and affordable digital cameras. The burgeoning digital culture and the rise of social media also enabled a mutual and productive relationship between Nawapol and his audiences. With the increased access to the internet, the growth of cinephile activities and fan culture helped promote his works and strengthen his authorial brand in the new public sphere.[32] Meanwhile, Nawapol was also an effective user of social media, allowing him to engage directly with the audiences and perform his own personal branding.[33]

Self-Branding

Nawapol's filmmaking career is closely intertwined with digital transformation, consistently reflected in his filmography.[34] Earlier discussions have shown how 'Sorry' employs the story of a workplace drama to explore the intersection of originality, inspiration, and the flow of information.[35] A recurring theme subsequently emerges in *The Master*— a hallmark of Thai cinema at the turn of the century— as Nawapol revisits the question of inspiration and access to information through hazy memories of the legendary Van Video.[36] In fact, during the year between the release of these two films, Nawapol actually made a career breakthrough with the hipsters' favourite *Mary is Happy, Mary is Happy* (2013). By weaving the same motif into a coming-of-age story, he created a memorable moment that resonated particularly with those in the audience who had lived through the 1990s. Here, fans of the golden era of Hong Kong cinema will appreciate Nawapol's tribute to the Hong Kong auteur Wong Kar Wai, whose rise to international prominence in the 1990s has turned his name into the auteur brand par excellence.[37]

The homage to Wong Kar Wai in *Mary is Happy, Mary is Happy* is noteworthy for what it means for contemporary film authorship. Nawapol's reference to Wong Kar Wai creates a moment of double self-reflexivity through the very act of referencing.[38] On one level, the film's visual and audio allusion to the stylistic cinema of Wong Kar Wai harks back to the Thai cinema of the 90s era. Recalling the discussion on Van Video, a significant aspect of the alternative cinema made accessible by the video piracy of the late 1990s was none other than Wong Kar

32 Interviewee K.

33 ibid.

34 By way of illustration, his first feature film, *36* (2012), revolves around the theme of memory with respect to the reliability of analog and digital technologies (i.e. film and digital cameras), while his most recent film, *Fast and Feel Love* (2022), makes a drastic change in direction to take on the fast-paced, meme-like humour of online viral videos.

35 See 'Ethical Choice' in Chapter 4.

36 See 'Global Doctrine and Local Knowledge' in Chapter 4.

37 For more discussion of Wong Kar Wai's auteurist status, see Wikanda, 'Asian Auteurs' (n 14).

38 Wikanda links the contemporary practice of citations and appropriations in Asian cinema, as exemplified in *Mary is Happy, Mary is Happy,* to the established tradition of self-reflexivity in European art cinema. See Wikanda, 'Why so Wong?' (n 2) 432–434. See also, András Bálint Kovács, *Screening Modernism: European Art Cinema, 1950–1980* (University of Chicago Press 2007).

Wai's entire oeuvre. His authorial presence in the development of contemporary Thai cinema helps to explain why the commercial pull of the Hong Kong auteur remains considerable, even though most of his famous films were made between the mid-1990s and mid-2000s.[39] It is fair to say that the name Wong Kar Wai still looms large in the minds of Thai cinephiles and filmmakers, while the internet and social media have helped his works to be discovered by younger generations. This continual branding of Wong Kar Wai lies at the heart of the next layer of reflexivity. Nawapol's tribute to Wong Kar Wai is also a reflexive gesture towards his own self-reflection.

The film scholar Wikanda Promkhuntong succinctly observes that *Mary is Happy, Mary is Happy* is marked by 'the duality of auteur-citing-fan and fan-citing-auteur.'[40] What she means by 'auteur-citing-fan' is the film's underlying concept. *Mary is Happy, Mary is Happy* owes its storyline to social media tweets by a real-life teenager, Mary Maloney, who counts among Nawapol's followers on Twitter. The end result is an experimental coming-of-age film that tells the story of a Thai teenager named 'Mary' who grapples with life's impermanence as she navigates the final year of school.

As for the 'fan-citing-auteur' homage, it occurs in a scene where the distraught Mary goes to the rooftop and finds solace in the act of pretending to smoke a cigarette while staring vacantly into space. Here, Mary's humorous act is reminiscent of what Wong likes to make his characters do, not to mention the scene's Wong-Esque visual style and the use of Wong's well-known soundtrack (the Yumeji's theme) in the background.[41] The scene concludes in typical Nawapol fashion when Mary is interrupted by a friend who has followed her to the rooftop to deliver a deadpan one-liner: 'There is no time for Wong Kar Wai.' It is evident that what Wikanda means by 'fan-citing-auteur' is a reference to the appropriation of Wong Kar Wai by both of his fans, that is, the real-life Mary Maloney and the fan-turned-filmmaker Nawapol.

When understood through the lens of reflexivity, the rooftop scene takes on a meaning beyond merely being a storytelling device or a tribute to Wong Kar Wai. More specifically, this scene implicitly addresses Nawapol's multifaceted identities as a fan, a cinephile, a filmmaker.[42] That Nawapol is a cinephile has already been addressed in relation to *The Master*, a film that could be described as a cinephile's love letter to the Thai cinema of the 1990s. And given his involvement in the cinephile community, it comes as no surprise that Nawapol is also a self-confessed

39 The popular *Chungking Express* was released in 1994, while *Happy Together* won him the Best Director award at the Cannes Film Festival in 1997 before he received the Palme d'Or for *In the Mood for Love* in 2000. See Wong Kar Wai's filmography on IMDB <https://www.imdb.com/name/nm0939182/> accessed 20 February 2025.

40 Wikanda, 'Why So Wong?' (n 2) 433.

41 ibid 434.

42 ibid 434–435.

fan of Wong Kar Wai.[43] Considering the 'auteur-citing-fan and fan-citing-auteur' conundrum, his on-screen reference to the Hong Kong auteur appears to create a self-reflexive moment in which he seeks to reconcile his multiple statuses by way of self-identification. To put it more generally, it is the construction of self through an engagement with the auteur brand that opens one's sense of self to the dialogic relations with one's own social, technological, and geographical milieu.

Brand Agency

Indeed, both Wong Kar Wai and Apichatpong have been influential figures for Nawapol.[44] And similar to Apichatpong, Wong's auteur status has benefited from recognition by Western cultural institutions—notably, the Best Director award at the 1997 Cannes Film Festival. But unlike Apichatpong, who has been closely associated with film festivals and art institutions, Wong's brand of auteurism has flourished in more commercial settings. A case in point is the endorsement he received from the celebrity director Quentin Tarantino, whose distribution company acquired the rights to his film *Chungking Express* (1994) and included his commentary as part of the DVD extras when the film entered the secondary market.[45] Similarly, the Oscar-winning Ang Lee spoke highly of Wong Kar Wai on the eve of the theatrical release of *My Blueberry Night* (2007), Wong's first English-speaking film.[46] In his introduction to the star of the evening, Lee said, 'I don't know any contemporary filmmaker/auteur that draws more interest, argument, articles, even essays, admiration and, as you say, imitations.'[47] More recently, and shifting the context from North America to Thailand, the name Wong Kar Wai has been mentioned constantly in the promotion of a Thai-language co-production, *One for the Road* (2021), for which he is credited as a producer alongside a Thai director.[48]

43 In a book he published in 2010, *ฮ่องกงกึ่งสำเร็จรูป* (*Instant Hong Kong*), Nawapol recounts his fan pilgrimage to Hong Kong, where he mainly traces Wong Kar Wai's filming locations. To promote the book, he also made a short video consisting of images and clips from the trip edited together in the style of Wong Kar Wai. See Nawapol Thamrongrattanarit, '*หนังสือ ฮ่องกงกึ่งสำเร็จรูป* Trailer' (YouTube, 5 July 2010) <https://www.youtube.com/watch?v=zM34DtwZEN0> accessed 20 February 2025.

44 See for instance Tuchchai (n 27).

45 Irene Lacher, 'Kindred Tarantino: the thunder rolls, out of Hong Kong' (*LA Times*, 3 March 1996) <http://articles.latimes.com/1996-03-03/entertainment/ca-42640_1_hong-kong> accessed 20 February 2025.

46 Ang Lee, 'A Pinewood dialogue with Wong Kar Wai' (Museum of the Moving Image) <http://www.movingimagesource.us/files/dialogues/3/71112_programs_transcript_html_303.htm> accessed 20 February 2025.

47 ibid.

48 Even the PR materials by Thailand's major cinema chain played up Wong's involvement. See '**หว่องกาไวเผย** One for the Road **คือหนังแห่งการเดินทางอย่างแท้จริง**' ('Wong Kar War reveals One for the Road is a true journey film') (*Major Cineplex*) <https://www.majorcineplex.com/news/wong> accessed 20 February 2025.

In this way, the commercial embeddedness of Wong's auteur brand resonates with what Timothy Corrigan terms the commerce of auteurism.[49] Writing in response to the New Hollywood era of the 1960s–1980s—when young directors such as Francis Ford Coppola and Martin Scorsese rose to prominence and became stars in their own right—Corrigan argued for film studies to re-evaluate the auteur concept.[50] His main reason was to keep pace with 'the business of being an auteur' as artistic recognition became intertwined with a star status and deployed as a commercial strategy in film distribution.[51] The more recent phenomenon of auteur branding in Thai cinema also indicates a similar shift, where the industry appears to turn towards a strong brand to cultivate loyal customers. Consequently, both Thai filmmakers and audiences now find themselves in a new business landscape—where it has become necessary to shift the analysis of auteurism from 'the auteur as the structuring principle of enunciation'[52] to 'the auteur as a commercial strategy for organising audience reception.'[53] In other words, it is the auteur as a star and the way the star status has been strategised in film marketing that deserves more attention.

Agent of Agency

It is fair to say that Corrigan chose to shed light on the commerce of auteurism to move the discussions beyond the romantic notion of the auteur as an autonomous figure.[54] This shifts attention away from the myth of originality, focusing instead on the necessity of publicity and the auteur's role as a commercial agent in film marketing and promotion. In this way, the commerce of auteurism effectively reveals the material conditions under which films are produced and consumed. This perspective seems relevant to Apichatpong as much as to Wong Kar Wai. This is because Corrigan's argument presents a relational concept of authorship in which the practice of auteurism is understood in terms of 'social agency' that predicates on 'the conditions of a cultural and commercial intersubjectivity.'[55] Consequently, his intersubjective approach is also apt for elucidating the nature of auteur-fan interactions in *Mary is Happy, Mary is Happy*. For as Corrigan suggests, the reference to Wong Kar Wai illustrates how an auteur brand serves as 'an agent of agency' not only for fellow filmmakers in their pursuit of an authorial voice but also for audiences in their quest for self-identity.[56]

As far as Nawapol is concerned, it is evident that his name has already assumed the status of a commercial auteur, and it is worth noting further how the auteur

49 Corrigan, 'The commerce of auteurism' (n 2).
50 ibid 48.
51 ibid 47.
52 ibid 45.
53 ibid 46.
54 See 'Authorship and Ownership' in Chapter 2.
55 Corrigan, 'The commerce of auteurism' (n 2) 47.
56 ibid 50.

Nawapol has also become an agent of public discourse. Not only does he possess a keen eye for the details of everyday life, but he also has a tendency to choose film subjects that resonate with life's circumstances.[57] This inclination is recognised by critics and fans, lending Nawapol's work a gesture of critical reflection towards the social reality off-screen. Consequently, Nawapol's auteur brand tends to foster in his audience a form of critical engagement that generates active contextualisation. Such responses can be observed in the reception of both *Mary is Happy, Mary is Happy* and *The Master*,[58] but a more interesting instance for the present discussion is what happened with his first studio production, *Heart Attack* (2015).

Because working with GTH meant his film would reach a wider audience than ever before, Nawapol positioned *Heart Attack* as a romantic comedy, even though it is more concerned with exposing the relentless demands of the creative industry. The main protagonist, a sleep-deprived freelance graphic designer, is instructed by the doctor—who is also his love interest—to strike a work–life balance, all while knowing that a younger, more ambitious newcomer could easily take his place.

In hindsight, it is hardly surprising that the film's reception turned out to be polarising. Nawapol's filmmaking style continued to endear his fans but proved too unfamiliar for GTH's mainstream audience.[59] Yet his auteur brand still sparked debates regarding the precarious employment in Thailand's creative sector. The film's publicity generated discussions on the deceptive allure of self-employment and the welfare issue facing creative workers, who had been treated like cogs in the big creative industry machine.[60] Suffice it to say, then, that Nawapol's auteur brand has served as a vehicle for collective agency in questioning the promise of the creative economy.

Brand Loyalty

From the discussion so far, it should be clear that the auteurist reputations of artists like Apichatpong and Nawapol carry more significance beyond the cultural and

57 On one occasion, he said 'When I make a movie, the story usually comes from an experience in my life.' See Pimchanok Phungbun na ayudhya, 'Death: (Non) existence' (*The Could*, 21 November 2017) <https://readthecloud.co/talk-18-nawapol/> accessed 20 February 2025.

58 A good example can be seen in the reviews, reflections, and a whole host of reactions in the 'Blogathons' organised by a group of veteran Thai cinephiles who run a Facebook page called 'Kafe Lumiere' to be an online community for those interested in alternative cinema. See <https://www.facebook.com/Kafelme> accessed 20 February 2025.

59 See also Anchalee Chaiwaraporn, 'Freelance/Freelance: Ham Puay . . .Ham Phak . . .Ham Rak Mo' in Mary Ainslie and Katarzyna Ancuta (eds), *Thai Cinema: The Complete Guide* (I.B. Tauris 2018) 191.

60 See for instance Ekasit Nunbhakdi, '**ฟรีแลนซ์ฯ: ร่างกายใต้บงการ**' ('Freelance: Docile bodies') (*Prachathai*, 6 September 2015) <https://prachatai.com/journal/2015/09/61244> accessed 20 February 2025; '**ควันหลงภ.ฟรีแลนซ์ฯ กับปัญหาสุขภาพจิตคนทำงาน**' ('Workers' mental health problems in the wake of the film "Freelance"') (Voice TV, 14 September 2015) <https://www.voicetv.co.th/read/258624> accessed 20 February 2025; Pattramon Sukprasert, 'Shining light on the freelance myth' (*Bangkok Post*, 16 September 2015) <https://www.bangkokpost.com/opinion/opinion/694724/shining-a-light-on-the-freelance-myth> accessed 20 February 2025.

commercial value they lend to film products. More than just reflecting the changing cultural and economic landscapes, auteur branding foregrounds the role of the fans, the audiences, and the consumers. This has been traced throughout the discussion, where it quickly became clear that branding revolves around creating a perception and garnering loyalty, and in this way, it creates a relationship of trust.[61] This role of trust also suggests that auteur branding mediates the relationships between filmmakers and audiences through the expression of authenticity, rather than the originality of expression.[62] In other words, staying 'on brand' seems more important than staying ahead or becoming original. However—and this is a necessary caveat—the value of an auteur brand is still realised at the box office or through other means of distribution.[63] Consequently, copyright law still has an important role in organising the relations between those involved in film distribution, including the audiences.

Therefore, it is important to further note that this spectatorial turn of authorship, if you will, dovetails thematically with another recent development in Thai cinema. In recent years, the quest for audience engagement has become a priority for Thai filmmakers. Film studios have come to regard film marketing as no less important than film production, so much so that they are willing to spend as much on marketing campaigns as on production.[64] If the discussion of auteur branding is anything to go by, one is justified in expecting that contemporary film audiences are not merely consumers but play an active role in Thai cinema.

II. Use as Production

Considering the discussion on auteur branding, it is not just the meaning of auteurism that has become visibly transformed. The notion of an audience also requires re-evaluation, given their indispensable role in the practices of auteur branding. The immediate question here is whether the audience can be placed on equal footing with the auteur. This question is pertinent to the legal conception of copyright, which otherwise operates on the distinction between authors and users.[65] Also pertinent to the question itself is the notion of creativity, which assumes a clear division between film production and consumption that is coextensive with a distinction between creation and use. This idea presents an image of creativity that reflects the so-called Creative Economy as well as representing the image of thought that informs the legal discourse. The scales appear to tilt against the audience.

That said, the audiences are well-positioned to reshape the meaning of filmmaking and redefine what copyright means in their relationship with filmmakers.

61 As discussed in Chapter 7, a trusting relationship is also central to an alternative perspective on copyright protection that emphasises the significance of social interaction and community relations.

62 See also Stefano Marzano, 'Branding=distinctive authenticity' in Jane Pavitt (ed), *Brand.new* (V&A Publications, 2000).

63 Film distribution is further discussed in 'Long Live Cinemas' in this chapter.

64 Interviewee A.

65 This author–user distinction is further discussed in 'The Public–Private Dichotomy' in Chapter 8.

This may evoke the kind of auteur–fan interactions seen in *Mary is Happy, Mary is Happy*, but with an emphasis shifted towards film audiences and the proliferation of meaning through what is otherwise mere consumption. As discussed in detail later, contemporary audiences could be considered producers in their own right, and understanding their role in contemporary Thai cinema can shed new light on the role and significance of copyright law. However, what needs addressing first is the notion of audiences as consumers. The issue this presents lies in the presupposition of a particular understanding of the creative process and copyright protection (i.e. incentives for creativity). More problematically, it implicates the logic of risk calculation that places the relationship between filmmakers and audiences in contention.

Creativity at Risk

In recent years, nobody seems to know where the future of Thai films lies. Local films have had a small prospect of profits, if they are produced at all, as film financing has also been hard to come by.[66] On the whole, Thai cinemagoers appear to prefer Hollywood blockbusters to local productions, and this is not just a matter of competition but also a problem of perception.[67] Choosing to play it safe, Thai studios and producers have stuck to old themes and formulas, apparently for so long that this has become a stigma.[68] The diminished confidence among local audiences is reflected in the prevalent idea that Hollywood films are worth a trip to the cinema but it is not necessary or worth it to pay to see Thai films in the theatre when online piracy is free, particularly as ticket prices continue to rise. Ironically, as films are primarily viewed as products, the issue of high ticket prices appears to reinforce social stratification rather than raising questions about access to culture.[69] Overall, it seems reasonable to suspect that the most urgent challenge facing Thai filmmakers is not that few people are watching Thai films, not least given that online streaming seems to be thriving.

Whether this is true or not, cinema going remains the lifeblood of the Thai film industry. The fact that few people watch Thai films at the cinema has placed the careers of Thai filmmakers in limbo.[70] Despite advancements in digital technology, the new modes and manners of film consumption have yet to displace the social activity of going to the cinema. Some might argue that it is only a matter of time, as change is already underway in the form of video streaming services, but

66 Thanayod Lopattananont, Voraluk Klasukon, and Saksit Thaweekul, '**ความสอดคล้องของโครงสร้างอุตสาหกรรมการผลิตภาพยนตร์ไทยกับยุทธศาสตร์การส่งเสริมภาพยนตร์และวีดิทัศน์ ระยะที่** 3 (พ.ศ. 2560–2564)' ('Coherence of Thai film industry and Thailand's strategies for film and video promotion, phase 3, 2017–2021') (Dhurakij Pandit University research paper, DPU 2020) 74.

67 ibid 77–78.

68 Interviewee A.

69 Criticism of the major cinema chains regarding the high cost of cinema tickets usually engenders the response that one gets what one pays for—it is business as usual.

70 Interviewee A.

be that as it may, cinema going appears poised to remain a significant social practice for the foreseeable future, and it is by examining the commercial practices of film distribution that one can begin to interrogate the discourse on copyright and creativity.

Long Live Cinemas

Historically, a theatrical release has always been a significant mode of film distribution in Thailand, though it is debatable whether cinemas have always been the primary outlet for films.[71] As with the changing technology of filmmaking, film distribution has not gone through the years unchanged. New practices on 'release windows' have usually indicated that the industry has discovered new ways to maximise a film's financial value through a new release sequencing (i.e. a window sequence) or through a new mode of making a film available to the public.[72]

The optical disc market, for instance, once played a significant role in Thai film distribution. A VCD/DVD release once constituted an important source of revenue after a film was released in cinemas and before it became available on TV.[73] However, the falling demand for VCDs and DVDs means that the film industry has had to revert to relying heavily on cinema ticket sales.[74] The significance of cinema attendance suggests that the popularity of illicit online access poses a more specific threat to the industry than the broad and simple claim that those responsible are stealing from Thai filmmakers.

Furthermore, a specific function of copyright emerges in the dynamic between film consumption and distribution. Here, copyright is not simply about exclusion because ultimately Thai filmmakers want the audiences to go to the cinema or, at the very least, watch the films through paid channels.[75] In this context, what is significant about the right to exclude is the ability to set the agenda in their relations with the audiences regarding how films are consumed. This is why copyright is crucial to the film distribution system.[76] The exclusivity of copyright serves to organise the relations among those involved in the film distribution process.

71 For a history of theatrical distribution in Thailand, see Unaloam Chanrungmaneekul, ***โรงหนัง สายหนัง ความ(ไร้)อำนาจของคนดูและศิลปิน ธุรกิจการฉายภาพยนตร์และสังคมไทย พ.ศ.** 2440–2561 (Cinemas, Distributors, and the (Absent) Power of Audiences and Artists: The Business of Film Exhibition and Thai Society 1897–2018)* (Thailand Research Fund 2020). For a historical mode of film exhibition that was once prevalent in rural Thailand, see Ingawanij, 'Itinerant cinematic practices in and around Thailand during the Cold War'.

72 For more detail on commercial strategies in theatrical distribution and exhibition, see Darlene C. Chisholm and Yu-Hsi Liu, 'Motion-picture industry' in Ruth Towse and Trilce Navarrete Hernández (eds), *Handbook of Cultural Economics* (3rd edn, Edward Elgar 2020) 341–345.

73 Interviewee H.

74 ibid.

75 Interviewee C.

76 Ronald Bettig's work may still offer a good starting point. See Ronald Bettig, *Copyrighting Culture: The Political Economy of Intellectual Property* (Routledge 1996).

Given that at one point the COVID-19 pandemic brought most activities in the film industry to a standstill, a pandemic-related controversy in Hollywood provides a striking illustration of the copyright nexus among various actors in the distribution landscape. Here, the decision of a Hollywood studio to release some films in cinemas and on a streaming service simultaneously, citing the uncertainty created by the global pandemic, upset cinema owners and a major film star whose earnings depended on box office performance.[77] The disagreement posed the risk of deadlocks and lawsuits because all these stakeholders had vested interests in the standard practice of release windows—through which their relations are framed and integrated via copyright agreements.[78]

The controversy surrounding simultaneous releases demonstrates how the exercise of copyright exclusivity is a matter of not exclusion but coordination. The Hollywood example suggests that cooperation and shared interests are pivotal to film distribution.[79] Just as this observation holds true for most relationships, the following discussion shows that it is certainly true for relationships in film production and consumption. Financing may indeed be the most urgent challenge facing Thai film production, but it takes more than an investment to make a successful film.

Risky Business

Considering the relational nature of film distribution, the claim that piracy kills Thai cinema immediately appears incomplete, if not skewed towards a distorted view of the industry. This typical claim regarding film piracy is notably silent on the ongoing exploitation of creative workers, otherwise echoed in Nawapol's *Heart Attack*.[80] Equally problematic is the way it treats audiences and fans as morally suspect consumers tasked with the responsibility of making the right choice.[81] And whatever choice they make will translate into the choice between self-interest and national interest, as the introduction of the Creative Economy policy has aligned the protection against piracy with the progress of the nation.[82]

All of this highlights how such claims about the demise of Thai cinema are overly simplistic and deliberately misrepresent the complex field of film production and consumption. The discourse of piracy presupposes investment as the nexus of the film industry. It assumes an economic model of creativity, viewing

77 For more detail, see for instance Sarah Whitten, 'Movie theatre owners are frustrated about streaming, but their survival depends on studios' (CNBC, 2 January 2021) <https://www.cnbc.com/2021/01/02/movie-theater-owners-are-frustrated-about-streaming-but-their-survival-depends-on-studios.html> accessed 20 February 2025; Ryan Faughnder and Meg James, 'Scarlett Johansson vs. Disney: How should talent be paid for streaming?' (*LA Times*, 3 August 2021) <https://www.latimes.com/entertainment-arts/business/newsletter/2021-08-03/wide-shot-disney-scarlett-johansson-nbc-olympics-tokyo-delta-variant-the-wide-shot> accessed 20 February 2025.
78 ibid.
79 See 'It Takes a Village' in Chapter 7.
80 See further discussion on workers' welfare and copyright in 'Burning Down the House' in Chapter 7.
81 See 'Moral Panic' in Chapter 5.
82 See 'The Politics of Creativity' in Chapter 5.

filmmaking as 'a largely economic activity—with calculable risks and outputs, necessary returns, and individual gains.'[83] Consequently, whatever poses a risk to film investors becomes a risk to the industry and a threat to Thai cinema.

As just seen, implicit in the death of Thai cinema is the notion of cinema that aligns with a commercial mode of filmmaking, where films are primarily perceived as products and film production as a commercial enterprise. Recalling the mass–indie divide, one thing that distinguishes commercial filmmaking from its independent counterpart is the cost–profit calculation of commercial film investment, which sharply contrasts with the important role of public and cultural institutions in financing independent films.[84]

In recent years, drawing up a budget for a commercial film project has become akin to solving a calculus problem. Investors commit specific funds that look increasingly disproportionate to the actual costs of filmmaking,[85] yet the investment always comes with a target profit, leaving the filmmakers responsible for working out everything else in between.[86] Furthermore, competition from Hollywood and the declining popularity of local films have driven Thai studios and producers to play it safe to ensure some financial return at the box office.[87] To this end, they have stuck to the once-successful formulas, apparently for so long that the repetition has turned into a stagnation and a stigma.[88]

The aversion to box office failure invites a comparison to the threat of piracy. For as much as the repetitiveness in Thai commercial cinema reflects a calculation against risk, the well-rehearsed argument that copyright law exists to provide creative incentives similarly presents a narrative of risk mitigation.[89] In other words, the law is required to intervene with the incentives of exclusivity so that the risk of piracy does not deter investors from putting money into film projects. In many ways, this does not seem to paint a controversial picture of filmmaking since films are expensive to make. The issue, however, lies in the fact that Thai commercial cinema has become out of touch with audiences, and this can be attributed to the logic of risk calculation too. The supposedly fail-safe strategy of cautiously repeating the same ideas, themes, and plots has inadvertently undermined the trust in Thai filmmakers and driven down the value of Thai production.[90]

Some may perceive a turning point in the recent shift in national film policy, as discussed in Chapter 5.[91] Others might point to the growing competition in the streaming market, where the rise of original content on platforms such as Netflix

83 Gibson, *Creating Selves* (n 1) 18.
84 Independent film financing is further discussed in 'Why So Serious?' in the next section.
85 Interviewee A.
86 ibid.
87 ibid.
88 See 'The Thai State and the State of Thai Cinema' in Chapter 5.
89 For more discussion on creativity, IP, and risk mitigation, see Gibson, *The Logic of Innovation*, 137–141.
90 See Thanayod, Voraluk, and Saksit (n 66) 77–78.
91 See 'The Thai State and the State of Thai Cinema' in Chapter 4.

has brought substantial investment to local productions and provided relative diversity to local offerings.[92] Yet more intriguing and indicative of the future of Thai film is arguably the recent emergence of regional *Isan* cinema that found success nationwide, much to everyone's surprise.

The rise of Thai regional cinema serves as a timely reminder of the difference between the logic of risk calculation and how filmmaking is inherently about taking risk. In 2017, the critical and commercial success of the micro-budget *Thi-Baan the Series* caught the film industry by surprise.[93] This dialect-speaking romantic comedy was swiftly followed by a series of *Thi-Baan* films that were so successful that the franchise placed *Isan* cinema on the national map.[94] The term '*Thi-Baan*' comes from the north-eastern *Isan* dialect and translates as 'villager' in English. As this translation suggests, the *Thi-Baan* franchise comes from a group of young *Isan* filmmakers who sought to tell the story of modern *Isan* life in their own voice.[95]

Unsurprisingly, their journey did not begin so smoothly because financing was hard to come by, not least because their films were *Isan* oriented.[96] It is true that the *Thi-Baan* series sits firmly within the popular genre of romantic comedy, but the way the *Thi-Baan* filmmakers presented the familiar plots and themes through the lives of *Isan* teenagers in their *Isan* environment initially made the franchise appear different if not actively foreign to general audiences.

The *Isan* orientation was certainly unusual for Thai mainstream cinema, particularly when comparing the *Thi-Baan* franchise with many studio productions that aimed to educate the audiences about the Thai nation and its unified culture.[97] The discussion in Chapter 4 already showed a parallel to how Thailand has become

92 See for instance Suchit Leesa-Nguansuk, 'Netflix to churn out local content' (*Bangkok Post*, 14 March 2018) <https://www.bangkokpost.com/business/1427890/netflix-to-churn-out-local-content> accessed 20 February 2025; Pornchai Sereemongkonpol, 'Netflix Thailand announces six Thai titles at "Tee Thai Tee Mun"' (*Bangkok Post*, 12 October 2022) <https://www.bangkokpost.com/life/arts-and-entertainment/2413038/netflix-thailand-announces-six-thai-titles-at-tee-thai-tee-mun> accessed 20 February 2025.

93 See for instance Kaewta Ketbungkan, 'How small Isaan films are going big in Bangkok' (Khaosod English, 20 March 2017) <https://www.khaosodenglish.com/life/arts/2017/03/20/small-isaan-films-going-big-bangkok/> accessed 20 February 2025. The *Thi-Baan* were not the first contemporary Northeast films to break into the mainstream, although they presented a major breakthrough, see Kong Rithdee, 'A wind from the Northeast' (*Bangkok Post*, 24 March 2017) https://www.bangkokpost.com/life/arts-and-entertainment/1220321/a-wind-from-the-northeast> accessed 20 February 2025.

94 So much so that a popular girl group, BNK48, joined the *Thi-Baan* filmmakers to create an *Isan*-themed film titled *Thi-Baan x BNK48* (2020). See Tatat Bunnag, 'A shining star in the North' (*Bangkok Post*, 24 January 2020) <https://www.bangkokpost.com/life/arts-and-entertainment/1842594/a-shining-star-in-the-north> accessed 20 February 2025.

95 See Sasiprapa Deerobrum, '**เปิดใจผู้กำกับ 'ไทบ้าน เดอะซีรีส์' หนังไทยสไตล์อีสาน ที่ม่วนคักจนหัวแฮง**' ('An open-hearted conversation with the director of "Thi-Baan the Series"') (Kaosod, 14 March 2017) <https://www.khaosod.co.th/lifestyle/news_253277> accessed 20 February 2025.

96 ibid.

97 For more discussion on Thai nationalism in mainstream cinema, see Adadol, 'Hyperbolic heritage' (n 357).

provincial to the West in how the Thai nation has made the provincial *Isan* its own backward Other—albeit the Other within.[98] The national breakthrough of the *Thi-Baan* franchise owed much to the filmmakers' belief that there would be a large audience to connect with the kind of stories they wanted to tell.[99] Hindsight is a wonderful thing, and whether one thinks these filmmakers have been proven right or simply fortunate, their belief reflects the drive to present the changing *Isan* identity, which has long suffered from misrepresentation.

Thus, it is quite fitting that the first *Thi-Baan* production was made possible by the financial support of a local *Isan* politician who had no experience in film investment and, apparently, no economic motives.[100] Quite possibly their initial difficulty in securing investors came from a lack of reputation on their part.[101] Yet the success of the *Thi-Baan* franchise still points to the fact that there are more stories waiting to be told and certainly a broad audience to connect with.

In light of the *Thi-Baan* discussion, the problem with the incentive argument lies in the logic of risk calculation that it reinforces. The case of the *Thi-Baan* franchise shows that risk calculation does not necessarily work in favour of creativity. In fact, one could argue that it is not about creativity at all, even if one identifies the creativity of commercial filmmaking in the development of a new product; if anything, the risk calculation of film investment is more concerned with selling a product. But to argue that copyright law has the instrumental purpose of encouraging creativity with financial incentives is to propagate the logic of risk calculation. This is because fundamentally, the argument that copyright provides incentives for creativity rests on two claims.[102]

The first is the empirical claim that creativity requires financial incentives. Although this claim cannot be properly assessed here, it is worth noting that reservations and context specificity have been recurring themes in empirical studies on copyright and creative incentives.[103] If anything, the ambiguity of the evidence serves to highlight the operation of the incentives argument on a normative plane in that the absence of clear evidence is not immediately relevant to the second, normative claim: that the purpose of copyright protection is to foster creativity. Operating concurrently on both empirical and normative planes allows the incentives argument to suspend the discrepancy, suggesting that the lack of an empirical

98 See 'What It Meant to be Thai' in Chapter 3. For a comparison to the times of European colonialism, see Thongchai, 'The Others within' (n 677).

99 Surasak said that the first *Thi-Baan* film specifically catered to *Isan* audiences, but they deeply hoped that a regional success would lead to a nationwide release. See Sasiprapa (n 1088).

100 See his interview with a Thai media source, '**กันดารคือสินทรัพย์ เบื้องหลังไทบ้านเดอะซีรีส์ ปั้น 2 ล้านเป็นหลายร้อยล้าน**' ('Hardship is asset: Behind Thi-Baan the Series that turned two million into hundreds of millions') (*The Standard*, 8 March 2020) <https://thestandard.co/podcast/thesecretsauce201/> accessed 20 February 2025.

101 ibid.

102 Abraham Drassinower, 'A note on incentives, rights, and the public domain in copyright law' (2011) 86 *Notre Dame Law Review* 1869, 1873–1874.

103 For more detail, see Springman (n 106) 32.

link only means that copyright law must be changed so that it fulfils the purpose of promoting creativity.[104]

But again, pointing this out is not meant to be an invitation to understate the importance of investment or to look past the injustice of free riding. Rather, it is an invitation to consider these issues and their roles in creative production without resorting to the language of risk calculation.[105] One might argue that shifting the discussion away from the role of law in the risky business of film also risks falling into the conventional art–commerce dichotomy. The pendulum may well swing back to the notion of film as art, with copyright law regarded as a protection for individual self-expression. Insofar as 'film as art' signifies a valorisation of individual expression that is disconnected from the social reality of filmmaking and film reception, it also becomes pertinent to ask the perennial question: What is wrong with entertainment?

Good Entertainment

In Thai cinema, there seems to be a line that separates art from entertainment, and this separation is coextensive with the mass–indie divide. In other words, the artistic sensibility of independent cinema is often juxtaposed with the crowd-pleasing entertainment of commercial films.[106] This dichotomy of art and entertainment is not simply a rhetorical device but reflects the reality of Thai cinema, as discussed later. However, the line that separates the two modes of cinema is not always clear. Therefore, when one attempts to delineate their boundaries, a fault line emerges, and it is here where a distinct role of copyright law can be observed.

As discussed in the context of auteur branding, the issue of agency calls attention to the business of being an auteur that transcends the mass–indie divide. A pertinent example is Nawapol, whose auteur brand has allowed him to work on both independent and commercial productions.[107] Furthermore, his auteur brand also reveals that auteur-driven agency is not always about the filmmakers. Just as Nawapol expanded his auteur status by crossing into commercial cinema, the publicity surrounding his first commercial venture, *Heart Attack*, also sparked debates on self-employment.[108] And while *Heart Attack* demonstrates how the commercial auteur can become an agent of public discourse, it also highlights the sociability of commercial cinema and the active role of the audiences. All of this suggests a realignment of the relationship between filmmakers and audiences, one that envisages a distinct function of copyright law.

104 As Drassinower has succinctly observed, 'it is perfectly possible to say (a) existing copyright law does not promote creativity; (b) copyright law ought to promote creativity; (c) we should therefore alter existing copyright law so as to make it live up to its own creativity promoting purpose.' See Drassinower, 'note on incentives' (n 1095).

105 Chapter 7 presents the concept of community resource as one way of doing so.

106 Interviewee A; Interviewee C; Interviewee F.

107 See 'Co-Authoring a Brand' in this chapter.

108 See 'Agent of Agency' in this chapter.

And with that, attention must now return to the business of being an auteur—this time with a focus shifted to its relationship with the rights in films. As discussed a bit later, the rise of auteur-driven films in Thai cinema has made Thai independent filmmakers noticeably mindful of where copyright ownership resides. However, rather than linking this back to the romantic ideals of creativity and selfhood, what stands out is the issue of agency. This shift in perspective brings relationships within the film industry to the forefront and highlights the mediating role of copyright law. Furthermore, it also opens up legal discussions to interesting practices in commercial cinema that might otherwise be overshadowed by concerns about risks.

Why So Serious?

With risk calculation characterising the commercial mode of filmmaking, Thai cinema has seen an increasing alienation of independent filmmakers in the commercial space. Today, becoming an independent filmmaker in Thailand not only means becoming independent of the studios, whether willingly or unavoidably, but also means becoming excluded from the principal distribution channel of theatrical screenings.[109]

As seen in Chapter 5, the film exhibition sector has been dominated by two major cinema chains that gravitate towards Hollywood blockbusters and other mainstream offerings.[110] This typically comes at the expense of independent films, with claims that the exhibition monopoly contributes to the lack of theatrical distribution faced by even award-winning films, such as those by Apichatpong.[111] However, when viewed from the audience's perspective, the situation seems to be more complex. For mainstream audiences, the challenges facing Thai independent filmmakers at home come from a simple reason: Their films are simply not entertaining. It is worth noting that not only are Thai independent films experimental in content but the political discontent they express can also be problematic.[112]

For Thai independent filmmakers, experimentation and politics seem to go hand in hand as they navigate the murky waters of both local and global film industries.[113] This hallmark of Thai independent cinema is epitomised by the career of its trailblazer, Apichatpong Weerasethakul. Apichatpong's filmography can be described

109 Interviewee C; Interviewee F.

110 See 'The Thai State and the State of Thai Cinema' in Chapter 5.

111 Unaloam, *Film exhibition* (n 71) 242–243.

112 Baumgärtel interestingly observes that 'if (mainstream) cinema has in the past played its part in shaping nations into 'imagined communities' in Benedict Anderson's sense,' then 'in countries like Malaysia, the Philippines, and Thailand, the emergence of an independent cinema in the last ten years corresponds roughly with a growing political discontent with how these countries are run.' See 'Global mediascape' (n 31) 23.

113 See Peerachai (n 16). See also Sopawan Boonnimitra, 'From the nightmarish to a dreamy state of being: The troubling present in Thai independent cinema after the 2014 Coup d'état' (FilmAsia2016, *Kobe*, October 2016); Sopawan Boonnimitra, 'Re-thinking politics in film: Thai independent cinema after the coup d'état 2014' (EuroMedia2016, Brighton, July 2017).

as one in which local histories of political and epistemic violence are revisited with the sensibility of experimental film, following in the tradition of transnational art cinema.[114] This intersection of local politics and transnational aesthetics also appears to be a recurring theme in the independent cinema of the younger generation.[115] Much like Apichatpong's upbringing in the oppressed *Isan*, these young filmmakers' lives have all but remained unaffected by decades of political turbulence under authoritarian rule. And with local funding still hard to come by, it only seems natural that these filmmakers have followed Apichatpong into the world of film festivals in search of creative agency.

Consequently, it is not surprising that the contours of the 'indie' sensibility in Thai cinema often reflect the kind of aesthetics favoured by festivals like the IFFR—the first to 'discover' Apichatpong and continuing to seek out new Thai talents.[116] The film festival circuit has become a platform for Thai filmmakers to negotiate and exercise political agency through the medium of auteur cinema.

As discussed in relation to auteur branding, one strategy for a film festival to distinguish itself is through co-branding, whereby a festival elevates its reputation by culturally consecrating its own funded director as an auteur.[117] In this way, co-branding is an auteur-driven process that begins at the funding selection stage, and it is here that Apichatpong's advice to Thai applicants sheds interesting light on the auteur-driven world of film festivals. When asked what made a film proposal successful, Apichatpong chose to emphasise the importance of self-expression.[118] He suggested that it was important for the applicant's own 'voice' to come through and that one should use the subject 'I' to convey everything from personal experience and individual consciousness.[119]

Apichatpong said that he was taught to do so in Chicago (where he attended film school) and noted that this was the Western way of conveying meaning.[120] Here, Apichatpong also contrasted the Western practice with the Thai approach to applying for public funding. He suggested that while a proposal to a film festival may only need some socio-political context to explain a story that should remain personal to the filmmaker, in Thailand, a typical film grant application would identify and prioritise a social objective to justify access to public funds.[121]

In this way, the practice of co-branding between festivals and filmmakers not only engages with the discourse of auteurism but also evokes the romantic ideal of creative genius. At first glance, what seems to follow from auteur-driven cinema is the notion that copyright law protects individual self-expression—that copyright represents a legal recognition of what is inherent to the relationship between

114 See Wikanda, 'Apichatpong' (n 10) 21.
115 Interviewee A.
116 For more detail on the effect of international film festivals, such as the IFFR, on the subject matter and aesthetic choices of Thai independent filmmakers, see Peerachai (n 16).
117 See 'Co-Authoring a Brand' in this chapter.
118 Sonthaya and Teekadech (n 16) 214–215.
119 ibid.
120 ibid.
121 ibid.

filmmakers and their work.[122] And indeed, there appears to be a growing sense of urgency among Thai independent filmmakers regarding the issue of who owns the rights to films.[123] Also added to this agitation is the fact that most of these filmmakers would likely agree that retaining the rights will not improve their financial situation in a meaningful way.[124] Even so, such an awareness of copyright law, familiar though it may be, does not necessarily indicate a belated universalisation of the romantic views on property and selfhood.[125] Instead of making such an assumption, it is better to consider copyright ownership in light of what has become evident from the discussion of auteur branding.

While it is wise to assume that various factors must have contributed to the growing recognition that copyright issues are not something to brush aside—and that different filmmakers may have different reasons for asserting their rights—an emerging theme in the independent production practices around copyright law is, once again, the agency of filmmakers. The exclusive rights allow independent filmmakers to set the agenda for how their films are used, making the topic of copyright law increasingly relevant to their strategies for personal branding. With film festivals playing a role from the stage of production through to distribution, the main gateway to the auteur brand is undoubtedly the film festival circuit, but each festival is a complex network of relationships that filmmakers must navigate.[126] And to negotiate their positions within this network, there may be situations requiring the intervention of copyright law, particularly when securing film funding is at stake.

Inasmuch as the branding of a given festival typically ties into its funding criteria, the task of raising funds for an independent film also requires the filmmaker's personal brand as well as copyright agreements. Furthermore, it is common for an independent production to rely on multiple funding sources, often combining grants from festivals and cultural institutions with foreign investments and, occasionally, personal funds.[127] As this observation suggests, a festival grant is hardly adequate for the cost of filmmaking, but what it also does is raise the filmmaker's profile, which in turn attracts further funding opportunities.[128]

Therefore, film financing is closely connected with personal branding, making it common for Thai independent filmmakers to take their projects through a circuit of film festivals to raise the funds as well as their profiles.[129] As a result, a situation of international co-production often arises from the international funding

122 See 'Authorship and Ownership' in Chapter 2.

123 Interviewee D; Interviewee F.

124 Interviewee C.

125 See 'Person, Property, and Empire' in Chapter 2.

126 For a good illustration using the example of the IFFR, see Marijke de Valck, 'Drowning in popcorn at the International Film Festival Rotterdam? The festival as a multiplex of cinephilia' in Marijke de Valck and Malte Hagener (eds), *Cinephilia: Movies, Love and Memory* (Amsterdam University Press 2005).

127 Interviewee F.

128 ibid.

129 Interview F. Interestingly, this theme also runs through nearly all interviews with Thai independent filmmakers presented in Sonthaya and Teekadech (n 16).

landscape. One challenge this poses for Thai independent filmmakers is the issue of coordinating with co-producers and investors.[130] Here, copyright law can serve as a mediating agent by structuring their relationships and interactions through defining and sanctioning the necessary agreements on ownership, rights distribution, territories division, and so forth.[131] In this way, the notion of agency not only foregrounds relationships in film production but also points to a significant role of copyright law in mediating relationships among those involved.

Let Me Entertain You

This relational perspective also makes discussions about copyright law more receptive to emerging practices in commercial cinema, which might otherwise be overshadowed by the risks of piracy and the incentives for exclusivity. More specifically, the issue of agency highlights the fact that those who read, watch, and listen also contribute to film culture. In this way, the change can begin with a greater focus on contemporary audiences whose contributions are often obscured by the notion of consumption. Given the level of engagement they have with the auteur brand, contemporary audiences are not mere consumers; they should be considered producers in their own right.

Similarly, shifting the focus to audiences will also move the discussion beyond both the incentives argument and what remains of romantic authorship. The primary concern will not be the creation of a new product or the protection of the author's property but rather the use of the product/property. However, this is 'use' as in 'user,' not as in 'useful,' and to use in this manner does not distinguish art from entertainment; therefore, it does not matter if pain makes better art or if entertainment is a mere pleasure. Indeed, pleasure is productive insofar as it produces new relations and connections, and the same applies to film as entertainment.

Audience engagement has become the focus of contemporary Thai cinema. Not only has the digital boom affected the mode and manner of film consumption, but perhaps more importantly, it has transformed the relationships between filmmakers and audiences. Averaging in their mid-20s when they made their first film, the *Thi-Baan* filmmakers were digital natives well-versed in participatory digital culture—so much so that even their solution to the challenge of film financing also involved a digital strategy[132]: When they struggled to find investors for the first

130 Apichatpong speaks from his experience of the difficulty in dividing ownership in the case of international co-production. See Sonthaya and Teekadech (n 16) 210–209.

131 For a brief discussion of copyright clauses in international co-production agreements, see Francisco Javier Cabrera Blázquez, Maja Cappello, Enric Enrich, Julio Talavera Milla, and Sophie Valais, 'The legal framework for international co-productions' (*European Audiovisual Observatory*, 2018) <https://rm.coe.int/iris-plus-2018-3-the-legal-framework-for-international-co-productions/168090369b> accessed 20 February 2025.

132 See an interview with Surask Pongsorn (director) organised by Thailand's National Innovation Agency (NIA), 'คุณสุรศักดิ์ ป้องศร ผู้จุดกระแส 'หนังไทบ้าน เดอะซีรีย์' ('Surask Pongsorn, the man behind the popular "Thi-Baan the Series"') (NIA Facebook Page, 25 January 2018) <https://www.facebook.com/watch/live/?ref=watch_permalink&v=1553552991348688> accessed 20 February 2025.

film, these young filmmakers decided to create a homemade film trailer and share it on social media to engage potential audiences.[133] This move successfully earned them an online presence that proved significant for how the film project unfolded.

Through social media, the *Thi-Baan* filmmakers were able to identify and connect with their target audiences, whose support helped them secure the necessary investment.[134] In fact, the young filmmakers dedicated much time and energy to fostering active participation from their fans and followers, with whom they sought to build a close relationship that eventually contributed to the film's financial success.[135] In the current digital environment, it is not just Hollywood but a whole host of online content with which Thai filmmakers have to compete for the audiences' attention. Advertising campaigns can be insufficient or far too expensive to be effective, and many Thai filmmakers appear to recognise the necessity of creating a social media presence to maintain a fan base and engage with potential audiences.[136]

Just as the bond of kinship is always two-way, another significant aspect of the digital kinship surrounding the *Thi-Baan* phenomenon was the rise of affective labour. The critical and commercial success of the *Thi-Baan* franchise can be attributed to the active participation of the audiences. The scant budget of the first *Thi-Baan* film meant that it was promoted on a shoestring, relying on the audiences who carried out the necessary work of promotion by expressing their affection online through reviews, comments, and memes.[137] This explains why publicity by word-of-mouth was celebrated in the media as the key to the unexpected success of the first *Thi-Baan* film.[138] The national breakthrough of the previously unknown *Isan* film also demonstrates that audiences indeed produce as much as they consume, and the embodiment of this form of social production can be found in all manner of online activities.[139] In the case of the *Thi-Baan* series, online reviews, discussions, and simple social media interactions, such as likes and shares, have been instrumental in establishing the *Thi-Baan* films as a new entertainment franchise.

Today, the '*Thi-Baan* universe' has become the media's description of an expanding multimedia output that encompasses film (including spin-offs), music (including soundtracks, music videos, and live performances), and social media (such as video clips and live streams)—all engaging and designed to foster further interactions.[140] Ultimately, at a time when Thai filmmakers still cannot earn a living

133 ibid.
134 ibid.
135 ibid.
136 ibid.
137 ibid.
138 See for instance '**ความสำเร็จ ไทบ้าน เดอะซีรีส์ และความเสี่ยงในตลาดหนัง**' ('The success of Thi-Baan the Series and the risks in film market') (Thai PBS, 23 February 2018) <https://www.thaipbs.or.th/news/content/270500> accessed 20 February 2025.
139 For further discussion, see 'Social Production' in Chapter 7.
140 See for instance Rattanapol Tipmanee, "**จักรวาลไทบ้าน' ในวันที่คนทำหนังไม่มีที่ทางทดเวลาบาดเจ็บ**' ('"Thi-Baan Universe" in an age when filmmakers do not get injury time') (*Way Magazine*, 10 December 2022) <https://waymagazine.org/thaibaan-interview/> accessed 20 February 2025. For the full breadth of the Thi-Baan universe, see official website <https://taibaan.com/> accessed 7 May 2025; official Facebook page <https://www.facebook.com/TaiBaanOfficial?locale=th_TH>

from feature films, the *Thi-Baan* filmmakers have been experimenting with the notion of film as a branding vehicle rather than a product as such.[141] Surasak Pongsorn, who emerged as the face of the group, explains that filmmaking can create a story for branding other potential products, from which the group can develop a business.[142] He provides one example from the second *Thi-Baan* film, in which a side story about a character developing a vegetable retail business was deliberately added with the hope that an actual retail franchise would follow.[143]

Another remarkable aspect of the *Thi-Baan* phenomenon was the proliferation of new meanings regarding the *Isan* identity and, by extension, what it means to be Thai. In parallel with its commercial success, the accessible entertainment of the *Thi-Baan* franchise proved conducive to a counter-discourse against the distorted representation of *Isan*. The portrayal of modern *Isan* life in the *Isan* voice has pushed back against decades of repression and misrepresentation by colonial Bangkok.[144] Even in mainstream media, this counter-movement is reflected in narratives attributing the surprise success of the first *Thi-Baan* film to the phenomenal reception it initially received in the peripheral region of *Isan* before the capital's multiplexes began to take notice.[145] This success story was described by the media as 'forest surrounding the city,' a well-known phrase originating from the policy of the Communist Party of Thailand, which envisaged a revolution that would proceed from the countryside to the city.[146] In this way, one can see that the discussions that arose from the on-screen projection of *Isan* life have interjected new ideas into the official discourse of what it means to be Thai.

At this point, it should be evident how the model of authorial self-expression is incapable of reflecting the role and contribution of audiences. Consumption is the new production, as it were, but this is not always recognised by copyright law, as it defines the role of audiences according to the conception of the creative process that rests on the author–user distinction.[147] In contrast, what has emerged from the discussion thus far is the mediating role of copyright law in the interactions among various actors in the production of Thai film culture. From this perspective, the

---

accessed7 May 2025; official YouTube channel <https://www.youtube.com/channel/UCiARyB-1wacrhQOhhT1K69Wg> accessed 20 February 2025.

141 Natee Meeprasert, '**สุรศักดิ์ ป้องศร** Make a movie like a "creative brand"' (*Creative Thailand*, 5 May 2018) <https://www.creativethailand.org/new/article/people/27917/en> accessed 20 February 2025.

142 ibid.

143 ibid.

144 See the Cold War politics around *Isan* identity in 'Identity Politics' in Chapter 3.

145 See for instance Prapt Bunpran, '**ไทบ้าน เดอะซีรีส์**' ('Thi-Baan the Series') (*Matichon*, 13 March 2017) <https://www.matichon.co.th/columnists/news_494156> accessed 20 February 2025.

146 ibid. See also '**ย้อนประวัติพรรคคอมมิวนิสต์แห่งประเทศไทย ในการเปิดตัวครั้งแรกหลังสงบนิ่งกว่า 30 ปี**' ('Tracing the history of the Communist Party of Thailand in the wake of its re-emergence after more than 30 years of inactivity') (BBC Thai, 31 March 2018) <https://www.bbc.com/thai/thailand-43603766> accessed 20 February 2025.

147 This legal distinction is further explored in 'The Public–Private Dichotomy' in Chapter 8.

function of copyright exclusivity is not merely to exclude but intertwines with the dynamics among various actors who form a web of productive relationships known as Thai cinema. Thai cinema, therefore, constitutes a locus of social production; its nature and relations to copyright law are the subjects of discussion in the next chapter.

Part IV

Community After All

7 Copyright in (Inter)Action

Today, arguing that film production is a collaborative process may no longer be controversial. However, the idea of collaboration is only a starting point for approaching filmmaking as a matter of social production.[1] The picture that emerged from the discussion in Chapter 6 is a multitude of productive relations encompassing various actors, from directors to cinema operators to audiences and many more. Furthermore, these relations do not just produce the material effects of sight and sound, unlike the linear, producer-consumer model that is collaboration. When the audiences identify with the *Isan* characters in *Thi-Baan*, empathise with the work-life balance dilemma in *Heart Attack*, or become intrigued by Apichatpong's unconventional aesthetics, simultaneously at work is the production of affects and the creation of meaning and value pertaining to such questions as what makes a good film.[2]

Indeed, the notion of a 'good film' in Thai cinema, tied closely to the mass–indie distinction, holds significant implications for what films will be made, who will watch them, and how they will be appreciated.[3] In other words, the discursive practices create resonance back on the material side and set things in motion.[4] This process of reflexive movements is duly reflected in the affective labour of fans, the creation of auteur brands, and, more generally, the repetition of specific stories, themes, and genres in Thai cinema.

For the same reason, the phenomenon of auteur branding also indicates the social nature of film production. Affection and affiliation have been significant to

1 For legal discussions on the collaborative nature of filmmaking, see for instance Dougherty, 'Not a Spike Lee joint?'; Handler, 'Continuing problems with film copyright'; Daniela Simone, *Copyright and Collective Authorship: Locating the Author of Collaborative Work* (CUP 2019).

2 The term 'affect' is adopted with reference to its usage in the work of Deleuze and Guattari, see Deleuze and Guattari, *A Thousand Plateaus,* 256–257. For Deleuze and Guattari, affects refer to the changes or variations that are the transitional products of an encounter or a coming together of bodies. Affects, therefore, describe the productive forces inherent in all forms of social interactions, and in this way, the idea of affect is pertinent to the topic of social production and the concept of familiar production, as discussed later in this chapter in 'Social Production.'

3 See the discussion of mass and indie films in 'Good Entertainment' in Chapter 5.

4 Deleuze and Guattari, *A Thousand Plateaus* (n 2) 6. See also Ian Buchanan, *Assemblage Theory and Method* (Bloomsbury 2021) 34.

DOI: 10.4324/9781003592037-12

the branding of Apichatpong, whose films have been admired and celebrated by the international community of cinephiles and the network of international film festivals.[5] In addition, the development of his auteurist status was simultaneously an exercise in branding on the part of the festivals. The IFFR, for instance, has built an international reputation as a discoverer of international talents with a specialisation in 'art, avant-garde, and auteurs' by way of self-positioning within the festival network.[6] With Apichatpong, the IFFR has been his long-time supporter with film grants, art commissions, and special events, as well as financing opportunities on its industrial front, namely the Cinemart.[7]

This kind of support may seem altruistic, but it can be a strategy of co-branding that creates a mutually beneficial relationship between festivals and directors, as can be seen in the IFFR's self-positioning and Apichatpong's trajectory as an auteurist director. It is fair to say that Apichatpong's films and his auteur brand are bound up with the way the cultural field of the film festival network sustains itself.[8]

In this way, the important thing about the back-and-forth movements between the material and the discursive is the way the interactions between different actors in Thai cinema both enable and condition Thai film production. Films are thus expressive of the connections and combinations that make up the creative assemblage in which they are produced. It also means the final product, or a finished film, neither marks a completion nor imposes an enclosure but becomes a new point of connection in the continuous production of effects, affects, and resonance. Consequently, films as finished products become unfinished when they are located and traced inside the creative assemblage of Thai cinema.

It is necessary to note here that the same social processes also produce a sense of community and belonging that pushes the meaning of social production to encompass the social of production, as just seen, and the social in production, as discussed next. Consequently, this brings into question the conventional site of value in the 'product' and the 'work' that currently constitutes the locus of control and protection for copyright law. Suffice it to say that a further discussion of these creative social processes crucially and constructively informs a re-conception of copyright as a community resource.

I. Social Production

As just mentioned, drawing attention to the social nature of film production raises a further question of whether films are conversely enmeshed in the production of the social world for what has come out of the interactions between those participating in the production and consumption of Thai films goes well beyond the

5 See 'Co-Authoring a Brand' in Chapter 6.

6 Marijke De Valck, *Film Festivals: From European Geopolitics to Global Cinephilia* (Amsterdam University Press 2007) 43.

7 Promkhuntong, *Film Authorship in Contemporary Transmedia Culture*, 47.

8 ibid 58–62.

economic production of consumer goods. Yet it would not be something new to suggest that film production sometimes plays a notable role in the reproduction of social and cultural institutions. Jean-Louis Baudry, for one, saw the ideological effects of cinematic apparatus in the latter's ability to imbue the spectators with the dominant ideology.[9] Other theorists have examined the link between cultural reproduction and the reproduction of social stratification.[10] Suffice it to say that the social production of films should be understood in relation to the role of film in social reproduction, but recognising the relationships between film production and social reproduction does not necessarily repudiate the agency of individual actors or deny the possibility of social change.[11]

A case in point is the crucial debates about identity and nationhood in response to the significant amount of online content produced in relation to the *Thi-Baan* franchise with its on-screen representation of *Isan*.[12] This portrayal of modern *Isan* life in the *Isan* voice pushed back against decades of repression and misrepresentation by colonial Bangkok. In this way, the *Thi-Baan* phenomenon changed the public discourse around *Isan*, as well as signalling the changing business landscape of Thai films. As already discussed, relationships with the audiences were integral to the success of the *Thi-Baan* franchise, where word of mouth reflected a social process that was both intimate and productive.[13]

Indeed, it was the production of meaning and value, which the films acquired through the emotional investment of the audiences, that was key to the franchise's popularity and financial success. This intimate, non-economic form of social production appeared to be driven by a sense of affiliation created through the on-screen projection of people's relationships with their immediate locality as well as the off-screen interactions, including the digital kinship between the *Thi-Baan* film-makers and their fans, which the films generated on social media. Moreover, the emergence of regional audiences that came with the films' immense success in the

9 Baudry pointed out specific operations of a camera, the nature of film editing, and, perhaps most crucially, the way the finished film was projected before the spectator—all of this was to support his contention that the ideological effect of cinema lied in its apparatus. See Jean-Louis Baudry and Alan Willian (tr), 'Ideological effects of the basic cinematographic apparatus' (1974) 28(2) *Film Quarterly* 39; Jean-Louis Baudry, Jean Andrews (tr), and Bertrand Augst (tr), 'The apparatus' (1976) 1(11) *Camara Obscura* 104.

10 For instance, Pierre Bourdieu, through his concepts of field and habitus, demonstrates 'the contribution made by the educational system to the reproduction of the structure of power relationships and symbolic relationships between classes, by contributing to the reproduction of the structure of the distribution of cultural capital among these classes.' See Pierre Bourdieu, 'Cultural reproduction and social reproduction' in Jeorome Karabel and A H Halsey (eds), *Power and Ideology in Education* (OUP 1977).

11 On the one hand, it is fair to say Baudry's apparatus theory has become obsolete, see Thomas Elsaesser, 'What is left of the cinematic apparatus, or why we should retain (and return to) it' (2011) 31(1-2-3) *Recherches Sémiotiques* 33. Meanwhile, it is also possible to argue that Bourdieu's analysis of social reproduction does not entirely deny the possibility of social change, see Lois McNay, 'Meditations on Pascalian meditations' (2001) 30(1) *Economy and Society* 139.

12 See 'Let Me Entertain You' in Chapter 6.

13 ibid.

regional market of *Isan* (which became a springboard to the subsequent distribution in Bangkok and elsewhere) also presents an opportunity for all Thai filmmakers to try to connect with the regional forms of sensibility and familiarity.[14]

Familiar Production

When viewed as an assemblage of productive relationships, these interpersonal activities around film production and consumption express a particular mode of social production that resonates with what Johanna Gibson calls familiar production:

> Familiar production is perhaps more concerned with the production of affiliative assemblages than with the particular products that may be produced through, and indexical of, those relations.[15]

Indeed, to be 'familiar' engenders an intimate sense of acquaintance and association such that to describe 'production' as familiar is to fold the economic (the production of goods and services) back into the social.[16] Thus, the concept of familiar production is attuned to the social of production. It encompasses the cultural circumstances of film production, as exemplified by the practices of auteur branding and the creative role of contemporary audiences.[17] This is why familiar production is not directed towards the creation of discrete objects such as film products.[18] And for the same reason, it is more concerned with the production of affiliations and associations, the kind of production that played a part in the struggle to liberate *Isan* identity and has opened up a new market of Thai regional cinema. As such, describing 'production' as familiar also indicates that this type of production is continuous and experiential in nature.[19] Indeed, familiarity—be it the familiarity of kinship, locality, or brand—is conducive to more interactions and hence more production of new meaning and value.

Understanding film production and consumption in terms of familiar production dislocates the product and producer from their privileged position. It shifts attention from the production of films as goods to the production of familiarity through films, and in this way, familiar production allows for the recognition of fluid relations among the participants in the Thai cinema assemblage. Their roles will not be reduced to the binary distinction between producer and consumer, or for that

14 See for instance Kong Rithdee, 'A wind from the Northeast' (*Bangkok Post*, 24 March 2017) <https://www.bangkokpost.com/life/arts-and-entertainment/1220321/a-wind-from-the-northeast> accessed 20 February 2025; Tatat Bunnag, 'A shining star in the North' (*Bangkok Post*, 24 January 2020) <https://www.bangkokpost.com/life/arts-and-entertainment/1842594/a-shining-star-in-the-north> accessed 20 February 2025.

15 Johanna Gibson, *Owned, an Ethological Jurisprudence of Property* (Routledge 2020) 298.

16 Gibson, *The Logic of Innovation*, 33.

17 See the discussion in Chapter 6.

18 Gibson, *Logic* (n 16) 37.

19 ibid 39–40.

matter, between author and user. But most importantly, familiar production moves social interactions to the foreground and a sense of community to the centre stage.

The production of familiarity resonates with the idea of community insofar as a community is a place where one feels at home—it is the familiar territory.[20] A territorial meaning of familiarity is reflected in an attachment to a geographical locality that characterises the notion of a community as understood traditionally and exemplified sociologically by the imagery of the pre-modern *Gemeinschaft*.[21] However, a community can also be 'something for people to think with' that can do away with the sharing of a locality while retaining the feeling of familiarity.[22] A sense of community can also arise when people feel at home in a situation of collective involvement or concern that has become their familiar territory. For this reason, social interactions can express a sense of community in various ways, based on a convergence of goals, a sharing of values, or a myriad of circumstances beyond geographical proximity.[23]

As discussed in relation to Thai cinema, one could say that the *Thi-Baan* phenomenon and the practices of author branding exemplify social groupings and allegiances underpinned by a sense of community. Taking another example from the Thai film industry, the 'feel-good' branding of GDH, the former GTH, also presents a case of community building by creating a familiar territory.[24]

The Bangkok-based GDH has often been a target of criticism from serious filmmakers and cinema goers, most of whom have deemed the studio's commercial style of filmmaking lacking in regional sensitivity and social commentary.[25] This criticism in itself is perhaps a testament to the success and popularity of GDH, whose executives have always insisted that the studio feels at home making films that communicate with large audiences rather than pursuing award-winning, auteurist cinema.[26] And indeed, GDH has been very successful with what it has professed to do, that is, moving the audiences with 'feel-good' films.[27] So much so that GDH has become a brand synonymous with feel-good films, and it is possible

20 The term 'territory' is adopted with reference to its usage by Deleuze and Guattari; see *A Thousand Plateaus* (n 2) 319–320. For Deleuze and Guattari, we are not territorial by nature, but territorialisation allows us to create for ourselves a place in nature, or to bring some order to chaos. In this way, territory is an act, not a space, and it is an expression of desire rather than of a function of instinct. See also Buchanan (n 1144) 97–98.

21 Cotterrell, *Law, Culture, and Society,* 43.

22 Cohen, *The Symbolic Construction of Community*.

23 See further discussion on this concept of community in 'Copyright's Community' in Chapter 8.

24 See for instance 'Thai film directors spread happiness' (*Bangkok Post*, 29 December 2021) <https://www.bangkokpost.com/life/arts-and-entertainment/2239407/thai-film-directors-spread-happiness> accessed 20 February 2025.

25 Interviewee D.

26 See an interview with a GDH executive in Siwaprak Jianwanalee, '**วรรณฤดี พงษ์สิทธิศักดิ์: หญิงสาวผู้อยู่เบื้องหลังความสำเร็จของค่ายหนัง** GTH (**และ** GDH)' ('Vanridee Pongsittisak: The lady behind the success of GTH (and GDH)') (*A Day Magazine*) <https://adaymagazine.com/yesterday-56/> accessed 20 February 2025.

27 ibid.

to say that feel-good cinema constitutes familiar territory for those working at the famous Thai studio, whose name is an acronym for 'Gross Domestic Happiness.'[28]

Seeing community relations in familiar production brings the idea of manners and courtesy into the sphere of production. In the same way that courtesy creates a better community, copyright law has furnished a language of manners for participants in the social production of Thai cinema. As will be seen, the need for manners also exists in the relationships of familiar production such that permission and attribution constitute a matter of courtesy or, one might say, the living law of a community.[29]

Artistic Copyright

Recalling the film 'Sorry,' the overall ambiguity of its stance towards unauthorised copying is a reflection of the changing social relations in Thailand after the turn of the century.[30] In 'Sorry,' the notion of theft constitutes a site for negotiating territorial disputes over the elusive borderlines of original and copy, creator and user, modern and traditional, Thai self and Western Other.[31] Property is thus territorial, and it is crucial to distinguish territorialisation from domination. As seen in the discussion of 'Sorry,' the adopted language of theft suggests an idea of property that is less about the object of one's ownership than the marking of one's territory—or as Deleuze and Guattari say,

> Property is fundamentally artistic because art is fundamentally *poster, placard*. As Lorenz says, coral fish are posters. The expressive is primary in relation to the possessive; expressive qualities, or matters of expression, are necessarily appropriative and constitute a having more profound than being. Not in the sense that these qualities belong to a subject, but in the sense that they delineate a territory that will belong to the subject that carries or produces them.[32]

From this perspective, the difference between Wor Wachirametee's moral imperative and the film's overall ambiguity becomes a reflection of two contrasting

28 Its mission statement says, 'GDH aims to create uniqueness and globally appealing content by elevating the quality of Thai films and TV series to a world-class level, and in doing so, creating smiles, laughter, pleasure, and greater gross happiness to the audience.' <https://www.gdh559.com/about> accessed 20 February 2025.

29 Eugen Ehrlich coined the term 'living law' to contrast with statutory enactment and judicial decision. It is 'the law which dominates life itself even through it has not been posited in legal propositions.' In other words, living law thus refers to social norms/normative structures of social life. See Eugen Ehrlich, *The Fundamental Principles of Sociology of Law* (Transaction Publishers 2002) 493. The idea of living law is further developed by Roger Cotterrell into a legal concept of community, which is fundamental to the concept of community resource to be developed later in this chapter.

30 See 'What Is Wrong Is Copying' in Chapter 5.

31 See 'Ethical Choice' in Chapter 5.

32 Deleuze and Guattari, *A Thousand Plateaus* (n 2) 316.

images of private territory. On the one hand, Wor Wachirametee's moral judgement of copying as theft reiterates a clear separation of individual boundaries, at least insofar as these are demarcated by copyright ownership.[33] This comes in contrast with the sense of ambivalence in 'Sorry,' a sense that evokes an image of overlapping boundaries.[34] Nawapol, unlike Wor Wachirametee, seems to ask whether boundaries were drawn simply to keep others out. The film not only addresses the inspiration–imitation conundrum but also opens it up to the broader question of how change occurs within culture and society.[35] In doing so, there is also an allusion to the idea of social agency, for 'Sorry' invites the viewer to consider the actions of these individual characters in the context of broader social relations.

As the story unfolds, it becomes clear that 'Sorry' does not tell a simple story of how copying is wrong because it is stealing. Imm may accuse Sun of stealing ideas from other filmmakers, but her accusation may well be interpreted as a claim of misattribution that does not target the taking of ideas per se. This caveat resonates with the senior members' arguments about how copying is not only inextricable to cultural progress but also allows the original work to reach a wider audience. In the end, both sides seem to show a recognition of overlapping territories that point to an appreciation of incremental innovation and community relations.

Indeed, the main point of contention lies in the way Sun uses others' ideas, and everyone in the room seems to acknowledge that he is guilty of acting against good manners. This suggests that the language of theft is not adopted simply to convey the sanctity of private property; the speaking of theft rather turns the problem of copying into a question of manners and courtesy. In other words, the argument over whether Sun is an idea thief shows a shared concern regarding the need to sustain interpersonal trust and safeguard familiar territory.[36]

II. Familiar Territory

The changing global film market has deterritorialised film production and distribution so much that the Thai film industry has seen a significant increase in the number of foreign productions and international co-productions.[37] Local production,

33 See 'Moral Panic' in Chapter 5.

34 Recalling that when Sun admits to stealing ideas, it is open to be interpreted as a confession to lying as much as copying because Imm has confronted him for claiming that the idea came to him in sleep. See 'Ethical Choice' in Chapter 5.

35 This happens when the senior members come to Sun's defence by shifting the argument to the social aspects of copying.

36 The idea of trust is central to the concept of community resource. This is discussed later in 'Mutual Trust' in Chapter 8.

37 See for instance Kim Seonghoon, 'Korea-Southeast Asia co-productions are booming' (*Korean Film Council*, 12 October 2017) <https://www.koreanfilm.or.kr/eng/news/features.jsp?blbdComCd=601013&seq=441&mode=FEATURES_VIEW> accessed 20 February 2025. See also '**สถิติการถ่ายทำภาพยนตร์ต่างประเทศในประเทศไทย**' ('Statistics on foreign film productions in Thailand') (*Department of Tourism*) <https://www.dot.go.th/chart-stat/category/4> accessed 7 May 2025.

too, has received growing interest from international audiences,[38] and this trend towards internationalisation has reterritorialised the mass-indie divide in Thai cinema.[39] Some signs of rapprochement can be seen in recent debates around government support for Thai filmmakers and the working conditions of Thai film crews.[40] Copyright-related issues, too, have transpired to be an area of shared concern.[41]

With more independent filmmakers seeking to sustain their artistic pursuits outside the studio system, copyright ownership and exploitation are no longer a subject of concern reserved for mainstream commercial films.[42] In addition, the viability of the industry at large has also been a common concern in public controversies concerning piracy and unauthorised copying.[43] As discussed below, many conventional and emerging practices concerning copyright ownership and exploitation indicate shared interests in the formation and continuation of alliances and associations. The discussion begins with common practices concerning copyright ownership, followed by copyright licensing and film distribution, and finally, public attitudes towards copyright infringement.

Build a House, Make a Home

First ownership answers a basic legal question that aims to put a name to the figure of the copyright owner who traverses between the realms of legal logic and social experience. In legal analysis, the identity of the copyright owner is a fundamental question insofar as ownership demarcates a private, enclosed territory from which other people are excluded. Although one can say the ownership language in the

38 See for instance Patrick Brzeski, 'Netflix Unveils Slate of Six Originals from Thailand' (*The Hollywood Reporter*, 11 October 2022) <https://www.hollywoodreporter.com/movies/movie-news/netflix-thailand-originals-1235238618/> accessed 20 February 2025; Zhao Ziwen, 'New Netflix movie The Lost Lotteries ushers in a slate of new Thai content—Will it boost Thailand's pop culture to compete with K-pop and K-dramas?' (*South China Morning Post*, 15 October 2022) <https://www.scmp.com/lifestyle/entertainment/article/3195998/new-netflix-movie-lost-lotteries-ushers-slate-new-thai> accessed 20 February 2025.

39 For instance, a roundtable discussion was organised as part of the Bangkok Asian Film Festival 2019 to build a bridge between studio-backed and independent filmmakers. See Chatrawee Sentanissak, '**คุยกับผู้จัด** Roundtable **กิจกรรมเพื่อเชื่อมหนังแมส-อินดี้/รุ่นใหญ่-รุ่นใหม่/ไทย-อาเซียน**' ('A conversation with the organisers of Roundtable, an even to connect mass-indie films/old-new generations/Thai-ASEAN') (The Momentum, 4 July 2019) <https://themomentum.co/roundtable-arthit-pimpaka/> accessed 20 February 2025.

40 See for instance Supawan Kongsuwan, 'The ugly truth: **ชั่วโมงการทำงาน ค่าแรง และความจริงที่เจ็บปวดของงานกองถ่าย**' ('The ugly truth: Working hours, wages, and the painful reality of film production') (The 101.World, 10 July 2020) <https://www.the101.world/the-ugly-truth-of-flimcrew/> accessed 20 February 2025.

41 This is particularly evident among young Thai filmmakers, for whom copyright issues are tied up with the future development of Thai cinema. See for instance Parichat Hantonsirisakul, '**ให้มันจบที่รุ่นเรา: การเมือง ประชาธิปไตย และคนรุ่นใหม่ในอุตสาหกรรมภาพยนตร์ไทย**' ('It is going to end with our generation: Politics, democracy, and the new generation in Thai film industry') (The Film Club, 12 December 2020) <https://filmclubthailand.com/film-interview/let-it-end-in-our-generation-politic-democracy-and-new-generation-in-thai-film-industry-part-1/> accessed 20 February 2025.

42 Interviewee C.

43 See 'Trusting Relationship' in this chapter.

film industry also entails the idea of exclusion, exclusion only constitutes one part of the broader picture.

That ownership of film copyright belongs to the studio is common knowledge in the industry.[44] Perhaps this is something to be expected from the viewpoint of film financing and commercialisation, but beneath the universality of impersonal logic and economic calculation lies a sphere of relationship. In Thai commercial cinema, the practices of first ownership often reflect a patron-client relationship between Thai directors and the influential figure of '*sia*' in the studio system.[45]

The *sia* is a powerful male figure who represents wealthy owners of film studios, but it is not just the wealth that makes these men influential. *Sia* does not only mean rich man: It implies a cultural status defined by his patronage over those who accept his sphere of influence.[46] As such, it is both his status and investment that underpin the nexus of contracts binding artists and creators to a film project with a 'hire of work' agreement.[47] Under Thai law, a hire of work binds the artist/creator to the hiring studio as a contractor working on a film that will become the studio's property.[48] It is, therefore, a reciprocal agreement, but one of a kind that does not necessarily reflect the kind of reciprocity that often characterises the actual relationship between Thai studios and directors.

For Thai directors, the opportunity to make a film is a consideration in itself, and it is a very significant one given the situation of local film productions.[49] In this regard, a hire of work appears to give legal effect to a different kind of reciprocity that is more personal and affective. This kind of relationship is essentially a clientelist exchange where a director seeks opportunity and support from the *sia* figure who picks a project to finance and obtains the rights to the film to seek returns on the investment.[50]

First ownership is thus determined by financial investment, but only arguably insofar as this arrangement will continue the reciprocal relationship between the parties involved.[51] This means that first ownership does not reflect a simple economic exchange where film directors merely trade their creative labour for remuneration. On the contrary, the common assumption that studios have the rights to films points to the recognition of shared interests: Film directors also stand to benefit when the studios are rewarded for taking financial risks.[52]

44 Interviewee A.

45 ibid.

46 One might even assert that the history of Thai cinema evolved from the adoption of an invention under royal patronage to the industrial support of film tycoons. For further information, see Unaloam Chanrungmaneekul, 120 **ปี ธุรกิจภาพยนตร์ไทย ในมิติประวัติศาสตร์เศรษฐกิจและสังคมไทย** (*120 years of Thai film business from the historical perspective of thai economy and society*) (Thailand Research Fund 2018).

47 'Hire of work' is a specific concept in Thai private law that refers to a form of service contract, and it is usually contrasted with an employment contract. See 'Burning Down the House' below.

48 TCA 1994, s 10.

49 Interviewee G.

50 Interviewee A.

51 However, reciprocity does not necessarily imply equal relations.

52 Box office success can also become a personal brand. For instance, Bangjong Pisanthanakun (Tong) is often referred to in Thai media as the 'billion (Baht) director' to refer to the total grossing of his

That said, this observation does not intend to make light of the unequal power relations that characterise a patron–client relationship. Indeed, inequalities of bargaining power can be problematic and a source of abuse, as discussed later.[53] The point being made here is the possible function of copyright ownership in aligning the interests of investors and creators such that it gives expression to a sense of affinity rather than causing them to hold each other at arm's length.

Compared with studio production, independent filmmaking is rather different. The practices of first ownership seem to vary because the financing landscape of independent cinema is quite diverse. Working outside the studio system means Thai independent filmmakers have to seek funding from various domestic and international sources, both private and institutional.[54]

The challenge of financing a film outside the studio system brings to the fore the role of film producers with their international network of financiers and distributors as well as their creative relations with film directors.[55] This distinct feature of independent cinema is reflected in how copyright ownership is determined between producers and directors. In general, consideration is given to, on the one hand, the nature of an independent film as the director's passion project that often deals with a personal subject and, on the other hand, the producer's years-long work of project management that goes from raising funds to production and distribution.[56]

Thus, determining copyright ownership appears to be a site for producers and directors to negotiate their working relationships. Unsurprisingly perhaps, there appears to be a presumption that the directors are the copyright owners because making an independent film is commonly viewed as a passion project that pursues personal ambition. Even so, this view not only does not preclude but even highlights the important role that film producers play in the process of turning ideas on paper into movies on screens.[57] In this regard, it is fair to say a producer is an indispensable bridge between dream and reality.[58]

With the director and producer bringing different things to the project, the dynamics of their relationship are such that one may see something akin to the mediation between art and commerce, albeit the commercial aspect is usually far

---

film *Pee Mak* that was released in 2013. See for instance '**โต้ง ผกก พันล้านปลื้ม**' ('Tong, the billion-baht director, delighted') (Thairath, 9 October 2014) <https://www.thairath.co.th/content/455447> accessed 20 February 2025.

53 See 'Burning Down the House' at the end of this chapter.

54 Interviewee F. See also Sonthaya Subyen and Teekadech Watcharathanin, ***ปฏิบัติการหนังทุนข้ามชาติ*** *(Operation: Transnationally Funded Films)* (Openbooks 2010).

55 Interviewee C; Interviewee F.

56 ibid.

57 For more detail from the perspective of a producer of Apichatpong's film, see Pimchanok Puksuk, '**โปรดิวเซอร์คือสะพานระหว่างความฝันและความจริง' สนทนากับ ดีอานา บุสตามานเต หัวหน้าทีมโปรดิวเซอร์แห่ง** Memoria (2021)' ('A producer is a bridge between dream and reality: A conversation with Diana Bustamante, the producer of *Memoria* (2021)') (The Film Club, 28 February 2022) <https://filmclubthailand.com/film-interview/diana-bustamante-memoria-interview/> accessed 20 February 2025.

58 ibid.

from lucrative and considered a matter of survival rather than profitable.[59] Particularly in recent years, the significance of commercial exploitation seems to have increased with the increasing competition for funding at international film festivals, which have so far been the primary source of financing for Thai independent cinema.[60] This means Thai filmmakers have to be more attuned to the working of film markets to keep the wheels of Thai independent cinema turning.[61] However, this in no way suggests that independent producers necessarily limit their role to the practical aspects alone. On the contrary, a producer–director relationship can be highly collaborative, such that both may agree to joint ownership to recognise the producer's voice when making a creative decision.[62]

So far, what appears to emerge from the identified practices of first ownership in commercial and independent filmmaking is the recognition of shared interests in developing relationships and good rapport. As such, these practices do not quite fit in the combative narrative of IP that valorises ownership acquisition and exploitation.[63] Quite the opposite, the point of establishing who owns the rights is to create and maintain a sense of affinity that will prolong alliances and associations. In this sense, copyright ownership can be seen as an expression of relationship commitment.

That said, the continuation of such relationships will come to nothing if the films do not reach the audience. Granted that those involved in film production have shared interests in the film's success, one may now wonder whether the same perspective extends to their relations with those who enter the picture after the production stage.[64] It is thus time for the discussion to turn to the practices of copyright exploitation in film distribution.

It Takes a Village

Although the financing studio is the copyright owner, the film's commercial success will not just be the studio's success but the success of many more people who

59 Interviewee F.

60 Interviewee C; Interviewee F.

61 ibid.

62 For instance, Interviewee F says, 'When I work with a director as a producer, I tell them that I also make creative input.' 'I see to the production until completion, and I take care of where the film goes, with creative considerations.' And for Interviewee F, this working relationship is expressed through copyright ownership: 'Suppose that I work on this project (as a producer), and I don't get any copyright; what does that say about my relationship (to the film)? I just collect my pay, and that is it. My work is done when the film is finished. But if you have the copyright, it means: OK, you're prepared to see it through.'

63 See the discussion about Thailand 4.0 at the beginning of Chapter 5.

64 In fact, it may not be appropriate to view film production and distribution as two discrete stages because film financing can come from pre-sales, which means selling the distribution rights of a future film based on an estimated value of the project. For more detail, see Martin Kanzler, 'Fiction film financing in Europe: A sample analysis of films released in 2019' (European Audiovisual Observatory, 2021) <https://rm.coe.int/fiction-film-financing-in-europe-2021-edition/1680a57229> accessed 20 February 2025.

have been involved in the enterprise.[65] Thai directors who work in the studio system may not own the rights to the films, but that does not mean they have no interest in how their films do at the box office. In this regard, what appears crucial to the reciprocal relationships that underlie and legitimise the practice of studio ownership, as discussed earlier, is the right to exploitation. Film studios are in the business of selling films, while filmmakers want the opportunity to make a film that audiences will see. Both, therefore, have shared interests in the exploitation of films, which brings our attention to the subject of film distribution.

Recalling the commercial practice of release windows, film studios with their exclusive rights do not benefit from exclusion per se but rather from the ability to set the conditions for how the films are distributed.[66] Vested with exclusive rights, studios can leverage these exploitation rights in contractual negotiations with other participants of film distribution. The language of contract law—deeply entwined with the notions of freedom and autonomy—may entice the conception of film distribution as a collection of atomised and impersonal exchanges.[67] This version of a contractual nexus gives an image of a film marketplace that cannot account for the business relations that underpin the nationwide system of commercial film distribution. Film studios, cinema owners, and regional distributors have long been the main actors in a national network of film distribution.[68] These actors are not mere counterparties to a transaction of the permission to use or a transfer of property; rather, they have shared interests in the overall enterprise of film distribution.

Nowhere can this be seen more clearly than in the problem of piracy. The two major cinema chains have played an active role by acting as the first line of defence against illegal recording in cinemas.[69] Camcording was once a significant source of unauthorised copies in the Thai market, so much so that the Thai legislature decided to introduce special measures against illegal recording in cinemas.[70] The discussions around the proposal threw light on how major cinema chains had worked

65 In this regard, it is worth comparing to a study of Australian film and television sector by Bowrey and Handler, who explain how copyright, combined with public policy and labour contract, is essential to the overall viability of the sector. See Kathy Bowrey and Michael Handler, 'Instituting copyright: Reconciling copyright law and industry practice in the Australian film and television sector' in Kathy Bowrey and Michael Handler (eds), *Law and Creativity in the Age of the Entertainment Franchise* (CUP 2014).

66 See 'Long Live Cinemas' in Chapter 6.

67 For a critical perspective on the legal concept of freedom of contract, see for instance PS Atiyah, *The Rise and Fall of Freedom of Contract* (Clarendon Press 2003).

68 For detailed discussion, see Unaloam Chanrungmaneekul, ***โรงหนัง สายหนัง ความ (ไร้) อำนาจของคนดูและศิลปิน ธุรกิจการฉายภาพยนตร์และสังคมไทย พ.ศ.*** *2440–2561 (Cinemas, Distributors, and the (Absent) Power of Audiences and Artists: The Business of Film Exhibition and Thai Society 1897–2018)* (Thailand Research Fund 2020) 154.

69 See for instance '**พณ. ผนึกโรงหนังจับมือแอบถ่ายติดวงจรปิดใช้เป็นหลักฐานเชือดละเมิดลิขสิทธิ์**' ('Ministry of Commerce joins hands with cinemas in catching illegal camcording by installing CCTVs for evidence of copyright infringement') (Komchadluek, 6 April 2011) <https://www.komchadluek.net/news/94175> accessed 20 February 2025.

70 See Copyright Act (No 3) BE 2558 (2015), s 3. See also Copyright Act BE 2537 (1994) (as amended up to Copyright Act BE 2565 (2022)), s 28/1.

closely with the right owners, with whom the admission revenue was shared, in a concerted effort to tackle the problem.[71] Such cooperation indicated a sharing of territories, as engendered by the recognition of shared interests between those involved in film distribution.

While sharing the admission revenue is a standard practice in the exhibition sector, Thai film studios have gone a step further by developing business partnerships with the major cinema chains.[72] These relationships help to explain why a recent expansion of multiplex cinemas in regional Thailand has been held as a positive development for the studios, which may now cut out the intermediaries in the regional markets.[73] Until recently, access to these markets had to go through the gateway of circuits that were under the control of regional distributors.[74] The presence of these regional distributors primarily meant the studios could not employ the revenue-sharing model and had to contend with selling their rights without knowing how much revenue the films might generate outside of Bangkok.[75]

These regional actors emerged historically from a lack of regional infrastructure and the geographical challenge facing Thai filmmakers in bringing their films to remote areas.[76] So as the film business flourished during the Cold War years, the division of regional circuits became integral to the landscape of Thai cinema, such that these regional distributors, with their financial resources, became influential in the film production business.[77] Although their continued presence may seem like a residue from the bygone era, not to mention a market barrier, their prominent role in Thai cinema history also provides another snapshot of shared interests among different actors in film production and distribution.

Unlike the studio executives, independent filmmakers seem to have little to celebrate about the increasing number of cinemas, given that the expansion of the big chains does not fix the problem of screen allotments.[78] Both major cinema chains and regional distributors seem to share the belief that independent films do not appeal to general Thai audiences and will not bring many people to the cinemas.[79] Partly this explains why film festival credentials have become crucial to Thai independent filmmakers and their prospects in the home market,[80] but from the audience

71 The distribution of box office revenue between copyright owners and cinema operators is between 50/50 and 40/60; see Unaloam, *Film Exhibition* (n 68) 185.

72 ibid 115.

73 A GDH executive is on record as saying that the branching out into regional areas presents a new opportunity to the studio: **‘ความท้าทาย ‘GDH—นาดาว’ สร้างโมเดลธุรกิจโตอย่างยั่งยืน’** (‘A challenge for “GDH-Nadao”: Building a sustainable business model’) (Marketing Oops!, 2 February 2020) <https://www.marketingoops.com/news/biz-news/gdh-and-nadao-bangkok-busienss-model-sustainable-growth/> accessed 20 February 2025.

74 Unaloam, *Film exhibition* (n 68) 180.

75 ibid 183–184.

76 ibid 34, 157, 166.

77 ibid 159.

78 Interviewee M.

79 Interviewee F.

80 ibid.

perspective, the limited theatrical outlets have become a recurring theme for those who lament a lack of diversity in cinema programmes, especially when one goes outside of Bangkok.[81] Against this landscape of mainstream distribution thus arose the informal network of independent grassroots screenings.

In towns and cities outside the capital, cinephiles and cinemagoers have taken matters into their own hands.[82] Within their localities, they have organised makeshift screenings of films that fall outside the remit of mainstream cinema. These localised events usually make use of whatever space is available and often aim to generate local participation through informal discussions and talks.[83] But despite a growing network of independent film exhibitors, to suggest that these grassroots activities are now changing the overall exhibition sector would be a mistake. Instead, it is the process, not the product, that defines the significance of this phenomenon.

In offering an alternative cinema-going experience, the provincial practice of grassroots screenings embodies the space of familiar production. On the one hand, there is the desire to promote familiarity with the world of alternative cinema that lies beyond mainstream distribution.[84] And because this desire has been pursued in the context of specific localities, grassroots screenings involve producing familiarity in more senses than one. That is, it is also an exercise in community building.

In provincial Thailand, the emergence of grassroots screenings has seen the development of local initiatives that not only aim to revitalise a sense of community but also seek to effect the regeneration of local communities.[85] One example of such initiatives is repurposing a century-old shophouse that aspires to breathe new life into a dying high street, which holds significance for local history and economy.[86] Interestingly, it is an initiative of this kind that marks the flight of alternative cinema from the territory of underground movements, recalling the emergence of

81 Interviewee M. See also 'Film directors urge more screening of Thai films in movie theatres' (*The Nation*, 12 March 2023) <https://www.nationthailand.com/thailand/general/40025488> accessed 12 March 2023.

82 Interviewee L; Interviewee M.

83 Interviewee M. See also Nopporn Sakdanares, "**หนังดูที่ไหนก็ได้**' 4 **พื้นที่ดูหนังที่ได้มากกว่าการดูหนัง**' ('Films can be watched anywhere; 4 screening spaces that offer more than watching films') (The Film Club, 23 February 2021) <https://filmclubthailand.com/film-interview/4-spaces-for-screening-film/> accessed 20 February 2025.

84 Here, the term 'alternative' is preferred to 'independent' to emphasise the substantive nature of a film (styles, subject matter, etc.) that falls outside prevailing commercial genres. By contrast, the *Thi-Baan* filmmakers have called themselves indie, but their films fit perfectly into the mould of mainstream romantic comedy.

85 See for instance Thida Palitpolkarnpim, '**ฝันของคนทำ** '**พื้นที่ฉายหนังอิสระ**': **รู้จัก** 'a.e.y.space' **ภารกิจพาหนังหลากหลายสู่สายตาคนหาดใหญ่**' ('The dream of an organiser of "independent screening space": Meet "a.e.y.space" and the quest of bringing a diverse selection of films to the people of Songkhla province') (The Film Club, 15 March 2022) <https://filmclubthailand.com/articles/special-article/indy-screening-space-a-e-y-space/> accessed 20 February 2025.

86 ibid.

Van Video and how this illicit enterprise transformed the country's cultural landscape in the late 1990s.[87]

Unlike the story of Van Video, the emergence of provincial grassroots screenings has taken alternative cinema overground in search of a wider audience. Recognising the value of continuity and consistency to the viability of their activities, these independent exhibitors appear willing to engage with legal and cultural institutions.[88] In this way, their practice of grassroots screenings represents a formalisation of alternative cinema, whose flight from the underground has been reterritorialised by industry standards and practices, including the practice of copyright licensing.[89] Nonetheless, it would be a mistake to simply view their engagement with copyright law as a matter of compliance when this is also conducive to building trust with the industry as well as the audiences and filmmakers. This suggests that one may seek to obtain screening permission not just to avoid liability but to engender a trusting relationship that is a building block of community relations.

Trusting Relationship

Perhaps the best sign of the growing legal consciousness is the constant controversies over online infringement. Gone are the days when all talks of respect for IP in the public sphere were meant to earn a measure of international respectability.[90] This was kept separated from the everyday reality of pirate consumption and circulation that everyone practised in the private sphere. Contrary to this public–private distinction was the recent branding of Thailand 4.0, which aspired to change individual behaviour for the benefit of an imagined community called the nation.[91]

As seen in Chapter 4, the pursuit of Thailand 4.0 was a quest for national development—it was a community-led project, as it were. This thus begs the question: Whose nation is it? The military junta had co-opted the notions of creativity and innovation, yoking them to the royal-nationalist narrative of Thai exceptionalism.[92] This 'official' nationalism, as Benedict Anderson calls it, narrates a relationship of indebtedness that presents the imagined Thai community as an embodiment of debt owed by every Thai person.[93] In this way, the necessary

87 See 'What Is Wrong With Copying?' in Chapter 5.

88 For example, 'Dude, Movie,' a group of independent exhibitors in the province of Chiang Mai, started off without a copyright license. However, they gradually had to do things by the rules to expand their connections and create opportunities. See Surapan Saengsuwan, 'Dude, Movie. **กลุ่มคนฉายหนังที่ใช้ป๊อปคัลเจอร์เปลี่ยนเชียงใหม่**' (Dude, Movie: A group of film exhibitors who use pop culture to change Chiang Mai) (*The Modernist*, 16 March 2022) <https://themodernist.in.th/dude-movie/> accessed 20 February 2025.

89 ibid.

90 See 'Inauthentic Self' in Chapter 4.

91 See 'Politics of Creativity' in Chapter 5.

92 Dr Suvit Maesincee, '**ถึงเวลาปฏิรูปขนานใหญ่รอบที่สอง**' ('It is time for the second great reform') (Facebook, 20 April 2006) <https://www.facebook.com/drsuvitpage/posts/1399691550337571:0> accessed 20 February 2025.

93 Anderson, *Imagined Communities*.

respect for copyright ownership becomes an obligation that arises from one's indebtedness to the nation, but the nation as an imagined community is just one of a myriad of community relations that constitute contemporary social life.[94] It must be possible to anchor such collective concerns in ideas other than indebtedness, and one such idea is trust.

What can be learned from public controversies around copyright infringement is the possibility of aligning the legal concept of infringement with a social relationship of trust. This learning opportunity presents itself when one carefully considers what copyright really means in these public discussions. This is not to say that one should examine whether the public understands the law correctly. Instead, it suggests that attention should be paid to what people really mean when they talk about copyright in the context of piracy or in the debates about imitation and copying.

In the context of Thai cinema, the consumption of pirate films may sometimes carry a sense of resentment against media tycoons and investors,[95] but there is usually public sympathy reserved for those working in the film industry. A standard line of argument is to deplore the injustice of free riding, citing loss of investment and lack of remuneration.[96] A sense of moral righteousness is at play here, no doubt,[97] but their interest in the predicament of the film industry often ties to their perception as audiences and fans who have an interest in the welfare of the filmmakers.

This perception also appears to inform the increasing public hostility towards creators who are deemed to be stealing from others. Again, it is worth recalling that the situation between Imm and Sun in 'Sorry' is essentially an audience calling out a filmmaker for taking someone else's work as their own. In real life, a situation like this is more observable in domains other than filmmaking. Particularly with music, an accusation of copying or imitating with reference to right infringement has become commonplace in mainstream media.[98] What is interesting about this trend is that the controversy often comes from the claim that the accused has

94 See further discussion on this point in 'Copyright's Community' in Chapter 8.

95 For an example of this sentiment, see Thanaporn Kohkaew, '**มองปัญหาลิขสิทธิ์-เศรษฐกิจ-สาธารณประโยชน์ ผ่านการดูเถื่อน**' ('Examine the copyright-economy-public interest conundrum through illegitimate consumption') (Prachatai, 2 March 2021) <https://prachatai.com/journal/2021/03/91924> accessed 20 February 2025.

96 See for instance '**ดูหนังออนไลน์-ซีรีส์เถื่อน: ฟรี ดูดเพลิน สูญหมื่นล้าน ฆ่าคนเบื้องหลัง**' ('Online consumption of pirated films and TV series: Free, fun, but costly and deadly to filmmakers') (*Thairath*, 4 April 2016) <https://www.thairath.co.th/business/599679> accessed 20 February 2025.

97 Not only is consuming pirated content considered morally dubious, but it is also deemed to encourage organised crime activities. See for instance Pitchaya K, '**ดูหนังผิดลิขสิทธิ์ = สนับสนุนเว็บพนันออนไลน์ทางอ้อม?**' ('Watching pirated films = indirectly supporting illegal gambling websites?') (Brandinside, 17 January 2023) <https://brandinside.asia/watching-illegal-streaming-sites-is-supporting-illegal-gambling-sites/> accessed 20 February 2025.

98 Claims of music plagiarism have been quite common for a long time, but what has just emerged is how they are now made with reference to copyright law as well. For an example of a discussion in popular media, see '**การลอกเพลง—ความเข้าใจผิด—ข้อควรระวังเรื่องลิขสิทธิ์**' ('Music plagiarism—misconceptions—copyright warnings') (*Pa-Ted Talk*, 29 December 2021) <https://www.youtube.com/watch?v=NWWka9rs5Vk> accessed 20 February 2025.

failed to credit those whose work is believed to have been copied.[99] In this way, it suggests that the act of copying is less problematic than the inauthenticity of misattribution and the deprivation of recognition.

In light of what was just discussed, one thing that appears to underlie most public controversies around alleged legal infringement is the issue of trust.[100] Whether it be the injustice of free riding or the inauthenticity of misattribution, it is fair to say that part of the public backlash is a response to an erosion of trust that views interpersonal trust as a public good.[101] As seen in this chapter, there is a sense of collective involvement in taking a stance against film piracy and expressing sympathy for those affected. These are part of a collective exercise in trust building expressed in the language of copyright law. Viewing public response from this perspective makes it possible to see how copyright law can contribute to a sense of community. It is the role of copyright law in building trust that turns overlapping boundaries among creators and users into the familiar territory of collective engagement. That said, it is also important to note that copyright law is also capable of creating mistrust.

Burning Down the House

The increased public attention to the economic potential of films has prompted critical discussions about the welfare of individual creators and workers.[102] Alongside the important subject of health and safety is another longstanding issue that has hitherto evaded public scrutiny. With talks of the film industry becoming the country's new economic engine, the issue of remuneration has been brought to public attention, and understandably so,[103] but what appears to be at stake is not just the well-being of creative workers. The future of the industry is also recognised to hang in the balance, primarily because the issue of low pay has been linked with underdevelopment in the field of screenwriting.[104]

The shortcomings in this field, which is otherwise crucial to the overall enterprise of filmmaking, have often been attributed to the vicious circle of inadequate

99 And this is linked to the misconception that giving credit legally excuses copyright infringement. See Athip Jittiruek, '12 **ความเข้าใจผิดเกี่ยวกับลิขสิทธิ์ของคนไทย**' (12 misconceptions about copyright among Thai people) (Prachatai, 8 January 2013) <https://prachatai.com/journal/2013/01/44561> accessed 20 February 2025.

100 Trust is also central to the concept of community resource, as discussed later in 'Mutual trust'.

101 For a sociological discussion about trust as a public good, see Barbara Misztal, *Trust in Modern Societies: The Search for the Bases of Social Order* (Polity 1996) 14–15.

102 See for instance Kongsuwan, 'The ugly truth'.

103 ibid.

104 See Thanayod Lopattananont, Voraluk Klasukon, and Saksit Thaweekul, '**ความสอดคล้องของโครงสร้างอุตสาหกรรมการผลิตภาพยนตร์ ไทยกับยุทธศาสตร์การส่งเสริมภาพยนตร์และวีดิทัศน์ ระยะที่** 3 (**พ.ศ.** 2560–2564)' ('Coherence of Thai film industry and Thailand's strategies for film and video promotion, phase 3 (2017–2021)') (Dhurakij Pandit University research paper, DPU 2020) 49–52.

remuneration and a lack of career prospects.[105] This situation is certainly not helped by the fact that Thai screenwriters usually have no proprietary rights in the product of their labour. Yet with their increasing discontent with low pay, they have become more vocal about the rights to the scripts, making copyright ownership a new battleground.

With the streaming market opening up new prospects for remakes and adaptations, Thai screenwriters have become mindful of the rights to the scripts, although they never had these rights to begin with.[106] Whether looking to submit a script to a film studio or hired to work on a new one, a standard contract that a screenwriter should expect is a hire-of-work contract.[107] Framing the legal relationship in this way is a common practice in the film industry and a problematic one at that.

The problem with a hire-of-work contract is not just that it places screenwriters outside labour protection law.[108] Their being independent contractors also means that these screenwriters do not have copyright ownership in the film scripts. Under the TCA 1994, if a work is created under a hire-of-work contract, it is the hirer who becomes the first copyright owner.[109] Perhaps unsurprisingly, a hire-of-work contract is a legal arrangement used with most artists and creators across the film industry.[110] In this regard, it is worth noting that these people do not enjoy any special economic safeguards under the TCA 1994.[111] Insofar as they are parties to a hire-of-work contract, the TCA 1994 treats them as property makers who have agreed to work for the pay. Their contest for copyright ownership looks like a battle that cannot be won.

Whether the right to the script is a battle that can be won or worth fighting at all, the very notion of a battle presents its own problem. For one thing, it turns the question of copyright ownership into a zero-sum game where one can only gain at the loss of the other. And with the stakes over ownership raised so high, the need for a battle further indicates an alienation of creative labour. Not only does one have to fiercely contest to benefit from the product of one's labour, but the very activity of creative labour, of working as a screenwriter, also seems to make one feel alienated and estranged.

A situation like this certainly does not help with the industry's shortage of screenwriters, not least because a contest for ownership is not zero sum but capable

105 Interviewee A.

106 ibid.

107 ibid.

108 In Thai law, a legal distinction is made between an employment contract under section 575 of the TCCC and a hire of work under section 587 of the TCCC. Conceptually, the latter is akin to a contract for services, which means the hired party does not qualify as an employee within the purview of Thai labour protection law.

109 TCA 1994, s 10.

110 See Creative Economy Agency (CEA), '**รายงานการศึกษาการพัฒนาอุตสาหกรรมสร้างสรรค์สาขาภาพยนตร์และวีดิทัศน์ ปี** 2564' (Creative Industries Development Report (film and audiovisual) 2021) (*CEA*, 2021) 40 <http://resource.tcdc.or.th/ebook/CEA.Film.Report.pdf> accessed 20 February 2025.

111 However, they are entitled to the rights of attribution and integrity under section 18 of TCA 1994.

of producing a net loss for everyone.[112] In other words, the screenwriters' scrambling for copyright ownership represents the tendency in the current legal framework to engender a relationship of mistrust. One can see the same problem of mistrust implicated in the polarisation in public discourse regarding respect for copyright.

Amplified by the effect of social media, respect for copyright has become a frequent topic of debate and controversy, and one that tends to generate polarising views. At one extreme lies the cynical conviction that copyright only serves the interests of big corporations. Here, the law is simply viewed as a tool for extortion and exploitation such that it can be easily brushed aside for want of legitimacy.[113]

This cynical outlook comes in stark contrast to the moralistic view that lies at the other end of the spectrum. Not defined by mistrust, it is plain and simple that use without permission is wrong, so much so that there almost seems to be a disregard for the inbuilt limitations and exceptions in copyright law.[114] It is possible that prejudice and misunderstanding partly account for the polarisation, especially when it comes to the finer points of law, but even so, what remains significant is the idea that property, including IP, should not be understood only in terms of the relations of persons to things.[115] What really is at issue in the discussion so far is the broader question of social interaction and collective involvement. This is reflected in the historical development of Thai copyright law as much as in the evolving role of copyright law in contemporary Thai cinema.[116]

Polarised as it may be, the public discourse on respecting copyright helps draw attention to the power of law to constitute social experiences.[117] Legal sociologists recognise this influence as law's ability to shape collective understandings of fundamental concepts such as property and contract, which then influence broader social practices and define the nature of social life.[118] With the Thai government promoting the combative narrative of IP, it becomes pertinent to ask what image of society is represented or assumed by copyright law.

112 The quality of screenplays is one pressing issue that threatens to hold back the development of the industry. See Thanayod, Voraluk, and Saksit (n 104) 75; CEA (n 110) 78.

113 A recent parliamentary debate serves as a good example. A member of the Opposition, Jirayu Houngsub MP, lambasted a Copyright Bill that would see Thai law align with the WIPO Copyright Treaty. Of the proposed amendments, Jirayu said they 'speak so little for common people' and went on to say that 'ordinary folks do not benefit from copyright. Most of the time, it is the merchants, entrepreneurs, and capitalists.' See House of Representatives Deb 27 January 2021, vol 25, year 2 (second session), no 15, 215–216.

114 A good illustration is Wor Wachirametee's moral teaching in 'Sorry.' See 'Moral Panic' in Chapter 5.

115 This point was already raised in the discussion of Chulayarnnon's film. See 'Life Imitating Art' in the Introduction.

116 As seen in the first three chapters, the relationship between nation-building, colonialism, and law constitutes a recurring theme in the discussions on the historical development of Thai copyright law.

117 For a brief discussion of this social power of law, see Roger Cotterrell, 'Law as constitutive' in Neil Smelser and Paul Baltes (eds), *International Encyclopedia of the Social and Behavioural Sciences* (Elsevier 2001) 8497–8500.

118 ibid 8498.

This is particularly evident when considering familiar production. The interplay between the material and discursive elements in contemporary Thai cinema highlights the creativity inherent in familiar production. This process is interactive and relational, generating new meaning and value through affiliations and associations. Film, therefore, is not merely a finished product to be passively consumed. It rather constitutes a point of connection within the dynamic and continuous production of Thai cinema's creative assemblage. This perspective underscores the potential for reimagining copyright law—one that values social interactions and mutual benefit over an antagonistic turf fight. If we agree that fostering collective engagement should be the priority of copyright law, then the key question becomes: How can we rethink copyright protection towards that aim?

8 Community Once More

Recalling Chulayarnnon's peculiar view on copyright and democracy, we have returned to where this book begins. While Chulayarnnon may not be consciously aware of it, his film invites us to reconsider what it means to protect copyright. This potential arises from the way the film draws a parallel between copyright ownership and ownership of a country. We first see Chulayarnnon ask whether a film belongs to the director, the funder, the audience, or the collector. Then, he poses a similar question about democracy, asking whether the country belongs to the government, the military, or the people. These two questions, though distinct, are supposedly connected through the problematic metaphors of reproduction and authenticity—a problem that this book employs in framing its exploration of Thailand's postcolonial conditions. However, despite the limitations of the film's analogy between copyright and democracy, the underlying concerns driving this unconventional comparison become evident if we can look past those two metaphors.

In an interview, Chulayarnnon explained that his film compares the small world of his art community to the larger world of Thai politics.[1] He emphasised that there is a connection between the copyright problem within his art community and the problem with democracy in Thai politics, framing both in terms of a contest for ownership. Taken literally, the connection may seem tenuous; after all, one cannot own a country in the same way that one owns a copyright. However, if we view copyright ownership as a relationship between the copyright owner and the art community, the analogy begins to resonate. In this context, the struggle for democracy can be understood as a fight to take collective ownership of the imagined community we call the nation. The notion of ownership, thus, stands in for a question of power relations.

In this way, when the film ponders who should be the copyright owner, it raises the deeper issue of how property relations should be organised among members of the art community. This shift in focus brings power dynamics of community relations into the consideration of what is typically considered individual rights.

1 See his interview with the Singapore International Film Festival (SGIFF), '100 times reproduction of democracy Q&A/SGIFF 2020' (SGIFF YouTube Channel, 22 January 2021) <https://www.youtube.com/watch?v=5kRhKXeFwA0&t=616s> accessed 20 February 2025.

DOI: 10.4324/9781003592037-13

Consequently, it opens the possibility to rethink what it means—both individually and collectively—to protect copyright. This insight has led the discussions in this book to look closely at the evolving practices in contemporary Thai cinema, and it has become clear that we need neither to assume the causality of the incentives arguments nor surrender to the transcendence of the author's rights. Chapter 7 showed that copyright law may see its role in facilitating social interactions and fostering collective engagement.

Still, the challenge for copyright theory lies in how to reconceptualise copyright protection in ways that can reshape the legal framework. Here, assistance will be sought from the work of Roger Cotterrell. Through his long-standing commitment to providing law and lawyers with sociological insights, he has created a specific concept of community that highlights the primary role of law in maintaining and supporting community relations. This chapter draws on his 'law-and-community approach' to develop the book's own concept of copyright as a community resource. This concept offers a new way of thinking about copyright protection, aiming to shift the existing copyright framework towards fostering trusting relations.

The development of this new perspective requires that we first examine the image of society and the understanding of social relations that are deeply embedded in copyright law, but where in the law should we look for such insights? The clue lies in the perennial legal discussions about striking a balance between public and private interests. Thus, we must turn our focus to the legal notion of balance and the specific image of society that this notion presupposes.

I. The Social in Copyright Law

The notion of balance is now recognised internationally. Its first appearance in international law came with the TRIPS Agreement of 1994, which subjects the whole spectrum of IP protection to 'a balance of rights and obligations.'[2] This was followed by the WCT 1996 and the recognition of 'a balance between the rights of authors and the larger public interest.'[3] The emerging distinction between private rights and public interest later found another expression in the context of regional integration. The 2001 InfoSoc Directive of the European Union is committed to safeguarding 'a fair balance of rights and interests between the different categories of right holders, as well as between the different categories of right holders and users of protected subject matter.'[4]

A theme that emerged from the institutionalisation of the balance notion is a fundamental distinction between 'private' and 'public,' with which a line can be drawn to delineate the scope of protection.[5] Considering that to balance is to draw

2 TRIPS Agreement, art 7.
3 WCT, preamble.
4 InfoSoc Directive, recital 31.
5 See Reto Hilty and Sylvie Nérisson, 'Overview' in Reto Hilty and Sylvie Nérisson (eds), *Balancing Copyright: A Survey of National Approaches* (Springer 2012) 1–3.

boundaries, and these lines will be redrawn over and over in the balancing act of law; what follows from the institutionalised notion of balance is a constant process of territorialisation that demarcates the private sphere of property rights from the public domain of use.[6]

The Public–Private Dichotomy

As reflected in the institutionalised notion of balance, what is inherent in the development of contemporary copyright law is the logic of public–private distinction.[7] This logic demarcates individual boundaries against social collectivity, and it can be observed in the concept of originality as well as in the principle that copyright law protects the expression of ideas, not the ideas themselves.[8]

Where the territory of a protected expression is already delineated, the public–private distinction is once again reaffirmed in the language of infringement and exception,[9] for inasmuch as copyright exceptions are considered to serve the public interest, the very notion of an exception presupposes the rule. In other words, an exception is a deviation from the standard and the usual, such that any exception to copyright infringement also presupposes and prioritises the private sphere of property.[10] Therefore, it is fair to say a conception of society reflected in the notion of balance is one that assumes a distinction between the public and private spheres.[11]

Furthermore, copyright law articulates the boundaries of public and private spheres through the concepts of the author and the user.[12] In other words, the public–private distinction is co-extensive with how the law draws a distinction between authors and users. This means that the territory of private property always precedes the public interest in use; it is the individual authors and their works that bring a public of users into existence in the first place. Furthermore, because the authors must always be identified and individualised, while users remain anonymous and homogeneous, the author–user distinction translates into the private sphere of identifiable individual authors constructed against a uniform public of anonymous

6 Rose, 'The author as proprietor,' 140–141.

7 ibid.

8 These legal ideas serve to 'mark your territory,' if you will, and this territorial possession is constituted by one's use of labour or with reference to one's personality. By contrast, see the notion of familiar territory in 'Familiar Production' in Chapter 7.

9 Rose (n 6) 140–141.

10 For instance, Sterling and Jacques interestingly note that limitations and exceptions contained in copyright law 'may be described as "internal restrictions," that is, actual or potential restrictions resulting from the provisions of [a national law or international/regional instrument] itself.' See JAL Sterling and Sabine Jacques, 'Limitations and exception' in Trevor Cook (ed), *Sterling on World Copyright Law* (6th edn, Sweet & Maxwell 2022) 491.

11 Perhaps unsurprisingly, this distinction does not only exist in copyright law. For a brief discussion of this idea in Western political thought, see Dana Howard, 'Public–private distinction' in Michael Gibbons (ed), *The Encyclopedia of Political Thought* (John Wiley & Son 2015).

12 See for instance Hilty and Nérisson (n 5) 1–3.

users.[13] In this way, the public–private distinction represents an antagonistic and unequal relationship where the individual authors try to defend their territory while the public of perfect strangers seeks to gain access.

This duality between the personality of the author and the anonymity of the user strikes a stark contrast with the myriads of associations and affiliations that constitute the assemblage of Thai cinema. Consider Nawapol, for example. His reference to *Wong Kar Wai* in *Mary is Happy, Mary is Happy* suspends the distinction between the author and the user, allowing him to perform multiple identities simultaneously: as a fan, a cinephile, and a filmmaker.[14] Similarly, the success of the *Thi-Baan* franchise owes much to the contributions of the audience, whose affective labour confounded the distinction between production and consumption and indeed between creation and use.[15]

One could point to the user concept as evidence of copyright law's inherent reflexivity towards the reality of creative production, but as long as the finished product—the creation of an authorial work—remains its primary focus, the law will fail to reflect on the biases and presumptions underpinning the author-user distinction. This is where the legal act of balancing reveals its limitations. Striking a balance involves making a value judgment outside the idea of balance itself, and the outcome can only be as sound as the premises informing it.[16] There needs to be a shift in focus—one that moves away from the originality of the work and the expression to appreciate the repetition of familiar production. The relationship between public and private spheres must be recast in terms of familiar territory. It is here where assistance can be sought from Cotterrell's concept of community.

Copyright's Community

Examining the legal act of balancing also reveals the tendency of copyright law to equate society with the nation. Copyright may be territorial in the sense discussed earlier when considered as a form of property. As a form of regulation, however, the territory of copyright law covers the same length and breadth as the nation-state. While this generally does not affect individual authors who may be foreigners, courtesy of the Berne Convention, it still means that the public of users is typically defined and limited by national borders. The nation, therefore, constitutes society, and the two become synonymous in copyright discourse. This implication has a peculiar resonance for Thailand, especially considering Thongchai's polemic against Thailand's rule of law discussed in Chapter 1; he contends that 'the rule by law' more accurately describes law's relationship to the Thai state, particularly

13 Gibson, *Creating Selves,* 127.

14 See 'Self-Branding' in Chapter 6.

15 See 'Let Me Entertain You' in Chapter 6.

16 For a similar assessment of the balance notion, see Abraham Drassinower, 'From distribution to dialogue: Remarks on the concept of balance in copyright law' (2009) 34(4) *Journal of Corporation Law* 991, 995–997. Drassinower interestingly argues that 'determinations as to what gets on the balance are prior to the balancing.'

considering the violence it has enacted in the name of the nation.[17] Indeed, the discussions in this book testify to this perspective. The role of law was evident in the rise of absolute monarchy in the late 19th century,[18] and the same can be observed in the persistence of authoritarianism in the 21st century.[19]

Interestingly, Thongchai's critique of Thai law has surprising resonances with Cotterrell's view on the relationship between law and society. Speaking from a sociolegal perspective, Cotterrell makes the following observation about law:

> The stability of the idea of law as essentially state law, the law of the nation-state, has depended on the continued possibility of treating state and nation as coterminous—having the same scope as in the nation-state concept. As long as these conditions prevailed, law could gain its conceptual unity from its inseparability from the idea of the nation, itself treated as simultaneously guaranteeing a social unity (society) and a political unity (the state).[20]

In contrast, Cotterrell argues for a pluralist conception of law that acknowledges the diversity of social life within and beyond the nation-state.[21] Though this view is far from a critique of postcolonial nation-states, unlike Thongchai's rule by law, his methods helpfully build a bridge between legal doctrine and interdisciplinary perspectives, as discussed in detail later. Furthermore, he also finds the public–private distinction increasingly implausible in legal thought, echoing earlier discussions on the limitations of the copyright balancing act.[22] So what then does he propose as an alternative conception of law and society?

This is where we bring the concept of community into the discussion. Cotterrell advocates for a sociological perspective on legal education and practice, which is to be assisted by his concept of community.[23] According to Cotterrell, this concept serves as 'an escape from traditional conceptions of the relationship between law, state, and political society.'[24] In his formulation, community refers to a form of collective involvement consisting of social relations that are not necessarily bound up with the nation-state and can be transnational or localised in nature. Given the cultural and intellectual connotations of the term community, it is important to recognise that his concept does not seek to bring back the distinction between

17 See Thongchai Winichakul, ***นิติรัฐอภิสิทธิ์และราชานิติธรรม ประวัติศาสตร์ภูมิปัญญาของ*** *Rule by Law* **แบบไทย** *(Legal-Privileged-State and Royalist Rule of Law: The Intellectual History of Thai-Style Rule by Law)* (Thammasat University 2020).

18 See 'Not So Romantic and Not Much of a Twin Birth' in Chapter 2.

19 See 'A Life No Less Civilised' in Chapter 3.

20 Cotterrell, *Law, Culture, and Society,* 66–67.

21 ibid 76–77.

22 Roger Cotterrell, 'Subverting orthodoxy, making law central: A view of sociolegal studies' (2002) 29(4) *Journal of Law and Society* 632, 637.

23 See Roger Cotterrell, *Sociological Jurisprudence: Juristic Thought and Social Inquiry* (Routledge 2017).

24 Cotterrell, *Law, Culture, and Society* (n 20) 65.

Gemeinschaft (community) and *Gesellschaft* (society) in classical sociology.[25] Cotterrell does not hark back to the bygone idea of a homogeneous, tightly knit community. His main concern is the regulation of social relations in all their variety, which means that

> [c]ommunity has to be drained of any residual romanticism and its different types identified insofar as they have a bearing on regulatory issues. Relations of community need to be seen as much more varied, flexible, fluid, and changeable than is envisaged in most appeals to community.[26]

To this end, Cotterrell's concept of community offers a schema of social relations. He organises social life in all its variety into four ideal types, namely, instrumental community, traditional community, community of belief, and affective community.[27] He develops this social schema by distinguishing social bonds into four types: a sharing of beliefs or values (community of belief), a convergence of goals generally seen in a commercial pursuit (instrumental community), a habitual or traditional form of relations that are usually linked to a geographical location (traditional community), and the kind of emotions generally found in family and friendship (affective community).[28]

These four categories are ideal types, which means they do not represent actual, empirical groups.[29] Instead, they form a comprehensive model in the sense that they can combine to exhaust all possible forms of social relations.[30] Essentially, these ideal types are not mutually exclusive; in reality, they exist as networks of community in countless combinations. In this way, Cotterrell's typology of community relations is not a system of social classification. It serves as an analytical construct that assists researchers in 'identifying different kinds of general regulatory problems that arise when law is seen as the regulatory aspect of the social.'[31] The law in question is not limited to that of the state, although state law arguably remains the focus.[32] Meanwhile, the nation—as an imagined community—becomes one among a multiplicity of communities that make up the social world.[33]

25 See Ferdinand Tonnies, *Community and Society* (CP Loomis tr, Routledge 1988).

26 Cotterrell, *Sociological Jurisprudence* (n 23) 181.

27 Cotterrell, *Law, Culture, and Society* (n 20) 68–70; he also indicates that his schema correlates with Max Weber's ideal types of social action: goal/purposive rational, value rational, affective, and traditional. See also Weber, *Economy and Society: A New Translation* (Keith Tribe ed/tr, Harvard University Press 2019) 101.

28 ibid.

29 Cotterrell, *Law, Culture, and Society* (n 20) 69; Weber (n 27) 96–99.

30 ibid.

31 Cotterrell, 'Community as a legal concept? Some use of law and community approaches in legal theory' in Cotterrell (ed), *Living Law: Studies in Legal and Social Theory* (Ashgate 2008) 8.

32 Cotterrell, *Law, Culture, and Society* (n 20) 76–77.

33 ibid 76.

In this way, Cotterrell's typology of community offers an interesting conceptual framework to replace the problematic public–private distinction. The community concept invites a discussion on how copyright law may facilitate a myriad of social relations that come with different regulatory needs.[34] By replacing the image of society as demarcated into public and private spheres, the individualistic and antagonistic characterisation of social life will give way to a myriad of associations and affiliations. Acknowledging the diversity of social life helps us to avoid seeing society in simplistic, binary terms. It shifts our attention away from fixed identities towards simultaneous participation in a variety of community relations. In other words, describing social life in terms of communal networks does not emphasise the act of marking boundaries; it acknowledges the overlapping of territories.

The implications of the community concept for copyright law extend well beyond disrupting the binarism of author and user. Lying behind the traditional distinction between the author and the user is the presumption of zero-sum competition. As discussed earlier, it is a general understanding that the task of copyright law is to strike a balance between public and private interests.[35] But insofar as this notion of balance presupposes the kind of author-user relationship discussed earlier, this understanding of balance looks increasingly out of touch with the proliferating digital environment.[36] By contrast, recognising that the social world is essentially a myriad of community relations highlights the shared interests among various social actors. This communal perspective places mutual trust at the heart of copyright protection. Later, how trust lies at the basis of familiar territory will be explored; it takes a trusting relationship for a sense of community to arise.

II. Community Resource

Evident in the charge of rule by law against the Thai state is a lack of trust. This is not surprising given the discussions of Thai law throughout this book. However, copyright law itself has also faced criticism for a lack of public trust. A good example of this is the controversy surrounding TRIPs and FTAs, as discussed in Chapter 4. Furthermore, the discussion of Thai cinema in Chapter 7 demonstrates how the law can contribute to a sense of mistrust within the community. Trust has, therefore, emerged as a critical juncture in the final stage of developing the concept of community resource.

34 For a similar attempt but in a different area of law, see Amanda Perry-Kessaris, *Global Business, Local Law: The Indian Legal System as a Communal Resource in Foreign Investment Relations* (Routledge 2016) 5–6.

35 See for instance Hilty and Nérisson (n 5); Martin Senftleben, 'From flexible balancing tool to quasi-constitutional straitjacket: How the EU cultivates the constraining function of the three-step test' in Jonathan Griffiths and Tuomus Mylly (eds), *Global Intellectual Property Protection and New Constitutionalism: Hedging Exclusive Rights* (OUP 2021).

36 See also Gibson, *Creating Selves* (n 13).

It is important to note here that the concept of 'community resource' is different from 'communal ownership.'[37] The term 'community' denotes collective concern and involvement, and it evokes a sense of belonging rather than asserting shared ownership—hence the term 'resource.' This construction allows for knowledge to still be private in entitlement while being communal in regulation.[38] It does not take away the author's rights but deploys them in service of community relations, where the author is also situated. This new perspective emphasises the role of copyright law in organising and encouraging social interactions. Copyright thus makes a resourceful community, and it does so by constituting a locus of regulation that supports and encourages trusting relationships.[39]

In this context, the proposed return to the idea of community is neither driven by a nostalgic longing for things past nor aligned with the notion of community as synonymous with indigenous or traditional groups. Instead, this is a return to 'the world of manners and relations,' as discussed earlier in the context of familiar production.[40] A productive synergy between familiar production and community relations presents itself in the idea of trust. This is where the kinship of familiar production can be articulated with the sociological perspective on associations and affiliations. Trust is the building block of community, Cotterrell explains.[41] This makes a trust-based reinterpretation concomitant with reconceptualising copyright as a community resource.

Mutual Trust

The prism of community shifts our perspective away from viewing social interactions in their individuality, which often highlights conflicts and competing interests. With an emphasis on collective involvement, it is the social bond rather than individual behaviour that is the focus of attention. This brings into discussion the reciprocity of community life. Community relations are not one-sided. They are dependent and elicited by an acknowledgement of shared interests—a convergence of interests both in terms of expected benefits (such as money, fulfilment, or respect) and mutual attention. In this regard, Gibson notes that

> [s]hared interests comprise fundamentally affiliative and empathetic relations and, as such, generate a genuinely ethical encounter. Trust is thus immanent to shared interests.[42]

37 However, the term 'community resource' does not reject the idea of cultural artefacts as property; rather, it entices and anticipates an alternative model of property, distinct from what Marilyn Strathern calls Western propertism.

38 In this way, community resource brings authors and users together on an equal footing. See 'The Public–Private Dichotomy' in this chapter.

39 See further discussion on this point in 'Mutual Trust' in this chapter.

40 Gibson, *Owned, an Ethological Jurisprudence of Property*.

41 Cotterrell, *Law, Culture, and Society* (n 20) 73.

42 Gibson, *Owned* (n 40) 258.

Indeed, Cotterrell, who reconceptualises community as a web of understanding, also locates the fundamental element of community relations in mutual interpersonal trust.[43] In conditions of community, Cotterrell observes that,

> [o]ne necessarily trusts the other person to exercise discretion in one's interests in a range of unknown and possible unforeseen eventualities, which could involve the disappointment of the trusting person; trusting someone invariably involves taking a risk.[44]

Considering the nature of trusting relationships, one may argue that a trust-based reinterpretation of copyright law turns the incentive argument on its head. Implicit in the claim that piracy kills Thai cinema, as discussed in Chapter 6, is the logic of risk mitigation that treats copyright protection as a necessary intervention to encourage risk-averse creators and investors to engage in creative production.[45] However, the exploration of Thai commercial cinema has demonstrated that the risk calculation of film investment is more interested in revenue than innovation, and this was responsible for the stagnation of Thai commercial films.[46]

In contrast, the decision made by the *Thi-Baan* filmmakers to take a chance with *Isan*-oriented cinema has led to new avenues of possibility for the film industry.[47] Risk-taking is, therefore, a key element in the success story of the *Thi-Baan* franchise. The same can be said for interpersonal trust, as trusting someone means taking the risk of relying on others to look after one's interests. In this regard, a trust-based reinterpretation shares the pessimism of the incentive argument concerning the prospects of free-riding. However, it does not share with the narrative of incentives the optimism of cost-benefit analysis, which purports to anticipate all possibilities of individual action, thereby defining the nature of social interaction.[48] On the contrary, the optimism of mutual trust lies in recognising familiar production as a sphere of becoming where new meaning and value emerge.

Furthermore, this trust-based conception of community does not shy away from the reality of power relations. It does not define community by shared essence that assumes homogeneity. Instead, it regards shared interests as defining relationships within a community such that power may breed suspicion, while trust can be empowering. From this perspective, trust and power are not mutually exclusive, for they both shape the dynamics of social interactions. An example of these dynamics can be seen in the clientelist relationships between some Thai film directors and studio owners, relationships that may be reciprocal but also are fraught with power

43 Cotterrell, *Law, Culture, and Society* (n 20) 73–76.

44 Cotterrell, *Law's Community*, 330.

45 See 'Risky Business' in Chapter 6.

46 ibid.

47 See 'Let Me Entertain You' in Chapter 6.

48 For further discussion on the economic analysis of copyright, see Anne Barron, 'Copyright infringement, "free-riding" and the lifeworld' in Lionel Bently, Jennifer Davis, and Jane Ginsburg (eds) *Copyright and Piracy: An Interdisciplinary Critique* (CUP 2010).

imbalances, leaving them open to abuse and exploitation. Situations like this suggest that copyright law, by conferring rights and imposing duties, may play a role in balancing power dynamics to foster trusting relationships. Indeed, Cotterrell argues that law may support and encourage mutual interpersonal trust, but only indirectly in shaping the empirical conditions of trusting relationships.[49] Interestingly, this proposition resonates with the discussions of contemporary Thai cinema in Chapter 7, where it can be further argued that copyright law facilitates mutual interpersonal trust in three ways.[50]

The first is through giving legal expression to trusting relationships, thereby reducing the risks of trusting through the guarantee of rights and duties.[51] This is evident in how relationships among directors, producers, studios, and audiences are mediated through the dynamics of authorship and ownership. Recognising the function of the film 'auteur' as a brand highlights the negotiation and collaboration inherent in the social construction of authorship. Similarly, the discussion on first ownership also shows how copyright law can help align the interests of filmmakers and investors. However, as discussed in Chapter 7, the discontent among screenwriters and the cynicism in the public also serve as reminders that the current copyright framework can also foster mistrust.[52]

Another way in which copyright law may support mutual interpersonal trust is by facilitating the participation of all actors, which helps to stabilise and reinforce their mutual trust.[53] One could say that copyright law already serves this function to an extent, as evidenced by the notion of public access currently safeguarded by the bulwark of copyright limitations and exceptions. However, the author–user distinction still poses a crucial challenge, rendering the necessary balancing act elusive. The discussion of balance showed that an unequal relationship is inherent in the author–user distinction and that it threatens to hinder the widening of participation.[54]

Finally, the legal instruments of licence and assignment can allow for coordination within and between different networks of community. Suffice it to say that coordination is indispensable to bridging gaps and resolving conflicts, which are conducive to trust.[55] Here, again, the discontent among the screenwriters serves as a warning sign. It demonstrates how a lack of protection for the weaker party can turn copyright issues into a zero-sum game. This will hinder rather than encourage trusting relationships.[56]

Considering these functions, the law-and-community approach provides a valuable lens for realigning the current legal framework with the kinship of familiar

49 Cotterrell, 'Subverting orthodoxy' (n 22) 643.
50 Perry-Kessaris (n 34) 13–17.
51 ibid 13.
52 See 'Burning Down the House' in Chapter 7.
53 Perry-Kessaris (n 34) 14.
54 See also Gibson, *Creating Selves* (n 13).
55 Perry-Kessaris (n 34) 16.
56 See 'Burning Down the House' in Chapter 7.

production. Insights from contemporary Thai cinema further illustrate this point. The discussion on the auteur brand is not a rejection of authorship but rather an exploration of how this concept can move beyond the myth of solitary genius. Branding is inherently dialogic and collaborative, involving not just filmmakers but also critics, institutions, and audiences. In this sense, authorship is a collaborative process, pointing to a potential role for moral rights in shaping brand relationships.[57] This relational perspective can shed new light on copyright as well. Consider copyright ownership, for example. Relationships among people involved in film production and distribution are shaped by how copyright ownership is defined, reflecting both collaborative dynamics and power relations.[58] This shows how ownership can serve as a tool for aligning interests and fostering trust, helping to establish common ground rather than merely excluding or asserting control.[59] Ultimately, what all of this suggests is that the change envisaged by the concept of community resource does not require that we tear everything down for the rebuild to begin.

So where do we begin? Always begin in the middle of things—just as this book dives into the rich and enticing experiences of contemporary Thai cinema.

Ethical Community

It is likely that discussing community regulation will evoke the notion of legal pluralism and the quest for a living law that is distinct from state law.[60] Indeed, this is

57 In this regard, moral rights, such as the right of attribution, would not originate from the individuality of the author but rather reflect the necessity of coordinating production and distribution relationships within the film industry, for instance, the credit system.

58 See 'Build a House, Make a Home' in Chapter 7.

59 In any case, the emphasis on trust-building suggests that copyright as a community resource is open to retaining the legal concept of the exclusive right as long as it serves community relations. A relevant example of what this might mean for legal doctrine is Ansgar Ohly's fairness-based, 'three-layer model' reconstruction of copyright law. Ohly's main contention focuses on the formalism of rights and exceptions in copyright law, particularly when viewed through a market-effect perspective. He contrasts this with trademark law and unfair competition law, which have prioritised the standard of fairness and currently appear more attuned to the actual effects of unfair practices. Ohly then proposes to articulate the relationship between copyright and the need for market sensitivity through the notion of fairness. The result is a model of layered protection: it begins with a blocklist of well-defined acts, followed by a layer of economic rights subject to a cognisable harm/unjust enrichment test, and rounded off with a general clause on unfair use. See Ohly, 'A fairness-based approach to economic rights' in Bernt Hugenholtz (ed), *Copyright Reconstructed: Rethinking Copyright's Economic Rights in a Time of Highly Dynamic Technological and Economic Change* (Wolters Kluwer 2018). Although his goal is different, his emphasis on market sensitivity makes copyright protection more relational, as the market itself can be seen as an expression of community relations. Meanwhile, his three-layered model also illustrates how the current framework could be changed to better accommodate diverse social interactions. So while Ohly limits his attempt at reconstructing copyright law to economic rights, his approach still offers a useful starting point.

60 Eugen Ehrlich coined the term 'living law' to contrast with statutory enactment and judicial decision, that is, state law. His concept of living law called attention to social norms/normative structures

the kind of project that Cotterrell's law-and-community approach lends itself to.[61] The community concept emerges from Cotterrell's attempt to recast society into communal networks so that one could look for law in the everyday experience of community life.[62] Law is thus referred to in a pluralist sense, and the main interest lies in laws below the state level. Consequently, the legitimacy and normative force of these laws will compel attention from the state as a matter of how to regulate the complexity and diversity of contemporary social life.[63] In this regard, one could say that Cotterrell elevates community into a source of law, as it were—and it is here where the concept of community resource makes a necessary departure from his law-and-community approach.

Cotterrell's primary concern has long been to advocate for a sociology of law that contributes to the understanding and interpretation of law.[64] He argues that empirical legal studies—whether referred to as legal sociology, law and society, or sociolegal studies—should engage directly with legal doctrine. This means they must address not only legal ideas but also legal values, thereby engaging with the moral significance of law. With his own concern with law's legitimacy in modern society, Cotterrell identifies the values of modern law as articulated in the work of the French sociologist Émile Durkheim.[65] Cotterrell finds a normative grounding for his law-and-community approach in Durkheim's moral individualism, a framework that upholds individual autonomy as a basis for collective solidarity.[66] Ultimately, for Cotterrell, law finds a moral calling in supporting community, as it were.

Indeed, the appeal of Cotterrell's community concept lies, to some extent, in the moral undertone of his law-and-community approach—a deliberate theoretical design which is intended to bridge the gap between legal doctrine and sociolegal inquiry. This, however, also limits its applicability in developing the concept of community resource. Cotterrell's law-and-community approach presupposes a stable and sustained communal network, as it must be possible to identify relations of community objectively; otherwise, there is no normative order or living law to speak of.[67] So while Cotterrell looks for law within relations of community, the concept of community resource puts the idea of community back into the framework of copyright law. This means the legitimacy of copyright protection will not arise from the normative force rooted in community structures but rather from

---

of social life. Thus, he proclaimed 'The sociology of law is the theoretical science of law [i.e. a theoretical study of law].' See Ehrlich, *The Fundamental Principles of Sociology of Law*, 25.

61 See Cotterrell, 'Community as a legal concept?' (n 31).

62 Cotterrell, *Law, Culture, and Society* (n 20) 65.

63 ibid 76–77.

64 See for instance Cotterrell, *Law's Community* (n 44); Cotterrell, *Law, Culture, and Society* (n 20); Cotterrell, *Sociological Jurisprudence* (n 23); Roger Cotterrell, *Jurisprudence and Socio-Legal Studies: Intersecting Fields* (Routledge 2024).

65 See Roger Cotterrell, *Emile Durkheim: Law in a Moral Domain* (Edinburgh University Press 1999).

66 Cotterrell, *Law, Culture, and Society* (n 20) 168–169.

67 See a similar critique in Reza Banakar and Alexandra Lort Phillips, 'Law, community and the 2011 London riots' in Richard Nobles and David Schiff (eds), *Law, Society and Community* (Ashgate 2014) 181.

the production of affiliations and associations. A trust-based reinterpretation transforms copyright law into a resource for familiar production, the smooth space of social and cultural becoming.[68]

To appreciate the significance of this transformation, it is worth noting again that what is at stake in the institutionalisation of copyright is not just the future of economic production. Equally important are the implications for the production of familiarity that allows a sense of self and belonging to rise from below. An important illustration of this potential is the emergence of regional Thai film.[69] The success of the *Thi-Baan* films not only offers a glimpse of how familiar production can shift the site of value from the products to the interactions. But such interactions—especially the discussions around the on-screen projection of *Isan* life—also interjected new ideas into the public discourse on what it means to be Thai. This holds a mirror up to the institutionalised image of the Thai self, one that depicts the populace of *Isan* as the Others within. And as such, it opens up the possibility of imagining the national community differently.[70]

Such opportunities for the proliferation of meaning and value that arise from familiar production make it a sphere of becoming—a dynamic space where relationships and identities are constantly renegotiated.[71] Once again, as Gibson highlights, 'in familiar production the way in which the user interacts with others and forms alliances and assemblages is as important as any particular product of those assemblages.'[72] In this context, Deleuze and Guattari remind us that:

> We know nothing about a body until we know what it can do, in other words, what its affects are, how they can or cannot enter into composition with other affects, with the affects of another body.'[73]

The cultivation of familiarity and kinship highlights the importance of participation and collaboration—*do with me*—in contrast to the persistence of coloniality in relationship of dominion, or *do as I do*.[74] By fostering new combinations that open up new possibilities, the kinship of familiar production embodies the ethical process of becoming, resisting the moral prescription of *do as I do*.

68 The term 'smooth space' comes from the work of Deleuze and Guattari. It is part of a conceptual pair that juxtaposes the imageries of the 'smooth' and the 'striated' with respect to the idea of 'space' that is not necessarily geographical. For Deleuze and Guattari, 'the sea is a smooth space fundamentally open to striation.' The sea is a smooth space because it lacks fixed referent points, but it is also subjugated to a striation for maritime navigation, which was integral to the European colonisation of the Americas and the global spread of colonialism. In this way, the smooth space of the sea is contrary to social divisions and hierarchies, whereby the image of the sea as an open water serves to illustrate a smooth space as a space of becoming. See Gilles Deleuze and Félix Guattari, *A Thousand Plateaus: Capitalism and Schizophrenia* (Brian Massumi tr, University of Minnesota Press 1987) 478–482.

69 See 'Let Me Entertain You' in Chapter 6.

70 By contrast, see 'Identity Politics' in Chapter 3 and 'Politics of Creativity' in Chapter 5.

71 Gibson, *The Logic of Innovation*, 39.

72 ibid.

73 Deleuze and Guattari, *A Thousand Plateaus* (n 68) 257.

74 Deleuze, *Difference and Repetition*, 23. See also 'Repetition and Learning' in Chapter 5.

Bibliography

I. Primary Sources

A. Published Primary Sources

Government Gazette (17 May 1847) Book 1
Government Gazette (19 August 1892) Book 9
Government Gazette (18 August 1901) Book 18
Government Gazette (29 April 1917) Book 34
House of Representatives Deb (29 September 1993) Vol 18, Year 2 (First Session), No 3
House of Representatives Deb (27 January 2021) Vol 25, Year 2 (Second Session), No 15
National Legislative Assembly Deb (16 June 1978) No 30
National Statistical Office, '**สมุดสถิติรายปี บรรพ** 29 (**พ.ศ.** 2512–2513)' (Statistical Yearbook, Chapter 29 (1969–1970)) (Bangkok 1970)
Police Department, '**คำชี้แจงของกรมตำรวจเกี่ยวกับภาพยนตร์ เรื่อง 'เดอะ คิง แอนด์ ไอ**'' (Police Department Clarification Regarding the Film 'The King and I') Sayamnikorn (Bangkok 19 August 1956)

B. Statutes and Instruments

1. Thailand

Author's Ownership Act RE 120 (1901)
Copyright Act (No 3) BE 2558 (2015)
Copyright Act BE 2521 (1978)
Copyright Act BE 2537 (1994)
The Protection of Literary and Artistic Works Act BE 2474 (1931)
Royal Decree to establish the Royal Society of Literature BE 2457 (1914)

2. United States

19 US Code § 2411 (1988)
US International Copyright Act (The Chace Act) (1891)

3. International, Regional, and Bilateral Instruments

Anglo-Siamese Treaty of 1925
Berne Convention, 1886, as Modified by the Paris Additional Act, 1896
Franco-Siamese Treaty of 1925

InfoSoc Directive 2001
Japanese-Siamese Treaty of 1924
Treaty of Amity and Commerce, 16 December 1920
TRIPS Agreement 1994
WIPO Copyright Treaty 1996

C. *Cases*

Donaldson v. *Becket* (1774) *Hansard, 1st ser.*, 17 (1774): 953–1003
Thai Supreme Court Decision No 2750/2537

D. *Unpublished Primary Sources*

National Archive of Thailand, Department of Royal Private Secretary Doc No Aor 20/1, **'พระราชหัตถเลขากรมหลวงเทวะวงศ์วโรประการกราบบังคมทูลพระบาทสมเด็จพระจุลจอมเกล้าเจ้าอยู่หัว เรื่องกฎหมายกอปีไรต์อเมริกัน'** (Letter from Prince Devawongse to King Chulalongkorn on US copyright law) (6 July 1893)
National Archive of Thailand, Ministry of Public Instruction Doc No Sor Thor 9.2/23, **'หนังสือจากพระยาวุฒิการบดีถึงอธิบดีกรมศึกษาธิการ เรื่องกฎหมายกอปีไรต์'** (Praya Wutthikarnbordi's letter to the Director of Education on the subject of copyright law) (12 March 1900)
National Archive of Thailand, Ministry of Public Instruction Doc No Sor Thor 9.2/23, **'หนังสือจากหลวงดำรงสาร ถึงพระเจ้าลูกยาเธอพระองค์เจ้ากิติยากรวรลักษณ์อธิบดีกรมศึกษาธิการ'** (Luang Damrongsan's letter to the Director of Education) (23 March 1900)
National Archive of Thailand, Ministry of Public Instruction Doc No Sor Thor 9.2/23, **'หนังสือจากหลวงชำนิบรรณาคมถึงขุนประพนธ์เนติประวัติ เรื่องการพิมพ์หนังสือแบบเรียนของกรมศึกษาธิการ'** (Luang Chamni-bannakom's letter to Khun Praponniprawat on printing government textbooks) (30 March 1900)
National Archive of Thailand, Ministry of Public Instruction Doc No Sor Thor 9.2/23, **'หนังสือจากกรมศึกษาธิการถึงกระทรวงธรรมการ'** (Memo from the Department of Education to the Ministry of Public Instruction) (17 January 1901)
National Archive of Thailand, Department of Royal Private Secretary Doc No Aor 20/2, **'พระราชหัตถเลขากรมหมื่นราชบุรีดิเรกฤทธิ์ถวายพระบาทสมเด็จพระจุลจอมเกล้าเจ้าอยู่หัว เรื่องขอพระราชทานอำนาจกอปีไรต์ในหนังสือทรงแต่ง** (Prince Rabi's letter to the King to request ad-hoc copyright)' (7 July 1901)
National Archive of Thailand, Department of Royal Private Secretary Doc No Aor 20/2, **'รายงานการประชุมเสนาบดีสภาตั้งแต่วันที่ 18 กรกฎาคม ถึง 5 สิงหาคม ร.ศ.** 120' (Minutes of the meetings of the Council of State) (18 July–5 August 1901)
National Archive of Thailand, Department of Royal Private Secretary Doc No Aor 20/2, **'ร่างพระราชบัญญัติว่าด้วยกรรมสิทธิ์ผู้แต่งหนังสือของกรมพระยาดำรงราชานุภาพ'** (Damrong's copyright bill)
National Archive of Thailand, Department of Royal Private Secretary Doc No Aor 20/2, **'หนังสือจากเจ้าพระยาภาสกรวงศ์ถวายพระบาทสมเด็จพระจุลจอมเกล้าเจ้าอยู่หัว เรื่องร่างพระราชบัญญัติกอปีไรต์ของกระทรวงธรรมการ'** (Chao Phraya Pasakorawong's letter to the King on MOPI's draft copyright law) (3 August 1901)
National Archive of Thailand, Department of Royal Private Secretary Doc No Aor 20/2, **'พระราชหัตถเลขากรมหมื่นราชบุรีดิเรกฤทธิ์ถวายพระบาทสมเด็จพระจุลจอมเกล้าเจ้าอยู่หัวทำความเห็นร่างพระราชบัญญัติกรรมสิทธิ์ในหนังสือ'** (Prince Rabi's letter to the King on his opinion about the copyright bill) (8 August 1901)
National Archive of Thailand, Department of Royal Private Secretary Doc No Aor 20/4, **'บาญชีรายชื่อผู้ขอกรรมสิทธิ์จดทเบียนกอปีไรต์'** (Copyright applicants register) (22 August 1901–6 October 1910)

National Archive of Thailand, 'Georges Padoux's Memorandum on the Question on Legal Education in Siam' (20 December 1913) Kor Tor 35.10/10

National Archive of Thailand, Miscellaneous documents of the sixth reign, Doc No Bor 10/10, '**ร่างประกาศตั้งนิรุกติสมาคม**' (Draft announcement to establish the society of language) (31 August 1916)

National Archive of Thailand, Ministry of Education Doc No Sor Tor 0701.35, '**รายงานประชุมกรรมการพิจารณาการออกกฎหมายคุ้มครองวรรณคดีและศิลปกรรม ครั้งที่** 1' (Minutes of the first meeting of the committee to consider the promulgation of the law to protect literary and artistic works) (31 May 1928)

National Archive of Thailand, Ministry of Education Doc No Sor Tor 0701.35, 'Prince Varnvaidya's report on the Copyright Conference' (25 June 1929)

National Archive of Thailand, Ministry of Education Doc No Sor Tor 0701.35, 'Memorandum on draft copyright law' (5 April 1930)

National Archive of Thailand, Ministry of Education Doc No Sor Tor 0701.5.1/6, '**รายงานการประชุมคณะกรรมการพิจารณาแก้ไขพระราชบัญญัติคุ้มครองวรรณกรรมและศิลปกรรมฯ ครั้งที่** 1/2516' (Minutes of the first meeting of the committee to amend the PLAWA) (30 March 1973)

Office of the Minister, Ministry of Education Doc No Sor Ror 0601/585, '**รายงานการประชุมคณะกรรมการพิจารณาแก้ไข พรบ คุ้มครองวรรณกรรมและศิลปกรรม พุทธศักราช** 2474 **ครั้งที่** 1/2517' (Minutes of the meeting of the committee to amend the PLAWA 1931, No 1/1974) (11 February 1974)

National Archive of Thailand, Ministry of Education Doc No Sor Ror 0601/585, '**รายงานการประชุมคณะกรรมการพิจารณาแก้ไข พรบ คุ้มครองวรรณกรรมและศิลปกรรม พุทธศักราช** 2474 **ครั้งที่** 4/2519' (Minutes of the meeting of the committee to amend the PLAWA 1931, No 4/1976) (9 November 1976)

National Archive of Thailand, Ministry of Education Doc No Sor Ror 0203/19130, '**คำชี้แจงประกอบร่างพระราชบัญญัติลิขสิทธิ์ พ.ศ.** . . .' (Explanatory notes on a draft Copyright Act) (9 September 1977)

II. Secondary Sources

A. Books

Alford W, *To Steal a Book is an Elegant Offense: Intellectual Property Law in Chinese Civilization* (Stanford University Press 1995)

Anderson B, *Imagined Communities: Reflections on the Origin and Spread of Nationalism* (revised edn, Verso 2006)

Aronczyk M, *Branding the Nation: The Global Business of National Identity* (OUP 2013)

Atiyah P S, *The Rise and Fall of Freedom of Contract* (Clarendon Press 2003)

Baker C, 'The 2014 Thai coup and some roots of authoritarianism' (2016) 46(3) Journal of Contemporary Asia 388

Baker C and Phongpaichit P, *A History of Thailand* (CUP 2014)

Baldwin P, *The Copyright Wars: Three Centuries of Trans-Atlantic Battle* (Princeton University Press 2004)

Ballano V, *Sociological Perspectives on Media Piracy in the Philippines and Vietnam* (Springer 2016)

Bamrungsuk S, *United States Foreign Policy and Thai Military Rule, 1947–1977* (Duangkamol 1988)

Barmé S, *Women, Man, Bangkok: Love, Sex, and Popular Culture in Thailand* (Rowman & Littlefield 2002)

Benkler Y, *The Wealth of Networks: How Social Production Transforms Markets and Freedom* (Yale University Press 2006)

Bettig R, *Copyrighting Culture: The Political Economy of Intellectual Property* (Routledge 1996)

Bhabha H, *The Location of Culture* (Routledge 1994)

Bhambra G, *Rethinking Modernity: Postcolonialism and the Sociological Imagination* (Palgrave Macmillan 2007)

Birnhack M, *Colonial Copyright: Intellectual Property in Mandate Palestine* (OUP 2012)

Boonchalermvipas S, ประวัติศาสตร์กฎหมายไทย *(Thai Legal History)* (Winyouchon 2005)

Bowring J, *The Kingdom and People of Siam*, vol 1 (OUP 1969)

Boyle J, S*hamans, Software, and Spleens: Law and the Construction of the Information Society* (Harvard University Press 1996)

Buchanan I, *Assemblage Theory and Method* (Bloomsbury 2021)

Cassel P K, *Grounds of Judgment: Extraterritoriality and Imperial Power in Nineteenth-Century China and Japan* (OUP 2012)

Chaiwaraporn A, ภาพยนตร์ในชีวิตไทย มุมมองของภาพยนตร์ศึกษา *(Cinema in Thai Life: A Perspective of Film Studies)* (Varaporn Publishing 2016)

Chaloemtiarana T, *Thailand: The Politics of Despotic Paternalism* (Silkworm Books 2007)

Chaloemtiarana T, *Read Till It Shatters: Nationalism and Identity in Modern Thai Literature* (ANU Press 2018)

Chanchira A, พระบามสมเด็จพระจอมเกล้าเจ้าอยู่หัวกับการพิมพ์หนังสือ *(King Mongkut and Publishing)* (Cremation Volume for Nai Banleu Chanchira 1972)

Chanrungmaneekul U, *120* ปี ธุรกิจภาพยนตร์ไทย ในมิติประวัติศาสตร์เศรษฐกิจและสังคมไทย *(120 Years of Thai Film Business From the Historical Perspective of Thai Economy and Society)* (Thailand Research Fund 2018)

Chanrungmaneekul U, โรงหนัง สายหนัง ความ(ไร้)อำนาจของคนดูและศิลปิน ธุรกิจการฉายภาพยนตร์และสังคมไทย พ.ศ. *2440–2561 (Cinemas, Distributors, and the (Absent) Power of Audiences and Artists: The Business of Film Exhibition and Thai Society 1897–2018)* (Thailand Research Fund 2020)

Cohen A, *The Symbolic Construction of Community* (Routledge 1985)

Cotterrell R, *The Sociology of Law* (2nd edn, Butterworths 1992)

Cotterrell R, *Law's Community: Legal Theory in Sociological Perspective* (Clarendon Press 1997)

Cotterrell R, *Emile Durkheim: Law in a Moral Domain* (Edinburgh University Press 1999)

Cotterrell R, *Law, Culture, and Society: Legal Ideas in the Mirror of Social Theory* (Aldershot 2006)

Cotterrell R, *Sociological Jurisprudence: Juristic Thought and Social Inquiry* (Routledge 2017)

Cotterrell R, *Jurisprudence and Socio-Legal Studies: Intersecting Fields* (Routledge 2024)

De Valck M, *Film Festivals: From European Geopolitics to Global Cinephilia* (Amsterdam University Press 2007)

Deazley R, *On the Origin of the Right to Copy: Charting the Movement of Copyright Law in Eighteenth-Century Britain, 1695–1775* (Hart 2004)

Deleuze G, *Difference and Repetition* (Paul Patton tr, Continuum 1968)

Deleuze G, *Spinoza: Practical Philosophy* (Robert Hurley tr, City Light Books 1988)

Deleuze G and Guattari F, *A Thousand Plateaus: Capitalism and Schizophrenia* (Brian Massumi tr, University of Minnesota Press 1987)

Deleuze G and Parnet C, *Dialogues II* (Hugh Tomilson and Barbara Habberjam trs, Continuum 1987)

Drahos P and Braithwaite J, *Information Feudalism: Who Owns the Knowledge Economy?* (Earthscan 2002)

Edelman B, *Ownership of the Image. Elements for a Marxist Theory of Law* (Elizabeth Kingdom tr, Routledge Kegan and Paul 1979)

Ehrlich E, *The Fundamental Principles of Sociology of Law* (Transaction Publishers 2002)

Ekun P, *Thai Education* (Suan Sunandha Rajabhat Institute 1999)

Engel D and Engel J, *Tort and Karma: Globalisation and Legal Consciousness in Thailand* (Stanford University Press 2010)
Eoseewong N, *Pen and Sail: Literature and History in Early Bangkok* (Silkworm 2005)
Executive Committee of the Eighth Congress of Far Eastern Association of Tropical Medicine, *In Siam: General and Medical Features* (Bangkok Times Press 1930)
Friedman L, *The Legal System: A Social Science Perspective* (Russell Sage Foundation 1975)
Frow J, *Time and Commodity Culture: Essays in Cultural Theory and Postmodernity* (Clarendon 1997)
Gervais D, *The TRIPS Agreement: Drafting History and Analysis* (5th edn, Sweet & Maxwell 2021)
Gibson J, *Creating Selves: Intellectual Property and the Narration of Culture* (Routledge 2006)
Gibson J, *The Logic of Innovation: Intellectual Property and What the User Found There* (Routledge 2014)
Gibson J, *Owned, an Ethological Jurisprudence of Property* (Routledge 2020)
Harding A and Pongsapan M (eds), *Thai Legal History: From Traditional to Modern Law* (CUP 2021)
Harrison R and Jackson P (eds), *The Ambiguous Allure of the West: Traces of the Colonial in Thailand* (Hong Kong University Press 2010)
Hell S, *Siam in the League of Nation: Modernisation, Sovereignty and Multilateral Diplomacy, 1920–1940* (River Books 2010)
Hemaratchata C, **คำอธิบายกฎหมายลิขสิทธิ์** *(A Commentary on Copyright Law)* (1st edn, Nitibunnakarn 1984)
Hemaratchata C, **ลักษณะของกฎหมายทรัพย์สินทางปัญญา** *(Characteristics of Intellectual Property Law)* (13th edn, Nititham 2022)
Herzfeld M, *Cultural Intimacy: Social Poetics in the Nation-State* (3rd edn, Routledge 2016)
Hobbes T, *Leviathan* (J C A Gaskin ed, OUP 2008)
Hunt M, *Thai cinema uncensored* (Silkworm Books 2021)
Jaijing N, ***ขุนศึก ศักดินา และพญาอินทรี การเมืองไทยภายใต้ระเบียบโลกของสหรัฐอเมริกา*** *2491–2500 (Warlord, Sakdina, and the Bald Eagle: Thai Politics in the American World Order, 1948–1958)* (Fah-diew-kan 2020)
Jenkins H, *Convergence Culture: Where Old and New Media Collide* (NYU Press 2006)
Jenkins H, Purushotma R, Weigel M, Clinton K, and Robison A, *Confronting the Challenges of Participatory Culture: Media Education for the 21st Century* (MIT Press 2009)
Jitjamnong D, **คุณค่าและคุณลักษณะเด่นของวรรณคดีไทยสมัยรัตนโกสินทร์ตอนต้น** *(The Value and Characteristics of Thai literature in the Early Rattanakosin Period)* (Thammasat University Press 1997)
Jitjamnong D, Jongsathitwattana S, Raksamanee K, and Phromsuttirak M, **พัฒนาการวรรณคดีไทย** (*Development of Thai Literature)* (Sukhothai Thammathirat Open University Press 1990)
Kakizaki I, *Rise of the Kingdom: The History of Thai Railways* (White Lotus 2012)
Kesboonchoo-Mead K, *The Rise and Decline of Thai Absolutism* (Routledge 2004)
King Chulalongkorn, ***การเสด็จประพาสยุโรปของพระบาทสมเด็จพระจุลจอมเกล้าเจ้าอยู่หัว ร.ศ.*** *116 (King Chulalongkorn's Visit to Europe in 1897)* (Department of Fine Arts 2008)
King Vajiravudh, ***เที่ยวเมืองพระร่วง*** *(Travels in Phra Ruang Country)* (Ministry of the Interior 1954)
Klein C, *Cold War Orientthongchaialism: Asia in the Middlebrow Imagination, 1945–1961* (University of California Press 2003)
Kotler P, Jatusripitak S, and Maesincee S, *The Marketing of Nations: Strategic Approach to Building National Wealth* (Simon & Schuster 1997)
Kovács A B, *Screening Modernism: European Art Cinema, 1950–1980* (University of Chicago Press 2007)

Kraivichien T, ***การปฏิรูประบบกฎหมายและการศาลในรัชสมัยพระบาทสมเด็จฯ พระจุลจอมเกล้าเจ้าหัวพระปิยะมหาราช*** *(The Reforms of Law and Judicial Administration During the Reign of King Chulalongkorn)* (Ministry of Justice 1968)

Landon K P, *Siam in Transition* (University of Chicago Press 1938)

Limsakul B, ***ผลการเจรจาแกตต์รอบอุรุกวัยต่อระบบการคุ้มครองทรัพย์สินทางปัญญาของไทย: รายงานการสัมมนาเชิงปฏิบัติการ*** *(The Impact of The Uruguay Round of GATT Negotiations on Thailand's IP Protection System: The Workshop Report)* (Thailand Research Fund 1994)

Locke J, *The Second Treatise on Government; and a Letter Concerning Toleration* (Mark Goldie ed, OUP 2016)

Loos T, *Subject Siam: Family, Law, and Colonial Modernity in Thailand* (Cornell University Press 2006)

Luang Saranaiprasas, ***พัฒนาการการศึกษากฎหมายในประเทศไทย*** *(The Development of Legal Education in Thailand)* (Thammasat University 1956)

Macmillan F, *Intellectual and Cultural Property: Between Market and Community* (Routledge 2021)

McCargo D, 'Network Monarchy and Crises of Legitimacy in Thailand' (2005) 18(4) The Pacific Review 499

McDonald N A, *Siam: Its Government, Manners, Customs, &c* (A Martien 1871)

Mehta U S, *Liberalism and Empire: A Study in Nineteenth-Century Political Thought and Practice* (University of Chicago Press 1999)

Ministry of Justice, *100* ***ปี กระทรวงยุติธรรม*** *(100 Years of the Ministry of Justice)* (Ministry of Justice 1992)

Misztal B, *Trust in Modern Societies: The Search for the Bases of Social Order* (Polity 1996)

Nye J, *Soft Power: The Means to Success in World Politics* (Public Affairs 2004)

O'Regan T, *Australian National Cinema* (3rd edn, Taylor & Francis, 2005)

Pang L, *Creativity and Its Discontents: China's Creative Industries and Intellectual Property Rights Offenses* (Duke University Press 2012)

Pattamanun U, ***การศึกษาเปรียบเทียบบทบาทต่างประเทศต่อการเปลี่ยนแปลงทางเศรษฐกิจไทย: ทศวรรษ*** *1960* ***และ*** *1990 (A Comparative Study of the Role of Foreign Countries in the Change in the Thai Economy: 1960s and 1990s)* (Institute of Asian Studies, Chulalongkorn University 2001)

Perry-Kessaris A, *Global Business, Local law: The Indian Legal System as a Communal Resource in Foreign Investment Relations* (Routledge 2016)

Peukert A, *A Critique of the Ontology of Intellectual Property Law* (Gill Mertens tr, CUP 2021)

Phongpaichit P and Baker C, *Thailand's Boom and Bust* (Silkworm Books 1998)

Phongpaichit P and Baker C, *Thaksin: The Business of Politics in Thailand* (Silkworm Books 2005)

Pope R, *Creativity: Theory, History, Practice* (Routledge 2010)

Puangpit N and Mulsilp W, ***หนังสือเรียน รายวิชาพื้นฐาน ประวัติศาสตร์ไทย ม.4—ม.6: ชั้นมัธยมศึกษาปีที่*** *4–6 (Coursebook for the Compulsory Subject of Thai History, Secondary School Year 4–6)* (Aksorn-charoen-tat 2015)

Puapongsakorn N and Ungpakorn P M, ***เอกสารประกอบการสัมมนาเรื่องผลกระทบของการเจรจารอบอุรุกวัยต่อประเทศไทย*** *(Materials for the Seminar on the Impact of the Uruguay Round on Thailand)* (Thailand Research Fund and Thailand Development Research Institute 1996)

Pueksom T, ***หยดเลือด จารึก และแท่นพิมพ์: ว่าด้วยความรู้/ความจริงของชนชั้นนำสยาม พ.ศ.*** *2325–2411 (Blood, Inscription, and Printing Press: The Conception of Knowledge/Truth of the Siamese Elite, 1782–1868)* (Illumination 2018)

Rachanuphap D, ***ตำนานหอพระสมุด หอพระมณเฑียรธรรม หอวชิรญาณ หอพุทธสาสนสังคหะ แลหอสมุดสำหรับพระนคร*** *(History of the Book Hall, the Palace Dhamma Library, the Buddhist Collection and the State Library)* (Cremation Volume for Phra Inthabenya (Sarakham Wattha) 1969)

Rajchagool C, *The Rise and Fall of the Thai Absolute Monarchy: Foundations of the Modern Thai State From Feudalism to Peripheral Capitalism* (White Lotus 1994)

Reungraklikid C, Sajjaphun R, and Jitjamnong D, *ทอไหมในสายน้ำ 200 ปีวรรณคดีวิจารณ์ไทย (Weaving Silk in Flowing Water: 200 Years of Thai Literary Criticism)* (2nd edn, A.N. Publishing 1998)

Reynolds C (ed), *National Identity and Its Defender: Thailand, 1939–1989* (Silkworm 1993)

Said E, *Orientalism: Western Conceptions of the Orient* (Penguin 1995)

Saunders D, *Authorship and Copyright* (Routledge 1992)

Senanan W, *The Genesis of the Novel in Thailand* (Thai-watana-panich 1975)

Simone D, *Copyright and Collective Authorship: Locating the Author of Collaborative Work* (CUP 2019)

Sivaraksa S, *อำนาจของภาษาและสถาบันวิชาการ: เพื่อใคร (The Power of Language and the Academy: For Whom?)* (Semmasikkhalai 1997)

Srisuwan U (Phrommachomphu A), *ไทยกึ่งเมืองขึ้น (Thailand, a Semicolony)* (Udomatham 1950)

Strathern M, *The Gender of the Gift: Problems With Women and Problems With Society in Melanesia Studies in Melanesian Anthropology* (University of California Press 1988)

Subyen S and Watcharathanin T, *ปฏิบัติการหนังทุนข้ามชาติ (Operation: Transnationally Funded Films)* (Openbooks 2010)

Suthersanen U and Gendreau Y, *A Shifting Empire: 100 Years of the Copyright Act 1911* (Edward Elgar 2013)

Suveeranon P and Tejapira K, *อัตลักษณ์ไทย: จากไทยสู่ไทยๆ และบริโภคความเป็นไทย (Thai Identity: From Thai to Thai-Thai and the Consumption of Thainess)* (Fah-diew-kan 2011)

Tamanaha B, *A General Jurisprudence of Law and Society* (OUP 2001)

Tantivasadakarn C, *นโยบายการค้าระหว่างประเทศของไทยในช่วงปี 2543–2549 (Thailand's International Trade Policy Between 2000 and 2006)* (Thailand Research Fund 2006)

Tejapira K, *Commodifying Marxism: The Formation of Modern Thai Radical Culture, 1927–1958* (Kyoto University Press 2001)

Tonnies F, *Community and Society* (CP Loomis tr, Routledge 1988)

Varathorn S, *ประวัติศาสตร์การประพันธ์นวนิยายไทย (The History of Thai Novel)* (Chareon-witkarnpim 1976)

Vella W, *Chaiyo! King Vajiravudh and the Development of Thai Nationalism* (University of Hawaii Press 2019)

Watson A, *The Evolution of Law* (Blackwell 1985)

Watson A, *Legal Origins and Legal Change* (Hambledon Press 1991)

Watson A, *Legal Transplants: An Approach to Comparative Law* (2nd edn, UGA Press 1993)

Watson A, *Society and Legal Change* (2nd edn, TU Press 2001)

Weber M, *Economy and Society: A New Translation* (Tribe K ed/tr, Harvard University Press 2019)

Williams J, *Gilles Deleuze's Difference and Repetition: A Critical Introduction and Guide* (Edinburgh University Press 2003)

Winichakul T, *Siam Mapped: A History of the Geo-Body of a Nation* (University of Hawaii 1997)

Winichakul T, *เมื่อสยามพลิกผัน: ว่าด้วยกรอบมโนทัศน์ของสยามยุคใหม่ (Siam at a Turning Point: On the Foundational Mentality of Siam in the Modern Era)* (Fah-diew-kan 2019)

Winichakul T, *นิติรัฐอภิสิทธิ์และราชานิติธรรม ประวัติศาสตร์ภูมิปัญญาของ Rule by Law แบบไทย (Legal-Privileged-State and Royalist Rule of Law: The Intellectual History of Thai-Style Rule by Law)* (Thammasat University 2020)

Woodmansee M, *The Author, Art, and the Market: Rereading the History of Aesthetics* (Columbia University Press 1994)

The Working Group on the History of Printing in Thailand, *สยามพิมพการ: ประวัติศาสตร์การพิมพ์ในประเทศไทย (Sayam Phimphakan: History of Printing in Thailand)* (Matichon 2006)

Wyatt D, *The Politics of Reform in Thailand: Education in the Reign of King Chulalongkorn* (Yale University Press 1969)
Wyatt D, *Thailand: A Short History* (2nd edn, Yale University Press 2003)

B. Book Chapters

Ainslie M, 'Post-war Thai cinema: Audiences and film style in a divided nation' in Gennari D T, Hipkins D, and O'Rawe C (eds), *Rural Cinema Exhibition and Audiences in a Global Context* (Palgrave Mcmillon 2018)
Anderson B, 'Introduction' in Benedict Anderson (ed) and Mendiones R (tr), *In the Mirror: Literature and Politics in Siam in the American Era* (Duangkamol 1985)
Armitage D, 'John Locke: Theorist of empire?' in Sankar Muthu (ed), *Empire and Modern Political Thought* (CUP 2012)
Bamrungsuk S, 'The development of the hybrid regime: The military and authoritarian persistence in Thai politics' in Chachavalpongpun P (ed), *Routledge Handbook of Contemporary Thailand* (Routledge 2020)
Banakar R and Phillips A L, 'Law, community and the 2011 London riots' in Nobles R and Schiff D (eds), *Law, Society and Community* (Ashgate 2014)
Barron A, 'Copyright infringement, 'free-riding' and the lifeworld' in Bently L, Davis J, and Ginsburg J (eds), *Copyright and Piracy: An Interdisciplinary Critique* (CUP 2010)
Baumgärtel T, 'I make films for myself:' Interview with Apichatpong Weerasethakul' in Baumgärtel T (ed), *Southeast Asian Independent Cinema* (Hong Kong University Press 2012a)
Baumgärtel T, 'Imagined communities, imagined worlds: Independent film from Southeast Asia in the global mediascape' in Baumgärtel T (ed), *Southeast Asian Independent Cinema* (Hong Kong University Press 2012b)
Bently L and Biron L, 'Discontinuities between legal conceptions of authorship and social practices: What, if anything, is to be done?' in van Eechoud M (ed), *The Work of Authorship* (Amsterdam University Press 2014a)
Bently L and Biron L, 'The author strikes back: Mutating authorship in the expanded universe' in Bowrey K and Handler M (eds), *Law and Creativity in the Age of the Entertainment Franchise* (CUP 2014b)
Bourdieu P, 'Cultural reproduction and social reproduction' in Karabel J and Halsey A H (eds), *Power and Ideology in Education* (OUP 1977)
Bowrey K, 'Law, aesthetics and copyright historiography: A critical reading of the genealogies of Martha Woodmansee and Mark Rose' in Alexander I and Gómez-Arostegui T (eds), *Research Handbook on the History of Copyright Law* (Edward Elgar 2016)
Bowrey K and Handler M, 'Instituting copyright: Reconciling copyright law and industry practice in the Australian film and television sector' in Bowrey K and Handler M (eds), *Law and Creativity in the Age of the Entertainment Franchise* (CUP 2014)
Chaiwaraporn A, 'Freelance/Freelance: Ham Puay . . . Ham Phak . . . Ham Rak Mo' in Mary Ainslie and Katarzyna Ancuta (eds), *Thai Cinema: The Complete Guide* (I.B. Tauris 2018)
Chakrabarty D, 'Belatedness as possibility: Subaltern histories, once again' in Boehmer E and Chaudhuri R (eds), *The Indian Postcolonial: A Critical Reader* (Routledge 2010a)
Chakrabarty D, 'The names and repetitions of postcolonial history' in Harrison R and Jackson P (eds), *The Ambiguous Allure of the West: Traces of the Colonial in Thailand* (HKUP 2010b)
Chisholm D C and Liu Y H, 'Motion-picture industry' in Towse R and Hernández T N (eds), *Handbook of Cultural Economics* (3rd edn, Edward Elgar 2020)
Cotterrell R, 'Law as constitutive' in Smelser N and Baltes P (eds), *International Encyclopedia of the Social and Behavioural Sciences* (Elsevier 2001a)
Cotterrell R, 'Is there a logic of legal transplants' in David Nelken and Johannes Feest (eds), *Adapting Legal Culture* (Hart Publishing 2001b)

Cotterrell R, 'Community as a legal concept? Some use of law and community approaches in legal theory' in Cotterrell R (ed), *Living Law: Studies in Legal and Social Theory* (Ashgate 2008)

De Valck M, 'Drowning in popcorn at the International Film Festival Rotterdam? The festival as a multiplex of cinephilia' in de Valck M and Hagener M (eds), *Cinephilia. Movies, Love and Memory* (Amsterdam University Press 2005)

Eckstein L and Schwarz A, 'Introduction: Towards a postcolonial critique of modern piracy' in Eckstein L and Schwarz A (eds), *Postcolonial Piracy: Media Distribution and Cultural Production in the Global South* (Bloomsbury 2014)

Falicov T, 'Migrating from South to North: The role of film festivals in funding and shaping Global South film and video' in Elmer G, Davis C, Marchessault J, and McCullough J (eds), *Locating Migrating Media* (Lexington Books 2010)

Feangfu J and Harrison R, 'Contested modernities and spectres of progress in twentieth-century Siam/Thailand' in Protschky S and van den Berge T (eds), *Modern Times in Southeast Asia, 1920s–1970s* (Brill 2018)

Ferrara F, 'The logic of Thailand's royalist coup d'état' in Chachavalpongpun P (ed), *Routledge Handbook of Contemporary Thailand* (Routledge 2020)

Foucault M, 'What is an author?' in Harari J (ed), *Textual Strategies: Perspectives in Post-Structuralist Criticism* (Cornell University Press 1979)

Freidman L, 'Some comments on Cotterrell and legal transplants' in Nelken D and Feest J (eds), *Adapting Legal Cultures* (Hart Publishing 2001)

Gibson J, 'The man behind the curtain: Developing film's double exposure of intellectual property' in Morris P S (ed), *Intellectual Property and the Law of Nations, 1860–1920* (Brill 2022)

Graziadei M, 'Comparative law, transplants, and receptions' in Mathias Reimann and Zimmermann R (eds), *The Oxford Handbook of Comparative Law* (2nd edn, OUP 2019)

Halle R, 'Offering tale they want to hear: Transnational European film funding as neo-orientalism' in Galt R and Schoonover K (eds), *Global Art Cinema: New Theories and Histories* (OUP 2010)

Handler M, 'Continuing problems with film copyright' in Macmillan F (ed), *New Directions in Copyright Law, Vol 6* (Edward Elgar 2007)

Hann C, 'Property: Anthropological aspects' in Wright J (ed), *International Encyclopedia of the Social and Behavioural Sciences* (Elsevier 2015)

Harding A, 'The eclipse of the astrologers: King Mongkut, his successors, and the reformation of law in Thailand' in Nicholson P and Biddulph S (eds), *Examining Practice, Interrogating Theory: Comparative Legal Studies in Asia* (Brill 2008)

Harding A, 'The legal transplants debate: Getting beyond the impasse?' in Breda V (ed), *Legal Transplants in East Asia and Oceania* (CUP 2019)

Harding A, 'Introduction' in Harding A and Pongsapan M (eds), *Thai Legal History: From Traditional to Modern Law* (CUP 2021)

Harrison R, 'Mind the gap: (En)countering the West and the making of Thai identities on film' in Harrison R and Jackson P (eds), *The Ambiguous Allure of the West: Traces of the Colonial in Thailand* (HKUP 2010)

Harrison R, 'Mummies, sex and sand: Bangkok gothic and the adventure fiction of 'Victorian' Siam' in Harrison R (ed), *Disturbing Convention Decentering Thai Literary Cultures* (Rowman & Littlefield International 2014)

Herzfeld M, 'The conceptual allure of the West: Dilemmas and ambiguities of crypto-colonialism in Thailand' in Harrison R and Jackson P (eds), *The Ambiguous Allure of the West: Traces of the Colonial in Thailand* (Hong Kong University Press 2010)

Hilty R and Nérisson S, 'Overview' in Hilty R and Nérisson S (eds), *Balancing Copyright: A Survey of National Approaches* (Springer 2012)

Howard D, 'Public-private distinction' in Gibbons M (ed), *The Encyclopedia of Political Thought* (John Wiley & Son 2015)

Ishii Y, 'The Thai Thammasat (with a Note on the Lao texts)' in Hooker M B (ed), *Laws of South-East Asia, Vol. 1, The Pre-Modern Texts* (Butterworth 1986)

Jackson P, 'Afterword: Postcolonial theories and Thai semicolonial hybridities' in Harrison R and Jackson P (eds), *The Ambiguous Allure of the West: Traces of the Colonial in Thailand* (Hong Kong University Press 2010a)

Jackson P, 'The ambiguities of semicolonial power in Thailand' in Harrison R and Jackson P (eds), *The Ambiguous Allure of the West: Traces of the Colonial in Thailand* (HKUP 2010b)

Jaszi P and Woodmansee M, 'Introduction' in Woodmansee M and Jaszi P (eds), *The Construction of Authorship* (Duke University Press 1994)

Karaganis J, 'Rethinking Piracy' in Karaganis J (ed), *Media Piracy in Emerging Economies* (Social Science Research Council 2011)

Kasemsup P, 'Reception of law in Thailand: A Buddhist society' in Chiba M (ed), *Asian Indigenous Law: In Interaction With Received Law* (Routledge 1986)

Kretschmer M, Bently L, and Deazley R, 'Introduction' in Deazley R, Kretschmer M, and Bently L (eds), *Privilege and Property: Essay on the History of Copyright* (Open Book Publishers 2010)

Lavik E, 'Romantic authorship in copyright law and the uses of aesthetics' in van Eechoud M (ed), *The Work of Authorship* (Amsterdam University Press 2014)

Leelamien D, 'การศึกษากฎหมายในประเทศไทยตั้งแต่การปฏิรูประบบกฎหมายและการศาลในรัชสมัยพระบาทสมเด็จฯ พระจุลจอมเกล้าเจ้าอยู่หัว' (Legal education in Thailand since the reform of Thai law during the reign of King Chulalongkorn)' in *100 ปี โรงเรียนกฎหมาย (A Hundred Years of the Thai Law School)* (Institute of Legal Education of The Thai Bar 1999)

Limapichart T, 'The Royal Society of Literature, or, the birth of modern cultural authority in Thailand' in Harrison R (ed), *Disturbing Convention Decentering Thai Literary Cultures* (Rowman & Littlefield International 2014)

Lobato R, 'The six faces of piracy: Global media distribution from below' in Sickels R (ed), *The Business of Entertainment (Vol. 1): Movies* (Greenwood Publishing 2008)

Loos T, 'Competitive colonialisms: Siam and Malay Muslim South' in Harrison R and Jackson J (eds), *The Ambiguous Allure of the West: Traces of the Colonial in Thailand* (Hong Kong University Press 2010)

MacDonald R, 'Film projection and the sacred geography of site-specific cinema in contemporary Thailand' in Menotti G and Crisp V (eds), *Practices of Projection: Histories and Technologies* (OUP 2020)

Manorom K, 'NGOs and civil society in Thailand' in Chachavalpongpun P (ed), *Routledge Handbook of Contemporary Thailand* (Routledge 2020)

Marzano S, 'Branding=distinctive authenticity' in Pavitt J (ed), *Brand New* (V&A Publications 2000)

McDuie-Ra D and Robinson D, 'Pirate places in Bangkok IPRs, vendors and urban order' in Fredriksson M and Arvanitakis J (eds), *Property, Place, and Piracy* (Routledge 2007)

McMahon M, 'Difference, repetition' in Stivale C J (ed), *Gilles Deleuze: Key Concepts* (McGill-Queen's University Press 2005)

Mungkandi W, 'Changing perceptions of Thai-US relations' in Neher C and Mungkandi W (eds), *US-Thailand Relations in a New International Era* (University of California 1990)

Ohly A, 'A fairness-based approach to economic rights' in Hugenholtz B (ed), *Copyright Reconstructed: Rethinking Copyright's Economic Rights in a Time of Highly Dynamic Technological and Economic Change* (Wolters Kluwer 2018)

Parivudhiphongs A, 'Creative industry policy in Thailand: A story of rise and demise' in Lim L and Lee HK (eds), *Routledge Handbook of Cultural and Creative Industries in Asia* (Routledge 2018)

Pattarakulvanit C, 'ปริศนาข้างหลังภาพ 'คณะสุภาพบุรุษ' (A mystery behind a picture of the 'Gentleman Group')' in Pattarakulvanit C (ed), *อ่าน(ไม่)เอาเรื่อง (Read Against the Grain)* (Kobfai 2002)

Peukert A, 'The colonial legacy of international copyright system' in Röschenthaler U and Diawara M (eds), *Copyright Africa: How Intellectual Property, Media and Markets Transform Immaterial Cultural Goods* (Sean Kingston Publishing 2016)
Phlainoi S, 'ครูเหลี่ยม ผู้เขียนนวนิยายไทยคนแรก (Khru Liam: The first Thai novelist)' in Samran N (ed), *ความไม่พยาบาท (non-vendetta)* (Dokya 2002)
Praya Nitisartpaisarn, 'ปาฐกถา เรื่องพระราชบัญญัติคุ้มครองวรรณกรรมและศิลปกรรม' (Lecture on the Protection of Literary and Artistic Work Act)' in Lekawichit L (ed), *รวมปาฐกถาซึ่งแสดงที่สามัคยาจารย์สมาคม ตั้งแต่ พ.ศ. 2470 ถึง พ.ศ. 2474 (A Collection of Lectures at Samakayacharn Society, 1927–1935)* (Bumrungnukulkij 1935)
Promkhuntong W, 'Apichatpong Weerasethakul' in Ainslie M and Ancuta K (eds), *Thai Cinema: The Complete Guide* (I B Tauris 2018a)
Promkhuntong W, ''Why so Wong': Transnational Asian cinema through the lens of cinephiles and transmedia fans' in Magnan-Park A H J, Marchetti G, and Tan S K (eds), *The Palgrave Handbook of Asian Cinema* (Palgrave 2018b)
Reekie S and Popattanachai N, 'Thai trust law' in Harding A and Pongsapan M (eds), *Thai Legal History: From Traditional to Modern Law* (CUP 2021)
Senftleben M, 'From flexible balancing tool to quasi-constitutional straitjacket: How the EU cultivates the constraining function of the three-step test' in Griffiths J and Mylly T (eds), *Global Intellectual Property Protection and New Constitutionalism: Hedging Exclusive Rights* (OUP 2021)
Seville C, 'British colonial and imperial copyright' in Alexander I and Gómez-Arostegui H T (eds), *Research Handbook on the History of Copyright Law* (Elgar Edwards 2016)
Spivak G C, 'Can the subaltern speak?' in Nelson C and Grossberg L (eds), *Marxism and the Interpretation of Culture* (Macmillan 1988)
Springman C J, 'Copyright and creative incentives: What do(n't) we know' in Dreyfuss R C and Siew-Kuan Ng E (eds), *Framing Intellectual Property Law in the 21st Century: Integrating Incentives Trade Development Culture and Human Rights* (CUP 2018)
Sterling J A L and Jacques S, 'Limitations and exception' in Cook T (ed), *Sterling on World Copyright Law* (6th edn, Sweet & Maxwell 2022)
Streckfuss D, 'The mixed colonial legacy in Siam: Origins of Thai racialist thought, 1890–19010' in Sears L (ed), *Autonomous Histories: Particular Truths, Essays in Honour of John Smail* (University of Wisconsin 1993)
Thepayasuwan B, 'หัวเลี้ยวของวรรณคดีไทย' (The turning point in Thai literature) in Social Science Association of Thailand (ed), *วรรณไวทยากรณ์ ชุมนุมบทความทางวิชาการ (Wanwaithayakon: A Collection of Academic Essays)* (Thai-wattana-panich 1971)
Tzouvala N, 'And the laws are rude . . . crude and uncertain: Extraterritoriality and the emergence of territorialised statehood in Siam' in Margolies D, Özsu U, Pal M, and Tzouvala N (eds), *The Extraterritoriality of Law: History, Theory, Politics* (Routledge 2019)
Warr P, 'Economic development of post-war Thailand' in Chachavalpongpun P (ed), *Routledge Handbook of Contemporary Thailand* (Routledge 2020)
Winichakul T, 'The Others within: Travel and ethno-spatial differentiation of Siamese subjects, 1885–1910' in Turton A (ed), *Civility and Savagery: Social Identity in Tai States* (Routledge 2000)
Winichakul T, 'Coming to terms with the west: Intellectual strategies of bifurcation and post-westernism in Siam' in Harrison R and Jackson P (eds), *The Ambiguous Allure of the West: Traces of the Colonial in Thailand* (Hong Kong University Press 2010)

C. Theses

Chongstitvatana S, 'The nature of modern Thai poetry considered with reference to the works of Angkhan Kalayanaphong, Naaowarat Phongphaibun, and Suchit Wongthet' (PhD thesis, University of London (SOAS) 1984)

Chunsaengchan P, 'Ruling aesthetics: Intermediality, media modernity and early Thai cinema (1868–1942)' (PhD thesis, University of Oregon 2020)
Copeland M P, 'Contested nationalism and the 1932 overthrow of the absolute monarchy in Siam' (PhD thesis, Australian National University 1993)
Ingawanij A, 'Hyperbolic heritage: Bourgeois spectatorship and contemporary Thai cinema' (PhD thesis, University of London (Birkbeck) 2006)
Limapichart T, 'Prescription of good books: The formation of the discourse and cultural authority of literature in modern Thailand (1860s–1950s)' (PhD thesis, University of Wisconsin-Madison 2008)
Limpichai S, '**บทบาทของธุรกิจเทปเพลงไทยสากลต่อการสร้างสรรค์ผลงานเพลง**' (The role of cassette tape business in music production) (Master's thesis, Chulalongkorn University 1989)
Pongsapan M, 'The reception of foreign private law in Thailand: The case study of specific performance' (PhD thesis, University of Edinburgh 2013)
Promkhuntong W, 'The East Asian auteur phenomenon: Context, discourse and agency surrounding the transnational reputations of Apichatpong Weerasethakul, Kim Ki-Duk and Wong Kar-Wai' (PhD thesis, Aberystwyth University 2017)
Ratchaburi C, '**ประวัติศาสตร์ธุรกิจเพลงลูกทุ่งไทย พ.ศ.** 2507–2535' (The history of Thai luk-tung music, 1964–1992) (Master's thesis, Thammasat University 1994)
Wannamethee P S, 'Anglo-Siamese economic relations: British trade, capital and enterprise in Siam, 1856–1914' (MPhil thesis, University of London (LSE) 1990)
Wuttipong N, 'The Thai popular music industry: Industrial form and musical design' (PhD thesis, University of Nottingham 2011)
Yensabai R, 'Competing narratives in cold war Thailand: Identity politics and the construction of foreign others' (PhD thesis, University of London (SOAS) 2019)

D. Articles and Papers

Aphornsuwan T, 'The West and Siam's quest for modernity: Siamese responses to 19th-century American missionaries' (2009) 17(3) South East Asia Research 401
Aree P, '**จากแอนนากับพระเจ้ากรุงสยาม ถึง** The King and I **ภาพสะท้อนแนวคิดเสรีนิยมและชาตินิยมแบบไทยๆ** (From Anna and the King of Siam to The King and I: A reflection of Thao-style liberalism and nationalism)' (1999) 2 Thai Film Journal 3
Atthasart C, '**ลิขสิทธิ์ภายในประเทศ**' (National copyright) (1984) 9(1) Chulalongkorn Law Journal 128
Barron A, 'Copyright and the claims of art' (2002) 4 IPQ 368
Baudry J L, Andrews J (tr), and Augst B (tr), 'The apparatus' (1976) 1(11) Camara Obscura 104
Baudry J L and Willian A (tr), 'Ideological effects of the basic cinematographic apparatus' (1974) 28(2) Film Quarterly 39
Bently L, 'Copyright and the death of the author in literature and law' (1994) 57 MLR 973
Bently L, 'R v The Author: From death penalty to community service' (2008) 32 Columbia Journal of Law and Arts 1
Bently L, 'The 'extraordinary multiplicity' of intellectual property laws in the British colonies in the nineteenth century' (2011) 12(1) Theoretical Inquiries in Law 162
Bhambra G, 'Postcolonial and decolonial dialogues' (2014) 17(2) Postcolonial Studies 115
Boonnak M, '**วิจารณ์ พรบ ลิขสิทธิ์ พศ** 2521' (A review of the Copyright Act 1978) (1979) 4(14) Journal of Business Administration 44
Boonnimitra S, 'From the nightmarish to a dreamy state of being: The troubling present in Thai independent cinema after the 2014 Coup d'état' (FilmAsia2016, Kobe, October 2016)
Boonnimitra S, 'Re-thinking politics in film: Thai independent cinema after the coup d'état 2014' (EuroMedia2016, Brighton, July 2017)

Boonyaketmala B, 'The rise and fall of the film industry in Thailand, 1897–1992' 6(2) East-West Film Journal 62
Bracha O, 'The ideology of authorship revisited: Authors, markets, and liberal values in early American copyright' (2008) 118 Yale Law Journal 186
Buruma I, 'Thailand's film-makers sink in a morass of money vs artistry' (1983) 122(43) Far Eastern Economic Review 53
Busbarat P, 'Thai–US relations in the post-Cold War era: Untying the special relationship' (2017) 13(3) Asian Security 256
Charoenvattananukul P, 'Window-dressing policy: Thailand's misuse of soft power as cursory practice' (2023) Asian Politics and Policy 1
Corrigan T, 'The commerce of auteurism: A voice without authority' [1990] New German Critique 43
Cotterrell R, 'Subverting orthodoxy, making law central: A view of sociolegal studies' (2002) 29(4) Journal of law and society 632
Craven M, 'What happened to unequal treaties? The continuities of informal empire' (2005) 74 NJIL 335
Desatova P, 'Thailand 4.0 and the internal focus of nation branding' (2018) 42(4) Asian Studies Review 682
Dougherty F J, 'Not a Spike Lee joint? Issues in the authorship of motion pictures under US copyright law' (2001) 49 UCLA Law Review 22
Drahos P, 'Global property rights in information: The story of TRIPS at the GATT' (1995) 13(1) Prometheus 6
Drassinower A, 'From distribution to dialogue: Remarks on the concept of balance in copyright law' (2009) 34(4) Journal of Corporation Law 991
Drassinower A, 'A note on incentives, rights, and the public domain in copyright law' (2011) 86 Notre Dame Law Review 1869
Du Plessis P and Suwanapech K, 'Law and identity: The case of the 'common law' of Scotland with comparative insights from Thailand' (2021) 1(1) Thai Legal Studies 47
Eimwattana B, 'ลิขสิทธิ์กับซอร์ฟแวร์ของสหรัฐอเมริกา' (Copyright and US software) (1987) 17(4) Thammasat Journal of Law 202
Ekiz O, 'My film in your pocket: an analysis of user interactions with films and copyright law' (2019) 9(2) QMJIP 196
Elsaesser T, 'What is left of the cinematic apparatus, or why we should retain (and return to) it' (2011) 31(1-2-3) Recherches Sémiotiques 33
Erlanger S, 'Thailand is the capital of pirated tapes' *New York Times* (New York, 27 November 1990)
Gibson J, "Gimme the prize': The author dysfunction' (2019) 9 QMJIP 127
Griffiths J, 'Dematerialization, pragmatism and the European Copyright Revolution' (2013) 33(4) Oxford Journal of Legal Studies 767
Halbert D, 'Intellectual property piracy: The narrative construction of deviance' (1997) 10(28) International Journal for the Semiotics of Law 55
Hamilton A, 'Video crackdown or the sacrificial pirate: Censorship and cultural consequences in Thailand' (1993) 5 Public Culture 515
Harding A, 'Global doctrine and local knowledge: Law in South East Asia' (2002) 15(1) International & Comparative Law Quarterly 35
Harrison R, 'Introduction: Cinema as an emerging field in South East Asian studies' (2006) 14(2) South East Asia Research 133
Harrison R, 'Somewhere over the rainbow': Global projections/local allusions in Tears of the Black Tiger/Fa thalai jone' (2007) 8(2) Inter-Asia Cultural Studies 194
Herzfeld M, 'The absent presence: Discourses of crypto-colonialism' (2002) 101(4) The South Atlantic Quarterly 899
Herzfeld M, 'The crypto-colonial dilemmas of Rattanakosin island' (2012) 100 Journal of the Siam Society 209

Higson A, 'The concept of national cinema' (1989) 30(4) Screen 36

Hoonpayon S, 'กฎหมายลิขสิทธิ์กับธุรกิจวีดีโอ' (Copyright law and the VHS business) (1984) 9(1) Chulalongkorn Law Journal 191

Ingawanij A, 'Itinerant cinematic practices in and around Thailand during the Cold War' (2018) 2(2) Southeast of Now: Directions in Contemporary and Modern Art in Asia 9

Janthimathorn S, 'กรรมการเซ็นเซ่อร์กับหนังต้องห้ามในเมืองไทย' (Censorship Board and the films banned in Thailand) (1972) 3 Social Sciences Review 26

Jaszi P, 'Toward a theory of copyright: The metamorphoses of 'authorship'' (1991) Duke Law Journal 455

Jaszi P, 'On the author effect: Contemporary copyright and collective creativity' (1992) 10 Cardozo Arts & Entertainment Law Journal 293

Jittareuk A, 'จาก 'เฮฟวี่' ถึง 'เมทัล': นักดนตรีเฮฟวี่เมทัลไทยจาก 'วัยรุ่นมืออาชีพ' สู่ 'ผู้ใหญ่มือสมัครเล่น,' 1970–2010' (From 'heavy' to 'metal': Thai heavy metal musicians, from 'young professionals' to 'adult amateurs,' 1970–2010) (2010) 22(1) Journal of Social Sciences, Chiang Mai University 231

Jory P, 'Books and the nation: The making of Thailand's national library' (2000) 31(2) Journal of Southeast Asian Studies 351

Kerdsint P, 'The dependence on international film festivals of Thai independent cinema' (EuroMedia2017, Brighton, July 2017)

Khopuangklang K, 'ระบบกฎหมายผสม' (Mixed legal system) (2007) 36 Thammasat Law Journal 568

Kraichitti S, 'The legal system in Thailand' (1967) 7 Wahburn Law Journal 239

Kuhonta E M and Sinpeng A, 'Democratic regression in Thailand: The ambivalent role of civil society and political institutions' (2014) 36(3) Contemporary Southeast Asia 333

Lee H and Cho Y, 'Introduction: Colonial modernity and beyond in East Asian contexts' (2012) 26(5) Cultural Studies 601

Legrand P, 'European legal systems are not converging' (1996) 45(1) International Comparative Law Quarterly 52

Legrand P, 'The impossibility of legal transplants' (1997) 4 MJECL 111

Lemley M, 'Romantic authorship and the rhetoric of property' (1997) 75 Texas Law Review 873

Limapichart T, 'The emergence of the Siamese public sphere: Colonial modernity, print culture and the practice of criticism (1860s–1910s)' (2009) 17(3) South East Asia Research 361

Lopattananont T, Klasukon V, and Thaweekul S, 'ความสอดคล้องของโครงสร้างอุตสาหกรรมการผลิตภาพยนตร์ไทยกับยุทธศาสตร์การส่งเสริมภาพยนตร์และวีดิทัศน์ ระยะที่ 3 (พ.ศ. 2560–2564)' (Coherence of Thai film industry and Thailand's strategies for film and video promotion, phase 3, 2017–2021) (Dhurakij Pandit University research paper, DPU 2020)

Lysa H, 'Extraterritoriality in Bangkok in the reign of King Chulalongkorn, 1868–1910: The cacophonies of semi-colonial cosmopolitanism' (2003) 27(1) Itinerario 125

Macmillan F, 'The cruel C: copyright and film' (2002) 24(10) EIPR 483

Masao T, 'Researches into indigenous law of siam as a study of comparative jurisprudence' (1905) 2 Journal of the Siam Society 14

Mattei U, 'Efficiency in legal transplants: An essay in comparative law and economics' (1994) 14(1) International Review of Law and Economics 3

McNay L, 'Meditations on Pascalian meditations' (2001) 30(1) Economy and Society 139

Meechoobot W, 'สยามกับสงครามโลกครั้งที่ 1' (Siam and the first world war) (2017) 39(1) Silapawattanatham

Mignolo W, 'The geopolitics of knowledge and the colonial difference' (2002) 101(1) South Atlantic Quarterly 57

Mignolo W, 'Delinking: The rhetoric of modernity, the logic of coloniality and the grammar of de-coloniality' (2007a) 21(2–3) Cultural Studies 449

Mignolo W, 'Introduction: Coloniality of power and de-colonial thinking' (2007b) 21(2–3) Cultural Studies 155

Musikawong S and Khumsupa M, 'Film is dangerous: Ten years of censorship in Thailand's cinema, 2010–2020' (2022) 30(1) South East Asia Research 377

Nagavajara C, 'Literature in Thai life: Reflections of a NATIVE' (1994) 2(1) South East Asia Research 12

Okediji R, 'The international relations of intellectual property: Narratives of developing country participation in the global Intellectual property system' (2003) 7(2) SJICL 315

O'Neill T N III, 'Intellectual property protection in Thailand: Asia's young tiger and America's growing concern' (1990) 11 University of Pennsylvania Journal of International Law 603

Pakdeethanakul J, '**ลิขสิทธิ์ระหว่างประเทศ**' (International copyright) (1984) 13(4) Thammasat Journal of Law 39

Pinyorat R, 'Civil groups want IP off trade-talks agenda with US' *The Nation* (Bangkok, 12 October 2014)

Pojanapitak T, '**การปรับตัวของหนังกลางแปลงในประเทศไทยต่อการฉายภาพยนตร์ในระบบดิจิทัล**' (The adaptation of Thai outdoor cinema to a digital cinema system) (2017) 35(2) Journal of Communication Arts 19

Quijano A, 'Coloniality and modernity/rationality' (2007) 21(2) Cultural Studies 168

Quijano A and Ennis M, 'Coloniality of power, eurocentrism, and Latin America' (2000) 1(3) Nepantal 533

Rahmatian A, 'Neo-colonial aspects of global intellectual property protection' (2009) 12(1) Journal of World Intellectual Property

Ricketson S, 'The birth of the Berne Union' (1986) 11 Columbia-VLA Journal of Law and the Arts 9

Rose M, 'The author as proprietor: *Donaldson* v. *Becket* and the genealogy of modern authorship' (1988) 23 Representations 51

Roy A, 'Copyright: A colonial doctrine in a postcolonial age' (2008) 26(4) Copyright Reporter 112

Sathaporn P, '**การฟื้นคืนชีพของกิจการฉายภาพยนตร์กับวัฒนธรรมการชมภาพยนตร์ในกรุงเทพฯ ทศวรรษ** 2490' (The revival of film screenings and film culture in Bangkok, 1947–1956) (2016) 3(2) Thammasat Journal of History 69

Sayre F B, 'The passing of extraterritoriality in Siam' (1928) 22 AJIL 70

Siamrath Weekly, '**วิเคราะห์ปัญหาพระราชบัญญัติลิขสิทธิ์ ฤาจะปิดประตูตีกันเอง**' (Analysing the problem with the Copyright Act, Will this turn into a domestic fight?) Siamrath Weekly (Bangkok, 9–15 October 1988) 15

Sivaraksa S, '**ศาสนาและวัฒนธรรม: วิกฤตและแนวโน้ม**' (Religion and culture: Crisis and tendency) (1994) 16(1) Silapawattanatham 103

Sucharitkul S, 'Thai law and Buddhist law' (1998) 46 AJCL Supp 69

Supapolsiri T, '**องค์ประกอบมูลฐานของงานอันมีลิขสิทธิ์**' (A fundamental element of a protected work) (1984) 9(1) Chulalongkorn Law Journal 173

Techaburana S, '**การเปลี่ยนแปลงและการขยายตัวของธุรกิจเพลงไทยสากลในทศวรรษที่** 2520' (The change and expansion of Thai pop music business in the 1980s) (2016) 3(2) Thammasat Journal of History 115

Tejapira K, '**ความเป็นไทยที่เปลี่ยนแปลง ตอน สาธารณกรรม**' (Thainess in a state of change: Profanation) Manager Daily (Bangkok, 5 November 1992)

Tejapira K, 'Post-crisis economic impasse and political recovery in Thailand: The resurgence of economic nationalism' (2002) 34(3) Critical Asian Studies 323

Teubner G, 'Legal irritants: Good faith in British law or how unifying law ends up in new divergences' (1998) 61(1) MLR 11

Ungpakorn G J, 'Why have most Thai NGOs chosen to side with the conservative royalists, against democracy and the poor?' (2009) 1(2) Interface 233

Viraphol S, 'Law in traditional Siam and China: A comparative study' (1977) 65 JSS 81

Vogenauer S, 'An empire of light? Learning and law-making in the history of German law' (2005) 64(2) Cambridge Law Journal 481

Watson A, 'Comparative law and legal change' (1978) 37 CLJ 313

Watson A, 'Legal change: Sources of law and legal Culture' (1983) 131 The University of Pennsylvania Law Review 1121

Winichakul T, 'The quest for 'siwilai': A geographical discourse of civilizational thinking in the late nineteenth and early twentieth-century Siam' (2000) 59(3) Journal of Asian Studies 528

Winichakul T, '**ประวัติศาสตร์ไทยแบบราชาชาตินิยม: จากจากยุคอาณานิคมอำพรางสู่ราชาชาตินิยมใหม่หรือลัทธิเสด็จพ่อของกระฎุมพไทยในปัจจุบัน**' (Royal-nationalist historiography: From the age of crypto-colonialism to a new royal-nationalism, or the Thai bourgeoisie's cult of the Father-King in the present) (2001) 23(1) Silapawattanatham (Art & Culture) 56

Woodmansee M, 'The genius and the copyright: Economic and legal conditions of the emergence of the 'author'' (1984) 17 Eighteenth-Century Studies 425

E. Online Sources

Arunmas P, 'B173m fake goods destroyed' (*Bangkok Post*, 27 August 2022) <https://www.bangkokpost.com/thailand/general/2378000/b173m-in-fake-goods-destroyed>

Banchanon P, '**วิเคราะห์ไทยแลนด์** 4.0: **วิสัยทัศน์ชาติที่ยังขาดรายละเอียด**' (Analyse Thailand 4.0: A vision lacking in detail) (*BBC Thai*, 6 January 2017) <https://www.bbc.com/thai/thailand-38527250>

Bangkok Post, 'PM trumpets 'soft power' of Thai delights' (*Bangkok Post*, 11 April 2022) <https://www.bangkokpost.com/thailand/general/2293202/pm-trumpets-soft-power-of-thai-delights>

Bangkok Post, 'Thai film directors spread happiness' (*Bangkok Post*, 29 December 2021) <https://www.bangkokpost.com/life/arts-and-entertainment/2239407/thai-film-directors-spread-happiness>

BBC, 'Oscars 2020: South Korea's Parasite makes history by winning best picture' (*BBC*, 10 February 2020) <https://www.bbc.co.uk/news/entertainment-arts-51440241>

BBC, 'Thailand protests: Risking it all to challenge the monarchy' (*BBC*, 14 August 2020) <https://www.bbc.co.uk/news/world-asia-53770939>

BBC, '**ย้อนประวัติพรรคคอมมิวนิสต์แห่งประเทศไทย ในการเปิดตัวครั้งแรกหลังสงบนิ่งกว่า** 30 **ปี**' (Tracing the history of the Communist Party of Thailand in the wake of its re-emergence after more than 30 years of inactivity) (*BBC Thai*, 31 March 2018) <https://www.bbc.com/thai/thailand-43603766>

BBC, '**รัฐบาลเร่งสร้าง** '**คนไทย** 4.0' **รองรับโลกยุคใหม่**' (Government to develop 'Thai 4.0' in preparation for the new age) (*BBC Thai*, 2 January 2017) <https://www.bbc.com/thai/thailand-38487137?ocid=socialflow_facebook>

Blázquez F J C, Cappello M, Enrich E, Milla J T, and Valais S, 'The legal framework for international co-productions' (*European Audiovisual Observatory*, 2018) <https://rm.coe.int/iris-plus-2018–3-the-legal-framework-for-international-co-productions/168090369b>

Brzeski P, 'Netflix unveils slate of six originals from Thailand' (*The Hollywood Reporter*, 11 October 2022) <https://www.hollywoodreporter.com/movies/movie-news/netflix-thailand-originals-1235238618/>

Bunnag T, 'A shining star in the North' (*Bangkok Post*, 24 January 2020) <https://www.bangkokpost.com/life/arts-and-entertainment/1842594/a-shining-star-in-the-north>

Bunpran P, '**ไทบ้าน เดอะซีรีส์**' (Thi-Baan the series) (*Matichon*, 13 March 2017) <https://www.matichon.co.th/columnists/news_494156>

Busan International Film Festival (BIFF), <https://www.biff.kr/eng/html/archive/arc_history.asp?pyear=2012&page_name=award>

Chetpayark K, '**ไม่มีประเทศไหนที่ทำรัฐประหารแล้วเจริญได้: มองข้อสรุปทางรัฐศาสตร์กับอ. ประจักษ์ ก้องกีรติ**' (No country has achieved progress after a coup) (*The Standard*, 3 February 2021) <https://thematter.co/%20social/coup-in-pol-sci-with-aj-prajak/134759>

Creative Economy Agency (CEA), '**รายงานการศึกษาการพัฒนาอุตสาหกรรมสร้างสรรค์ สาขาภาพยนตร์และวีดิทัศน์ ปี 2564**' (Creative industries development report (film and audiovisual) 2021) (*CEA*, 2021) <http://resource.tcdc.or.th/ebook/CEA.Film.Report.pdf>

Deerobrum S, '**เปิดใจผู้กำกับ 'ไทบ้าน เดอะซีรีส์' หนังไทยสไตล์อีสาน ที่ม่วนคักจนหัวแฮง**' (An open-hearted conversation with the director of 'Thi-Baan the Series') (*Kaosod*, 14 March 2017) <https://www.khaosod.co.th/lifestyle/news_253277>

Department of Intellectual Property (DIP), <https://www.thailandipfair.com/>

Department of State, 'Mobile development unit PROP, 22 May 1969' (USAID) 2 <http://pdf.usaid.gov/pdf_docs/pdaad616b1.pdf>

Department of Tourism, '**สถิติการถ่ายทำภาพยนตร์ต่างประเทศในประเทศไทย**' (Statistics on foreign film productions in Thailand) (*Department of Tourism*) <https://www.dot.go.th/chart-stat/category/4>

Economic Reform Committee, '**รายงานของคณะกรรมาธิการขับเคลื่อนการปฏิรูปประเทศด้านเศรษฐกิจสภาปฏิรูปแห่งชาติ เรื่องการปฏิรูประบบทรัพย์สินทางปัญญา**' (Report by the ERC on the reform of intellectual property system) (*National Reform Council*, June 2016) <https://dl.parliament.go.th/handle/20.500. 13072/478808>

Faughnder R and James M, 'Scarlett Johansson vs. Disney: How should talent be paid for streaming?' (*LA Times*, 3 August 2021) <https://www.latimes.com/entertainment-arts/business/newsletter/2021-08-03/wide-shot-disney-scarlett-johansson-nbc-olympics-tokyo-delta-variant-the-wide-shot>

Festival de Cannes, <https://www.festival-cannes.com/en/f/lung-boonmee-raluek-chat/>

Frater P, 'Thailand's censors get heavy with horror film 'Hoon Payon'' (*The Variety*, 10 March 2023) <https://variety.com/2023/film/news/thailand-censorship-horror-film-hoon-payon-1235549168/>

FTA Watch, <http://www.ftawatch.org/about>

GDH 559, <https://www.gdh559.com/about>

Hantonsirisakul P, '**ให้มันจบที่รุ่นเรา: การเมือง ประชาธิปไตย และคนรุ่นใหม่ในอุตสาหกรรมภาพยนตร์ไทย**' (It is going to end with our generation: Politics, democracy, and the new generation in Thai film industry) (*The Film Club*, 12 December 2020) <https://filmclubthailand.com/film-interview/let-it-end-in-our-generation-politic-democracy-and-new-generation-in-thai-film-industry-part-1/>

Harrison R, 'Traveling in Siamese time and space' (*Docalogue*, November 2020) <https://docalogue.com/railway-sleepers/> accessed 1 March 2023

Harvey R, 'Thai prime minister defends rise to power on Facebook' (*BBC*, 7 June 2011) <https://www.bbc.co.uk/news/world-asia-pacific-13685253>

Head J, 'The mystery of the missing brass plague' (*BBC*, 20 April 2017) <https://www.bbc.co.uk/news/world-asia-39650310>

Homsab C, '**อุตสาหกรรมหนังเกาหลี: สตาร์ทพร้อมไทย 15 ปีผ่านไปถึงฝั่งออสการ์**' (Korean film industry: Started off at the same time with its Thai counterpart and reached the Oscar 15 years later) (*Way Magazine*, 30 July 2020) <https://waymagazine.org/the-cinema-of-south-korea/>

Hookway J, 'Why a stolen democracy plaque is gripping Thailand' (*Wall Street Journal*, 25 April 2017) <https://www.wsj.com/articles/why-a-stolen-democracy-plaque-is-gripping-thailand-1493112247>

IMDb, <https://www.imdb.com/>

International Film Festival Rotterdam (IFFR), <https://iffr.com/en/about-us/mission-vision>

Jagan L, 'Thailand's struggle with goods piracy' (*BBC News*, 13 December 2001) <http://news.bbc.co.uk/1/hi/world/asia-pacific/1709267.stm>

Jianwanalee S, '**วรรณฤดี พงษ์สิทธิศักดิ์: หญิงสาวผู้อยู่เบื้องหลังความสำเร็จของค่ายหนัง GTH (และ GDH)**' (Vanridee Pongsittisak: The lady behind the success of GTH (and GDH)) (*A Day Magazine*) <https://adaymagazine.com/yesterday-56/>

Jitmongkolthong S, 'First virtual broadcast of a counterfeit-goods destruction ceremony in Thailand' (*Tilleke&Gibbins*, 7 December 2020) <https://www.tilleke.com/insights/first-virtual-broadcast-of-a-counterfeit-goods-destruction-ceremony-in-thailand/>

Jittiruek A, '12 ความเข้าใจผิดเกี่ยวกับลิขสิทธิ์ของคนไทย' (12 Misconceptions about copyright among Thai people) (*Prachatai*, 8 January 2013) <https://prachatai.com/journal/2013/01/44561>

Kafe Lumiere, <https://www.facebook.com/Kafelme>

Kanzler M, 'Fiction film financing in Europe: A sample analysis of films released in 2019' (*European Audiovisual Observatory*, 2021) <https://rm.coe.int/fiction-film-financing-in-europe-2021-edition/1680a57229>

Ketbungkan K, 'How small Isaan films are going big in Bangkok' (*Khaosod English*, 20 March 2017) <https://www.khaosodenglish.com/life/arts/2017/03/20/small-isaan-films-going-big-bangkok/>

Khaosod Online, "เพื่อไทย' ชำแหละ 7 ปีรัฐประหาร ประเทศถอยหลัง 'ประยุทธ์' ไม่ทำตามสัญญา ปฏิรูปการเมือง-ปราบโกง ล้มเหลว' ('Pheu Thai' lambasts seven years since coup: Country going backwards, 'Paryuth' going back on promises, political reform-combating corruption floundering) (*Thairath*, 22 May 2021) <https://www.khaosod.co.th/politics/news_6412448>

Kohkaew T, 'มองปัญหาลิขสิทธิ์-เศรษฐกิจ-สาธารณประโยชน์ ผ่านการดูเถื่อน' (Examine the copyright-economy-public interest conundrum through illegitimate consumption) (*Prachatai*, 2 March 2021) <https://prachatai.com/journal/2021/03/91924>

Komchadleuk, 'พณ. ผนึกโรงหนังจับมือแอบถ่ายติดวงจรปิดใช้เป็นหลักฐานเชือดละเมิดลิขสิทธิ์' (Ministry of Commerce joins hands with cinemas in catching illegal camcording by installing CCTVs for evidence of copyright infringement) (*Komchadluek*, 6 April 2011) <https://www.komchadluek.net/news/94175>

Komchadleuk, 'อภิสิทธิ์เน้นศก.สร้างสรรค์เพื่อพัฒนาปท.ให้เข้มแข็ง' (Abhisit focuses on a creative economy to strengthen the country)' (*Komchadluek*, 31 August 2009) <https://www.komchadluek.net/news/26619>

Kongsuwan S, 'The ugly truth: ชั่วโมงการทำงาน ค่าแรง และความจริงที่เจ็บปวดของงานกองถ่าย' (The ugly truth: Working hours, wages, and the painful reality of film production) (*The 101.World*, 10 July 2020) <https://www.the101.world/the-ugly-truth-of-flimcrew/>

Lacher I, 'Kindred Tarantino: The thunder rolls, out of Hong Kong' (*LA Times*, 3 March 1996) <http://articles.latimes.com/1996-03-03/entertainment/ca-42640_1_hong-kong>

Lee A, 'A pinewood dialogue with Wong Kar Wai' (*Museum of the Moving Image*) <http://www.movingimagesource.us/files/dialogues/3/71112_programs_transcript_html_303.htm>

Leesa-Nguansuk S, 'Netflix to churn out local content' (*Bangkok Post*, 14 March 2018) <https://www.bangkokpost.com/business/1427890/netflix-to-churn-out-local-content> accessed 1 March 2023

Lefevre A S, 'Thai army chief calls on all to protect monarchy' (*Reuters*, 17 December 2014) <https://www.reuters.com/article/us-thailand-politics-idUSKBN0JV13K20141217>

Lingg A, 'Mon rot fai/Railway Sleepers' (*Berlin International Film Festival*, 2017) <https://www.berlinale.de/en/2017/programme/201716963.html>

Maesincee S, 'ถึงเวลาปฏิรูปขนานใหญ่รอบที่สอง' (It is time for the second great reform) (*Facebook*, 20 April 2006) <https://www.facebook.com/drsuvitpage/posts/1399691550337571:0>

Major Cineplex, 'หว่องกาไวเผย one for the road คือหนังแห่งการเดินทางอย่างแท้จริง' (Wong Kar War reveals One for the Road is a true journey film) (*Major Cineplex*) <https://www.majorcineplex.com/news/wong>

Meeprasert N, 'สุรศักดิ์ ป้องศร Make a movie like a 'creative brand'' (*Creative Thailand*, 5 May 2018) <https://www.creativethailand.org/new/article/people/27917/en>

MGR Online, 'เปิดโมเดล Creative economy อัด 2 หมื่น ล. ดัน 15 อุตสาหกรรมสร้างสรรค์' (Unveiling the creative economy model: Injecting 20,000 million (THB) to push 15 creative industries forward) (*Manager Online*, 5 December 2009) <https://mgronline.com/smes/detail/9520000146841>

MGR Online, 'ต้าน FTA ไทย-สหรัฐ!' (No to Thai-US FTA) (*Manager Online*, 18 January 2006) <https://m.mgronline.com/politics/detail/9490000006951>

Ministry of Culture, 'ยุทธศาตร์การส่งเสริมอุตสาหกรรมภาพยนตร์และวีดีทัศน์ ระยะที่ 3 (พ.ศ. 2560–2564)' (Strategies for film and video promotion, phase 3, 2017–2021) <https://filmcommittee.m-culture.go.th/th/db_63_filmcommittee_9/8579>

Montlake S, 'Making the cut' (*Time Magazine*, 11 October 2007) <https://content.time.com/time/subscriber/article/0,33009,1670261,00.html>

National Electronics and Computer Technology Center (NECTEC), <http://internet.nectec.or.th/webstats/internetuser.iir?Sec=internetuser>

National Innovation Agency (NIA), 'คุณสุรศักดิ์ ป้องศร ผู้จุดกระแส 'หนังไทบ้านเดอะซีรีย์'' (Surask Pongsorn, the man behind the popular 'Thi-Baan the Series') (*NIA Facebook Page*, 25 January 2018) <https://www.facebook.com/watch/live/?ref=watch_permalink&v=1553552991348688>

National News Bureau of Thailand (NBT), 'Government eyes soft power as revenue source' (*National News Bureau of Thailand*, 13 March 2022) <https://thainews.prd.go.th/en/news/detail/TCATG220313171829419>

NESDB and Thailand Creative & Design Centre (TCDC), 'รายงานการศึกษาเบื้องต้นเศรษฐกิจสร้างสรรค์' (A preliminary study on creative economy) (May 2009) <https://www.nesdc.go.th/article_attach/CreativeEconomy.pdf>

NESDB, 'แผนพัฒนาเศรษฐกิจและสังคมแห่งชาติ ฉบับที่ 12 พ.ศ. 2560–2564' (12th National Economic and Social Development Plan, 2017–2012) 3 <https://www.nesdc.go.th/ewt_dl_link.php?nid =6422>

Nunbhakdi E, 'ฟรีแลนซ์ฯ: ร่างกายใต้บงการ' (Freelance: Docile bodies) (*Prachathai*, 6 September 2015) <https://prachatai.com/journal/2015/09/61244>

Office of the National Economic and Social Development Board (NESDB), 'แผนพัฒนาเศรษฐกิจและสังคมแห่งชาติ ฉบับที่ 1 พ.ศ. 2504–2506' (First National Economic and Social Development Plan, 2017–2012) <https://www.nesdc.go.th/ewt_dl_link.php?nid=3776>

Office of the US Trade Representative (USTR), ''Special 301' on intellectual property' (25 May 1989) <https://ustr.gov/sites/default/files/1989%20Special%20301%20Report.pdf>

Pajee P, 'Thai film industry in crisis' (*The Nation*, 15 March 2023) <https://www.nationthailand.com/lifestyle/30284197>

Palitpolkarnpim T, 'ฝันของคนทำ 'พื้นที่ฉายหนังอิสระ': รู้จัก 'a.e.y.space' ภารกิจพาหนังหลากหลายสู่สายตาคนหาดใหญ่' (The dream of an organiser of 'independent screening space': Meet 'a.e.y.space' and the quest of bringing a diverse selection of films to the people of Songkhla province) (*The Film Club*, 15 March 2022) <https://filmclubthailand.com/articles/special-article/indy-screening-space-a-e-y-space/>

PaTedTalk, 'การลอกเพลง—ความเข้าใจผิด—ข้อควรระวังเรื่องลิขสิทธิ์' (Music plagiarism—misconceptions—copyright warnings) (*Pa-Ted Talk*, 29 December 2021) <https://www.youtube.com/watch?v=NWWka9rs5Vk>

Pawakapan P, 'ความล้าหลังของการเกณฑ์ทหาร' (The backwardness of conscription) (*Prachatai*, 19 February 2019) <https://prachatai.com/journal/2019/02/81102>

Phoonphongphiphat A, 'Thailand 4.0: Are we ready?' (*Bangkok Post*, 2 January 2017) <https://www.bangkokpost.com/business/1173133/thailand-4–0-are-weready->

Phungbun naayudhya P, 'Death: (Non) existence' (*The Could*, 21 November 2017) <https://readthecloud.co/talk-18-nawapol/>

Pisuthipan A, 'Lessons from Korea on soft power' (*Bangkok Post*, 28 March 2022) <https://www.bangkokpost.com/opinion/opinion/2286226/lessons-from-korea-on-soft -power>

Pitchaya K, 'ดูหนังผิดลิขสิทธิ์=สนับสนุนเว็บพนันออนไลน์ทางอ้อม?' (Watching pirated films= indirectly supporting illegal gambling websites?) (*Brandinside*, 17 January 2023) <https://brandinside.asia/watching-illegal-streaming-sites-is-supporting-illegal-gambling-sites/>

Post Today, 'นายกไม่รับข้อเสนอยุบสภา 15 วัน' (Prime Minister rejects the suggestion to dissolve the parliament) (*Post Today*, 23 March 2010) <https://www.posttoday.com/politics/19545>

Puksuk P, "โปรดิวเซอร์คือสะพานระหว่างความฝันและความจริง' สนทนากับ ดีอานา บุสตามานเต หัวหน้าทีมโปรดิวเซอร์แห่ง Memoria (2021)' (A producer is a bridge between dream and reality: A conversation with Diana Bustamante, the producer of *Memoria* (2021)) (*The Film Club*, 28 February 2022) <https://filmclubthailand.com/film-interview/diana-bustamante-memoria-interview/>

Rakthinkamnerd R, 'ย้อนรอยยุคทองของ 'ซีดีเถื่อน' จากเฟื่องฟูสู่ต่ำสุดหลังรัฐประหาร' (Tracing the Golden Age of 'Illegal CDs': From its ascendancy to the demise after the 2009 Coup) (*TCJI*, 24 April 2016) <https://www.tcijthai.com/news/2016/04/scoop/6167>

Rithdee K, 'A wind from the Northeast' (*Bangkok Post*, 24 March 2017) https://www.bangkokpost.com/life/arts-and-entertainment/1220321/a-wind-from-the-northeast>

Rojmethakul S, 'กทม เปิดตัวการ์ตูน-หนังสั้นรณรงค์หลักสูตร 'โตไปไม่โกง'' (Bangkok Metropolitan Authority unveils animation and short films for the 'Growing Good' school curriculum) (*Isranews*, 2 November 2012) <https://www.isranews.org/investigative/278-thaireform/thaireform-slide/17441>

Rooney D, 'The legend of Suriyothai' (*Variety*, 29 September 2002) <https://variety.com/2002/film/reviews/the-legend-of-suriyothai-1200545836/>

Saengmanee P, 'Outdoor cinema is exercise in soft power' (*Bangkok Post*, 25 July 2022) <https://www.bangkokpost.com/opinion/opinion/2353281/outdoor-cinema-is-exercise-in-soft-power> accessed 1 March 2023

Saengsuwan S, 'Dude, movie. กลุ่มคนฉายหนังที่ใช้ป๊อปคัลเจอร์เปลี่ยนเชียงใหม่' (Dude, Movie: A group of film exhibitors who use pop culture to change Chiang Mai) (*The Modernist*, 16 March 2022) <https://themodernist.in.th/dude-movie/>

Sakdanares N, "หนังดูที่ไหนก็ได้' 4 พื้นที่ดูหนังที่ได้มากกว่าการดูหนัง' ('Films can be watched anywhere,' 4 screening spaces that offer more than watching films) (*The Film Club*, 23 February 2021) <https://filmclubthailand.com/film-interview/4-spaces-for-screening-film/> accessed 1 March 2023

Secretariat of the Prime Minister, ***วารสารไทยคู่ฟ้า*** (*Thai-khu-fah Journal*) (issue 31, 2016) 20–21 <https://www.thaigov.go.th/ebook/contents/detail/18#book/>

Secretariat of the Prime Minister, ***วารสารไทยคู่ฟ้า*** (*Thai-khu-fah Journal*) (issue 33, 2017) 2 <https://www.thaigov.go.th/ebook/contents/detail/74#book/>

Sentanissak C, 'คุยกับผู้จัด Roundtable กิจกรรมเพื่อเชื่อมหนังแมส-อินดี้/รุ่นใหญ่-รุ่นใหม่/ไทย-อาเซียน' (A conversation with the organisers of Roundtable, an even to connect mass-indie films/old-new generations/Thai-ASEAN) (*The Momentum*, 4 July 2019) <https://themomentum.co/roundtable-arthit-pimpaka/>

Seonghoon K, 'Korea-Southeast Asia co-productions are booming' (*Korean Film Council*, 12 October 2017) <https://www.koreanfilm.or.kr/eng/news/features.jsp?blbdComCd=601013&seq=441&mode=FEATURES_VIEW>

Sereemongkonpol P, 'Netflix Thailand announces six Thai titles at "Tee Thai Tee Mun"' (*Bangkok Post*, 12 October 2022) <https://www.bangkokpost.com/life/arts-and-entertainment/2413038/netflix-thailand-announces-six-thai-titles-at-tee-thai-tee-mun>

Shinawatra T, 'คำแถลงนโยบายของคณะรัฐมนตรี' (Cabinet's policy statement) (*Royal Thai Government*) <https://www.thaigov.go.th/aboutus/history/policy/11>

Sketchors, <http://www.chulayarnnon.com/profile.html>

Sukprasert P, 'Shining light on the freelance myth' (*Bangkok Post*, 16 September 2015) <https://www.bangkokpost.com/opinion/opinion/694724/shining-a-light-on-the-freelance-myth>

Supreme Court, <http://deka.supremecourt.or.th/>

Taibaan, <https://taibaan.com/>

Taibaan, <https://www.facebook.com/TaiBaanOfficial?locale=th_TH>

Taibaan, <https://www.youtube.com/channel/UCiARyB1wacrhQOhhT1K69Wg>

Thai PBS World, 'Bangkok organises outdoor cinema festival to boost local economy' (*Thai PBS World*, 8 July 2022) <https://www.thaipbsworld.com/bangkok-organises-outdoor-cinema-festival-to-boost-local-economy/>

Thai PBS, 'ความสำเร็จ ไทบ้าน เดอะซีรีส์ และความเสี่ยงในตลาดหนัง' (The success of Thi-Baan the Series and the risks in film market) (*Thai PBS*, 23 February 2018) <https://www.thaipbs.or.th/news/content/270500>

ThaiPR.NET, 'กทม. ร่วมกับนิด้าและองค์กรเพื่อความโปร่งใสในประเทศไทย เดินหน้ารณรงค์โครงการกรุงเทพเมืองสีขาว 'หลักสูตรโตไปไม่โกง'' (Bangkok Metropolitan Authority together with NIDA and FACT seek to promote the Bangkok White City Project: The 'Growing Good' school curriculum) (*RYT9*, 7 November 2012) <https://www.ryt9.com/s/prg/1524871>

Thairath Online, ''โต้ง' ผกก พันล้านปลื้ม' (Tong, the billion-baht, delighted) (*Thairath*, 9 October 2014) <https://www.thairath.co.th/content/455447>

Thairath Online, 'ดูหนังออนไลน์-ซีรีส์เถื่อน: ฟรี ดูดเพลิน สูญหมื่นล้าน ฆ่าคนเบื้องหลัง' (Online consumption of pirated films and TV series: Free, fun, but costly and deadly to filmmakers) (*Thairath*, 4 April 2016) <https://www.thairath.co.th/business/599679>

Thamrongrattanarit N, 'Sorry, A film by นวพล ธำรงรัตนฤทธิ์' (Nawapol Thamrongrattanarit) (*Youtube*, 4 January 2013) <https://www.youtube.com/watch?v=XRhPZM9lKyk>

Thamrongrattanarit N, 'หนังสือ ฮองกงกึ่งสำเร็จรูป Trailer' (*YouTube*, 5 July 2010) <https://www.youtube.com/watch?v=zM34DtwZEN0>

The Nation, 'Film directors urge more screening of Thai films in movie theatres' (*The Nation*, 12 March 2023) <https://www.nationthailand.com/thailand/general/40025488>

The New York Times, 'Thai cabinet resigns over US copyrights' (*New York Times*, 30 April 1988) <https://www.nytimes.com/1988/04/30/world/thai-cabinet-resigns-over-us-coprights.html>

The People's Information Centre, April–May 2010 Crackdown, 'Truth to justice: A fact-finding report on the April–May 2010 crackdowns in Thailand' (July 2012) <http://www.pic2010.org/en-report/>

The Standard, 'กันดารคือสินทรัพย์ เบื้องหลังไทบ้านเดอะซีรีส์ ปั้น 2 ล้านเป็นหลายร้อยล้าน' (Hardship is asset: Behind Thi-Baan the Series that turned two millions into hundreds of millions) (*The Standard*, 8 March 2020) <https://thestandard.co/podcast/thesecretsauce201/>

Thongterm A, 'รายงานพิเศษ: สุวิทย์ เมษินทรีย์ สานความฝันเป็นความเชื่อ แล้วลงมือทำ' (Special report: Suvit Maesincee, turn a dream into belief and make it happen) (*Matichon*, 1 February 2017) <https://www.matichonweekly.com/column/article_23242>

Thungkasemvathana P, 'Masterly delve into the video age' (*Bangkok Post,* 5 December 2014) <https://www.bangkokpost.com/life/arts-and-entertainment/447358/masterly-delve-into-the-video -age>

Tipmanee R, ''จักรวาลไทบ้าน' ในวันที่คนทำหนังไม่มีที่ทางทดเวลาบาดเจ็บ' ('Thi-Baan Universe' in an age when filmmakers do not get injury time) (*Way Magazine*, 10 December 2022) <https://waymagazine.org/thaibaan-interview/>

USOM, 'A brief history of USOM support to the office of accelerated rural development, September 1969' (USAID) 1 <http://pdf.usaid.gov/pdf_docs/Pdacr645.pdf>

USTR, '2013 out-of-cycle review of notorious markets' (*USTR,* 12 February 2014) <https://ustr.gov/sites/default/files/FINAL-PUBLISHED%202013_Notorious_Markets_List−02122014.pdf>

Voice Online, 'ควันหลงภ.ฟรีแลนซ์ฯ กับปัญหาสุขภาพจิตคนทำงาน' (Workers' mental health problems in the wake of the film 'Freelance') (*Voice TV*, 14 September 2015) <https://www.voicetv.co.th/read/258624>

Whitten S, 'Movie theatre owners are frustrated about streaming, but their survival depends on studios' (*CNBC*, 2 January 2021) <https://www.cnbc.com/2021/01/02/movie-theater-owners-are-frustrated-about-streaming-but-their-survival-depends-on-studios.html>

Wiengin N, 'คุยกับ เต๋อ-นวพล จดหมายรักถึง "ร้านแว่นวิดีโอ"' (A conversation with 'Ter-Nawapol': A love letter to 'Van Video') (*Matichon TV,* 4 December 2014) <https://www.youtube.com/watch?v=_eYj9lOrBF0&t=1s>

WIPO, 'Treaties and contracting parties' <https://www.wipo.int/wipolex/en/treaties/parties/remarks/TH/15>

Wongkitrungrueng T, **'นวพล ธำรงรัตนฤทธิ์ ผู้กำกับ 36–กับยุค ๓๖ ช็อต ที่ผ่านพ้นไป'** (Nawapol Thamrongrattanarit, the director of 36, and the bygone era of 36 shots) (*Sarakadee*) <https://www.sarakadee.com/magazine/338-issue/>

Wongwudthianan S, 'Copyright and what's right' (*Bangkok Post*, 11 December 2013) <https://www.bangkokpost.com/opinion/opinion/384200/copyright-and-what-right>

WP, **'ความท้าทาย** 'GDH—**นาดาว' สรางโมเดลธุรกิจโตอยางยั่งยืน'** (A challenge for 'GDH-Nadao': Building a sustainable business model) (*Marketing Oops!*, 2 February 2020)<https://www.marketingoops.com/news/biz-news/gdh-and-nadao-bangkok-busienss-model-sustainable-growth/>

Ziwen Z, 'New Netflix movie The Lost Lotteries ushers in a slate of new Thai content: Will it boost Thailand's pop culture to compete with K-pop and K-dramas?' (*South China Morning Post*, 15 October 2022) <https://www.scmp.com/lifestyle/entertainment/article/3195998/new-netflix-movie-lost-lotteries-ushers-slate-new-thai>

Filmography

Chidgasornpongse S, *Railway Sleepers* (2016)
Cromwell J, *Anna and the King of Siam* (1946)
Kar-Wai W, *Happy Together* (1994)
Kar-Wai W, *In the Mood for Love* (2000)
Kar-Wai W, *My Blueberry Night* (2007)
Lang W, *The King and I* (1956)
Rich R, *The King and I* (1999)
Siriphol C, *A Cock Kills a Child by Pecking on the Mouth of the Earthen Jar* (2013)
Siriphol C, *100 Times Reproduction of a Cock Kills a Child by Pecking on the Mouth of the Earthen Jar* (2017)
Siriphol C, *100 Times Reproduction of Democracy* (2019)
Tennant A, *Anna and the King* (1999)
Thamrongrattanarit N, *36* (2012a)
Thamrongrattanarit N, *Sorry* (2012b)
Thamrongrattanarit N, *Mary is Happy, Mary is Happy* (2013)
Thamrongrattanarit N, *The Master* (2014)
Thamrongrattanarit N, *Heart Attack* (2015)
Thamrongrattanarit N, *Fast and Feel Love* (2022)
Weerasethakul A, *Uncle Boonmee Who Can Recall His Past Lives* (2010)
Yukol C, *Suriyothai* (2001)

Index

100 Times Reproduction of a Cock Kills a Child by Pecking on the Mouth of the Earthen Jar (Siriphol) 2, 16
100 Times Reproduction of Democracy (Siriphol) 1–6, 11, 16, 201

Accelerated Rural Development (ARD) programme 96–97
agency 8, 12, 53, 76, 83, 102, 103, 153, 154–163, 170–171, 172, 173, 174, 183, 187
agents 8, 59, 63, 85, 156n21, 161–162
Agreement on Trade-Related Aspects of Intellectual Property Rights (TRIPS) 27, 87, 93, 98, 112–113, 119, 120, 202, 207
ahangan 69
Anderson, Benedict 15n78, 87, 94, 101–102, 107, 171n112, 195
Anglo-Siamese Treaty of 1855 (Bowring Treaty) 30, 32, 36, 48, 49, 51, 65
anti-piracy 99, 101, 142, 144
Asian Financial Crisis [AFC] ('Tom Yum Kung' crisis) 121, 135
auteur branding 17, 21, 153, 161, 163, 170–173, 181, 184
authenticity 2, 3–5, 11, 67, 163, 197, 201
Author as Proprietor, The (Rose) 57, 60
authorship 5, 17, 19–20, 38, 57–59, 60–65, 60n22, 66, 67–70, 72, 74, 76, 81–85, 87, 108, 152–163, 174, 210–211
Author's Ownership Act (AOA) [Amendment] of 1914 40–42, 45, 58, 86n220, 108, 109
Author's Ownership Act of 1901 (AOA) 25, 32, 37–42, 44–47, 49–50, 57, 76, 77–78, 81, 82–86, 86n220, 101, 108
autonomy 11, 48,65, 153, 192, 212
Ayutthaya Kingdom 70–71, 72

Baudry, Jean Louis 183
belatedness 13–14, 21, 134, 140, 143, 144–146, 148, 150–151
Berlin Act of 1908 47
Berne Additional Protocol of 1914 47
Berne Convention 32, 35, 46–47, 46n163, 49, 50, 86n220, 109, 109n141, 115, 205
Bhabha, Homi 11, 12
Bhambra, Gurminder 51
Birnhack, Michael 17
books: book trade 81–83; as commodity 79–81; piracy 83–84; role in modern education 78–79, 81; Siamese law 80, 84–85
Boonak, Marut 100–101, 110
Bowring, John 65
Bracha, Oren 62–63, 66
Bradley, Dan Breach 36, 79–80
brand agency 160–161
branding 17, 154–163, 170–171, 172; *see also* auteur branding
brand loyalty 162–163
Brenner, Yul 29, 30
Buddhism 71, 72–74

Central Intellectual Property and International Trade Court (CIPIT) 120
Chace Act of 1891 35–36
Chakrabarty, Dispesh 13–14, 85
Chaloemtiarana, Thak 74, 102
Chart, Sart, Kasat ('Nation, Religion, and King') 9
Chidgasornpongse, Sompot 91–92
Chiemcharoen, Wimol (Tomyantee) 111
Chulalongkorn, King of Siam (Rama V) 25, 29–40, 43, 48, 51, 55, 66, 68, 75, 77, 78–80, 82, 83–84, 91–92, 108, 136
Chungking Express (Wong) 160

cinema: 16mm film era 93, 117; art cinema 170–171; audience engagement 174–175; authorship/branding 16–17, 154–163; belatedness of 140–151; commercial cinema 170–171, 174–177; development 94–95; emergence 92–93; film consumption/distribution 165–170; film financing 173–174; future of 197–200; imagery of Thai-sakon 117–118; independent cinema 17, 171–174; national cinema 16–17; national strategies for establishment of film industry 137–140; production 15–17, 163–177, 181–195, 197–200; *see also* individual filmmakers/films
Civil and Commercial Code (TCCC) 34–35
co-branding 155–156, 172–173
Cold War 6, 7, 51, 92–94, 96, 98, 101–111, 116, 136, 193
colonial modernity 8–10, 28–56, 57, 58–59, 68, 73, 75, 85–87, 92, 125
community 5–7, 15, 20, 205–207, 208, 209
community regulation 211–213
community relations 208–211
community resource 20, 22, 182, 202, 207–213
consumer brand 156–158
consumerism 93, 98, 103, 109, 110–111, 116–118
Coppola, Francis Ford 161
copyright law: colonial copyright 17; colonialism and making of 26–56; community resource 20; copyright registration 77–78; decolonial jurisprudence 10–11; film protection 19–20; introduction 35–42; modernising 98–101; post-WWII development 98–101; as social/legal institution 14–15; *see also* authorship; Author's Ownership Act (AOA) [Amendment] of 1914; Author's Ownership Act of 1901 (AOA); Berne Convention; intellectual property (IP); literary property; ownership; Paris Additional Act of 1896; property; Protection of Literary and Artistic Works Act of 1931 (PLAWA); romantic authorship
copyright scholarship 19, 46, 58, 60n22, 87, 114–116
Corelli, Marie 74–75
Corrigan, Timothy 161
Cotterrell, Roger 20, 106–107, 202, 204, 205–210, 212
creative economy 10, 19, 113, 122–123, 127–129, 134, 162, 163, 166
creativity 164–165
crypto-colonial 53–54, 63, 67, 75, 79, 104, 108–109, 125–126, 140
cultural commodities 110
cultural intimacy 126–127, 129, 148

Damrong Rachanuphap, Prince, son of Mongkut, King of Siam 25, 37–38, 81
Darunowat (journal) 82
decoloniality 11–12, 54–55
Deleuze, Giles 13, 14, 85, 145, 146n94, 149, 150–151, 150n118, 181n2, 185n20, 186, 213, 213n68
Department of Intellectual Property (DIP) 119
difference 13, 14, 85–87, 143, 146n94
Divine Nymphs, The (Khru Liam) 66–67, 150
Donaldson v. Becket (1774) 58, 61
DVDs 2, 165

economic development 97–99; *see also* kanphattana (development)
economic nationalism 122
education reform 39–40, 77, 78–79, 83, 84
English law 33–35, 37, 58, 86
Erlanger, Steven 123–124
ethical community 211–213
extraterritoriality 31–33, 36, 46, 48, 49–50, 65

familiar production 20, 184–186, 194, 200, 204, 208, 209
Fichte, Johann Gottlieb 60–61
Film Censoring Council 139
Foucault, Michel 59–60
Free Trade Agreement (FTA) 120, 122, 207
Friedman, Lawrence 63

Genius and the Copyright, The (Woodmansee) 57, 60
Gibson, Johanna 20, 184, 208, 213
globalisation (loka-phiwat) 16, 17, 27, 86–87, 112, 114, 121–123, 136, 144
Gross Domestic Happiness (GDH) 185–186
GTH 162, 185
Guattari, Félix 181n2, 185n20, 186, 213, 213n68

Hammerstein, Oscar 28
Harrison, Rachel 19, 67
Heart Attack (Thamrongrattanarit) 162, 166, 170, 181
Herzfeld, Michael 53, 54, 126
Higson, Andrew 16
hire-of-work contract 198
Hubert Bals Fund (HBF) 155
hybridity 11–13, 19, 53, 74–76, 85, 104, 108, 146, 150, 151

identity 9, 11–14, 54, 64, 73, 109, 117, 126, 145, 150, 153, 169, 176, 183, 184, 188; *see also* national identity; Thai identity; Thainess
imagined community 5, 9, 15n78, 107, 127, 195–196, 201, 206
InfoSoc Directive of the European Union of 2001 202
Ingawanij, Adadol 54, 117, 124
intellectual property (IP) 10, 17, 18, 48, 49, 50, 87, 100, 110, 112–113, 114, 118–123, 125, 127, 128, 133–134, 136, 140, 143, 147, 191, 195, 199, 202
International Copyright 47–48
International Federation of Phonograms and Video Producers 123
International Film Festival Rotterdam (IFFR) 155–156, 172, 182
internationalism 103
International Monetary Fund (IMF) 121, 122, 124
intertextuality 3–4
Isan 96, 97, 104, 105, 168–169, 172, 175–176, 181, 183–184, 209, 213

Jackson, Peter 52, 75–76
Jitjamnong, Duangmon 69, 72
Jory, Patrick 78
judicial system reform 33, 52

kanphattana (development) 93, 94, 97–98, 101, 102–105, 108, 114, 145, 149
khon-roon-mai 121
Khru Liam: Divine Nymphs, The 66–67, 150; Non-vendetta 74–75
King and I, The (film) 28–30, 31, 51, 102, 103
kinship 175, 183, 184, 208, 210–211, 213
Kittikachorn, Thanom 98, 138
klao-klon 69–70
knowledge 7, 8, 9, 11–12, 14, 17–18, 29, 30, 36, 42, 44, 51, 55, 56, 59, 65, 67, 70, 71, 72–73, 78–79, 82, 83, 104, 108, 113, 122–129, 143, 149, 208

labour theory 64
Lak-witthaya (journal) 42–43, 71
language 10, 21, 44–45, 49, 62–63, 64, 65, 69, 74, 85–86, 136, 140, 144, 147, 149, 170, 186, 187, 188, 192, 197, 203
law-and-community approach 106–107, 202, 210–213
League of Nations 48, 49
Lee, Ang 160
legal education 33–34
legal irritants 107–108
legal transplants 34, 59, 85, 105–108, 110, 120, 151
Legrand, Pierre 106
Leonowens, Anna 28, 29, 30, 102
Limapichart, Thanapol 44
literary property 37–39, 57, 58, 59–76, 77, 84–85
literature 42–45, 58–59, 65–74, 77, 84–85, 115
living law 186n29
Locke, John 64
Loos, Tamara 26, 28, 29, 55, 73, 83n207

Maesincee, Suvit 135–136, 137
Marketing of Nations, The (Maesincee) 136
Mary is Happy, Mary is Happy (Thamrongrattanarit) 158–159, 161–162, 164, 204
Master, The (Thamrongrattanarit) 140–143, 147, 148, 158, 159, 162
Mignolo, Walter 8, 11–12
mimicry 12, 74
Ministry of Public Instruction (MOPI) 37, 40, 83–84
mistrust 20, 197, 199, 207, 210
Mittraphap ('Friendship') Highway 96, 105
modernity/coloniality 11–13, 19, 54–56, 58, 87, 96, 139
Mongkut, King of Siam (Rama IV) 28–30, 81, 102, 136
Motion Pictures Export Association of America 95
Muay Thai 137
music business 99
Music of Association of Thailand (MAT) 99, 101
mutual interpersonal trust 20, 209, 210
mutual trust 20, 208–211
My Blueberry Night (Wong) 160

Nagavajara, Chetana 70
Nangsu-Wachirayan (journal) 82
national cinema 16–17
national cultural heritage 110
National Economic and Social Development (NESD) Plan 97–98
national identity 16, 104, 110
nationalism 9–10, 29, 32, 41–43, 45, 57, 75, 108, 122, 124–125, 126, 195
National Legislative Assembly (NLA) 100–101, 104, 111
nation branding 133
Non-vendetta (Khru Liam) 74–75

official nationalism 9–10, 195
One for the Road (Poonpiriya/Wong) 160
opium ban decree 79–80
Orientalism 11
originality 2, 4–5, 11, 20, 63, 67, 85–86, 86n220, 148, 158, 161, 163, 203, 204
ownership 1–2, 4–5, 10, 38, 45, 47, 57–58, 60–65, 60n22, 77, 84–85, 113, 134, 136, 146–147, 149, 171, 173–174, 186–191, 192, 196, 198–199, 201, 208, 210–211; *see also* Author's Ownership Act (AOA) [Amendment] of 1914; Author's Ownership Act of 1901 (AOA)

Pantip Plaza 125–126
Parasite (film) 139
Paris Act of 1971 98
Paris Additional Act of 1896 49
Pax Britannica 51–52
People's Party 3–4, 50–51
personhood 63–65
Phatsakorawong, Chaopraya 39
Phillips, Matthew 103–104
Phromwaranurak, Prince of Siam 82
piracy 10, 21, 40, 83, 84, 86, 94, 95, 99, 112–129, 141–142, 144, 145, 148–149, 148n102, 158, 164, 166–167, 174, 188, 192, 196, 197, 209
pleng-string 101
poetry 68–71, 93
power/knowledge 70, 113
Prajadhipok, King of Siam 50
Presley, Elvis 101
print capitalism 32, 49, 76, 78–83
print technology 36–37, 58
Priority Watch List country 118–119
Promkhuntong, Wikanda 159
property 1–2, 61, 82, 108, 113, 147, 173, 174, 186–187, 189, 192, 198, 203, 204; *see also* intellectual property (IP); literary property
property relations 18, 113, 152, 201
proprietary personhood 63–65
Protection of Literary and Artistic Works Act of 1931 (PLAWA) 47, 49, 86n220, 98, 100, 109–110
public–private dichotomy 203–204
Pueksom, Taweesak 72–73

Quijano, Aníbal 8, 11, 54–55, 76

Rabi of Ratchaburi, Prince 25, 31, 33–34, 37–39, 77, 80–81
radio 99
Railway Sleepers (Chidgasornpongse) 91–92
railway system 91–93
Rajchagool, Chaiyan 31
Ratchakitchanubeksa (journal) 82
repetition 13–14, 13n69, 20, 85–87, 137, 143, 145, 148–151, 167, 181, 204
representation 11–14
reproduction 2–3
reung-pralom-lok 77
Richard, Cliff 101
Rogers, Richard 28
romantic authorship 5, 58, 59, 61–63, 62n34, 62n36, 67, 85, 108, 153, 174
Rose, Mark 57–58, 60, 84, 85
royal nationalism 29, 42–43, 45, 57, 75, 125
rural development 96–97

Said, Edward 11, 12
sakon 124–127
Samakom-kaephasa/Society for Language Correction 44, 45
Scorsese, Martin 161
screenwriters 198–199
self-branding 158–160
Siriphol, Chulayarnnon: 100 Times Reproduction of a Cock Kills a Child by Pecking on the Mouth of the Earthen Jar 2, 16; 100 Times Reproduction of Democracy 1–6, 11, 16, 201
Sivaraksa, Sulak 116
siwilai 7, 12, 29, 32, 40, 53–54, 66–67, 71, 73, 75, 78, 84–85, 93–94, 97, 101, 103–104, 104n95, 108, 125, 149
Smith, Samuel J. 36
social agency 161–162
social media 16, 135, 157–158, 159, 175, 183, 199
Songkran 137

'Sorry' (Thamrongrattanarit) 143–144, 146–148, 187
Special 301 Report 118–119
spiritual–material bifurcation 72–74, 103
Spivak, Gayatri 11, 12
Strathern, Marilyn 64
subalterns 11, 13, 75
Suriyothai 117
Suriyothai (film) 117

Tarantino, Quentin 160
Tejapira, Kasian 26, 52, 116–117, 121
Teubner, Gunther 107–108
Thai Copyright Act of 1978 (TCA 1978) 98–101, 103, 104–105, 107, 108, 109, 110–111
Thai Copyright Act of 1994 (TCA 1994) 100, 119, 198
Thai identity 58, 76, 103–104, 124, 137; *see also* Thainess
Thailand 4.0 133–135, 137, 195
Thainess 9, 13, 18, 42–43, 44, 59, 70, 103–104, 137, 151
Thai-sakon 117–118, 124, 137, 154
Thalok-witthaya (journal) 71
Thamrongrattanarit, Nawapol: assemblage of Thai cinema 151; Heart Attack 162, 166, 170, 181; Mary is Happy, Mary is Happy 158–159, 161–162, 164, 204; Master, The 140–143, 147, 148, 158, 159, 162; self-branding 157–160; 'Sorry' 143–144, 146–148, 187
Thanarat, Sarit 93–98, 101, 102–104, 108, 138–139
Thawee-panya (journal) 71
Thi-Baan 168–169, 174–176, 181, 183, 185, 204, 209, 213
Three-Seal Code 33
Tinsulanonda, Prem 119
trademarks 49
trade names 49
trade treaties 30, 31–32, 48, 58, 120, 122
translations 42, 47, 49–50, 65–67, 71, 74, 79n174, 86n120, 109n141, 150
trust 20, 22, 163, 167, 187, 195–197, 197n100, 202, 207–211, 213, 219
trust-based reinterpretation 208, 209, 213

UK Copyright Act of 1842 37
US Congress 35
US Generalised System of Preferences (GSP) 119
US Trade Representative (USTR) 118
trust law 35n76, 146n93

Vajiravudh, King of Siam 31, 32, 40, 41–45, 48, 50, 57, 58, 75, 108
Van Video 140–143, 148, 158, 195
VCDs 165
Vejjajiva, Abhisit 128–129
Vella, Walter 42
Vendetta (Corelli) 74–75

Wachirametee, Wor 144–146, 186–187
Wachirayan (journals) 82–83
Wachirayan Library 36–37, 78, 82–83
Wachirayan-wiset (journal) 36
Wannakhadi-samoson/Royal Society of Literature (RSL) 44–45, 58
Watson, Alan 40, 105–106
Weerasethakul, Apichatpong 154–157, 160, 161, 162, 171–172, 181–182
Wilson, Woodrow 48
Winichakul, Thongchai 7, 28, 29, 53, 55–56, 73, 103, 204–205
WIPO 109, 110
WIPO Copyright Treaty (WCT) of 1996 202
Wong Kar Wai: auteur brand 158–161; Chungking Express 160; My Blueberry Night 160; One for the Road 160; reference by Thamrongrattanarit 204
Woodmansee, Martha 57–58, 60–61, 85
writing 72–74
Wyatt, David 51

Yensabai, Rungchai 103–104

Kolibri 360 GmbH
Ferdinand-Jühlke-Straße 7
99095 Erfurt, Deutschland
produktsicherheit@kolibri360.de